DAILY LIFE OF
THE ETRUSCANS

Daily Life of

THE ETRUSCANS

Jacques Heurgon

Translated from the French by James Kirkup

THE MACMILLAN COMPANY

NEW YORK

1964

MADE AND PRINTED IN GREAT BRITAIN

CONTENTS

ILLUSTRATIONS

between pages 148–149

MAPS

To

MONSIEUR JEROME CARCOPINO

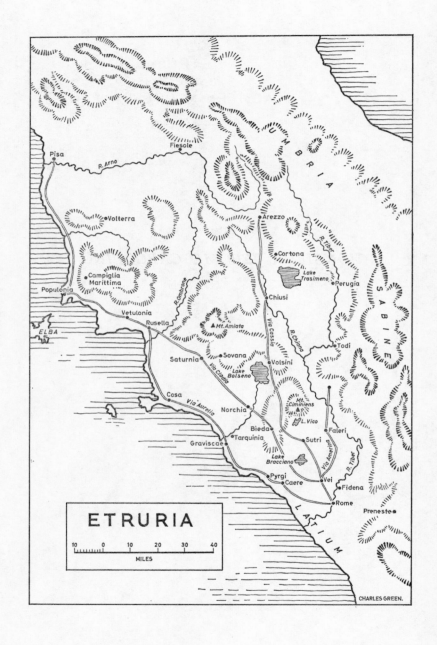

ETRURIA

10 0 10 20 30 40
MILES

Pisa
R. Arno
Fiesole
Volterra
Arezzo
Campiglia Marittima
Cortona
Lake Trasimeno
Perugia
Populonia
Vetulonia
R. Ombrone
Chiusi
Rusella
ELBA
Mt. Amiata
Via Cassia
Saturnia
Sovana
R. Chiana
Todi
Via Clodia
Lake Bolseno
Volsini
Cosa
Via Aurelia
Norchia
Mt. Ciminus
L. Vico
Faleri
Bieda
Graviscae
Tarquinia
Sutri
Lake Bracciano
R. Tiber
Pyrgi
Vei
Fidena
Caere
Rome
Preneste

UMBRIA
SABINE
LATIUM

CHARLES GREEN.

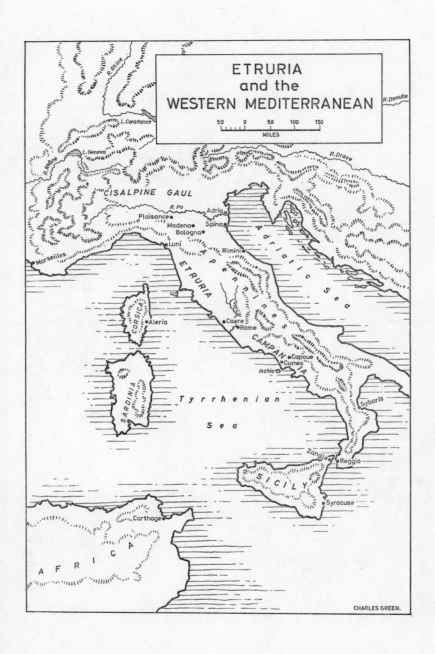

ETRURIA
and the
WESTERN MEDITERRANEAN

50   0   50   100   150
MILES

R.Rhine

R.Danube

L.Constance

L.Geneva

R.Drave

R.Rhone

CISALPINE GAUL

R. Po
Plaisance•
Modena•   Adria•
Bologna•   Spina•
•Luni

Marseilles•

•Rimini

ETRURIA

A
p
e
n
n
i
n
e
s

Adriatic Sea

CORSICA
•Aleria

•Caere
•Rome

CAMPANIA

•Capoue
•Cumes
Ischia•

SARDINIA

Tyrrhenian

Sea

Sybaris•

Zancle•
•Reggio

SICILY

•Syracuse

•Carthage

A F R I C A

CHARLES GREEN.

INTRODUCTION

The word Etruscan might *a priori* seem to many people the very last one to be associated with the idea of 'daily life'. The mere sound of the word tends to induce in certain people a trance-like state which almost discourages any attempt to approach the subject in a realistic manner. Our contemporaries, fascinated by an art whose marvels were little known until they were revealed by the memorable 1955 exhibition at the Louvre and the subsequent publication of numerous illustrated books on the subject seem inclined to look upon the creators of that art as men who, if ever they existed, did so outside the bounds of space and time. They are the children of mystery and the sons of night, and the dazzling fibulae which served to hook up their women's garments perhaps shine all the brighter for being seen in a setting of impenetrable dark. In the eyes of many people the Etruscans belong more to the domain of myths than to the pages of human history. Our aim here is to show that, unlike the Arimaspians and the other Hyperboreans, the Etruscans really existed.

It is no easy task: literary evidence about them is rare, their language, to say the least, obscure, and the data presented by their artefacts are uncertain. The Etruscans who still survived at the time of Augustus were, in the words of Dionysius of Halicarnassus, 'a very ancient people resembling no other either in language or customs'.[1] To this it may be added that, though they did not hide themselves away behind an iron curtain they were by nature proud and reserved, unwilling to reveal their secrets to outsiders. Above all, it must be understood that the Etruscans neither saw nor painted things as they are. Possessing a deep store of popular wisdom and a marked gift for observation and expression which in the end came into their own, they first

I

of all nobly surrendered themselves to a passionate admiration for the most beautiful thing they knew – Greece. It was they who introduced abroad and imitated all aspects of Greek civilization, and in so doing lost their own way a little. Thus there arose in Italy that strange and generous impulse, which was to be found again at all periods of history, on the walls of Pompeian houses and in the palaces of Renaissance princes, to re-create in everyday life the constant and multiform presence of an ideal Hellas. Venetians in the sixteenth century and Campanians in the first re-lived the loves of Ariadne and the labours of Hercules as if they were their own. The middle classes at Herculaneum opened up the walls of their narrow dwellings with immense perspectives, in trompe-l'oeil style, of Hellenistic colonnades. The Etruscans in the days of the Tarquins were already living in a dream that at every step brought them into contact with the gods.

But our attempts to see their real face and to observe them in their ordinary lives have been in a large measure frustrated by the narrow-minded and impatient attitude of their historians. A welter of theories and interpretations has merely succeeded in blurring the outlines of things. It is sometimes thought that there are only two main problems and that if these were solved everything else would be explained. For some scholars the main problem is that of the origin of the Etruscans: when it is known where they come from, they say, we shall know what sort of people they were. The second problem is that of their language: it is commonly believed that the Etruscan tongue is quite unintelligible and even indecipherable. But if a bilingual text of some extent were to turn up, or if a cryptographer of genius were to come along, those mysterious strangers would at once seem closer to us, and less inscrutable.

Let us first of all, in order to centralize our aims, attack these two problems. A brief historical exposition of the Etruscan people and a linguistic outline of what is involved when we come to the interpretation of their texts will allow us to determine more precisely the extent of our aims in the present study. But let us be clear on this point: the obscure beginnings, in the Orient or elsewhere, of the distant ancestors of those who one day, settling between the Tiber and the Arno, were to become the Etruscans, will concern us much less than their civilization as it developed on Italian soil, and which is above all considered as the first great civilization in Italy. On the other hand, a knowledge of the Etruscan tongue, which might afford us solid but limited results, can be acquired only after long and patient study; our knowledge of this language moreover is much more advanced than is generally supposed, and a great number of small inscriptions offer precious insights which – and this will be perhaps one of the more original contributions made by this little book – can be made use of within reason.

WERE THE ETRUSCANS OF ORIENTAL ORIGIN?
The Etruscans have always inspired myth-makers. Ever since the days of antiquity numerous myths have been related about them, and in these truth was inextricably mixed up with false-hood. One of these myths, which was supposed to demonstrate the peculiar ways of the Etruscans, must be recalled here, in the words of Herodotus:[2]

'. . . In the reign of Atys son of Manes there was a great scarcity of food in all Lydia. For a while the Lydians bore this with what patience they could; presently when there was no abatement of the famine, they sought for remedies, and divers plans were devised by divers men. Then it was that they invented the games of dice and knuckle-bones and ball, and all other forms of pastime, except only draughts, which the Lydians do not claim to have discovered. Then, using their discovery to lighten the famine, they would play for the whole of every other day, that they might not have to seek for food, and the next day they ceased from their play and ate. This was their manner of life for eighteen years. But the famine did not cease to plague them, and rather afflicted them yet more grievously. At last their king divided the people into two portions, and made them draw lots, so that the one part should remain and the other leave the country; he himself was to be the head of those who drew the lot to remain there, and his son, whose name was Tyrrhenus, of those who departed. Then one part of them, having drawn the lot, left the country and came down to Smyrna and built ships, whereon they set all their goods that could be carried on board ship, and sailed away to seek a livelihood and

3

a country; till at last, after coasting along many nations in turn, they came to Ombrici, where they founded cities and have dwelt ever since. They no longer called themselves Lydians, but Tyrrhenians, after the name of the king's son who had led them thither.'

Such, in the words of a Greek writing in the fifth century before Christ and whose authority was scarcely ever disputed afterwards, were the origins of those whom he called in his own language Tyrrhenians (whence the name Tyrrhenian Sea given to that part of the Mediterranean along the western coast of Italy). The Romans named them *Tusci* (whence the name Tuscany) and *Etrusci* (whence the term the Etruscans). And Herodotus' account, leaving out of consideration the obviously legendary details embellishing it, was accepted even by modern scholars, for the hypothesis of the Etruscans' oriental origin allowed them to understand better the more or less organically oriental characteristics of that civilization.[3]

By this we do not mean the objects, customs or beliefs that may have been introduced by the regular routes of commerce and intellectual exchanges. It has indeed been said that future archaeologists, digging among the ruins of eighteenth-century boudoirs, will probably find a suspicious amount of broken porcelain from China: they would be wrong to infer from this that a wave of yellow-skinned invaders had swept over western Europe at that period. In the same way, the history of Etruscan civilization opens with a so-called orientalizing period which extended over the whole of the seventh century, and many of whose traits can be explained by foreign importations: such as that Egyptian faience vase, found at Tarquinii, and bearing the cartouche of the Pharaoh Bocchoris (720–714), Phoenician scarabs of smalt, ivory amulets, amber beads, bronze and gold pins, and, later, in the first Etruscan temples, the principles of terra-cotta frieze decoration similar to that used everywhere in the Creto-Asiatic world – all these things really only go to prove the venturesome spirit of merchants and the hold of culture on primitive peoples. But there is a more profound correspondence whose significance cannot be explained away by superficial influences.

For example, one is impressed by the affinities of religion

linking the Etruscans with the ancient empires of the Orient. In particular, they earned the admiration of other races all through their history for their skill in the interpretation of omens. No other region in the ancient world knew such an obsession with telling the future, nor had such experience of the observation of celestial phenomena, the interpretation of thunder-claps and divination from the intestines of their victims, such a passionate desire to know the will of the gods. Only the ancient magi of Assyria and Chaldea, themselves past masters in astrology and hepatoscopy, were their equals. So that there is a great temptation to consider the Etruscans as the remote but faithful heirs of the latter. A sheep's liver in bronze in the museum at Piacenza has its convex side divided into forty-four compartments, each one marked with the name of a god; it resembles strikingly about thirty terra-cotta livers, compartmented in the same way and marked with inscriptions, which were discovered at Mari on the central Euphrates and which date back to the first part of the second millennium.

Then the Etruscan language itself also constitutes a mystery which might show signs of solution if the hypothesis of the oriental origin of those who spoke it were accepted. Etruscan does not belong to the Indo-European family of languages; it is fundamentally different from Latin, Oscan, Umbrian, Celtic, Greek and Sanskrit; but it seems to contain certain grammatical peculiarities which are found in the dialects of western Asia Minor, Lycian, Carian, Lydian. A funerary stele unearthed by French archaeologists in 1885 on the island of Lemnos in the northern Aegean and dating from the sixth century BC, that is, from a period when the Athenian conquests had still not resulted in the introduction of Greek, presents an epigraphic text whose authenticity and significance have been confirmed by recent discoveries and which, if it is not written in Etruscan, is at least the text most closely resembling Etruscan ever read outside Italy. This is not the place to mention points of vocabulary and morphology which establish a very close link between the two languages. But we must remember that, according to Herodotus, the Tyrrhenians had in the course of their migration 'coasted along many nations': it is just conceivable that they may have left behind a part of their contingent on Lemnos.

Is the case not proved, then, and what is it that prevents a growing number of etruscologists from accepting the Herodotus theory? First of all because it resembles too many of those fables of antiquity which tended to link the birth of any western Mediterranean civilization with a population-shift from the east. Herodotus' version of the exodus of Tyrrhenus and his companions and of their settling in Etruria is not *a priori* more worthy of credence than Virgil's accounts of the voyages of Aeneas and his companions after the sack of Troy had forced them to flee the shores of Phrygia and find a new home for themselves at the mouth of the Tiber. But what increasingly prevents archaeologists today from accepting the hypothesis of oriental origins is the difficulty they have in finding any sufficiently precise break in the succession of cultures in central Italy to allow of the intervention of a foreign people.

For a long time this was believed to have taken place about 700 BC, at a moment when the orientalizing influence of which we have spoken replaced the civilization that had reigned for two centuries and which we call the Villanovan culture because it was first studied closely in the region of Bologna, at Villanova. This culture is characterized, in the early part of its development, by cremation of the dead, whose remains were contained in cinerary urns shaped like small houses or in ossuaries made of two superimposed truncated cones and by the geometrical decoration of objects; then, at a more advanced stage, by the appearance, together with the rite of cremation, of grave burial – without any new ethnic factor having supervened to cause the change – and by the gradual enrichment of funerary furnishings. Now it is becoming ever clearer, notably at Caere (Cerveteri), at Tarquinii and at Bolsena where Raymond Bloch's diggings have revealed the site of ancient Volsinii, that the orientalizing civilization appears nearly always in those places which were centres of Villanovan culture, following it without a break, the Etruscan chamber tombs for example developing by natural evolution from the former inhumation tombs. So that one arrives at the conclusion that if oriental elements did reach the Tyrrhenian coast of Italy they were numerically of small importance and did not sensibly modify the centres of population; in fact, one wonders if the Villanovans were not already Etruscans. But at Bolsena

6

(ancient Volsinii) itself the foundations of huts from the preceding civilization have just been laid bare – the civilization marking the end of the Bonze Age, belonging to a type called Apenninic because it extended over a large part of the peninsula's dorsal range. In fact, one no longer knows exactly where one is nor where to place these awkward intruders in the scale of Italian pre-history and proto-history, unless along with Herodotus we set their arrival in a legendary thirteenth century BC, which means, in that part of Italy, that they are lost in the mists of time.

THE THEORY OF AUTOCHTHONOUS ETRUSCANS

It is at this point, when the traditional hypothesis begins to fade away into a rather depressingly vague perspective, that another solution presents itself, one whose sole supporter among the ancients was Dionysius of Halicarnassus, and one which has long been considered heretical by modern scholars. 'In fact,' says our historian, 'those people who declare that the Etruscans did not emigrate from anywhere and were always there have a chance of coming closest to the truth.'

The partisans of the theory supporting the autochthony of the Etruscans do not waste fire on sterile criticism of the opposing side. They have positive views to put forth and an overall interpretation of all aspects of the problem, among others of cultural and linguistic relationship of the Etruscans with certain oriental peoples, which is no less convincing than that of their opponents. To the concept of a progress in techniques and beliefs through communication by sea and land, they oppose the idea of a resurrection after a long entombment. The Etruscans, they say, were not new arrivals in Italy, but the first occupants of a land which had been wrested from them by Indo-European invasions; yet these had not wiped them out completely nor had they broken their spirit. The birth of Etruscan civilization in the sixth century therefore is held to be simply the re-emergence – after a slow re-conquering of the interior and under various influences including those of the Orient and Greece – of the irrepressible descendants of indigenous Bronze Age inhabitants.

'If the seed withereth not . . .' The hypothesis of Etruscan autochthony obstinately pursues the subterranean course of a Mediterranean community which the influx of great blond

7

barbarians, Italians or Greeks, might have temporarily subdued but which went on struggling for freedom under the conqueror's heel. Etruscan legends contain a ready-made symbol to explain the origins of their religion, and one is astonished that so little weight has been given to it: it is said that a Tarquinian plough-man one day dug more deeply than usual in the earth and saw a little man come out of the hole who looked like a child but had the wisdom of an old man. He was called Tages and revealed to those who had collected round him the secrets of what was termed the *Etrusca disciplina*.[4]

Thus a dualism which was no longer really horizontal – between Orient and Occident – but vertical would seem to be the true explanation of the ancient primitive world. One must imagine, at the outset, in Italy, as also in Minoan Crete, a civilization dominated by the importance of Chthonian cults and by the pre-eminence of women; then, after vast upheavals, the marriage of Heaven and Earth, Indo-European strength with Mediterranean grace, the conquest of an agricultural society by war-lords. And if survivals of the first community reappear only in certain isolated parts, this is because its disappearance was like the sub-merging and disintegration of an entire continent. The links between Etruscan and Caucasian, between Lydian and the dialect of Lemnos are understandable if one considers that an 'Etrusco-Asianic' language was once used in Italy, in the Balkan peninsula, on the islands of the Aegean and in Asia Minor and was then driven back to the furthest bounds of its domain by the linguistic pressure of the invaders.

But here again, as in the hypothesis of oriental migration, we recognize the simplifying characteristics and grandiose outlines of myth. As we said at the beginning, the very word Etruscan evokes in the minds of our contemporaries the idea of mythological beings. Either the sacred wisdom of the empires of the Orient were transplanted in Tuscany after a mysterious voyage across the seas, or a Mediterranean civilization, submerged for a time by Indo-European invasions, reappeared after germinating for centuries. These are broad and dizzying perspectives and we may choose, according to our temperament, whichever one appeals most to us, or else refuse to make a choice – and that is what many scholars today feel impelled to do. But if the interest we have in the Etruscans were confined to that, we would be ill-advised to write an account of their daily life which necessarily requires a more precise and unassuming focusing of the lens.

ETRUSCAN CIVILIZATION: THE FIRST GREAT CIVILIZATION IN ITALY
Fortunately the Etruscan problem does not limit itself, as has so long been thought, to the so far insoluble problem of origins. Indeed, it has recently been remarked that even if this problem were to be solved the real questions would only just be beginning.[5] After all, the history of France is something more than the history of the origin of the Franks. The history of the Etruscans is not the inevitable unfolding of corollaries at the end of a theorem demonstrated once and for all, but the gradual formation of an organism whose shape becomes defined in relation to its *milieu* and circumstances. In any case, the Etruscan nation did not appear at Caere or Tarquinii in the guise of a well-defined and unalterable people.

It was only from the seventh century onwards, on Italian soil, making contact with other people and at grips with peculiar natural and climatic conditions that this nation achieved self-awareness. Those elements, probably decisive, from which it derived its singularities and its language gradually merged during the five or six centuries of its existence into an ensemble which alone may be termed Etruscan. We catch a shadowy glimpse of this nation at the start; but we have a good view of it at the finish for that culture which was formed from the seventh to the second centuries in Etruria was nothing less than the first great Italian civilization.

It is indeed a striking thought that the same region of central Italy has twice, in the shape of ancient Etruria and modern Tuscany, been the source of civilization in Italy. Since the seventh century BC and from the fifteenth century onwards, in the dawn of antiquity as well as at the beginning of modern times, the same region of the peninsula has been distinguished by exceptional qualities. The birth and the re-birth or Renaissance of Italy had the same cradle. It is a remarkable coincidence, and perhaps it is more than a coincidence. Are we to believe that the landscape, the light and the climate of Tuscany, enjoying a more tonic atmosphere than the heavy air of the Roman

9

Campania, produced the same miracle twice? Michelangelo, Vasari tells us, attributed 'whatever good he might have in his nature to the lively and subtle air one breathes in Arezzo'. Are we to assume that Dante, Machiavelli and Leonardo da Vinci inherited, despite the effects of invasions and the mixture of races, the centuries-old spirit of the ancient Etruscans? There are astonishing correspondences and resemblances: for example, the angels of death which keep watch at the foot of the cinerary urn of Arruns Volumnius at Perugia seem to be guarding a tomb of one of the Medici. Raymond Bloch, in one of his charming little works,[6] has juxtaposed the head of a young man coming from Cerveteri (Caere) and dating from the fifth century with that of Donatello's St George. It is difficult to tell which is Etruscan and which is Tuscan.

These remarks make us wonder whether the 'Etruscan mystery' can be confined solely to the origins of the race or whether it is repeated right through the nation's history in its most recent manifestations. We shall do well to allow the sort of enchantment inspired by the contemplation of the intangible to dissipate itself, and to bring our faculties to bear upon things much closer to us, upon a world where real men and women (who though strange are not much different from the Italians of old and more recent times) may be observed in the actual surroundings of their everyday life.

HISTORICAL SUMMARY

It will be helpful to retrace the main outlines of the Etruscans' history from the point in the seventh century when the country between the Arno and the Tiber and between the Apennines and the Tyrrhenian Sea seemed first to be touched with the rays of a new dawn. From Populonia to the south of Livorno to Caere to the north of Rome a series of princely tombs piled with golden ornaments, silver plate, bronze chariots, figures and decorations of ivory come to light in the cemeteries, sometimes in the very mounds themselves of the inhumation tombs: signs of a sudden prodigious increase of wealth[7] which soon extends to all the cemeteries and which in any case, right from the start, overflows the southern limits of Etruria. In fact, at Praeneste (Palestrina) in Latium the Bernardini and Barberini tombs, identical to and contemporaneous with the Regolini-Galassi tomb at Caere, suddenly illuminate, with equal splendour, the strategic point commanding the road to Campania.

Today it can no longer be doubted that this rapid transfiguration of the Villanovan world was connected with the discovery by the Greeks of the metal deposits of Etruria. We shall discuss later in greater detail the conditions under which the copper, iron, aluminium and perhaps tin mines were exploited. The Greek colonization of the west (in the eighth century when the Chalcidians in 770 established their first advance post on the island of Ischia) was directed towards the discovery of basic materials whose exploitation and exportation determined the economic progress of those who were in control of the mines.[8] Populonia has been called the Pittsburgh of the ancient world. Or, if we prefer a comparison which today might appeal even more to our imaginations, we might say the Etruscan gold was also, at the outset, a black gold. Iron from the island of Elba played more or less the same rôle for the Etruscan lucumones as oil does today for the Emirs of the Persian Gulf.

Etruria, then, was at the start a country suddenly favoured by great fortunes and in consequence was a civilization which came to birth under Greek and oriental influences, developing in heterogeneous surroundings. In this respect Praeneste is as Etruscan as Caere, though its population and dialect are Latin: a silver vase of the Bernardini tomb bears a Latin inscription. But otherwise it is incontestable that to the north of the Tiber the inhabitants of that country speak in general the same tongue and are united, ethnically, by the closest links. But all the same there is great diversity between one town and another: each city has its own peculiar characteristics, its rites and traditions, its industries and arts; and political disunity is to be one of the constant features of Etruscan history. They did not shape themselves into a *nation* all at once.

Later, probably towards the middle of the sixth century BC, they formed, after the example of Asia Minor's league of Ionian cities, a confederation of twelve peoples united by political and religious solidarity.[9] These twelve peoples or cities, *duodecim Etruriae populi*, were, if one can venture to proffer an official list, Veii, Caere, Tarquinii, Vulci, Rusellae, Vetulonia, Volsinii,

Clusium, Perugia, Cortona, Arretium and Volterra and they held periodically in a federal sanctuary situated in the territory of the Volsinii at the temple of Voltumna or Vertumnus a solemn assembly (*concilium Etruriae*); there the delegates discussed the nation's interests and elected to protect these a 'magistrate of the Etruscan nation' or *zilath mechl rasnal*, which means in Latin *praetor Etruriae*. Despite the dissensions which continued to agitate them, the Etruscans in the future at times pooled their military resources for the prosecution of common enterprises and for carrying out extremely ambitious plans.[10]

So it was that having become aware of their political unity and not content with clearing and fertilizing the territory which nature – or Jupiter, as they claimed – had given them, they crossed its frontiers and created an Empire which at one time covered almost the whole of the peninsula: to the north in the valley of the Po at the end of the sixth century they founded a new Etruria of twelve cities including Marzabotto at the mouth of the Reno, Bologna, which they called Felsina, Parma, Modena, Ravenna, Spina, Adria, Melpum which is perhaps Milan, and Mantua where Virgil was born. And these places, when the Gauls invaded Italy at the beginning of the fourth century, were the first to bear the brunt. To the south, they conquered Latium and placed Rome under their domination: the tradition of the annals has it that from 616 to 509 the Etruscan dynasty of the Tarquins reigned there, and the most recent archaeological finds confirm this, though they sometimes place the dates rather later (550–475).[11] They advanced even further and the Etruscan Campania, which came into being opposite Cumae, round Capua, Nola, Nuceria and Pompeii (where just before the outbreak of war Etruscan inscriptions were found), Sorrento, Salerno – as well as twelve other towns, it is said – established immediate contact with *Magna Graecia*.

But the maritime strength of the Etruscans was in no way inferior to their land forces. Their most ancient cities, Vetulonia, Vulci, Tarquinii and Caere are found only a few kilometres from the coast where small ports, Graviscae for Tarquinii, Pyrgi for Caere, sheltered their vessels, whether merchant or battle ships. It is as sailors or rather as pirates that the Etruscans first appear in the stories of the Greeks: but the word 'pirate' which really means 'adventurer' indicates the jealous disposition of rivals who looked upon all competition as disloyal. The Etruscans had for a long time waged war on Greek shipping in waters over which they had control. Bound by very ancient ties with the islands across the water, notably Sardinia, they checked Greek colonization in the southern part of the peninsula. Soon, in order to resist the progress being made by Phocaean thalassocracy which founded Marseilles and became mistress of the far West, they united with Carthage in an alliance so close that in the words of Aristotle 'the Etruscans and the Carthaginians had once formed a single nation'. The Phocaeans, having successfully established themselves in Corsica, were driven from that island about 535 following a memorable naval battle off Alalia (Aleria) in which they were defeated by the combined Etruscan and Carthaginian fleets.

This date marks the apogee of Etruscan greatness. Shortly after that the Etruscans were to begin their slow decline. At the end of the century, in *circa* 509, the Tarquins were expelled from Rome, Latium recovered its independence and Campanian Etruria was cut off from Etruria proper. In 480 the Carthaginians at Himera lost all hopes of conquering Sicily. In 474 the Etruscan fleet suffered defeat from the Syracusans at Cumae which put an end to their domination of the Tyrrhenian Sea.

It was not an irremediable catastrophe; it did not cut short the vital force of a whole race nor did it extinguish their resourceful spirit. Tarquinii and Caere lost a considerable part of their prosperity as a result, but the closing of their outlets on that side gave a great stimulus to Etruscan expansion eastwards to the Adriatic: the organization of northern Etruria, the growth of Marzabotto and Etruscan Bologna, the beginnings of prosperity in Adria and Spina at the mouth of the Po all coincide with the turn of the sixth century. The interior of northern Etruria in contact with the fresh forces of that province took over henceforward the naval lead that had belonged to the south.

In Etruria, as in the whole of central Italy, this date marked the beginning of a kind of complex and confused Middle Ages during which there were obscurely worked out those political, religious and technical elements whose most well-known centre was republican Rome. It was a vast experiment conducted with simultaneous solidarity at Tarquinii, Volsinii, Arezzo, Tusculum and Rome and in which various peoples, at peace and at war, sought by reciprocal exchanges to find a solution to the problems, both spiritual and material, which presented themselves to all.[12] In the formation of this cultural *koinè* the conquests which Rome was to effect in the fourth and third centuries did not stop Etruscan institutions from continuing in some places with paradoxical vigour and from contributing, more than anything else, to the civilizing of the conqueror. At the end of the fourth century the great Roman families usually sent their sons to Caere as they were later to send them to Athens to finish their education and it was the Roman senate which in the middle of the second century took measures to guarantee the continuation and preservation, should the Etruscan nobility lose interest in it, of the *Etrusca disciplina*. Veii was destroyed in 396, and Volsinii in 265, but other cities more fortunate than these, reduced to the state of allies continued to struggle on together and to carry on, at least nominally, the administrative and priestly duties they had performed when they were independent. Right to the end of the Republic there were *zilath mechl rasnal* at Tarquinii, and there even emerged under the Empire the old title of *praetor Etruriae*. At the beginning of the first century, the François tomb at Vulci proclaimed with greater piety than ever the exploits of heroes who had been the glory of that city. Under Constantine the federal games in the sacred wood of Volsinii were still being religiously celebrated.

This is why the chronological boundaries of our study cannot be narrowly defined. Putting aside Tyrrhenian pre-history or proto-history, we should like to observe the living Etruscans – this Mediterranean world slowly vanishing, this Roman world slowly growing – at their height, in the sixth century. But no one will grudge us the assistance of more ancient evidence – the treasures buried about 650 at Caere and Praeneste – nor indeed that of the most recent finds. It is from the fourth century that figured monuments become more explicit and their inscription more numerous; and even after the Roman conquest which infinitely increases our knowledge it is permissible to extract from documents, taking full account of their date, evidence which enlightens us about ancient Etruria. We shall often notice that the Etruscans, though displaying a very receptive enthusiasm for superior modes of civilization, meaning Greek civilization, show throughout their history an irreducible conservatism, a jealous guarding of ancestral habit, a proud fidelity to their own nature. It was not for nothing that Dionysius of Halicarnassus, in the reign of Augustus, called them a 'very ancient people'. They demonstrate a specific slowing-down of the historical process which makes the princes of Norchia and Perugia, wearing the purple-bordered toga of the Roman knights towards the end of the Republic, authentic contemporaries of the Tarquins.

Let us stress here a fact which may not be at once evident to all our readers: it would be wrong to imagine that Etruscan history abruptly stopped with the entry on the scene of other actors, the Romans, or that the Etruscan people disappeared with the Roman conquest which destroyed a few of its towns and deprived it of some of its political freedom. A people does not die out so easily. There were of course massacres and displacements of the population. But when Volsinii and Falerii were destroyed there arose at their gates *Volsinii novi* and *Falerii novi* where the survivors of the catastrophes settled and went on living, perpetuating, in new forms, their ancient traditions. It has often been believed, by those who put their faith in certain rhetorical exaggerations, that the Samnites had been exterminated in the social war. Ettore Pais has effectively demonstrated that under the Empire the municipal magistrates of Samnium were the direct descendants of the Samnites of the golden period whose families had never died out completely. This is even more the case with the Etruscans, whose civilization was highly regarded in Rome and who, as Horace says, 'Vanquished, vanquished their vanquisher'. Indeed in certain cases it was the Romans who took measures to preserve Etruscan rites and customs. The roll-call of Etruscan proper names has come down through the centuries with a consistency which proves the persistence in the same ancient rites, in the same palaces, of the same great families from whose members Roman history has selected its poets and even its emperors. And though a long decadence perhaps undermined their diehard singularities, it did not affect their irreducible vitality. And it is not without significance that even during the Augustan era the Etruscan language was spoken and engraved on the tombs at Perugia.

WHAT WE KNOW ABOUT THE ETRUSCAN LANGUAGE

It perhaps comes as some surprise that we should so often make reference to the evidence of inscriptions in the Etruscan tongue in order to obtain reliable information about institutions and manners. It must not be thought that we belong to those who periodically flatter themselves that they have 'pierced the mystery', reputed to be 'insoluble', of that language. But our knowledge of Etruscan is much less limited than is supposed and it would seem that the public is not properly acquainted with the conditions posed by this problem. Salomon Reinach once published *Eulalia, or Greek without Tears*, and *Cornelia, or Latin without Weeping*; there is perhaps room now for a *Tanaquil, or Etruscan without Trickery*.

Etruscan is not hidden from our understanding by the veil of a special writing which would have to be deciphered before we could go any further, as Champollion deciphered the Egyptian hieroglyphics or as Ventris and Chadwick more recently, in a resounding discovery, deciphered the ideograms of the Mycenaean syllabary called Linear B. To everyone's surprise, it was realized that the *unknown* signs engraved, between 1450 and 1200 BC on the tablets of Mycenae and Pylos concealed a *known* tongue, which was no other than archaic Greek. But no such difficulty attends the reading of Etruscan: it can easily be read by means of an alphabet very similar to our own, because it was this, derived from the Greek alphabet, which the Latins borrowed before transmitting it to us. However the words which we can *read* so easily cannot be *understood*: they belong to a tongue which, apart from a few loan-words, resembles neither Greek nor Latin nor any known language.

Does this mean that we must abandon for ever all hope of understanding it? (Discounting the likelihood of the chance discovery of a bilingual, Etruscan-Latin text similar to the Rosetta Stone which, being trilingual, allowed a scrutiny of three parallel versions in hieroglyphics, demotic and Greek of the same text and thus gave early nineteenth-century Egyptology a fine start.) We have long been in possession of brief bilingual Etrusco-Latin inscriptions in which a romanized Etruscan gives evidence of a double civil status. It is possible that one day, while exploring the forum at Vulci or the pile dwellings of Spina archaeologists may unearth a long inscription detailing on both sides of the stone, in two languages, the clauses of a treaty or of some important public law. Such a discovery would considerably enrich our lexicographical knowledge, but it would be wrong to imagine that it would illuminate completely an area which until then had been shrouded in the deepest dark. It would be a great step forward; but meanwhile, a large part of the area has already been mapped.

Indeed we cannot ignore the long, patient and fruitful work performed by several generations of linguists who, conscious of the limitations within which they worked but determined to exploit them to the full, made etruscology an authentic science whose methods are constantly becoming more precise. By scrutinizing carefully some ten thousand epigraphic texts, of which only a small number are of any length, they have succeeded in conquering certain isolated reefs in an ocean of uncertainties and taking these as their points of departure, are proceeding from the known to the unknown and making constant progress.[13]

In order to reassure the sceptics, let us consider here as examples three epitaphs from Tarquinii:

1 Larth Avles clan avils huth muvalchls lupu;[14]
2 Velthur Larisal clan Cuclnial Thanchvilus lupu avils XXV;[15]
3 Larth Arnthal Plecus clan Ramthasc Apatrual eslz zilachnthas avils thunem muvalchls lupu.[16]

An examination of hundreds of formulae of this kind in which there reappear, always in the same place, identical words, has allowed us to establish, down to the last details, the indisputable meaning of the inscriptions. They begin with proper names which are often known to us through their Latin equivalents (*Lars, Aulus, Tanaquil*, etc.): they are the names of the dead person, of his father and sometimes of his mother. They terminate with the words *avils lupu* preceded or followed by a number written in figures or in letters (*thu* and *huth*, for example, have been proved to be names of numbers on two of the faces of a die). The third inscription introduces, in the middle, two words of which one, *eslz*, is the name of a number or numeral adverb, while the other is derived from the magistrature, the term *zilath*, as we have already seen, meaning *praetor*.

According to this analysis, the following translations are not only possible, but irrefutable: the only words open to other interpretations are the names of numbers:

1 'Larth, son of Aulus, died at the age of fifty-four years';
2 'Velthur, son of Laris and of Tanaquil Cuclni, died at the age of twenty-five years';
3 'Larth, son of Arnth (= Arruns) Plecu and of Ramtha Apatrui, having twice been praetor, died at the age of forty-nine (*undequinquaginta*) years.'

Documents of this nature therefore show us without any doubt names indicating parental relationships (*clan*: 'son'; elsewhere *sec*: 'daughter'; *puia*: 'wife'), the substantive meaning 'year' (*avil*), the verb signifying 'to die' (*lupu*). The third epitaph shows us the existence of a copulative conjunction -*c*, post-positioned like the Latin -*que*. They furnish us with yet other morphological indications, notably concerning the -*s* and -*al* inflections of the genitive case. Doubts still remain concerning the interpretation of the names of numbers, which it must be agreed will one day be resolved. But after all that, though we must admit that Etruscan is certainly a difficult language, we can see that its gradual decipherment is not dependent upon a miracle, but simply a matter of time.

Etruscology is now in possession of a vocabulary which, not counting proper names, consists of about two hundred word-roots: a certain number of these come from ancient glosses; but the majority are derived from textual exegesis, and their number is growing steadily every year. One day Emil Vetter picked out from certain Tarquinian epitaphs the formula of the date used by eponymous magistrates corresponding to the Latin *Cn. Fulvio P. Sulpicio consulibus*.[17] On another occasion Santo Mazzarino, proceeding from the Etruscan *tular*, meaning 'limit', elucidated in the inscription, on a *cippus* or truncated column at Perugia, relating the facts of a litigation between neighbouring proprietors, a whole series of terms taken from legal language.[18]

Knowledge of a language however is not measured by the number of words whose meaning one knows or can guess at. Etruscan is one of those whose grammar we are beginning to master. It is a grammar which obeys complex and at times disconcerting rules:

nevertheless we now have at our disposal a fairly well-established system of phonetics, a morphology with its own paradigms of declension and conjugation, and even the elements of a syntax and stylistics. What is holding up scholars today is not the question of whether Etruscan is related to Basque or to Caucasian, but whether such and such a form is a genitive or a locative, whether another is an active or a passive. Interpretation no longer depends on tracing a word which in some obscure context suddenly seems to be explained by its resemblance to Greek, Latin or Lydian and thereafter drawing vertiginous conclusions; the tendency now is to analyse the word morphologically and phonetically before allowing the supposed relationship to have any value. Thanks to this method considerable results have been obtained which sometimes are highly relevant to the history of Etruscan civilization; and we are allowed consequently to extract from technical journals, *Glotta* or *Studi Etruschi*, certain data which may help us in our attempt to reconstruct Etruscan life.

CHAPTER ONE

THE PHYSICAL TYPE

Evidence of medical biology – The evidence of monuments with figures – Etruscans and Tuscans – Life-expectancy of the Etruscans

What makes an Etruscan? Faced with the wonderment that these strange people's customs inspired in the ancients and indeed in the moderns, we must first of all ask ourselves if, like Montesquieu's Persian, there was not 'in his physiognomy something admirable'. Was there an Etruscan type which allowed one to recognize at first sight among the Mediterranean crowds the pirate from Caere, the augur from Tarquinii, the courtesan from Pyrgi? It is not unimportant that we should know with whom we are dealing in the pages to come and so we must find out if those people whom we wish to surprise about their daily tasks had their own unmistakable look.

THE EVIDENCE OF MEDICAL BIOLOGY

The problem is not a new one and numerous scholars, archaeologists, anthropologists and biologists have shown interest in it. Most of them were bent on proving the oriental origin of the Etruscans. Recent articles by Sir Gavin de Beer, director of the Victoria and Albert Museum,[1] have even made use of the evidence of blood-groups. The percentage of the four groups into which humanity is divided shows a remarkable stability in each race and reunites, for example, over the centuries, the Jewish colonies of Holland and Russia. The Romanies of Hungary present more or less the same picture as the Hindus from whom they are descended. Now it has been observed that maps of geographical distribution reveal in central Italy a zone – corresponding roughly to the boundaries of Tuscany – in which the proportion of groups A and B is greater by about five per cent to that of the neighbouring populations to the north and south, and this would seem to relate the descendants of the Etruscans to the oriental peoples – Armenians, Hindus, Romanies.

Inspired by these findings, the Ciba Foundation organized a conference in London in 1958 at which the origins of the Etruscans were discussed from a medical-biological point of view.[2] Representatives of archaeology and the natural sciences attempted to co-ordinate their methods and findings. In fact, the scientists were extremely cautious and in general their reports steered clear of any definite answer, particularly concerning the oriental origin of the Etruscans. Before breaking up, the conference passed a resolution submitting that a detailed investigation into blood-group proportions should be made in Etruria and the surrounding areas.

But for the last century at least anthropologists have been measuring skulls from Etruscan cemeteries, always aware that the material at their disposal was very scanty and that the periods dominated by the rites of cremation were excluded from their observations. Giuseppe Sergi studied systematically forty-four skulls taken from tombs in seven Etrurian towns and identified thirty-four dolichocephalics and mesocephalics and ten brachycephalics: the long and medium-sized skulls would have belonged to invaders from the Orient, and the large skulls to the indigenous population. To which it was objected that this verdict on the skulls was more or less the same as that on the skulls of the Mediterranean race which flourished over the whole of southern Europe from neolithic times.[3] The facts present a picture of such complexity that one is alarmed by the intrepid assurance of certain anthropologists' generalizations:

'The Etruscan skulls are notably smooth in surface relief, with little in the way of browridges; the side walls of the vaults, seen from above, are not parallel, as with the longer Mediterranean forms, but converging with the greatest breadth in the parietals and a narrow forehead; the orbits are high and rounded, and the nose narrow.'

From which Sir Gavin concludes: 'It is easy to recognize in the

anthropologists' descriptions the type of the couple on the sarcophagus of Cerveteri: long face, thin nose, forehead high and
narrow without bulge, head rather long in shape.'[4]

This terra-cotta sarcophagus from Cerveteri (Caere) and dating
from the second half of the sixth century is well known. There
are in fact three almost identical examples of it, one of which is
in the Louvre, the second in the Museo di Villa Giulia in Rome
and the third (forgery) in the British Museum.[5] It would be
pointless to give a lengthy description of this couple reclining
side by side on the funerary banquet-bed, with their delicate
features, their discreet smiles. We shall see that the presence of
the wife reclining beside her husband who lays his right arm
tenderly across her shoulder, would probably have seemed an
impermissible audacity in Greece, but among the Etruscans such
a pose was common. The dead wife wears on her head the
tutulus shaped like a sutar-loaf which was the favourite head-
dress of Etruscan women in the archaic past, and on her feet she
has the *calcei repandi* or slippers with turned-up toes which was
also the national style of footwear. But despite the pose and
certain details of costume which we could show are of Ionian
origin, the faces resemble almost exactly those one sees on contemporary monuments in Greece and Asia Minor. The woman
seems to be related to the first Attic *Korai*, and as for the man,
to quote M. Charles Picard, 'with his jawline beard, his oval,
almost triangular face, his oblique eyes, his abundant hair spread
freely over his shoulders, this Tyrrhenian could easily have been
born on the shores of the Aegean'.[6]

THE EVIDENCE OF MONUMENTS WITH FIGURES

Then must we conclude that the sarcophagus at Cerveteri gives
us a faithful portrait of bygone Etruscans, and must we imagine
the princes and princesses at the court of the Tarquins as this
couple is represented here in clay? That would be to forget the
imperious power of art, whose contemporary aesthetic has taught
us that it imposes the laws of its own vision on the facts of life.
Nature, it is said, imitates art much more than art reproduces
reality. That the Impressionist period, reacting against academic
beauty, should have preferred in the bathers of Renoir, the dancers
of Degas and the nymphs of Rodin, an animal grace in keeping

with their sensuality does not mean that French girls in 1880 all woke up one morning with slant eyes, flat noses and full lips, nor that a colony of Tahitian women settled on the banks of the Seine in the wake of Gauguin. How much more general and tyrannical was the influence in Etruria of the Ionian style! With the rich stuffs of Miletus and the black-figured amphorae of Attica or Clazomenae, with the technical resources of their artisans and the very form of their gods the Etruscans had imported from Asia Minor or Greece the sloping brow, the straight nose, the almond-shaped eye and the peculiar smile, concepts of ideal beauty to which they tried to conform during their lifetime and which in any case determined the image of what they wished to appear like after their death. So that those funerary sculptures from the archaic period are merely masks.

It is certainly tempting to seek more authentic evidence in later monuments, when a certain Etruscan realism, brought about by the easy handling qualities of terra-cotta, though not before attempting here and there other stylized forms, finally abandoned those old-fashioned masks. This evidence tempted, on the eve of the last war, certain German scholars who wanted to prove their *Rassentheorie*, or racial theories of Nazism. But by choosing as they pleased whatever features seemed best to fit their aims, they arrived at very different conclusions. One of them, looking at cinerary urns surmounted by statues of the dead persons, had been struck by the fact that some of these sometimes had hooked noses.[7] So he proceeded to class the Etruscans among the aquiline races, and Professor Fischer went around finding these noses everywhere, drawing them in cafés and photographing Italians of 1938 whose noses, like eagles' beaks, seemed to him incontestably Etruscan. He found them everywhere, but particularly at Chiusi, the home land of Porsenna. And also at Volterra and at Tarquinii. Very few at Perugia. And none at all at Viterbo. Could it be, the professor asked himself in all seriousness, that the history of Viterbo, a city so long the subject of quarrels between Pope and Emperor and overrun by so many foreign invasions, explains this physiognomic upset and the disappearance of all aquiline noses? But the echoes of this communication to the Berlin Academy of Science had scarcely died away before an article in the review

Klio claimed that the fundamental and distinctive character of the Etruscan race, and the proof of its oriental origin, lay in its obesity.[8]

The responsibility for this should be laid to Catullus and Virgil who, without apparently having tipped each other the wink, denounce the *obesus Etruscus* and the *pinguis Tyrrhenus*.[9] Catullus, invoking the various peoples of Italy, places between the Umbrian and the Latin of Lanuvium, 'sun-tanned and full-toothed' the 'obese Etruscans'. Virgil, in more elevated tones, describes a sacrifice celebrated to the music of a flute when 'a gross Tyrrhenian blew upon the ivory instrument near the altars'. Moreover the sarcophagi of the second and first centuries would provide our poets with an appropriate plastic commentary. They represent the dead man reclining on one elbow with a wine-cup in his hand in the attitude of someone at a banquet and in these figures the sculptor's eye for realistic detail has not overlooked, indeed has rather exhibited with a kind of implacable complacency as it sags over the robe's wide-open panels the plenitude of a majestic corporation.

Similarly, certain scholars have claimed that primitive Etruscans, judging by the emaciated proportions of the effigies on the sarcophagi at Cerveteri, were extremely skinny, and that they were succeeded later, following ethnic transformations and social revolutions which allowed the autochthonous population to reassert themselves, by the stout, stocky form of the Italians. Other scholars were amazed to discover on steles and ancient bronzes Etruscans with squat bodies: these, they claimed, were the authentic Etruscans, shipped straight over like a host of pot-bellied Sileni, from Caria in Asia Minor, while the elegant slimness of the figures at Cerveteri were thought to reveal, in southern Etruria, the existence of a distinct race, the Pelasgians which were claimed to have come from Crete and the Grecian Islands. As if the squat and the slim forms of the human body had not existed simultaneously or alternately – as has long been proved – in the vagaries of the Ionian style! But this did not prevent Ernst Bux, in 1942, from attributing to the Etruscans a 'square stature' which he was pleased to distinguish in the Emperor Vespasian, born of an incontestably Sabine father but of a mother who perhaps was Etruscan; a stature which moreover, as he saw fit to remark, has been preserved to the present day in half the population of Tuscany.

But let us leave these incongruous theories and return to the obesity of the Etruscans: we cannot ignore the evidence of the poets, above all when it is confirmed by obviously contemporary funerary representations. But has the poets' testimony not been overrated? In the excellent catalogue which Reinhard Herbig collated on these later Etruscan sarcophagi,[10] we have found only a small number, three or four, which show this peculiarity. Even here, distinctions must be made. One of them, coming from San Giuliano near Viterbo, is all the more impressive because the figure is lying on its back and the monumental stomach, culminating in the centre, rises from the body in proud independence. It was thought to be a woman who had died in pregnancy. But it is more reasonable to take into account a tendency towards stylistic deformation which the Etruscan sculptors of that period were fond of displaying, and which, achieving a geometric simplification of masses, has actually been called cubist: more exactly, it was called stereometric, because it sought to combine spherical as well as cubic volumes. It is certainly from this school, so foreign to the Greek taste and so contrary to the usual forms of Etruscan art, that the sarcophagus at San Giuliano derives, in which it is impossible to see a faithful representation of any individual.

Yet another, in the tomb of the noble Partunu family at Tarquinii, shows stretched along the lid the body of an old man whose flesh, in contrast with the hollow cheeks and deeply-wrinkled neck, is soft and plump; but as M. Herbig rightly remarks, this happens to many intellectuals at the end of their days.

The only truly obese Etruscan is the one in the museum at Florence. A big bag of flesh, he has been called, displaying his rotundity before us with a sort of cynical innocence. A wreath of flowers round his shoulders, a bowl in his outstretched right hand, the golden seal-ring of the knights on the third finger of his left hand, this man, aged about fifty or so, has a small head with no hint of plumpness; the top of his head is bald but the temples are still well thatched; his big, vague eyes are wide open, and his mouth seems fresh and young. He does not seem to be aware of his colossal *embonpoint*, but if he were to rise from his couch several servants would be needed to support him. The nudity of his navel, the centre of his world, is almost indecent, but he does not care. By exhibiting a belly of generous proportions this descendant of the ancient *lucumones* proclaims, without shame and even with a kind of family pride, his satisfaction at leaving this life with a full stomach, in death which preserves to the last the appearance of a banquet.

But it is this very feature which gives the sarcophagus at Florence its value and justifies to some extent the words of the Latin poets. It does not show us the Etruscan as such, nor the eternal Etruscan, but one Etruscan from the period of decadence, one of those great Tuscan landowners whose political independence had been suppressed but whose social privileges had been confirmed by Rome and who, administering from afar their *latifundia* for which there was abundant manual labour, were henceforward devoting their lives, in their Perugian or Tarquinian palaces, to proud memories of past glories and to the pleasures of *dolce far niente* and a well-laden table.

At the same period, in Rome, sumptuary laws were passed in an ineffective attempt to compel moderation at table. Cato the Censor deprived of their public horse those *equites* who were too corpulent to ride. Attacking an obese Roman, he said: 'How can the State make any use of a man's body which from neck to waist is all belly?'[11] The satirical poet Lucilius used the whole range of his Rabelaisian vocabulary to describe big eaters: *mandones*, *comedones*, *lurcones* – gormandizer, glutton, guzzle-guts – who stuffed themselves with legs of pork, with choice asparagus and cauliflowers, with shrimps and giant sturgeon. And he ended with the sarcastic invocation: *Vivite ventres!* 'Ye bellies, I salute you!'[12] Meanwhile Laelius the wise, Scipio Aemilianus' *alter ego*, was singing the praises of vegetarian frugality and the philosophical superiority of sorrel[13] and itinerant preachers went about repeating that gluttony was like Circe the enchantress, could change old men into beasts and that a big belly is incompatible with an active mind: 'How can they attain wisdom if their hearts are crammed with filth and wine?'[14] Thus Roman humour and Greco-Roman ethics let loose their barbs and their condemnations against obesity as a manifest expression of vice and as the Etruscans for reasons which we shall examine later, had the reputation for luxury and debauch, it was natural, as soon as their degeneration began to provide a target, that they should appear in the ill-natured eyes of their masters and rivals as the very embodiment of *mollitia*. But this was more of a moral judgement than a physical portrait. The Etruscan became known as *obesus* just as he was known elsewhere as *segnis* or *ignavus*. We shall return to this point.

ETRUSCANS AND TUSCANS

It now hardly requires much effort to dissipate the fog behind which the stylizations of the ancients and the categorical spirit of the moderns have hidden the Etruscan type from us. In fact, the thing that comes to the fore in the majority of portraits, as soon as the authority of Greek models begins to lose its hold, is a refreshing realism; a liking, shared by both artists and clients, for a scrupulously exact representation of individual features and of the smallest and most private details. The man who had a sculpture made of himself to decorate his sarcophagus no doubt insisted first and foremost on a good likeness, down to the last wart, because it was his fervent hope that he would live on in this other self of stone or terra-cotta. The sculptors themselves, leaving to the Greeks the marble which lends itself to idealization and noble effects, had learnt their trade by modelling common clay which they worked not with bated breath and with prudent chisel as did the sculptor his marble, but with a freedom of movement and improvization which enabled them to seize the individual look, the typical gesture; and this freedom of treatment was extended to their bronzes and even to their sculptures in alabaster and travertine.

A striking example of this general tendency is given us by a school of vase-painters which flourished at Volterra in the third century; these painters took a mischievous pleasure in ornamenting the flanks of their vases not with the idealized, dreamy profiles suggested by Greek models but with sketches, almost caricatures, done in a few brush-strokes with a proletarian vigour, of prosperous citizens seen at the market or taking their evening stroll along the *corso*: the fiery-eyed girl with the candid face, the shrew with pinched nostrils, the self-satisfied sporting type, the frosty intellectual, the round-cheeked boy and the old lady with her head-scarf tied round her neck and under her chin; the latter was chosen by historians of Etruscan ceramics as representative of one of the painters of that particular school, who is termed the Nun-painter.[15]

So that if one looks at this gallery of portraits which are as true to life as any, one finds a great diversity of human types and faces, delicate or vulgar, energetic or sluggish, cunning or stupid, and on which nature has inscribed all possible psychological combinations. And this race has physically nothing which makes them appear foreign to us, nothing which might inspire in us a feeling of difference, attraction or repulsion such as we experience at the sight of certain peoples; and they have nothing of the accepted 'oriental' appearance. In fact, once the orientalizing masks have been torn away, they appear as present-day Italians, and give an almost hallucinating impression of consanguinity with the inhabitants of the peninsula. There is not one Caliph of Baghdad, not one Merchant of Venice among them: instead, they are Tuscan peasants, *condottieri*, Roman priests and emperors, young Bonapartes; and, on an urn from Volterra which shows us two happy sixty-year-olds, we might be looking at Ovid's Philemon and Baucis or Giuseppi Giusti's Taddeo and Veneranda. Therefore there is nothing to stop us, as we wander in imagination through the streets of Tarquinii and Veii, from lending our visions of their former inhabitants the same physical types as we see today among the strollers along the Lungarno.

One last trait completes the illusion: the women were considerably smaller than the men.[16] Their skeletons have been measured and compared: the medium height for men was 1 m. 64., and for women 1 m. 55. It is comforting to know that the signs of gynaecocracy which we shall mention later did not mean that the women had the stature of guardsmen, that a capable woman like Tanaquil, though she might dominate her husband temperamentally, did not crush him with her superior physique, and that Tarquin, when he spoke to Tanaquil, had to bend his head a little towards her.

LIFE-EXPECTANCY OF THE ETRUSCANS

After these remarks about the physical constitution of the Etruscans, it may be of interest to make known a few unpublished facts about their expectancy of life. Demographic studies are now in full swing and these can attempt an explanation, by their new methods, of population problems in the Greco-Roman world. Attempts have been made to evaluate 'the expectancy of life at birth' in Egypt, North Africa, Spain and at Bordeaux: documentary evidence is provided by funerary inscriptions which very frequently indicate the dead person's age.[17] We have large numbers of Etruscan epitaphs. What can we learn from them on this subject?

We have not used in this survey those texts which transcribe in letters the names of numbers. The correct interpretation of these is still in dispute, and though etruscologists have now reached some measure of agreement in establishing the sequence of the first ten numerals – *thu, zal, ci, huth, mach, sa, cezp-, semph-, nurph-* and *zar*, – there is still some doubt concerning the respective values of *huth* and *sa*, four or six, and of *cezp-* and *semph-*, seven or eight.[18] Now as the names of the tens, from thirty to ninety, are formed from the units from three to nine, the use of these inscriptions (about twenty in all) might risk an error sometimes multiplied by ten. Did *Ramtha Matulnai* die at the age of forty-five or sixty-five?[19] Did *Larth Tute* die at the age of sixty-two or eighty-two?[20] There is no way yet of being quite sure.

But we have at our disposal some one hundred and thirty funerary inscriptions in which the age of the dead person is indicated in numbers and here no doubt is possible. Nevertheless we have disregarded those in which worn stone or cracks have made interpretation uncertain. That leaves us with one hundred and thirteen, sufficient to help us towards some conclusions.

These one hundred and thirteen inscriptions are of late date: they belong to the last two centuries of the Etruscan world, from about 200 to 50 BC. They nearly all come from Tarquinii and Volterra, the only two towns where the habit of indicating age on epitaphs was widespread. But within these limits, they bring to life a numerous population, of varied and healthy types, and in which all ages and all conditions of man are represented.

There is little *Ravntza Urinati*, daughter of Arruns, aged two, little *Sethre Ceisinies Masu* (in Latin, Caesennius Maso), who lived to the age of three, and little *Agatinia Annia*, daughter of Lucius, who died at the age of four. They are so touching, those diminutives with their tender, caressing note (*Agatinia*, and

Ravntza from *Ravntu*), as is the dignity with which those babies already bear all the onomastic attributes of grown-ups – gentilicial name, sometimes a *cognomen*, and then the name of the father who recognized them as his own.[21]

Beside these 'premature dead' for whom Virgil's hell and presumably the Etruscan hell also contained a limbo, we see the venerable *Larth Vestarcnies* moving slowly towards a tomb laden with honours; he died at the age of eighty-four, not very different probably from his compatriot – though there were three centuries between them – of the same name and perhaps the same family, the consul Vestricius Spurinna, whose green and smiling old age has been described by Pliny the Younger.[22] Between these two extremes come children, about thirty young men and women snatched away between the ages of twenty and thirty, in the prime of life; then there are the proud, fulfilled mothers; and a grandfather whose double success as a family man and as a politician is marked by three stages: three sons, mayor of his little town at twenty-eight, six grandchildren, died at the age of sixty-six.

And in case it is thought that these documents illumine only a limited aristocracy, let us add that a good number of them relate to slaves or freed men. One of the greatest families in Volterra was that of the Caecina, in which Cicero, at the end of the Republic, found intimate friends whose religious knowledge he praises highly, and whose political errors he excuses: they kept a large number of servants whose epitaphs have their place in this statistical survey.[23] (Not counting that woman called *Larthi Lautnei*) who died at the age of thirty-three, and whose name (*lautni*) expressly denotes someone of servile origin.)[24]

What conclusions can we draw? The total number of years lived by these one hundred and thirteen persons was 4,620, and the average length of life was 40·88 years. The average length of a man's life was 41·09 years; of a woman's, a little less – a fact which is met with all over the ancient world – 40·37 years. Our figures are considerably higher than that which is usually given (twenty-five years) but they agree with conclusions recently come to for other countries or towns: 45·2 for North Africa, 36·2 for Spain, 35·7 for Gallo-Roman Bordeaux. Naturally they have only an approximate value. They do not take into consideration infant mortality and therefore perhaps should be reduced by what has been reckoned as one-sixth. But we can appreciate their full significance when we realize what striking proof they give of the vitality of the Etruscan people even in the days of their decline, when we remember that life-expectancy at birth round about 1800 in Europe was thirty years: today it has risen to sixty-five. In Italy in 1900 it reached 44·2 years for men and 44·8 years for women; and in 1950, respectively, 53·7 years and 56 years.[25]

CHAPTER TWO

THE MORAL TEMPER

*The gossip of Theopompus – The judgement of Posidonius –
The Roman view*

Dionysius of Halicarnassus, who had devoted critical reflections
and thorough-going researches to the Etruscans, does not say that
this people differed physically from others, but states that it was
distinguished from the rest of humanity by its morals. Should
we therefore believe that nature or history had dowered this race
with a peculiar moral temper which set it apart from the rest of
humanity?

We must treat with caution what the Greeks have to say on
this subject. They had never forgotten the state of desperate
enmity which had existed between them and the Etruscans who
had allied themselves with the Carthaginians in order to dispute
the Greeks' access to and mastery of the western Mediterranean.
The fear they had of Etruscan pirates, coupled with the cruelty
of the indigenous inhabitants, had long prevented them from
advancing further, and had set an impenetrable frontier to their
colonial expansion which in Italy stopped at Cumae, Pozzuoli and
Naples.

Doubtless the Greeks of Phocaea in Asia Minor had succeeded
in forcing the blockade and opened a route to the distant shores
of Andalusia and Provence, where, towards 600, they founded
Marseilles. But in 535 their maritime empire foundered at the
battle of Alalia (Aleria) off the shores of Corsica: the joint Etruscan
and Carthaginian fleets chased them out of Corsica and Sardinia:
the survivors took refuge at Marseilles or went to settle at Velia
(Elea) in Lucania; those prisoners who had the misfortune to fall
into the hands of the Etruscans of Agylla or Caere suffered a

punishment which roused the wrath of the gods and froze the blood of the Greek historians. They were conducted out of the city, according to Herodotus, and stoned to death.[1]

Other texts, taking their information from the same author, described tortures even more abominable, which they attributed to the Etruscan pirates in general, although Virgil held the impious Mezentius, king of Caere, responsible: 'Shall I tell you of his unspeakable slaughters? His savage, tyrannical acts? May the gods bring them down upon his head and upon his race! He went as far as to bind living people to dead bodies, hands against hands, mouth against mouth, and these victims of a new form of torture, drenched in pus and poisoned blood, died slow deaths coupled in this wretched way.'[2]

The image the Greeks formed of the Etruscans was a reflection of the horror of those merciless wars and those monstrous cruelties which seemed to reveal, in its taste for other people's sufferings, not so much primitive brutality as sadistic refinement. And this image was all the more dismal because it was coloured by jealousy as well as by hatred. The Etruscans shared with the Milesians of Asia Minor and the Sybarites of Greece the dangerous honour of offering less fortunate rivals who willingly looked upon poverty as a virtue the precocious wonders of a brilliant culture: the same 'weakness' or *mollitia* preyed upon all three peoples, who were all accused of indulging in 'luxury and gluttony' and of joining in a sort of league founded on a common love of pleasure. According to the Sicilian historian Timaeus, all ills sprang from the woollen mantles of Miletus: 'The Sybarites wore mantles made of wool from Miletus, and from this sprang the friendship between the states. The Sybarites loved the Etruscans above all the other peoples of Italy and among those of the Orient had a special preference for the Ionians, because these, like themselves, were fond of luxury.'[3] When Sybaris was destroyed in 510, all adult Milesians shaved their heads as a sign of mourning.

Apart from these moralistic considerations, it has long been established what the economic reasons were that led to the Milesians, Sybarites and Etruscans getting to know and like each other. Sybaris was one of the principal ports of transit through which Ionian merchandise and culture made their way to Tuscany. It certainly did not enjoy the exclusive monopoly which has been attributed to it; the Chalcidian cities of the Sicilian straits, Rhegion and Zancle (Messina) were its strong competitors.[4] It is no less certain that the Sybarites and the Etruscans enjoyed a mode of life of which only the less honourable aspects were remembered because of the malevolent exaggerations of rivals.

THE GOSSIP OF THEOPOMPUS

It so happens that, by a great stroke of misfortune, the picture of Etruscan manners has been painted, *ne varietur*, by a writer as false-tongued as he is eloquent, Theopompus. He was writing in the middle of the fourth century. Etruscan maritime power had died out a century before, under the attacks led by Hiero of Syracuse in the waters round Cumae. The danger this fleet had represented to the Greeks was long past: it was now permissible to laugh at this detested, envied and vanquished enemy. Now Theopompus, whether he was writing about Athenian demagogues, Persian tyrants or barbarian kings had usually, as Cornelius Nepos has well said,[5] the wickedest tongue in all literature (*maledicentissimus*): he was particularly fond of scabrous anecdotes and bits of spicy gossip. But his malicious falsehoods have been accepted as authoritative. They were piously collected by the philosophers and historians, by grave Aristotle[6] and romantic Heraclides Ponticus,[7] and by that Timaeus of Taormina[8] whom Nepos also ranks among the most wicked-tongued of authors. Let us cast a glance, though not one of total credulity, at this fragment of Theopompus which Athenaeus transcribed word for word in his *Learned Banquet*.[9]

'Theopompus, in Book XLIII of his *History*, says that the Tyrrhenians possess their women in common; these take great care of their bodies and exercise naked, often along with men, sometimes among themselves; for it is not shameful for them to show themselves naked. They sit down to table not beside their own husbands but beside any of the guests, and they even drink to the health of anyone they please. Moreover they are great wine-bibbers and very beautiful to behold. The Tyrrhenians bring up together all those children that are born to them, heedless of who their father may be. These children live in the

same manner as their protectors, passing the most of their time
in drinking and having commerce with all the women indifferently. There is no shame for a Tyrrhenian to be seen committing
a sexual act in public or indeed submitting to it, for this too
is a custom of the country. And so removed are they from regarding the act as shameful that when the master of the house
is engaged in making love and he is called for, they say: "He
is doing so-and-so," referring to the act quite impudently by
its name. When there are gatherings of family or friends, this
is how they do: first of all, when they have finished drinking
and are ready for bed and while the torches are still lighted the
servants bring in sometimes courtesans, sometimes handsome
boys, sometimes their own wives. When they have taken their
pleasure of the women or the men, they make strapping young
fellows lie with the latter. They make love and pursue their
pleasures in full view of everyone, but usually surround their
couches with small frames of woven branches over which they
drape their cloaks. They certainly have much commerce with
women, but they always enjoy themselves much better with
boys and young men. The latter are in this country quite
beautiful to behold, for they live lives of ease and their bodies
are hairless. Moreover, all the barbarians who live towards the
west cover their bodies with wax and shave themselves; and
among the Tyrrhenians there are even many establishments
and practicians for this purpose, as common as barbers in our
own land. When they go there they lend themselves to the
work without any reserve, without having any shame of being
seen, even by passers-by.'

THE JUDGEMENT OF POSIDONIUS
We shall see later how much to credit of this libidinous chatter,
but for the moment it would be as well to counter it with the
evidence supplied by the philosopher Posidonius of Apamea who,
at the end of the second century, had brought back from his long
voyages in the west a much more equitable view of Etruscan
manners: at that time the old naval rivalry which had for so long
disturbed the judgement of the Greeks was no more than very
ancient history; and Posidonius' was a mind of a quite different
class from that of Theopompus. This Stoic had no special

liking for soft living and luxury, which he condemned very severely in the towns of his native Syria. But he knew the right way to look at things, could dispose under a subtle lighting the facts of virtues and vices and here and there was able to distinguish causes from effects. This is what Diodorus Siculus, writing under Caesar, gives us of that intelligent report:[10]

'The Etruscans, who formerly were distinguished for their energy, conquered a vast territory and there founded many important towns. They also disposed of powerful naval forces and for a long time enjoyed mastery of the seas, so much so that the one which washed the western shores of Italy was called by them the Tyrrhenian. They perfected the equipment of their land forces by inventing what is called the trumpet, which is of the greatest utility in war and was named by them Tyrrhenian; they also devised marks of honour for the generals who led them, assigning to them lictors, an ivory throne and a toga bordered with purple. And in their houses they invented the peristyle which is a great convenience in that it deadens the uproar caused by their great crowds of servants. The majority of these discoveries were imitated by the Romans, who perfected them and introduced them into their civilization. They encouraged the progress of letters, science, nature and theology and developed to a higher degree than any other people the interpretation of thunder. This is why today they still inspire those who are masters of nearly all the world (that is to say, the Romans), with such deep admiration, and why they are employed today as interpreters of the celestial signs. As they inhabit a land fertile in fruits of all kinds and cultivate it assiduously, they enjoy an abundance of agricultural produce which not only is sufficient for themselves but by its excess leads them to unbridled luxury and indolence. For twice a day they have tables sumptuously dressed and laid with everything that can contribute towards delicate living; they have coverings embroidered with flowers and are served wine in quantities of silver bowls, and they have at their call a considerable number of slaves. Some of the latter are of a rare beauty; others dress themselves in clothes more magnificent than befits their station of servitude, and the domestic staff have all kinds of private dwellings: as have indeed most of the freed men. In general they have abandoned the valiant steadfastness that they prized so much in former days, and by their indulgence in banquets and effeminate delights they have lost the reputation which their ancestors won in war, which does not surprise us. But what served more than anything to turn them to soft and idle living was the quality of their land, for, living in a country that produces everything and is of inexhaustible fecundity, they are able to store up large quantities of fruit of every kind. Etruria is indeed very fertile, extending for the most part over plains separated by hills with arable slopes and it is moderately well-watered, not only in the winter season, but also during the summer.'

We notice that unlike Theopompus, Posidonius as a matter of course attributed to the Etruscans the merit of manly courage (*andreia*), as Virgil was to do later: *Sic fortis Etruria crevit* 'Thus it was that valiant Etruria grew.'[11] He paid additional tribute to their fertile genius and enumerated the many arts in which they had deployed an incontestable vigour. Nevertheless he recognized that they had degenerated, and under the influence of a too-generous climate, had lost the energy for which they had once been so highly praised. The image of the Etruscan passing his time in drinking and loose living (*anandroi*) was therefore nothing more than the image of irremediable decadence in a type of humanity which was dragging out its days in the idleness to which the Roman conquest had reduced it.

It is probable that it was in Rome itself that Posidonius had formed this new opinion of Etruscan manners, one so different from that which the philosophers and historians of Greece had put about. For the Romans, after five centuries of intimate, neighbourly interchanges, really knew much better a people from whom they had borrowed so much. And though they might let loose a satirical shaft or two – inspired by the Greek tradition or by contemporary reality – on the loose conduct of Etruscan women or the obesity of its musicians, it was not sensuality which seemed to them the basis of the Etruscan character.

THE ROMAN VIEW

When the Romans of the last years of the Republic thought about the Etruscans, they had in mind the concept of a great power brought low, of fabulous, vanished riches but above all – would you believe it? – the virtues of a rustic folk, bronzed by working in the fields and animated by a deep sense of piety. Livy said they were 'a nation attached more than any other to religious practices, because they excelled in their knowledge and conduct of them'.[12] And the etymologists racked their brains trying to detect in the name Etruscan (*Etrusci* or *Tusci*) a symbol which would indicate this vocation. They related *Tuscus* to the Greek *thusia*, which means 'sacrifice'[13] and had no doubt that *caerimoniae*, 'ceremonies', came from the name of the city of Caere.[14]

Indeed few peoples have been more deeply obsessed by the will of the gods. Their daily existence, public or private, was a forest of symbols through which their diviners had the task of guiding their anxious steps. In their detailed observation of lightning or examination of the liver of victims, in the careful interpretation of natural catastrophes or abnormal births, in all the phenomena which were reported to them at all seasons these diviners or *haruspices* read what the future had in store and sometimes were even able to influence the future when it looked black. They had confided their secular experience to very learned books, the *Books of Fate*[15] of which numerous fragments have come down to us in Latin, and their prestige even in foreign lands was such that Rome, very early on, had habitually turned to them when her own pontiffs and the oracle of Apollo at Delphi were not able to clarify the future sufficiently. We shall return further on to whatwas called *Etrusca disciplina*,[16] the sacred science of the Etruscans, but something would be lacking, probably something essential, in our presentation of the *homo Etruscus* if we did not stress strongly enough this anguished preoccupation with the supernatural.

One of the most celebrated tombs in Etruria is that of François de Vulci, whose frescoes are perhaps not anterior to the beginning of the first century before our era. On one of the walls of the atrium there rises in profile the figure of a young man with black hair, draped in a dark blue cloak ornamented with embroideries. His name, *Vel Saties*,[17] is inscribed above his head: perhaps he was

38

the owner of the tomb, but at any rate he was certainly an actual person. 'We are in the presence,' it has been said, 'of the most ancient full-length portrait in European painting.'[18] On his left crouches a dwarf, *Arnza*, 'little Arruns' who holds on his left hand, attached to a string, a bird which has been identified as a woodpecker. The scene represents an augural consultation, caught at a moment of extreme dramatic tension, the moment when the bird is about to take flight. And already *Vel Saties* is getting ready to follow its course across a sky heavy with omens. We are struck by the anxious expression in those lifted eyes and in those parted lips: it is a gripping pictorial translation of that phrase of Livy's: *gens ante alias dedita religionibus.*

An ardent and sombre piety which senses in every object a hidden significance and which the ritual books load with the weight of grand cosmic laws, that is the fundamental insight the Etruscans give us about themselves and which Roman evidence confirms; this insight offers a total contrast to the double image that the Greeks had of the Etruscans and which, even taking into account the exaggerations and deformations of spiteful minds, must have contained some truth. We must assume that in the Etruscans there was an underlying cruelty which is revealed in the horror of certain of their tortures and in the persistence, right into historical times, of their human sacrifices. On the other hand they were overflowing with sensuality and enjoyed a liberty of morals which was hardly controlled by the Roman conquest. But these three contradictory notions might just be reconciled if we consider them as characteristic of a humanity still deeply engaged in the pre-hellenic reign of the unconscious and which, despite the passionate interest which Greek civilization exercised upon it, nevertheless remained, with tenacious obstinacy, a humanity that reached back beyond reason and beyond wisdom. The Etruscan world was able to receive with enthusiasm the missionaries of the dionysiac religion, but it seems difficult to imagine that the lessons of Socrates found favour with it. It remained, despite itself, the faithful heir of ancient powers, oriental if one wishes, or Mediterranean, but whose survival conferred on its culture the characteristics of a brilliant archaism.

CHAPTER THREE

ETRUSCAN SOCIETY

I

THE RULING CLASS

Etruscan society is an archaic society which, while neighbouring
societies gave way slowly and not without resistance to the
necessity for transforming their structures, strove to maintain,
with a rigid conservatism, an organization which despite the
anachronism one can call feudal.

In Rome since the sixth century according to traditional
chronology, but doubtless later in reality, the copyhold system
attributed to King Servius Tullius had broken primitive duality.
Shortly after the beginning of the Republic, in 493, the lower
classes created tribunes to be responsible for their defence against
the oppression of the patriciate and who gradually assured them
access to all magistracies. Certainly the new governing class, the
Roman nobility, was trying to monopolize the magistracy. None-
theless it opened its ranks to representatives of Italian families,
and new men were perpetually being voted to the Senate. The
upward movement of the lower classes, though restricted, went
on without a pause. A rich bourgeoisie or middle class, the
Roman knights, came into being and made itself into a third
estate between the senatorial nobility and the *humiles* or lower
classes. But Etruscan society never knew, right up to its final

extinction, anything but masters and slaves, and that too must be defined more precisely as *domini* and *servi*.

THE KINGS

The ruling class is naturally better known to us than the others: writers of epic poetry and history confine themselves to those of the upper class. And first of all, at the summit of the hierarchy, there appear very early at the head of the peoples of Etruria the kings, who, however, cannot be proved to have presided over the origins of the race.

We know the names of several of these kings. Rome, during its Etruscan period, was governed by the dynasty of the Tarquins, who originated in Tarquinii. But no less celebrated was Porsenna, king of Clusium (Chiusi) whom the common peril had elevated to the rank of federal king of all the nation. After the expulsion of the Tarquins, he tried to set them on the throne again, laid siege to Rome and doubtless took the city, though pious legends tend to draw a veil over this defeat. Horatius Cocles, one against a hundred, braved the enemy attack while the Sublicius bridge was being cut, the bridge across which, coming from the Janiculum, the enemy intended to swarm into the city. Mucius Scaevola, having crept into the enemy camp to kill Porsenna, burned his hand in a brazier rather than reveal the secret plot. Clelia, with a group of young girls whom the king was keeping as hostages, escaped by swimming the river and they arrived back home safe and sound.

In fact it is probable that the first Roman consuls were merely prefects of Porsenna;[1] but these fine tales which enchanted the annalists and have furnished subjects for innumerable Latin prose compositions, contributed indirectly, right to this very day, to the glory of Porsenna, whose memory was still so vivid at the end of the Roman Republic, when Varro described the gigantic tomb which he had had constructed under the town of Clusium, with its interior labyrinth and its superposed terraces, supporting enormous pyramids.[2] Alas! archaeologists have found no trace of it.

But Caere had also had its kings, one of whom was the famous Mezentius, 'the mocker of the gods', to whom Virgil, as we have seen, attributed the responsibility for the monstrous deaths and tortures which the pirates of Agylla inflicted on their prisoners. A Latin inscription recently discovered at Tarquinii mentions, though the mutilation of the stone prevents us from reading his name, a king of the Caerites, *Caeritum regem*:[3] the dimensions of the break did not allow the insertion of his name. At Veii, we know of a whole series of kings: a certain Morrius, if the name is not a corruption, Thebris, who is said to have given its name to the nearby Tiber, Propertius, the same name as that of the elegiac poet[4] – and the number of these kings proves that the local traditions at Veii were no less imposing than those at Rome concerning its dynasties. But above all – and here we tread firmer ground – Lars Tolumnius, who, in 432, perished by the hand of the Roman consul Cossus: the inscription relating to these *spolia opima*, seized from an enemy chief, and which Cossus had hung up in the temple of Jupiter Feretrius on the Capitol, was still legible in the days of Augustus.[5] Now the existence of the *gens* Tolumnia has been confirmed four times in the last thirty years by epigraphical discoveries in the diggings at the temple of Portonaccio at Veii, where, during the first half of the sixth century, a *Velthur Tulumnes* and a *Karcuna Tulumnes* offered two vases to the divinity,[6] and where later, in the third century, at a time when Veii was subdued by Rome and Etruscan had been replaced by Latin, a certain *L. Tolonios* offered up two more to Minerva and Ceres:[7] the family, dethroned for the past two hundred years, nevertheless still survived in faded grandeur among the local gentry. One might cite again the obscure Arimnestos, 'king of the Etruscans' who is known to us through the ex-voto, a throne, recalling his munificence, in the sanctuary of Zeus at Olympia.[8] And we must not forget that, judging by the testimony of the poets he protected, Maecenas, the minister of Augustus, was directly descended from royal ancestors, the Cilnii, who had reigned at Arezzo.[9]

We know besides the title and insignia of these kings. They were called in Etruscan *lauchme* or *lauchume*, a word which has been transcribed into Latin as *lucumo*, for: *lucumones reges sunt lingua Tuscorum*;[10] but sometimes the Romans took this generic title for a name of an individual, just as others take the Piraeus to be a man. One Etruscan *lucumo*, who according to legend had been the ally of Romulus in his war against the Sabines, was called Lucumo by Cicero and Lygmon by Propertius.[11] Lucumo was also the name which Livy gave to Tarquinius the Elder before he settled in Rome and had himself inscribed there under the three names of Roman civilian status, Lucius Tarquinius Priscus.[12] This kind of confusion, of which we shall find another example later on in the case of Servius Tullius, was probably encouraged by the fact that after the downfall of the kings the same name, Lauchme or Lauchume, or in a derived form *Lauchumni*, *Lauchumsnei*, had in fact become, notably in the regions of Perugia and Chiusi, a family name as banal as our own King and Prince.[13] Under the Empire there was a lady at Volterra called Laucumnia Felicitas. Let us point out besides that even under the republican régime the religious functions of the ex-king were carried out (as in Athens they were carried out by the arkhōn basileus and in Rome by the *rex sacrorum*) by a magistrate who retained that title (*lucairce=regnavit*[14]) and who perhaps lived in a *Regia* (locative *lauchumneti* in the ritual of Zagreb[15]).

THE INSIGNIA OF SOVEREIGNTY

As for the insignia of royalty, they are enumerated by Dionysius of Halicarnassus in the account he gives us of the conquest of Etruria by Rome under the rule of Tarquinius the Elder. The ambassadors of the Etruscan league then awarded him 'the insignia of sovereignty with which their own kings were invested. They brought him a crown of gold, a throne of ivory, a sceptre bearing an eagle on the top, a tunic of purple with gold figuring and a mantle of purple adorned with embroideries, similar to that worn by the kings of Lydia and Persia'.[16] We shall have to come back when we are studying Etruscan costume and its Roman survivals to these two pieces, upper and lower garments of the royal robes, and which we recognize as the *tunica palmata* and the *toga picta* (sometimes decorated with a sprinkling of golden stars) of the Roman triumpher who, on ascending the Capitol, sported for one day the purple, the crown and the sceptre of the kings. With slight variations, this text of Dionysius of Halicarnassus is confirmed by painted plaques from Caere, which are in the Louvre:[17] on these an Etruscan king, contemporary with the Tarquins, is seated before the statue of a goddess and is holding a sceptre in his left hand: his seat, lacking arms and back, is not the 'throne' of which Dionysius incorrectly spoke, but the folding stool, decorated with plaques of ivory, which was known in Rome as the curule chair (*sella curulis*), on which sat the magistrates when dispensing justice. He is wearing characteristic shoes, with up-curving toes, the same as those we have already noted on the sarcophagi of the same period from the same city. Finally he is wearing, over a white, short-sleeved tunic which falls no lower than his upper thighs (therefore quite different from the long, flowing tunic of the oriental monarchs) a mantle of purple adorned with embroideries, also very short, the sort of little toga that was called the *trabea*.

But an even more definite manifestation of sovereignty was provided by the lictors who, carrying fasces over their shoulders, walked before the king. We are assured that each of the twelve Etruscan kings had one lictor at his disposal, but when in the event of war the supreme power was delegated to only one of them, this king was entitled to all the twelve lictors with their fasces. There were indeed twelve fasces brought to Tarquinius by the Etruscans, along with other royal insignia, as tokens of the submission, not of one particular city, but of the entire nation. And we know that in the Roman republic each of the two consuls, heirs of kings, had the right to twelve lictors.

This bundle of rods with an axe in the middle which the Etruscans handed down to certain Roman magistrates as a symbol of their coercive power or *imperium* is well documented among the oldest records in their history. According to a poet of the Flavian era, Silius Italicus, whose *Punica* reveal here and there, amid much Virgilian imitation and rhetorical inflation, precious traditions probably going right back to Cato's *Origines*,[18] it was the Etruscan city of Vetulonia that invented the curule chair, the *toga praetexta* (that is, with a purple border), the military trumpet and the fasces:

> Vetulonia, formerly the pride of the Lydian race, was the first city to place the twelve fasces at the head of processions and to add to them the silent menace of the axes.[19]

Now by a curious coincidence it was at Vetulonia that there was discovered, in a seventh century tomb, the most ancient example of such fasces, an ex-voto in iron, in miniature proportions and displaying this peculiarity, that, unlike the Roman fasces, the axe in the middle of the rods is a double-headed axe, a bipennate one.[20]

The axe had always played a considerable part in primitive religions, and the civilizations of the Orient and the Mediterranean have given it a prominent place in their religious symbolism. In it is concentrated, it has been said, 'all that is divine in a storm, in human blood, in immolated victims'. But it was above all in Crete that the double-headed axe had been the object of a general cult: it was placed in tombs, dedicated in sacred grottoes and represented at the side of gods in rites and ceremonies.[21]

The bipennate fasces from Vetulonia, found likewise in a tomb, cannot be dissociated from Aegean practices. Yet the association with double-headed axes, which is even more closely connected with the attributes of a Roman magistrate, suggests a significance more political than religious: some leader, perhaps a king, having died, his followers had wanted to bring back to his last resting-place the power with which he had been invested in his lifetime.

But as if fate wanted to confirm a second time the evidence of Silius Italicus, it was once more at Vetulonia that a contemporary stele (end of seventh century) was discovered showing a bipennate axe, flourished like a commander's baton in the right hand of a warrior wearing a big-crested helmet and carrying a circular shield.[22] And the inscription, one of the most ancient, if not the most ancient of all Etruscan inscriptions, tells us the name of this person, *Aveles Feluskes Tusnuties*, or in Latin, Aulus Feluscus the Victor or the Terrible or the Valorous (the exact meaning of his surname is uncertain), in memory of whom one of his brothers-in-arms, *Hirumina Phersnachs*, Herminius of Perugia, had set up a stele.[23]

THE CONDOTTIERI

Here apparently it is no longer a question of rightful kings, but rather of those *condottieri* who are glimpsed at the beginnings of Etruscan history, roaming across the countryside at the head of their bands of mercenaries, giving their services now to Perugia now to Vetulonia, just as in the fifteenth century Erasmo de Narni, called the Gattamelata, whose equestrian statue by Donatello stands in Padua, brought victory over the Visconti to the Most Serene Republic, which awarded him the baton of a general.

If history tells us nothing about this Aulus Feluscus, the prowess of other Etruscan captains, celebrated in epic verse, has left a few traces on later art and literature. As late as the Roman era people still remembered the two legendary heroes of Vulci, the brothers Caelius and Aulus Vibennae.

Their historical existence, or at any rate that of their *gens*, even has epigraphical testimony, as in the case of the royal family of the Tolumnii.[24] In the same sanctuary at Veii, one Avile Vipiiennas or Aulus Vibenna, towards the middle of the sixth century – at a moment when archaeology proves that Vulci was at the height of her power – consecrated a *bucchero* bearing an Etruscan votive inscription. A century later, the same names, Avles V(i)pinas, appear on a cup with red figures which an Etruscan artist, apparently from Vulci, had painted in imitation of an Attic cup from the school of Duris: it can be seen in Paris in the Musée Rodin.

Caelius and Aulus Vibennae were accredited with numerous exploits: on a mirror and on various funerary urns of the third century they can be seen entering, sword in hand, the sacred wood in which prophesies a certain Cacus who adopts the lyre and the attitude of Apollo and whom they are going to force to reveal their destinies.[25] This destiny was to take them to Rome. Scholars living at the end of the Republic even believed that one of the seven hills, Mount Caelius, took its name from Caelius Vibenna, who was said to have given assistance to one of the kings of Rome, Romulus (others said Tarquinius) and as a reward obtained the right to settle there with a colony of his own people.[26] A mutilated fragment of Verrius Flaccus, which stops just as it is about to reveal an important secret to us, alluded to the arrival of the two brothers in Rome and their appearing before Tarquinius. They were accompanied by a mysterious personage, of whose name only the first three letters remain: *Max* . . . This is what the commentators have deciphered: *Volci entes fratres Caeles et A. Vibenna [e . . . ad] Tarquinium Romam se cum Max [. . . contulerunt]*: 'The brothers from Vulci Caeles and Aules Vibennae went to Rome to see Tarquin with Max . . .'[27]

The Etruscan historians, if we are to believe the emperor

Claudius,[28] told a different story: it was Servius Tullius, whose reign, by Roman tradition, comes between those of Tarquinius the Elder and Tarquinius Superbus, who must have been in close touch with Caelius Vibenna. He had been 'the most constant friend of Caelius Vibenna and his inseparable companion in all his adventures'. These, it appears, ended in disaster: Servius, driven from Etruria 'with the remnants of Caelius' army', had to go into exile in Rome and there had lived on Mount Caelius, which he named in memory of his 'leader'. Thereafter he reigned, 'to the very great good of the Roman State', under the name of Servius Tullius, 'for in Etruscan he was called Macstarna' or Maxtarna: he was the unknown person mentioned by Verrius Flaccus.

Now one of the most dramatic episodes in the combats which Caelius and Aulus Vibennae, aided by this faithful ally, had to enter into and which is depicted in the wall-paintings in the François tomb at Vulci itself[29] was the freeing of *Caile Vipinas* or Caelius Vibennae, whose bonds were cut by faithful *Macstrna* (Macstarna, Maxtarna). Beside them several warrior couples are still fighting, and their names are inscribed above each figure: *Larth Ulthes* or Lars Voltius, is slaying *Laris Papathnas Velznach*, or Lars Papatius of Volsinii; *Rasce* or Rascius is slaughtering *Pesna Arcmsnas Sveamach*, Pesius Arcumnius of Sovana; *Avle Vipinas*, Aulus Vibennae himself, is massacring an adversary whose name *Venthical . . . plsachs* is mutilated but perhaps designates a man from Falerii. Last, and not least, *Marce Camitlnas*, Marcus Camitilius, is running his sword through *Cneve Tarchunies Rumach*, Cnaeus Tarquinius of Rome, thus one of our Tarquins, though the first name, Cnaeus, shows that he was not the Lucius who is recorded in history. In any case, we notice that in all these curious combats only the vanquished carry any indication of their country. Caelius and Aulus Vibennae, Macstarna, Lars Voltius, Rascius and M. Camitilius did not need, at Vulci, to have their origins clearly stated. The others were the leaders of a foreign coalition which was composed of contingents from Volsinii, Sovana, Falerii and perhaps Rome. They had succeeded for a while in holding Caelius Vibenna prisoner. But Macstarna had arrived with Aulus at the head of a relief army and by reversing the situation had saved his leader and his friend.

There is much more that could be said about this amazing man Macstarna. According to Roman tradition, he had come to Rome as an ally to place his strong sword at the service of Tarquinius; but in the Etruscan version of events he was among the enemies and indeed the murderers of Tarquinius. Then, at the end of his adventures, he had seized one of the hills of Rome and by means perhaps far from peaceful, the throne, whose vacancy goes unexplained. It is clear that the Romans, in order to save face, had tried (as they had so often done, for example in the case of Porsenna) to disguise as benevolent concessions a blistering defeat. But for the Etruscans Macstarna was an embarrassing hero whom they allowed only to play the part of a Pylades. This was because at Vulci he was still a foreigner, as his name, of Latin origin, proves.

In fact, this has long since been recognized: Macstrna, the original spelling on the François tomb, is no other, if one takes away the final -na, the usual *gentilicium* suffix,* then the Latin substantive *magister*: Etruscan does not stress, or stresses irregularly, the interior vowels, and in its orthography confuses the voiced guttural *g* with the unvoiced guttural *c*: *Macstrna* is *mag(i)st(e)r-na*.[30]

Here the Etruscans have made the same mistake as the Romans did when they took the title '*lucumo*' to be the name of a person. They transformed into a proper name that was in fact the title of a Roman or Latin magistrate. For in Latin the word *magister*, 'master' (and *magistratus* is directly derived from this), originally meant various 'magistratures'. In classical times there was still the *magister equitum*, 'master of the horse', who was the dictator's adjutant; but it is not so widely known that the dictator was originally called *magister populi*, 'master of the people'. It has been supposed,[31] not without reason, that Macstarna, whom historians identify with Servius Tullius, owed his legendary prestige to the fact that he had come forward as the first dictator in the Etrusco-Roman world – one of those plebeian, revolutionary chiefs who, when the monarchial régime in Italy as in the whole of the Mediterranean was tottering on its foundations, rose into

*The *gentilicium nomen* is in Latin the family name (*gens*) which, preceded by the first name and followed by the surname or *cognomen*, forms with these the *tria nomina* or three names under which a citizen is registered: the Etruscan system of names is more or less the same.

prominence as the bearers of a new ideology, as the men who unthroned kings, as the liberators of the people on the threshold of the republican age. Is he really the one for whom the Roman annals have made a place between the two Tarquins, at the end of their gallery of kings? In defence of this identification it is pointed out that Servius Tullius, whose very name evokes a servile (or foreign) birth, was held to be the founder of all republican Rome's democratic institutions and the man who, in the words of the tragic poet Accius, *libertatem civibus stabiliverat*, 'had established the liberty of the citizens'. And indeed from then on, from the end of the sixth century, the whole of central Italy, in Rome, but also in Tusculum in Latium, in Tarquinii in Etruria, in Assisi among the Umbrians, was to undertake, in peace and in war, a common laboration of the political forms of the future.

THE MAGISTRATES

Henceforward texts and monuments allow us to perceive ever more clearly the outlines of an aristocracy very jealous of its privileges and intent on retaining the government of the city.[32] The authors mention several times those whom Livy designates as *principes*, 'the great ones'; they constitute a class (*ordo*) called upon to deliberate in the Senate which, to the exclusion of what might have corresponded to the *comitia centuriata* or *comitia tributa* of Rome, is the one political assembly of the Etruscan state. They elect among their members a *princeps civitatis* who, having replaced the king, fulfils the functions of president of the republic and is elected annually; to assist him he has magistrates, also elected annually, composing a collegium which recalls that of the Nine Archons in Athens. Epigraphy illuminates a little the gaps left by historians concerning these magistrates' titles, careers and the special privileges which certain of them enjoyed. It acquaints us with about forty *cursus honorum*, often very complicated, with the enumeration of diverse charges whose significance and connexion we are beginning to understand.

It must be realized that these inscriptions are generally fairly late, that the oldest of them go back no further than the fourth century, and that the majority date from a period when, having entered willy-nilly into the Roman alliance, the Etruscan cities

49

had seen their political responsibilities considerably reduced and the victor's institutions contaminating their traditions. The Etruscan *principes* still proudly displayed their medals, but this was a mere relic of the past and doubtless all that remained to them of powers which Rome, even in strictly municipal limits, was tending to mix with her own magistracies. For example, in picturesque Tuscania, which, between Tarquinii and Viterbo, lifts its crenellated walls, its medieval turrets round two admirable Romanesque churches, a third century sarcophagus celebrated an illustrious personage whose name unfortunately is mutilated; but he had been pontiff, *prutanis* and generalissimo of his country, perhaps duumvir also in some institution, and he had died, laden with honours but not with years, at the age of thirty-six! Nevertheless this attachment to the vanity of titles tells us something about a period in which they carried their full weight.

Leaving aside many sacerdotal or administrative dignities which are still no more than names to us, let us turn our attention to those magistracies which seem to have been accorded special prestige, because they implied effective participation in the government. There has indeed been discovered in Etruscan a family of words derived from the root *zil-* which signifies 'to govern': *zilc* or *zilath* is, like the Latin *magistratus*, the magistracy or the magistrate; *zilachnve*, *zilachnuce* mean, in the perfect, 'has exercised the magistracy of *zilath*'. Several *zilath* devoted themselves to the governing of the city; their numbers are unknown to us, but they worked together in the sort of assembly which we have compared to that formed by the nine Athenian *Archons*. The jurisdiction of several of these was sometimes clearly defined: just as in Athens distinctions were made between the king-*archon*, the *archon polemarch*, the *archon eponymus* and six undifferentiated *thesmothetae*, here we encounter a *zilath* who was so to speak a minister of religious affairs, another concerned with the protection of commoners, a third who was perhaps entrusted with the interests of the nobility. Certain *zilath* bore the particular title of *maru*, which we find, with various meanings, in the institutions of other Italian peoples, notably among the Umbrians of Assisi and Foligno, and which furnished the Mantuan, Virgil, P. Vergilius Maro, with a *cognomen* inherited from the Etruscan traditions of his native city. The *maru* were both priests and magistrates and they have been equated in certain respects with the Roman *aediles* or town councillors. Finally the president of the group of *zilath* was sometimes designated by this one name, as a *zilath* properly speaking, and sometimes by the term *purth* or *purthne*, which perhaps comes from the *prutanis* of the Greeks: this was the first *zilath*, or one might say the first minister, and in the *interpretatio Latina* the Romans translated it as praetor, that is, in the old sense of the word, the chief of State.

Such were the principal magistracies within the city. But on the national level, when the twelve peoples of Etruria met in the federal assembly, they elected as head of their league a supreme *zilath*, a fact given epigraphical authority in the denomination *zilath mechl rasnal*, that is, *zilath* of the Etruscan people (we know that Rasenna was the name which the Etruscans called themselves in their own language): until the end of the Roman Empire there were *praetores Etruriae*.

Proceeding from these elementary data, the epigraphists were able to decipher some *cursus honorum* which bring to life a number of brilliant careers. An inscription from Vulci tells us that *Larth Tute*, son of Arruns and of *Ravnthu Hathli*, had been *zilath* seven times, having been *purth*, that is, president, once, and that he died at the age of seventy-two.[33] Another, probably his son *Sethre Tute*, son of *Larth* and of *Vela Pumpli*, had been *zilath* and had died at the age of twenty-five, during the year in which he was president.[34] We can see from these two examples that one could hold the same magistracy several times, and reach very high positions at a very early age.

An inverted *cursus*, that is, enumerating the facts in descending order, beginning with the most recent and most distinguished offices, was lately identified as: . . . *Larisal Crespe Thanchvilus Pumpnal clan zilath mechl rasnas marunuch cepen zilc thufi tenthas marunuch pachanati ril LXIII.*[35]

This Crespe, whose first name we do not know, son of *Laris* and of *Tanaquil Pumpni*, had been: 1. *marunuch pachanati*, that is, *maru* of the brotherhood of Bacchus; 2. *zilc thufi*, either *zilath* for the first time, or first *zilath*; 3. *marunuch cepen*, titular head of some public religious office; 4. *zilath mechl rasnas*, president of the Etruscan league. He died at the age of sixty-three.

OFFICIAL PROCESSIONS

The number of examples could be greatly increased; those which we have given will at least have given us a glimpse of the workings of the complex machine. But we shall see it portrayed in even more concrete fashion if we add to these epigraphic testimonies the pictorial commentary offered by sepulchral bas-reliefs and paintings.[36] Indeed a good number of sarcophagi, on whose lids are stretched the effigies of the defunct ones, display, above the epitaph which pays tribute to their grandeur, the funeral cortege conducting them to the Great Beyond. But these *zilath* and *maru* and *purth* have no desire to meet the infernal divinities wearing the simple clothes of everyday life. Their last journey, preserved in stone for the edification of posterity, must have the solemn aspect of a triumphal procession, and they must proceed beyond the grave bearing the insignia and surrounded by the escort befitting their rank. So one sees them – on the *nenfro* sarcophagi of Tarquinii, on the alabaster urns of Volterra and on a few remnants of fresco – mounted on a chariot of ceremony to which are harnessed two or four richly caparisoned horses: they wear the tunic and a sort of toga, and, on their heads, a crown still retaining touches of gilding. Behind them march servants carrying baggage, not just the bag containing items necessary for a journey but also the great register, the writing tablets, the cylindrical boxes for holding rolls, symbols of their administrative functions, and above all the curule chair on which they are majestically enthroned, and, who knows, may still be, among the judges of the infernal regions.

Even more impressive is the front of the procession. That is usually where there parades a band of musicians blowing enormous horns and long, straight or curved trumpets accompanied on occasion by a player on the cithern or the flute. Then there come those who are given the task of clearing the way for the magistrate's chariot: first an apparitor, in Latin a *viator*, holding in his right hand one of the symbols of power, a lance, or else holding horizontally, pointed forward, a baton to keep the crowd at bay; then come the lictors, in varying numbers, most often two, sometimes three and even four. So far it has been impossible to define the connexion which perhaps existed between this number and the importance of the magistracies held by the dead man. But this does not alter the fact that these lictors are, in the Etruscan republics as in Rome, the descendants of those who, as we have seen, headed the king's procession. Only the fasces which they carry on the left shoulder, as the traditional insignia of his *imperium*, appear here always lacking the axe which originally was inseparable from its bundle of rods.

Is this, as has been surmised, because the Roman conquest had reduced the Etruscan magistrates' powers of coercion and that the visible symbol of their dominion over the life and death of citizens had been ended? In Rome, too, the consul P. Valerius Publicola was credited with the passing of a law in 509 which allowed any Roman condemned to death to make an appeal to the people and with the symbolic act of taking the axes out of the fasces: *secures de fascibus demi iussit.*[37] In reality the law *de provocatione* is not anterior to 300: after that date the lictors of Rome carried, within the walls, where the sovereign rights of magistrates ended, only fasces without axes. It is interesting to note that those in Tuscania did the same, probably as soon as the third century.

Moreover certain reliefs at Volterra which are sculpted in an alabaster that lends itself to a more precise rendering of details show in addition to the fasces a thin wand carried by the lictors; it might also be a lance, and they seem to be endeavouring to keep it balanced upright in front of them, like a candle, either in the free left hand or in the right hand already carrying the fasces. Now this attribute, loaded with a significance which escapes us now but whose slightness compensates for its practical uselessness, is found in late Roman scenes where an appeal is being made to the public: the magistrate's apparitor, leaning two rods on his left shoulder, holds vertically, with his right hand, a lance, emblem of sovereignty. All this apparatus demonstrates that the Etruscans, even after their fall, remained faithful, at least in their funereal iconography, to the antique symbols of their power.

But we can learn even more from these processions, not only about the *zilath* and their ceremonials, but about the rites with which Rome surrounded her own magistrates. For the Etruscan symbolism of the *imperium*, from which we know that the Romans had borrowed, was of an infinite richness; it included, besides those they retained, many insignia which they did not know how to use. In the paintings on the tomb of the Typhon at Tarquinii. and on that of the *Hescana* at Orvieto,[38] mingling with the crowd of musicians and lictors, are heralds carrying over the left shoulder a sort of caduceus whose points are twisted together, and which has no likeness in the pictures we have of public life in Rome.

II

THE SERVANT CLASS

Below the masters, there was hardly any other class in Etruria but the slave class, though this slavery, as we shall see, had its degrees. The palaces in the cities, the farms in the countryside, the mines and workshops in the industrial zones were swarming with an immense slave population that emerges from the shadows here and there in sculptured monuments and in the pages of the historians.

THE HOST OF SERVANTS

First of all, a whole world of servants – that is what the *familia urbana* was later to be called in Rome – peopled at Tarquinii and Volsinii the dwellings of the rich. Among the Etruscans, this *familia* was so numerous that the reason sometimes given for the existence of the *atrium* or courtyard at the centre of the house was that the master's apartments might be separated from the commons and protected from 'the uproar caused by the host of servants'.[39] From the sixth century one sees on the tomb frescoes pictures of servants busy round the couches of banqueters: cup-bearers jumping to re-fill cups, a young servant-girl fanning her mistress, kitchen-hands kneading dough or putting dishes in the oven; not forgetting the little boy bringing a chair, another teasing a cat under the table, another fallen asleep curled up in a corner. Fundamentally all these domestics resemble very closely those who attended on the feasts of imperial Rome and these paintings might be given an appropriate commentary, albeit satirical and exaggeratedly low in tone, in a famous letter by Seneca on how to treat slaves:[40] 'An insolent fashion decrees that at supper the master shall have a whole troupe of slaves standing round him . . . We are reclining on our festive couches. One slave wipes up gobbets of spit from the floor. Another slices up rare fowls: his expert hand, passing in a flow of precise movements from the breast to the rump, carves off delicate slivers. The young cup-bearer, attired like a girl, endeavours to belie his age . . . Nevertheless the wretched slaves do not have the right to move their lips, even to speak. The rod silences all murmurings. No exception is made, even for involuntary sounds, fits of coughing, sneezings, hiccups. They spend the whole night standing there, silent and without a bite of food.' Here Seneca is showing us the reverse side of the picture; the Etruscan world however is sometimes presented in a more humane light. Certain slaves are referred to by name, they have a personality. It would seem that the living had believed they were giving pleasure to the dead man by surrounding him beyond the grave with the attentions of his own servants, and, as Seneca says, of his 'humble friends'.

They are also slaves who, in the same frescoes in the Tomb of the Augurs or of the Triclinium, devote their talents to the amusement of guests or participate in the funeral games held in memory of the dead man: athletes and pugilists, acrobats and jugglers, but above all flute-players, dancers and ballerinas, perhaps actors. These, according to Posidonius, were more sumptuously clad than befitted their station as slaves.[41] We shall later describe these magnificent robes and cloaks whose brilliant colours are known everywhere now through the vogue for Etruscan painting; but those who wore them were still slaves.

Livy has a significant passage on this subject. The scene takes place at the beginning of the fourth century, shortly before the siege and destruction of Veii. The federal assembly of the twelve peoples had met at Volsinii in the temple of Voltumna, to elect the supreme head of the league and to celebrate its great annual feast. One of the candidates was a nobleman from Veii, and it was he who this time contributed more than any other to the brilliance of the games. Nevertheless he was beaten, and his defeat in the elections upset him so that right in the middle of the spectacle he suddenly called in the artists 'who were almost all his slaves': *artifices, quorum magna pars ipsius serui erant, ex medio ludicro repente abduxit.*[42] Such an interruption of the sacred ceremonies was a grave scandal: Etruscan piety never forgave

55

him. One can imagine, like an episode from some very ancient Comic Romance, the return, all along the via Cassia, of the melancholy procession of chariots and carts carrying the disappointed troupe, with their glittering costumes locked away in boxes.

THE PEASANTS

The country slaves were quite different, and doubtless very numerous too; they were known as the *familia rustica*. Here we must not let our judgement be led astray by what Plutarch tells us of Tiberius Gracchus' impressions when, in 137, he crossed Etruria to rejoin the Numantia front in Spain; 'he was struck by the desolation of the countryside, where there lived, in the fields and on the pastures, only foreign and barbarian slaves'.[43] This testimony concerning maritime Etruria – for Tiberius Gracchus of necessity followed the coastal route, the via Aurelia – might possibly be applicable in the case of the Tuscan Maremma and the least fertile part of Etruria; but above all its reference is temporally very restricted: it defines exactly the demographic state, not only of Etruria, but of the whole of central Italy in the second century BC, when, as a consequence of various political and economic factors which the historians have brought to light, the disappearance of the small rural holding and the development of the system of *latifundia* had produced from one end of the peninsula to the other a depopulation of the countryside and the use of slave labour to guard the flocks. 'Foreign and barbarian slaves': the expression is extremely apt, and in these two adjectives we can identify, not only Greeks, but mainly Carthaginians, Sardinians, Gauls and Spaniards whom the wars had cast up in their thousands in the slave-markets. But in primitive Etruria the population of the Etruscan countryside must have had a different look.

Once again it is to Livy we are indebted for some very valuable indications. At the end of the fourth century a Roman legion, led by the consul Q. Fabius Rullianus, made its way through the dense Ciminian Forest, in the region of Viterbo, and came out in the opulent cornlands of central Etruria. The family traditions of the Fabii paint their great man's prowess in glowing colours, but behind these glorious pictures there are a number of authentic little details. It matters very little whether it was the consul's brother or half-brother who, on a reconnaissance mission with a single slave, triumphed over all the traps set by man and nature. It is a story, but the details are astonishingly correct. This Roman knew Etruscan, for he had been brought up at Caere in a *gens* with whom the Fabii exchanged hospitality.

In order to avoid being captured by the enemy, the two emissaries had borrowed native clothes. 'They set off disguised as shepherds and equipped with rustic weapons, carrying each a sickle and two hunting-spears.' And in fact when the rest of the legion followed in their tracks they encountered only small detachments of Etruscan peasants hastily mobilized by the local lords: *tumultuariae agrestium Etruscorum cohortes repente a principibus regionis eius concitatae.*[44]

So when the Romans entered the Etrurian regions of Chiusi, Arezzo and Perugia, they found a landscape of cultivated fields lying between dense forests (cereals and timber have always been the principal products of Chiusi); and, in this setting, a sedentary population, very primitive and practising an economy as yet undifferentiated as it was based on sheep-raising ('disguised as shepherds'), on agriculture (the sickle for cutting corn) and on hunting (the two boar-spears). But these peasants, if the alert was given, owed military service to the local princes, and, carrying their tools in the guise of arms, formed improvised troops whose combat value seems to have been mediocre.

Dionysius of Halicarnassus gave these Etruscan peasants a name which is merely metaphorical but nevertheless very accurate. He was writing about the course of one of the legendary wars between Rome and Veii, which the annals traditionally assigned to the year 480 or thereabouts. Veii was in danger, and appealed for help to the league of twelve. 'Reinforcements arrived from all over Etruria,' says Livy.[45] But the Greek historian, using the same source material but writing more expansively, says precisely: 'The most powerful princes came from all over Etruria, bringing with them their *penestes*.'[46]

This name traditionally meant, in Thessalia, indigenous populations reduced to slavery by the conquerors after the Dorian invasions: attached to the soil as the helots in Sparta, they were compelled, in exchange for guarantees against violence and

57

eviction, to do agricultural labour and military service. Demosthenes tells us of a Thessalian noble, Menon of Pharsalos, who, on the occasion of an expedition launched by Cimon against the city of Amphipolis, had placed at the disposal of the Athenians, besides twelve talents of silver, 'three hundred horsemen recruited from among his penestes'. It was the same situation as that in which the *lucumones* called together their vassals to the defence of Veii. In comparing the latter with the penestes of Thessalia, Dionysius made quite clear that they were free men whose dependence on their lords was based on *clientela*;[47] but he suggested that, contrary to what went on in Rome, the Etruscan masters treated their people with contempt, giving them degrading tasks to perform, beating them and treating them as badly as if they had been real slaves sold by public auction in the great markets of Greece or Asia. Dionysius of Halicarnassus, though he upholds the thesis of the Etruscan people's autochthonous existence, provides, in his account of the *penestes*, an argument in favour of those who see in the serfs of the Etruscan countryside the descendants of Villanovans exploiting lands (which they had to pay rent for) that the invaders had seized from them.

When he reproaches the Etruscan princes with inflicting on their *penestes* tasks unworthy of free men, we think of those particularly arduous tasks, the digging of quarries and mines, which were always, in antiquity, given to slaves. The marble quarries of Luna (Carrara) were not opened before the end of the Roman republic. But it is evident that the mining industry which, in Populonia and in the Campigliese, was the foundation of Etruscan power, had to fall back on a large amount of slave labour and that the arms and tool factories could only work at full stretch if they had at their disposal numerous *familiae* of metal workers. (In Arezzo alone, these factories were able, in 205, to equip the fleet of Scipio Africanus with three thousand bucklers and as many helmets, fifty thousand javelins, *gaesa** and long lances, not counting the axes, spades and scythes.)

Juvenal describes the punishments meted out to those pampered and indolent city slaves when they misbehaved. They were sent into darkest Lucania to labour in the fields, or *in Tusca ergastula*, (into the Tuscan slave prisons).[48] Here some scholars might be

*The *gaesum* was a sort of javelin, of Gaulish origin.

tempted to take *ergastulum* in its primary sense, that of the Greek *ergastèrion*, 'workshop', of which it is merely a modified transcription. And certainly there must have been in Populonia, at the mouth of the Po, and in the Etruscan campagna, ergastula of this nature – hutments or vaults in which miners were locked for the night, or labourers engaged in draining the marshes. But the life led in these places was so atrocious that 'ergastulum' became a synonym for 'slave prison', in which there were prisoners or *vincti* whose manacles were never loosed. Thus Martial, at the end of the first century AD could write, not without rhetorical exaggeration, that the *latifundia* of Etruria rang with the clanking of innumerable chains.[49]

THE SLAVE REVOLTS

As we have seen, literary texts furnish us with only rare and uncertain evidence about the lower levels of the Etruscan population. Nevertheless they insist upon the frequency and violence of social disorders which, from the end of the fourth century, agitated the most populous cities of Etruria: in Arezzo,[50] the ostentation of the Cilnii, distant ancestors of Gaius Maecenas, provoked an armed insurrection, and a little later revolts broke out in Volsinii, whose mighty ramparts above Bolsena have been identified by M. Raymond Bloch.[51] A similar revolution took place in the mysterious *Oinarea* or *Oina*, which we do not know whether to identify with Volterra, Orvieto or Volsinii itself: but in the *Mirabiles Auscultationes* attributed to Aristotle, we have the testimony, almost contemporaneous, of a third century Greek.[52]

The fall of Volsinii was related by Livy in a book now unfortunately lost; but several of his followers or abbreviators, among them Valerius Maximus, Florus, Cassius Dio,[53] have preserved for us the substance of his account, whose historical value, despite moralizing intentions and peripeteia, is considerable.

Volsinii in 280 had had to submit to Rome. For obscure reasons which Livy declared were the effects of lengthy indulgence in soft living and pleasure but which also probably contained elements of despair and disgust, the local nobility had lost interest in the management of its affairs and had left the responsibility to the slaves.

More aware politically, the Pseudo-Aristotle discerned in the events which occurred in exact parallel at Oinarea, the threat of tyranny which nobles of liberal tendency had hoped to avert by relying on the slave class.

At any rate, the Volsinians had, in a hasty democratic evolution, emancipated their slaves on a massive scale, and, in the absence of those assemblies which in Rome served to express and canalize popular opinion, had at once opened access to their senate for the affranchised slaves. These had not hesitated to seize, by trickery, the whole of the government. The Pseudo-Aristotle declares that they exercised power in alternation every year.

The traditional account of Livy did not cover up the excesses in which the mob had indulged: the new masters proceeded to carry out land reforms and redistribution of property, forbade the former free men to attend meetings and banquets (that is, withdrew the right of free association), married the daughters of their masters (that is, abolished those restrictions on the inter-marriage of upper and lower classes which stayed in force in Rome until the reign of Augustus). It is even added, though this may be calumnious exaggeration, that they passed a special law licensing their attacks on the modesty of widows and married women and forbidding any young girl to marry a free man before her virginity had been taken by one of the new rulers.

It was in these desperate circumstances that the nobles had appealed to the Romans for help. And here the annalists' imaginations were given free course. They related complacently the arrival of secret ambassadors who insisted on being received by the Senate in a private dwelling-house, so that none of the proceedings might become public. As bad luck would have it, a Samnite, guest of the master of the house, concealed himself on the premises, overheard the entire discussion and denounced the plot. On their return the ambassadors were arrested, tortured and executed.

That was in 265. Then the consul Q. Fabius Gurges was sent to Volsinii, and, having skirmished with the army which was sent out against him, laid siege to the city. He had been mortally wounded and was replaced by a *consul suffectus*,* P. Decius Mus who had to repel a vigorous attack from the besieged city. Its

Consules suffecti was the title given to consuls who took the place of those who died in office or were unable to carry out their commitments.

defenders did not give in until famine forced them to the following year. The consul M. Fulvius Flaccus triumphed over the Volsinians, *de Vulsiniensibus*,[54] on November 1, 264. The affranchised men had been massacred in their prison, the surviving nobles had their rights restored to them but were transferred to the site at Bolsena. Volsinii itself was destroyed, and its two thousand bronze statues gave Rome a new adornment.

THE AFFRANCHISED

In the preceding passages we have not concealed our sense of being at a loss to explain precisely the bonds of dependence which subjected the lower classes of Etruria to the aristocracy of the *principes*. In fact, one hardly knows what name to call them by: slaves, serfs, clients, affranchised men?[55] The ancients themselves were reduced to approximations whose inexactitude they must have been well aware of. The Greeks, avoiding the term *douloi*, only used the expressions *oikétai* and *thérapeuontes*, which in their tongue actually signified 'domestics' and 'servants'. As if the revolt at Volsinii could have been carried out only by kitchenhands and musicians! Only once, as we have seen, Dionysius of Halicarnassus, dealing with country serfs, has recourse to a metaphor which shows fairly clearly the inadequacy of the current terminology: he had to go as far as Thessalia to find a word which corresponded to the condition of those rural masses. So ancient were the Etruscans, who resembled no one else! If it is permissible to apply to their *penestes* the definition which Dionysius had given beforehand, they were free men but were treated like slaves. Writing in Rome at the beginning of the Roman Empire, Dionysius was unable to find in that disconcerting society the juridical forms, well-known and clearly codified, of the *mancipium*, or master's right of ownership of a slave as it was defined in Roman law. If the legal status of rural labourers seemed to him more like that of a client with regard to his patron, he could not blink the fact that their real status was scarcely better than that of the slaves. Such were the problems which the study of a strange and archaic civilization set a historian accustomed to viewing things in relation to the categories of his time and of his adopted country.

Livy has fewer scruples, and does not hesitate to affix the

forthright name of *servi* to all and sundry – the peasant bands who rose up in 196 against the landowners as well as the dancing troupe of a *lucumo*.[56] And Valerius Maximus writes that it is the *servi* who, imprudently admitted to the Volsinian senate, drove their former masters from the government: this is a deceptive abbreviation, missing out the intermediate stages of affranchisement. Others, Orosius and Aurelius Victor, do not do this and speak judiciously of *libertini*.[57] But here again a difficulty awaits us: it is not certain that the affranchisement in Etruria was the same thing or had the same effects as the Roman *manumissio*.

A small number of bilingual Etrusco-Latin texts have established the equivalence of the Latin word *libertus* and the Etruscan word *lautuni*, which is usually syncopated into *lautni*. A cinerary urn from Perugia, for example, has inscribed on its lid:

L. SCARPVS SCARPIAE L. POPA,[58]

which means *Lucius Scarpus Scarpiae libertus popa*, 'Lucius Scarpus, freed man of Scarpia, victimary', the *popa* being an inferior priest, the executioner who led the victim to the altar and killed him by hitting him over the head with a mallet. This man had been affranchised by a woman named Scarpia whose gentilitial name he had taken.

On the body of the urn itself there appears:

Larth Scarpe Lautuni,

where the same person appears with his Etruscan first name (*Larth*), his name derived from the name of his mistress, and the qualification *lautni* of which *libertus* is the translation. So one is tempted, in the very numerous Etruscan inscriptions where the term *lautni* figures (or its feminine form *lautnitha*) to translate automatically: *Avle Alfnis lautni* by 'Aulus, freed man of Alfius', and *Velia Tutnal lautnitha* by 'Velia, freed woman of Tutia'.[59]

The origin of *lautni* is known: it is derived from the word *laut(u)n* which corresponds exactly to the Latin *familia*. Now *familia*, in good Latin, does not mean at all what is meant by our 'family': it meant first of all 'the community of slaves and servants living under the same roof', then, by extension, 'the entire house, master, wife, children and servants living under the master's dominion'.[60]

The sense of the words evolves by a perpetual and complex movement of meaning; the *familia*, which at first comprised only the slaves to the exclusion of the free members of the family, ended by including only the latter, to the exclusion of the slaves, while at the same time *familiaris* became coloured with moral nuances and finally expressed the charm of intimacy. When Seneca, in the letter we quote, congratulated his correspondent on living *familiariter*, that is, living 'en famille' with his slaves, because he invited them to dine with him, he was playing on the two meanings, ancient and modern, of the adverb. A little further on he writes: 'Will you at least remember how far our fathers went in doing away with everything that could arouse hatred for the master or cause the degradation of the slave: they called the master the "father of the family" (*pater familias*); the slaves were "the people of the family" (*familiares*).'

Etymologically, the translation of *lautni* would be *familiaris*, that is, 'slave'. It is remarkable, and characteristic of the natural incompatibilities dividing the two societies, that it should be interpreted by our bilingual experts, at the moment when the Etruscan world, drawing to its close, was abdicating more and more its own personality, remodelling it on that of the conqueror, in the sense of 'affranchised man', that is 'ex-slave'.

But the contradiction is perhaps not as profound as it at first appears. For in Rome itself the affranchised man remained in a state of dependence on his former master, whose first name and surname he took as if he were his son. And though henceforward he escaped the confines of his former *familia*, there are plenty of tombs in which the master has reserved a place *sibi libertis libertabusque posterisque eorum*, 'for him, for his affranchised men and women, and for their posterity'. Among the Etruscans, it seems, at least during the late period of the inscriptions we refer to, the *lautni* occupied within the *familiae*, whose coherence remained unaltered, a relatively privileged situation. This was not the obscure host of slaves of the lowest rank, those who barely had a name or a burial-place; they are at a fairly high level in the hierarchy of the humble, having acquired through personal merit or the favour of their master, the enjoyment of a measure of liberty which, transposed into terms of Roman law, made them *liberti*. It is possible, indeed it is probable that this liberty was confirmed by a juridical act of emancipation analogous to the *manumissio*. The essential thing is that they did not leave the *familia*, that they even constituted its essential element, and the only one that mattered, the rest not being worthy of mention.

We have a fine example of this persistent solidarity in Etruscan slave families in the following account which dates to 91 BC. That year, threatening omens heralded the wrath of the gods, offended, in the estimation of rich landed proprietors, by the policy of agrarian reform in which the Gracchi, some forty years before, had taken the initiative and which, so long excluded from Etrurian soil, seemed about to strike it directly.

'In the land of Modena, two mountains clashed together with a great noise, advancing and then retreating, whilst flames and smoke rose up between them into the heavens, in broad daylight, and from the via Aemilia a great crowd of Roman knights with their *familiae*, and travellers too witnessed the spectacle. The shock destroyed all the houses in the place and killed a multitude of animals that were there.'[61]

This account of an earthquake, as the Etruscan *haruspices* had written it in their books, from which it had passed on to Pliny the Elder, is admirable in its picturesque precision, and every detail deserves a brief comment. Who does not know the via Aemilia, the great Roman highway which, from Rimini to Placentia, takes in the immense and fertile plain to which it has given its name, Emilia? Anyone who has travelled along it, from Bologna to Modena and from Reggio to Parma, through the fields of maize and past opulent farms with their mulberry walks, with the first ramparts of the Apennines to the south, where inviting roads lead towards Tuscany, will have no difficulty, even though modern culture has modified the landscape a little, in imagining the scene. . . The disaster he will situate in the valley of Frignano. Here there were numerous *villae* which crumbled into ruins; sheep-farming was practised on a large scale, and the *Campi Macri*, near Modena, were famous woollen markets: those sheep would be the *animalia* that were crushed and perished. And the road is black with people. Here let us quote from Pliny's text:

spectante e via Aemilia magna equitum Romanorum familiarumque et viatorum multitudine. Doubtless, as was natural, travellers (*viatores*) passing by on foot, on horseback or in those carriages which the Cisalpine Gauls had made widely popular in their many forms, stopped to stare. But above all the local population was there, comprising, significantly, only two elements, Roman knights (*equites Romani*) and their people (*familiae*). Now these Roman knights, in 91 BC, were no other than the descendants of noble Etruscans who had become Roman citizens and whose fortunes placed them in the rank of knight. They were still the same rich landed proprietors, here raisers of sheep, whose properties were touched neither by Roman colonization nor by Gracchian policy. And all round them stood compact groups of people (no category of freed men having been mentioned at all) which the Naturalist does not bother to divide into their various elements: the *familiae*.

COMPOSITION OF THE SLAVE PERSONNEL

Fortunately Etruscan epigraphy helps us to make a deeper analysis, and illuminates from within the darkest corners of individual existences and the composition of these groups.

There was one of these, somewhere in the country between Chiusi, Montepulciano and Lake Trasimene, whose funerary inscriptions acquaint us with about fifteen of its members. It was the *alfni* family,[62] whose name, despite its suffix, has nothing specifically Etruscan about it: it was formed on the radical *alb-* in Latin, *alf-* in Osco-Umbrian, which signifies 'white'. One encounters Albii and Alfii or 'Whites' throughout the peninsula, and it is possible that the ancestor of the *alfni* arrived one day from Umbria or Campania to seek his fortune at Chiusi.

In the last century before the Christian era, the *pater familias* was cremated in a fine urn of travertine on which, for the first time, his civil status was inscribed in Etruscan and in Latin:

Vl. Alfni. Nuvi. Cainal
C. ALFIVS. A. F. CAINNIA. NATVS.[63]

In his native tongue he was called *Vel Alfni Nuvi*, with an Etruscan first name and two names of which the second belonged no more than the first to Etruscan onomatology. It was simply,

65

transcribed into Etruscan, a name derived from the adjective *novus*, 'new', which was met extensively in southern Italy and elsewhere: which confirms the connexions of the *Alfni* with a region outside Etruria.

But the thing that reveals this person's fidelity to national traditions is the mention of his mother *Cainei*, *Cainal* in the genitive.

In order to have himself inscribed in the registers of the Roman census, *Vel Alfni Nuvi* had exchanged his first name, decidedly inassimilable, of *Vel* for the common one of Caius; he kept only the first of his names and gave his father's first name in the customary abbreviated form *A(uli) f(ilius)*, 'son of Aulus'. But he insisted, even in Latin, on retaining the name of his mother, *Cainnia*.

Now the *Alfni* possessed a large and picturesque band of servants; the epitaphs of certain of these, painted in red on urns or pots, give us confused glimpses of their persons.

There were servants like *Aule Alfnis lautni*, or Aulus, the *lautni* of Alfius. *Venzile Alfnis lautni* had been given a name which was a fond diminutive of the first name *Venel*: this seems to betray the affection of the master for the little slave born in his house (*verna*). A tile, indicating a neighbouring ossuary, introduces us to an Arruns Alfius who was a dyer, *fulu*, in Latin *fullo*. There were female servants, like Vibia, *lautnitha* of Alfius, and, in Latin, *Alfia Q(uinti) l(iberta) Prima*, or again that *Larthi Alfnis lautnitha Percumsnas*, otherwise 'Larthi, *lautnitha* of Alfius, wife of Percumsna', which is a name like 'Perconius' or 'Pergonius'. The little terracotta urn which held her remains was found about ten kilometres to the west of Chiusi, at Sarteano, where Larthi had married and was buried beside her husband Vel Percumsna, son of Arruns. Another, *Sleparis Alfnis l(autnita) Achlesa*, bore a name, *Sleparis*, which was believed to be a transcription of the Greek Cleopatra: but it is more likely to express one of the special duties she had to discharge in the house; others were put in charge of the crockery (*urnasis*), of the beds (*hupnis*) or of the table (*aklchis*).[64] But this *lautnitha* of Alfius was also married, and had as her husband *Achle*, or Achilles.

This was not the only slave or freed man of Greek origin in the family. A terracotta urn contained the remains of yet another *lautni* of Alfius and whose name, *Pilunice*, is quite transparently *Philoneicos*. A cippus preserved, in Latin, the memory of *Amethystus T. Alfi Hilari servus*, 'Amethystus, slave of Titus Alfius Hilarus', *servus* being, as indeed was *libertus*, an approximate translation of *lautni*.

The entire slave onomasticology of inner Etruria, from Chiusi to Perugia, is studded like this with Greek names easy to decipher from their phonetic deformations and orthographic peculiarities: a widespread name was *Antipater* (Antipater), *Apluni* (Apollonius), *Archaza* (Arcadius), *Atale* (Attalus), *Evantra* (Evander), *Herclite* (Heraclides), *Licantre* (Lycander), *Nicipur* (Nicephorus), *Pherse* (Perseus), *Philutis* (Philotis), *Tama* (Damas), *Tinusi* (Dionysos), *Tiphile* (Diphylos), not forgetting several *Zerapiu* (Serapion) whose Egyptian origin is at once evident.[65]

But naturally maritime Etruria, if the epigraphical harvest was as abundant or as communicative, would not speak another language. At Caere, where a more precocious romanization had brought about a general use of Latin but not the disappearance of the ruling *gentes*, what a lot of *cognomina* of Greek and oriental origin we find in the large family of the Magilii, doubtless descendants of the *Macla* or *Macula* who flourished already in the days of independence! Philemon and Laïs, Philip and Chelido (the swallow), Hébénè, black and precious as the wood she was named after; and there is even a Jew, *L. Magili L. l. Aciba*, whose surname was merely the transcription of the proper name Jacob, in Hebrew Aqiba.[66]

The sources of recruitment of this slave population, whose numbers since the end of the third century had shown a massive rise, were not so much provided by the raids of Etruscan pirates as by the carrying-off of war prisoners by Roman generals. Of 150,000 Greeks whom Aemilius Paulus brought back in 167 from his campaign in Epirus, most were sent to Tuscan ergastula; of the 50,000 Carthaginians whom Scipio Aemilianus sold in 146 after the destruction of their city, a large number were doubtless sent to Etruria where they may have helped to spread certain agricultural techniques which the great Punic agronomist Mago had described and which the Etruscan agronomist Saserna and his son must have studied. We should have liked to discover among the inscriptions in Etruria traces of Carthaginian slaves and deformations of names like Hanno or Muthumbal with which Plautus' *Carthaginian* has made everyone familiar. So far we have had no luck. They are concealed perhaps under Greek names, slave merchants having the tendency to make frequent use of those appellations which were at a premium. Or they might even have gone under specific Etruscan denominations, harmless first names like *Cae* (Caius) or *Aule* (Aulus), and finally under the curious *Lethe*, feminine *Lethi* or *Lethia*, which, it has been recently proved was frequently used to designate persons of servile condition, rather as in Latin the word *puer* was used to denote young boy slaves – a sort of common name that remained attached to the slave who used it as a first name, or even as a family name which he passed on to his children.[67]

If we cannot identify the Carthaginians and the Sardinians whom Tiberius Gracchus doubtless encountered in large numbers along the via Aurelia, there are other 'strangers' and other 'barbarians' whose presence in Etruscan families is gradually being revealed, and in an unmistakable way, by the analyses carried out by researchers.

At the gates of Perugia there is a tomb in which an apparently prosperous family had deposed the urns of at least nine of its members: it is the Tomb of the Veneti, in Etruscan *Venete*. One of these, for example, was called:

Se. Venete La. Lethial clan[68]

which can easily be interpreted as:

Sethre (first name) *Venete*, *clan* (son) of *Larth* (*Venete*) and of *Lethi*.

The eponymous ancestor of the *Venete* had certainly come from the north, from the region of Este and Padua, where flourished the people who have given their name to Venetia and Venice. Horse breeders, merchants and sailors, the Veneti, whose religion, art and language related to Latin are beginning to emerge in the light of history, had succeeded, alone of all Cisalpine peoples, in preserving their independence in the face of Etruscan colonization. Livy, who was one of them, never misses an opportunity to recall this with pride. But they had not surrounded themselves with an unbreachable wall: exchanges, either through war or through peaceful relations were inevitable. At Este there was a certain *Voltiomnios* (Voltumnius), a *Carponia* and other Etruscans.[69] Similarly there were *Venete* at Perugia, and also at Chiusi and Bomarzo (Polimartium), for whom in former days the ethnic name was used as a personal name.

Had the first *Venete* at Perugia come of his own free will to settle? It is possible that he had been a prisoner of war and a slave, and later affranchised, either he or his descendants. In any event, nothing of the *Venete* in this tomb recalled their humble origins. But the father of *Sethre Venete, Larth Venete*, had married *Lethi*, whose name betrays a more or less indirect descent from slaves. We shall meet her a little later under another aspect of the *familia*.

Epigraphy gives us another glimpse, at Perugia or Chiusi, of other Veneti whom the linguist recognizes by their characteristic names: *Ustiu, Autu, Tita*; and along with them, originating at the other extremity of the Cisalpine region, some Ligurians: a *lautni* bearing the name of *Lecusta* (Ligustius),[70] a freed woman called in Latin *Salassa Grania* after the Salassians of the Vale of Aosta.[71] We shall not mention the Mantuans, since Mantua was an Etruscan colony, from which, not surprisingly, one *Manthuate* and one *Manthuatnei*, a woman, had returned to die in the land of their fathers.[72] What we must look for in particular among the peoples of the north are the Gauls.

It is well known that for centuries they had mingled with the Etruscans in a war for the possession of that Cisalpine region which, Etruscan at first, was finally called Gaul; and the cities of Etruria proper never ceased to tremble at the threat of invasion by the Gauls, who, before reaching Rome in 390, sacked those very cities. For a long time, when Rome was still only a small state hemmed in by its own hills, they had to fight on two fronts, against the Greeks (that is, the Syracusans whose fleet was ravaging their coasts), and against the Gauls whose irresistible pressure was with difficulty held back at the Apennines. There was a striking expression of this double nightmare in the barbaric rite which, at certain critical junctures, required the wrath of the gods to be appeased by burying alive, in the forum of the city, a Greek man and woman and a Gaulish man and woman; these poor wretches were selected from the anonymous crowds of Greek and Gaulish slaves at the nearest *ergastulum*.

The vast human reservoir of the Gauls must have contributed in great measure to swell the ranks of Etruscan slave classes. Perhaps the majority, like our hypothetical Carthaginians, disguised themselves under banal names, *Cae*, *Aule*, and so on, or under the qualification *Lethe*. But sometimes a corner of the veil is lifted.

A cippus at Volterra warns us of the nearby presence of the tomb of Mogetius, *lautni* of Cneuna, *Mucetis Cneunas lautunis*. The master has a family name, *Cneuna* or *Cnevna*, formed on the first name *Cneve*, in Latin *Cnaeus*. But in *Muceti*, *Mogetius*, the linguists are unanimous in recognizing a Celtic name often found in the three Gauls and even as far afield as Mainz or Mayence, which name, Mogontiacum, is formed from the same root, 'great'.[73]

THE REAL CONDITION OF ETRUSCAN SLAVES

Besides the origins of slave personnel, our inscriptions reflect in miniature but sometimes with a fascinating precision, the conditions they lived under. And here again, naturally, we know nothing about the very lowest classes. It was not until the slave became a *lautni* that he got a voice, a name, an ossuary. We said previously that he was often called *Lethe*, but this knowledge comes down to us through others; he himself remains mute. The *lautni* are more communicative, and tell us, among other things, about their marriages.

Thana Laucinei (or, if we so wish, Thana Lucinia in Latin) was the *lautnitha* belonging to two brothers, *Vel* and *Tite*: we assume that she had been their undivided property before being emancipated by them both, and that they had both remained her masters. Hence the inscription, on a cheap terracotta jug:

Laucinei Thana Velus Tites lautnitha.[74]

But on the tile drawing the passer-by's attention to the tomb, she was described as:

Thana Laucinei Lethesa = *Thana Laucinei*, wife of *Lethe*.[75]

Let us not inquire if they were united by legal bonds. Nevertheless we notice here that the wife has a right to the same title as women of free birth, with the qualification of *puia, conjunx: Caia puia Lachus, Caia*, wife of *Lachu*, which is perhaps a transcription of the Greek *Lachôn*.[76] Moreover freed men on occasion married outside their respective families and then the women followed the man to his abode: we have seen *Larthi Alfni* leaving Chiusi for Sarteano after her marriage. But there were misalliances; not only between free-born men marrying freed women, but sometimes – we have two very clear examples of this – free-born women who lived in concubinage with a *lautni*.

A single urn from Chiusi, which is now in the Louvre, contained the mingled ashes of *Hasti Ecnatei*, whose first and family names indicate a very honourable birth (there had been Egnatii in the Roman Senate since the second century), and of a *lautni* whose name is no less rich in significance: *H. Ecnatei Atiuce lautnic*.[77] Although the copulative particle *-c* (in Latin *que*) is placed after the second of the two co-ordinated terms, this can clearly be deciphered as: *Hastia Egnatia Antiochusque libertus*, 'Hastia Egnatia and the freed man Antiochus'. A degrading union, such as the revolutionaries of Volsinii dreamed of at the time of their brief seizure of power, but which, in a more recent Etruria, no longer caused any scandal and was advertised in the cemeteries, although this *Atiuce*, Antiochus, must have come fresh from heaven knows what slave-market on the Syrian Orontes.

It really does seem that henceforward the *familiae* of Chiusi and Perugia were the settings for rather rapid social rises. We have already cited one Diphylos who, with another Greek named Damas, had been part of the Velcii household. He was laid to rest at Chiusi, next to his wife Pollia, herself doubtless a *lautnitha: Tiphile, lautni Velches Puliac*, or: *Diphylos, Velcii libertus et Pollia*. They had one son, who is designated thus on a cinerary urn: *Ath. Tiphile. Palpe. Pulias*, or *Arruns Diphilus Balbus, Pollia natus*. Thus, in the space of one generation, *Tiphile* had become a name preceded by the most classical of all Etruscan first names, *Arnth, Arruns*, and which is followed by a surname borrowed from Latin (*Balbus*, the Stammerer). In conformity with the usages of good society, the matronymic is mentioned, but there is no allusion to the father, since legally that Arruns is *nullo patre*. Wait a few years more and we shall find, in Latin characters, the epitaph of one *Ar. Tibile, P.L. Arruns Diphilus Publii libertus* – the *gens* created so recently already has its own freed men.[78]

THE CLIENTS

It was a rise in the social scale which did not stop with the attainment of the status of *lautni* and the conquest of liberty. Even higher than the *lautni* can be distinguished the category of the *etera*, who, in the family tomb, had a place of honour. For example, in the Tomb of the Veneti, the urn of *Se. Venete La. Lethial clan* was flanked by another which belonged to *La. Venete La. Lethial etera*,[79] and whose inscription was no different from the first excepting in the name *Larth* instead of *Sethre* and the substitution of the word *etera* for the word *clan* (son). Elsewhere, in the tomb of the Titii Petronii, there were ranged against the rear wall, side by side, the urns of the eldest son and of the *etera* of the *pater familias*. The *etera* formed a privileged class, but not an independent one, for one is always the *etera* of somebody. At Tarquinii, a special magistrate, *zilatheterau*, was put in charge of their interests.[80]

We are more and more inclined to agree that these *etera* were clients, and high-class ones. Many attempts have been made to explain their name. We have proposed[81] among several etymologies which have been suggested, that it is a loan word from the Greek *hétairos, hétaros*, a companion in arms. The Etruscan legend, formed in the image of Homeric epic, is very keen on these bonds of military companionship which, as we have seen, united Macstarna and Caelius Vibenna. And moreover the institution of the clientela is part of all ancient societies in their primitive state. The Roman nobility had its clients, whom Dionysius of Halicarnassus sometimes calls *hétairoi*, and the Gaulish aristocracy had its own, called in the Celtic tongue *ambacti*; it is curious that the historian Polybius, writing of the Cisalpine Gauls against whom the Etruscans had fought so long, translates *ambacti* by *hétairoi*.[82] Of the Etruscans, too, he might have said that they knew no other outward sign of personal credit and power than a large train of servants and *hétairoi* gathered round a man. There is a good chance that if they gave their clients the name of *etera* they had borrowed it, along with so many other terms of civilization, from the Greeks.

But we also see in Etruscan inscriptions at Chiusi and Perugia the qualification of *lautneteri*, which is, quite undoubtedly, composed of *lautn* and *etera*. Thus *Salvi Precus lautn eteri* would mean *Salvius, lautneteri* from *Preco*.[83] It is natural to suppose that in this case it was a question of a *lautni* in an Etruscan family who had been promoted to the enviable condition of *etera*. Livy by chance furnishes us with the Latin equivalent when he mentions a *cliens libertinus* of the tribune of the plebs called P. Rutilius.[84].

CHAPTER FOUR

THE ETRUSCAN FAMILY AND THE RÔLE OF WOMEN

Family life – The status of women – The freedom they enjoyed – Their political authority – Mediterranean survivals – Archaeological confirmation – The culture of Etruscan women – Their privileges beyond the grave

---

FAMILY LIFE

The Etruscan family – and we now use the word in its usual restricted sense – the human group formed by father and mother surrounded by their children and grandchildren, is not distinguishable in any way from the Roman family or the Grecian family. It knew neither the communal sharing of wives which Strabo[1] describes in the Arab world and Caesar[2] attributes to the Celts in the British Isles; nor marriage between brother and sister which was recommended in the very ancient Orient and was still practised in the Egypt of the Ptolemaic dynasty; nor, apparently, the polygamy recognized by Assyrian laws, nor the uterine filiation that flourished in the matriarchal societies, among the Lycians for example, who, according to Herodotus, called themselves by their mother's and not by their father's name.[3]

As far back as we can go, the Etruscans seem to have had solid and well-united families. They did not contest the authority of the *pater familias* which the Romans accorded to the family head; the filiation in their inscriptions is definitely paternal.

One religious personality in Tarquinii, at the beginning of the second century, called himself *Laris Pulenas*, son of *Larce*, nephew of *Larth*, grandson of *Velthur*, great-grandson of *Laris Pule Creice*.[4] In the same period, one Scipio in Rome called himself *L(ucius) Cornelius, P(ublii) f(ilius), L(ucii) n(epos), P(ublii) pron (epos)*.

74

Thanks to these inscriptions, we know the principal parental terms in Etruscan. We know that *clan* meant 'son', *sec* 'daughter', *puia* 'wife', and that *tusurthi(r)* signified 'the married pair'. We discover that 'grandfather' was *papa* (cp. the Greek *pappos*), and 'grandmother' *ati nacna*, literally 'dear mother', 'brother' was *thuva* and 'nephew' *papacs*. The great-grandson was the *prumaths*, and the grandson the *nefts*, which greatly resembles the Latin *nepos*. *Nefts* and *nepos*, *papa* and *pappos*: these concordances or borrowings go to prove that there were deep affinities between the Etruscan family and the Graeco-Roman family.

What could be more respectable than this example of regularity in family life, the epitaph of the Petronii at Perugia, banal as one of our own funeral announcements, inscribed on an urn whose lid bears the reclining statues of the husband and wife: Vel Titius Petronius, son of Vel and of Anneia Spurinna, rests here with his wife Veilia Clantia, daughter of Arruns? Beside this, another urn contained the remains of their son Lars Titius Petronius, son of Vel and Clantia, and of his wife, Fasti Capenia, daughter of Vel and of Coesidia, wife of Tarchi.[5] Doubtless here it is a question of relatively recent inscriptions (second century), but it is the same language which would have been used on the great mass-produced sarcophagi of the sixth century if epitaphs had been written on them for the anonymous couples of Caere stretched beside one another on the funerary couch, and whose attitude, at once dignified and informal, the affectionate protectiveness of the husband, the tender confidence of the wife, express in the most universal sense what we call married bliss.

These texts and figured representations are a far remove from the scurrilous gossip of Theopompus.

THE STATUS OF WOMEN

Perhaps one detail will have been noticed in the inscriptions we have just quoted, a detail which distinguishes Etruscan civil status: the women are provided with a first name. The most illustrious Roman matron was never referred to in Latin inscriptions as more than Claudia or Cornelia; even an empress was still plain Livia. But Etruscan women were given individual first names, *Ramtha*, *Tanaquil*, *Fasti*, *Velia*, which gave a more rounded expression to their personality in the bosom of the family. Again,

while the Latin onomastic formula only mentions, after the first
and the family names, the first name of the father: *M(arcus)*
Tullius M(arci) f(ilius), Etruscan epigraphy regularly adds the
mother's name, sometimes even accompanied by her first name.
A praetor of Tarquinii called himself *Larth Arnthal Plecus clan*
Ramthasc Apatrual, or 'Lars, son of Arruns Pleco and of Ramtha
Apatronia'.[7] And this tradition was so strongly rooted in national
habits that it survived the romanization of the Latin inscriptions
in Etruria, where the mention of the mother's name completes –
which to an authentic Roman would have seemed a pointless
luxury – the indication of the father's name. Some inscriptions
from Montepulciano, still under the Empire, acquaint us with a
certain *A. Papirius L.f. Alfia natus*, or 'Aulus Papirius son of
Lucius, born of Alfia'. And a certain *L. Gellius C. f. Longus Senia*
natus, 'Lucius Gellius, son of Caius, born of Senia'.[8] And this
particularly would be sufficient, even outside Etruscan territory,
to reveal the origins of a sister-in-law of the emperor Claudius,
Vibia Marsi filia Laelia nata, 'Vibia, daughter of (Vibius) Marsus,
born of Laelia'.[9]

These were uses which, in their tenacious singularity, point
to a feature of Etruscan life we cannot ignore, though we must not
exaggerate its importance. For it is obvious that it was the
patronymic which had the first place in inscriptions, and that in
Tarquinii or Perugia as in Rome it was the father's name that his
sons and daughters received when they were born. The matronymic only takes second place. But the care that is taken not to
omit it, and at the same time the attribution of a special first
name of their very own to the women, are signs, among many
others, of the particular consideration they enjoyed. Let us not
try to seek a quick explanation: let us take the facts.

THE FREEDOM THEY ENJOYED

Yet in the opinion of the Greeks and Romans, Etruscan women
had a rather bad reputation. Serious authors, like Aristotle,
repeated the tales of Theopompus and accused them of banqueting
with men, lying with them under the same cloak.[10] Comic authors
like Plautus claimed that they collected their dowries by making a
commercial exploitation of their charms.[11] Need we remark that
this has been seen as an argument in favour of the race's oriental

origin? But why should the case of Etruscan debauchery be sought in the sacred prostitution of Babylon? Lydian women, it appears, gave themselves to all and sundry. But so did the women of Cyprus and even of Locri in Greece itself. We must remember in all this that the Etruscan way of life offered in this respect many opportunities for ill-natured criticism and from the point of view of morals in antiquity it sometimes created a scandal. For, taking into account the relaxations which time had brought about in the severe living-conditions of Greek women under Dorian law and in their primitive seclusion in the *gynecaeum*,[12] the Etruscan woman enjoyed no less liberty and rights, which, for a narrow-minded Greek – and there were some, after all – seemed to authorize the very worst misbehaviour.

The Greek woman and the Roman woman lived in the shadow of their homes; but the Etruscan woman 'went out' a great deal. We see her everywhere, in the forefront of the scene, taking a considerable place in it and never blushing for shame, as Livy says of one of them, when exposing themselves to masculine company. In Etruria it was a recognized privilege for ladies of the most respectable kind, and not just for courtesans as in Greece, to take part with men in banquets where they reclined, as the men did, beside their male hosts on the couches of the Triclinium, whereas even in private parties represented on Attic *steles* the wife remains modestly seated, the better to serve her lord and master. But Etruscan women were not afraid to have themselves painted in such company in the numerous frescoes at Tarquinii, in the Tomb of Leopards and in the Tomb of the Triclinium (fifth century), conventionally adorned with blond hair (the men have black hair) and wearing a heavy embroidered mantle over their tunic. In this costume they attended dances, concerts, sports events; they even presided, as a painting in Orvieto shows, perched on a platform, over boxing matches, chariot races and acrobatic displays[13] – whereas at Olympia only the priestess of Demeter had the right to attend the games.[14] Such participation in public and private life on the part of the Etruscan women could appear indiscreet; it roused the suspicions of neighbouring peoples and gave fuel to the hostile propaganda of their enemies.

Livy gives us some admirable examples of this enviable or at any rate different women's situation which provoked such astonished disapproval in Greece and Rome. Livy, despite the summary judgements on his work which appear sometimes in learned manuals, is one of the most intelligent historians of antiquity. The feeling he has for psychological realism certainly equals that which is more willingly attributed to Tacitus. Writing under Augustus, he had collected in the tradition of his predecessors a quantity of very ancient facts which he always endeavoured to understand, to motivate and explain according to the character of the men concerned in them. Now it so happens that in the second part of his Book I, he had to recount the history of the three Etruscan kings, Tarquinius Priscus, Servius Tullius and Tarquinius Superbus, who had reigned in Rome in the sixth century. All this part of his work stands out from the whole because of certain new characteristics: the style is much less dense, the story is richer in human truth and more given to dramatic effects. After all the vague fables and long accounts of wars, there suddenly appears a living dynasty of *condottieri*, painted in the liveliest colours; it bounds on the scene and for more than a century engages in a complex game of intrigues and violence. This was because, at the origins of this tradition, the obscure data of Etruscan historiography offered themselves to the narrator in a second-hand state; they had already been used, exploited and remodelled by the first Roman annalists, but nevertheless still contained, in a fossilized condition as it were, irreducible and unassimilated facts. Livy does not always seem to get the meaning: in his view these are monstrosities or oddities whose more profound significance he does not realize, but which we are able now to interpret more precisely.

For example, in chapter LVII he tells a marvellous anecdote. We are in the reign of Tarquinius Superbus: the young princes, his sons, are at the siege of Gabii in Latium, and the fall of the city is expected:

'Here in their permanent camp, as is usual with a war not sharp but long drawn out, furlough was rather freely granted, more freely however to the leaders than to the soldiers; the young princes for their part passed their idle hours together at dinners and drinking bouts. It chanced, as they were drinking in the quarters of Sextus Tarquinius, where

Tarquinius Collatinus, son of Egerius, was also a guest, that the subject of wives came up.'[15]

The subject is a common one and has been taken up many times by the novelist and the dramatist: a conversation in the mess or in a stalag: a number of men thrown on their own company seek to supplement the idleness of captivity by talking about women: each one praises the merits of his own, and from this spring drama, desire, jealousy. What Livy does not mention, seeming not to be interested in it (though it interests us profoundly) is that the young princes' wives are of Etruscan blood like themselves, except the wife of Tarquinius Collatinus, who is Roman. It is the virtuous Lucretia's very purity which is to inspire in Sextus Tarquinius, a blasé Don Juan, a passion and a violence that are to incite rebellion and the expulsion of the kings.

So 'the subject of wives came up, and every man fell to praising his own wife with enthusiasm, and, as their rivalry grew hot, Collatinus said there was no need to talk about it, for it was in their power to know, in a few hours' time, how far the rest were excelled by his own Lucretia. "Come! If the vigour of youth is in us let us mount our horses and see for ourselves the disposition of our wives. Let every man regard as the surest test what meets his eyes when the woman's husband enters unexpected." They were heated with wine. "Agreed!" they all cried, and clapping spurs to their horses were off for Rome. Arriving there at early dusk, they thence proceeded to Collatia, where Lucretia was discovered very differently employed from the daughters-in-law of the king. These had been seen at a luxurious banquet, whiling away the time with their young friends. [*Cum aequalibus*, in the text, does not indicate their sex.] But Lucretia, though it was late at night, was busily engaged upon her wool, while her maidens toiled about her in the lamplight as she sat in the hall of her house. The prize for the contest in womanly virtues fell to Lucretia.'

This confrontation is not, for us, as it was for Livy, just one between dissipation and virtue, but between two ways of civilization. The rather timorous discretion of the historian will have been noted – how he glides rapidly over the princesses' occupations:

79

the tombs of the Leopards and of the Triclinium leaves us in no doubt that they would have handsome youths with them, and as for the way they passed the time, we know that they were 'heavy drinkers'.[16] But this brief evocation of the life of Etruscan women has been kept to the last, the better to bring out by immediate contrast the image of Roman Lucretia sagely by the hearth at evening, by candlelight winding and spinning amid her toiling women and above all, for this attitude is the essential thing, not reclining on a festive couch, but seated, *sedentem*.

Pudica, lanifica, domiseda: such are the epithets customary on funerary inscriptions which Roman husbands composed in praise of their wives. They could imagine no finer rôle for them than to spin wool and keep house. '*Domum serauit, lanam fecit*', soberly concludes the most celebrated of these epigrams.[17] The Etruscan ideal and Etruscan manners were different. One can imagine, when the two societies mingled, what domestic conflicts must have taken place. When a young Roman brought a fiancée from Chiusi or Arezzo and introduced her to the *pater familias*, her replies to questions on manners were not always satisfactory. The foreign girl was not home-keeping enough, did not sit up straight on her chair and so on. And when a Fabia or a Claudia married into a family in Volterra or Vulci, her sisters-in-law must have laughed at her prudery. But it was the Romans who finally triumphed, and from the fourth century onwards, in the paintings at Tarquinii, we see that the Etruscan women had learned to sit properly on chairs, like civilized creatures.

THEIR POLITICAL AUTHORITY

But they not only enjoyed more liberty than Roman women in their pleasures. In civil society also they played a preponderant rôle which Roman matrons could not pretend to, despite the moral authority their virtues gave them. This is what comes out again admirably in the portrait of Tanaquil which Livy has painted for us, not without astonishment at the part this extraordinary woman took in promoting the rise of her husband, Tarquinius Priscus.

He was the son of a Corinthian Greek, Demaratus, whom a revolution had driven from his country and who had come and settled in Tarquinii. The extent of Corinthian commerce along the shores of Etruria in the middle of the seventh century, largely confirms the truth of such a legend.[18] In Tarquinii, Demaratus married an Etruscan woman who gave him two sons: one of these, whom Livy calls Lucumo, married Tanaquil.

'The self-confidence implanted in his bosom by his wealth was heightened by his marriage with Tanaquil, who was a woman of the most exalted birth, and not of a character lightly to endure a humbler rank in her new environment than she had enjoyed in the condition to which she had been born. The Etruscans looked with disdain on Lucumo, the son of a banished man and a stranger. She could not endure this indignity, and forgetting the love she owed her native land, if she could only see her husband honoured, she formed the project of emigrating from Tarquinii. Rome appeared to be the most suitable place for her purpose; amongst a new people, where all rank was of sudden growth and founded on worth, there would be room for a brave and strenuous man.'[19]

There could be nothing more solemn nor yet more informal than the arrival of the emigrant family, the future Tarquinius and his wife Tanaquil, when, having piled all their household goods on a chariot, they came one day in sight of Rome; one can almost feel one is following them along what was later to be the via Aurelia, and, at the last turning on top of the Janiculum, looking down with them, on a Rome spread out over the mouth of the Tiber, which doubtless was not the Rome of a thousand domes which one goes to view today from that celebrated balcony, nor even the Rome which Augustus, in the days of Livy, began to construct of marble but simply, lying there in the golden light, a primitive Rome with peasant villages perched on the seven hills. It was indeed to be the work of the Tarquins to turn it into a true city and into the Eternal City.

And it was there, as they halted for a moment, wondering what destiny would have in store for them, that the wondrous event occurred: a bird, an eagle, came circling down round Tarquinius' head, snatched off his pointed cap, circled round again for two or three times, then returned and replaced it firmly, *apte*, on the head of the man whom Jupiter thus designated as called upon to reign. He was somewhat frightened, but 'Tanaquil, versed, as Etruscans usually are, in the interpretation of celestial signs', reassured him. 'She embraces her husband, and exhorts him to cherish great and high hopes.' Heartened by this incident, and confirmed in their ambitions, Tarquinius and Tanaquil went on their way, and, having found a lodging, went to the police station where Tarquinius had himself registered under the curious name of Lucius Tarquinius Priscus, which means, by the delicious anachronism of tradition, Lucius Tarquinius *the Elder*, to distinguish him from those who were to follow.[20] A Roman tradition, based on Etruscan data, which is determined to honour the future king with the *tria nomina* of a real Roman citizen, and relegates to anonymity the woman who nevertheless had been the interpreter and maker of his fate.

Some thirty-seven years later, at the death of Tarquinius, Tanaquil again played a determining rôle in the strange accession of Servius Tullius whose hidden future she had divined while he was still a little boy, and who had become her son-in-law. Using her irresistible authority, she passed over her own sons and presented him as their new king to a populace that was at first unwilling to accept him.[21] This fresh intervention, which only reaches us now wrapped in obscure magical practices and mixed up with specious erudition, nevertheless reveals in the Etruscan queen a strange political primacy which would have eclipsed the brilliance of the men whose power she had made possible if she had not been, from the Roman point of view, a mere woman. Generations of historians ever since Fabius Pictor, who was the first, at the beginning of the second century, to delve into Etruscan sources for the material of his books, had done all they could to bring this virago down to the common level of Roman matrons, subjecting her retrospectively to the all-powerful *pater familias*. Tanaquil who, we may be sure, attended in her native city of Tarquinii banquets and games in the company of men, had finally, in Rome or at least in the complaisant imaginations of those who had adopted her, been brought to bear the traditional distaff. Young married couples at their wedding ceremony used to invoke her name, for she had been a model of conjugal honesty: the proof of this was that she had been an 'excellent spinner', *summa lanifica*. And Varro had seen, miraculously preserved in the temple of Semo Sancus on the Quirinal hill her spindle and distaff, still wound with wool.[22]

There could be no question of using etruscology to explain every authoritarian woman in history. But there was one, at the court of Augustus, who, though the days of Tanaquil had long since passed, seemed to bring her tradition alive again. She was called Urgulania, and her name, recently discovered on an inscription at Tarquinii, clearly indicates her origin. Tacitus, in various passages of his Annals, has traced a portrait in the grand style of that haughty and dominating personality.[23] She had acquired, thanks to the friendship of Livia, wife of Augustus, a considerable position 'which placed her above the law'. 'Called as a witness in a case which was being heard in the Senate, she declined to appear: a praetor was sent to question her at her home.' She succeeded in escaping a previous accusation by addressing herself directly to the imperial palace. Later she makes an appearance as an old lady who would suffer no stain on her family honour. One of her grandsons had thrown his wife out of the window: in order that he should be spared the ignominy of certain conviction, Urgulania sent him a dagger.

This Etruscan woman of imperious character and inflexible pride had a husband of whom one knows nothing but that he was called Plautius. In order to establish the fortune of her descendants, she made full use of the exceptional credit and excessive power which were hers through her links with the empress.

She first used her *nimia potentia* to get her son, M. Plautius Silvanus, appointed to a consulship in the year 2 BC, which he had the honour to share with Augustus himself. Silvanus had a brilliant career which is outlined for us in an inscription on the mausoleum he had made for himself and his family at Ponte Lucano near Tivoli:[24] the epitaphs of other members of his family tell us something about its history.

He himself had married Lartia, whose name, based on the first name *Lars*, *Lartis*, has an obvious Etruscan character. For Urgulania kept up an unfailing fidelity to her own race both in herself and in those around her.

The eldest of her four grandchildren, M. Plautius Silvanus (the same name as his father), a praetor, had conjugal difficulties

83

as we know. But the woman he defenestrated was called Apronia, and this is also an Etruscan name. The second son, Aulus Plautius Urgulanius, died at the age of nine before his grandmother had had time to marry him off. But the third, P. Plautius Pulcher, did not escape. We are able to follow him all through a slow and painful career which, despite the protections he enjoyed, rose no higher than a praetorship. But he also had married an Etruscan princess, *Vibia Marsi filia Laelia nata.*

Urgulania, who practised, as we can see, a policy of rigorous endogamy within the Etruscan aristocracy, tolerated only one misalliance: this was in order to marry her granddaughter Urgulanilla to one of Livia's grandsons, the future emperor Claudius.

This boy was the 'idiot' of the imperial family: despised by all, ridiculed in public, he set his grandparents a difficult problem. We have the fragment of a letter from Augustus to Livia in which the ageing emperor expresses his embarrassment. What was to be done with this poor creature, *misellus*, now that he had attained the age to accede to the magistracies? The best thing they could think of, to teach him good manners, was to entrust him to M. Plautius Silvanus – he who had thrown his wife out of the window – and to marry him off to Urgulanilla. And Claudius, introduced into the Etruscan discipline, became a great scholar: he composed a history of the Etruscans in twenty volumes. It is clear that the son-in-law and brother-in-law of the authentic representatives of the principal Etruscan *gentes* of the time, having access to family archives jealously guarded within the severe walls of Tuscan palaces at Tarquinii, Volterra, Chiusi and Perugia had found there his vocation as etruscologist; and at the same time we can see that the fragments of his *Tyrrhenica* which have come down to us, take on, if they are placed in this perspective, an unexpected value.

MEDITERRANEAN SURVIVALS

But returning from the *nimia potentia* of Urgulania to the over-weening ambition of Tanaquil, we cannot fail to notice, more or less effaced or muddled by prejudiced historians, traces of a social status for women that was very different from that existing in Rome. It was on this that ninety years ago a German scholar, contemporary and friend of Nietzsche, J. J. Bachofen, had based his ingenious – and inadmissible – *Sage von Tanaquil*, in which he defined Etruscan society as an example of *Mutterrecht* or matriarchy, surviving into historical times.

A fairly pure form of *Mutterrecht* is described by Herodotus in his account of the Lycians of Asia Minor:

'They call each other by their mother's name, not by their father's. If one of them inquires of a neighbour what his name is, the person questioned will give his genealogy on the maternal side and enumerate the maternal ancestors of his mother. If a woman citizen marries a slave, the children of the marriage are considered to be of good stock; but if a male citizen, even were he the greatest of all, marry a foreign woman or a concubine, the children would enjoy no consideration whatsoever.'[25]

But sociologists distinguish between the matriarchy of a régime (of which Egyptian and perhaps Cretan society showed fairly clear signs, and which, closely allied to systems where relationship was passed down on the maternal side, cannot be quite compared with them), and that of female domination or gynaecocracy. And we can well imagine that in both cases the eminent dignity of the *mater familias* had been one of the distinctive traits of the Mediterranean societies before the Greek and Italian invasions had put in their place the reign of the male.

It cannot be denied that Etruscan society in many respects has elements of both matriarchy and gynaecocracy. What we have related above about the attention given to the matronymic in civil life recalls certain features of matriarchy. The case of Maecenas, the minister of Augustus, whose ancestors had reigned at Arezzo, is very curious in this respect. He was called *C. Maecenas C.f.*, but all his noble connexions seem to have come to him from his mother's side, by which he was related to the illustrious *gens* of the Cilnii, and it was for this reason that Augustus, ignoring the name of his paternal ancestors, called him affectionately *Cilniorum smaragde*, 'emerald of the Cilnii'.

But if there was a form of *Mutterrecht* among the Etruscans, it existed in a very adulterated form. It was the father's name which was given to children. If Tarquinius Priscus had lived in a rigorously matriarchal city, there would have been no reason for him to emigrate.[26] Among the Lycians 'if a woman citizen marries a slave, the children of the marriage are considered to be of good stock'. In Tarquinii, the son of an Etruscan woman and of a Corinthian would have no difficulty in realizing his ambitions, and Tanaquil's pride would not have had to suffer from a misalliance which did not encroach upon her privileges.

What is the final word? There is a phrase of Cicero's that goes very far: reproaching Cato with the abstract intransigence of his dogmatism, he objected to him that he did not live 'in the ideal Republic of Plato, but in the filthy city of Romulus'.[27] We do not find in Etruscan society either a theoretical *Mutterrecht* or an ideal gynaecocracy, but simply one stage in a long development, an unstable equilibrium of antagonistic forces in full evolution and which is given its full significance only if we compare it with what we observe in Greece and Rome. We have already noted several times that Etruscan civilization was an archaic civilization. Its feminism, strange as it may seem to us, is not so much a recent conquest as a distant survival threatened by Graeco-Roman pressures; it recalls in many respects the Crete of Ariadne and the paintings of Cnossos more than the Athens of Solon and Pericles. But the social state, of which it seems to retain many of the characteristics, if it was ever realized in its pure form, had a for a long time, in the Etruria of the seventh or sixth centuries, felt contrary influences which denatured it. Human societies can never be defined with absolute precision. In Etruscan society, the *pater familias* laid down the law, but the *mater familias* had her say also, and her word was often the last one.

Let us open our Livy again: in the accession to power of Tarquinius Superbus, his wife Tullia played a rôle analogous to that which Tanaquil had played in the accession of his predecessors, Tarquin the Elder and Servius Tullius.[28]

Servius Tullius had had two daughters, Tullia the elder and Tullia the younger, of whom history – Roman – has not preserved the first names. The one was violent and the other timid. In order to consolidate his throne, Servius Tullius had married them to the two sons of Tarquinius the Elder: two very ill-assorted households. The violent daughter had married a gentle man, the timid daughter had married a violent one. Then Tullia the violent one fell in love with her violent brother-in-law. Gentle Tarquinius and gentle Tullia were assassinated. The remaining pair, by marriage, united their double violence, assuring Tarquinius Lucius, the future Superbus, the royal crown.

Now in this story which Livy tells as if it were some tragedy in the tradition of Aeschylus' *Oresteia*, there are some details that give us pause. Servius Tullius, in the Curia, had just been furiously assaulted by his son-in-law Lucius Tarquinius and had been cast down from the throne. Tullia was awaiting in her palace the outcome of this dramatic scene: but she could not wait for news, and went out. 'It is believed, inasmuch as it is not inconsistent with the rest of her wickedness, that this deed was suggested by Tullia. It is agreed, at all events, that she was driven in her carriage into the Forum, and nothing abashed at the crowd of men, summoned her husband from the Curia and was the first to call him king.' [*Regemque prima appellavit.*][29]

These words: 'she was the first to call him king' are perhaps one of those fossils, embedded in a very ancient tradition, of which we have already spoken; the whole context is psychological interpretation, and, in a certain sense, literature. One thing is certain, as Livy says: the proclamation of the king by the queen. Livy, to whom this kind of accession seemed very suspect, expends great ingenuity in explaining it through the personality of Tullia. His Lucius Tarquinius himself is profoundly shocked by it, like the good Roman he is according to his Roman biographers. He orders Tullia, in very sharp words, to 'leave such a tumultuous crowd' and to go back home. But it seems that the generating kernel of the story was an immemorial usage in which the Etruscan woman, as in Cretan and Egyptian society, had the status, incomprehensible to Livy, of 'king-maker' – as if the legitimate monarchy depended on the queen's designation and consecration of the monarch. *Regemque prima appellavit.*

In a preceding chapter, one small phrase embarrasses the editors very much.[30] Tullia, as we have seen, despised her younger sister because she was of a gentle and timid disposition, and she never stopped telling her brother-in-law how unworthy of him such a wife was. The one who had been given the energetic and violent husband 'lacked feminine audacity', *muliebri cessaret audacia*. This 'feminine audacity' seems to have shocked most of the editors of Livy. When the historian, in the picture which inspired David, shows the Sabines dashing into the midst of battle to separate their confronted fathers and husbands, and says that they triumphed through their *muliebris pavor*, the timidity of their sex, no one can find any objection. When Sallust, in his account of Catiline's conspiracy (*De Catilinae Conjuratione*), evokes the image of lovely Sempronia, full of wit and talents and effrontery, and declares that this young lady had committed more than one ill deed with a manly audacity, this *virilis audacia* is found quite satisfactory by everybody. But Tullia despises her sister because she lacks 'feminine audacity', and most editors assume that the text here is corrupt. An English editor suggests that *audacia* should be corrected to *ignavia*: *muliebris ignavia* would make everything quite all right. 'Tullia despises her sister because her feminine cowardice makes her irresolute.' M. Jean Bayet suggests we should read *muliebriter cessaret audacia*: 'because woman as she was, she lacked courage'. But it is wise to keep to the original manuscript, as Conway and Walters have so rightly done in the Oxford edition, and profit from its lesson. Perhaps Livy did not exactly realize the importance of what he was saying. Perhaps he did not find the sources transmitted to him altogether clear. But we must take the reality as it stands. It is a woman speaking: Tullia is not in revolt against her own sex; she does not disown her sisters; she does not consider herself to be an exceptional being free from all feminine weakness. Only she has particular ideas regarding the feminine temperament which are not incompatible with a sort of specific audacity, energy and ambition, the *audacia muliebris* which animates Etruscan women like Tanaquil and Tullia the Elder in the dynasty of the Tarquins.

ARCHAEOLOGICAL CONFIRMATION

Now that these traditions which Livy echoes should not have been empty fables but should correspond – though imaginary in so far as details of events and persons were concerned – to a state of civilization in which the woman exercised prerogatives which were withdrawn from her later on is something which archaeology confirms in a decisive manner, not only in paintings where we see Etruscan women participating with men in numerous aspects of social life, not only in the epitaphs where the matronymic often is given a prominent place, but in certain evidences, not sufficiently noted before, which are provided by the contents and the disposition of the tombs.

At least some of these among the most ancient and most luxurious, which had revealed to a dazzled nineteenth century the extent of the Etruscan princes' riches, had in fact been constructed for princesses. In the case of the Regolini-Galassi tomb at Caere,[31] which dates from about 650, there is no doubt at all: the *hypogeum* comprised a funerary chamber at the end of a long corridor, in the walls of which two alcoves had been fashioned: in the one on the right, along with arms and a ceremonial chariot there lay, in an urn surmounted by a horse, the ashes of a warrior; in front, in the antechamber, another man was buried surrounded by very rich furnishings, with much silver and bronze plate, part of which flowed over into the left-hand alcove; but in the funerary chamber proper there was stretched, on the ground covered with gold, silver and ivory, alongside her throne, the bejewelled skeleton of a woman: it was above all for her that the tomb had been destined, and quite by chance we even know her name from the inscriptions that were engraved on the silver cups and goblets: she was called *Larthia*.

We cannot help wondering what was the relationship between the three dead people, though we are unable to reach any solid conclusion. In any case it was Larthia who had first right to the tomb. A queen, accompanied or rejoined in death by a prince of her own family inhumed in the antechamber and by a warrior whose cremated remains were placed in the right-hand alcove, Larthia would make a good heroine for a novel. The two different kinds of funerary rites – inhumation and cremation – the different styles of life which the arms of one, the precious objects of the other reveal between a soldier and a courtier would fire the slowest imaginations. Has not a great scholar been tempted to suppose that the warrior was the enemy of the prince inhumed in the antechamber, or else a slave sacrificed to appease his shade? That Larthia herself, the supposed widow of the prince, had been constrained, like Hindu women, to follow her husband beyond the grave? And why not? In a more sober fashion, Luigi Pareti, the most recent exegetist of the Regolini-Galassi tomb, concludes: 'The traces of matriarchy which have been claimed in Etruria have doubtless been exaggerated; nevertheless in the archaic era a princess at Caere had been able to occupy the same state of sovereignty as Roman tradition still accords Tanaquil the wife of Tarquinius the Elder, who is said to have brought about the accession to the throne of Rome first of all of her husband, then of her protégé Servius Tullius.'[32]

But perhaps Larthia was no exception. It so happens that the Bernardini tomb at Praeneste, more or less contemporary with the Regolini-Galassi tomb at Caere, and which has delivered up no less a number of marvels, has just arisen from the anonymity in which it had lain so deeply buried. While cleaning one of the great silver cups from that tomb, there was discovered a *graffito* which reveals a proper name, *Vetusia*.[33] A Latin name, which, by virtue of the phonetic transformation known as rhotacism, is perpetuated after the fourth century under the form Veturia. There were still Vetusii at the consulate in Rome at the beginning of the fifth century. And the Latin style of this name causes no surprise at Praeneste, a Latin city. What we must remember in all this is that the one proprietary name which until now has been discovered in the Bernardini tomb is that of a woman, Vetusia.

Incidentally, the curious will not fail to wonder why, at Caere as at Praeneste, it was only on their silver plate that Larthia and Vetusia had their proof of ownership engraved. The evidence from the Bernardini tomb consists, as yet, of only one piece. But in the Regolini-Galassi tomb the name of Larthia was repeated on five goblets, six cups and a small silver amphora, whereas her companion in the antechamber had his name engraved on none of the silver cups belonging to him and not one of the fibulae, bracelets and pieces of gold leaf which adorned the princess bore the slightest trace of *graffiti*. The period – mid seventh century – is that in which in Greece, Athens, Aegina and Corinth began to mint coins in that metal. Was there a risk of silver acquiring a venal quality in the process of smelting which might attract robbers? Was an Etruscan princess's dowry counted in so many pieces of silver plate? In the present state of our knowledge, we cannot tell.

But we shall notice that, even later, at the end of the sixth and at the beginning of the fifth centuries, at a time when Caere would be at the height of her power, the women among the aristocracy had still not given up, if not their pretensions to royalty, at least their rights to luxury articles of plate. This has been revealed by the study, among others, of a tomb in the necropolis of the Banditaccia explored at the beginning of this century by Raniero Mengarelli; this tomb is called the Tomb of the Grecian Vases.[34] We shall have to return to this tomb when we discuss the Etruscan house, faithfully reflected in funerary architecture; this tomb which, in its plan and decoration, testifies to the already classical taste of those for whom it had been constructed, though they surmounted it by a vast tumulus which covered the three neighbouring tombs of their ancestors. Some one hundred and fifty Attic vases with black or red figures of a severe style and of an often signal quality which accumulated there during two or three generations prove the enthusiasm with which, from 550 onwards, when the Tarquins reigned in Rome, a great family at Caere collected ceramic products and in general the most refined objects of Hellenic civilization.

THE CULTURE OF ETRUSCAN WOMEN

Among the materials in the Tomb of the Grecian Vases there are three pieces signed by the potter Nicosthenes – two amphorae with black figures and one *pyxis* with red figures. Now the two amphorae which represent different subjects, one a procession of animals, the other dances of Silenoi and Bacchantes, but which have, as if deliberately, the same height exactly – 31 centimetres – both carry, engraved on the base, the name of their owner, and this name is *mi culnaial*: 'I belong to Culni'. And this *Culni* was a woman. Besides this, *Culni* saw fit to inscribe her name on two decanter vases of the type known as *olpè*; these, too, have black figures and can be dated, as can the amphorae of Nicosthenes, round about 530. Other *graffiti* were looked for but only one more was found in the whole collection, on the base of a third *olpè*, and this *graffito* reads *mi atiial*: 'I belong to Ati'. So two women, *Culni* and *Ati*, lend the tomb a little of the personality associated with living people. But they do it, and especially *Culni*, in a singularly expressive way. *Culni* loved Attic vases; she preferred signed examples; she had a fondness for the graceful curve of Nicosthenes' amphorae. One amphora by Nicosthenes is all very well; but two, each measuring thirty-one centimetres, suggests some aesthetic purpose. These twin amphorae were destined to echo one another, placed on either side of some doorway. *Culni* had a feeling for symmetry which accords well with the architectural features of the tomb where she was interred. Etruscan women of the second half of the sixth century, while their husbands, strangely absent, scoured the high seas, fought at Aleria and lapidated Phocean prisoners, seem to have played an active part in the progressive hellenization of their country.

Naturally there exist proprietary marks which bear the names of men, though these are very rare in Caere. On the other hand, in Greece we do not find, as far as we can infer from the ceramic inscriptions of the *agora* of Athens or that of Olbia, similar marks emanating from a woman. In Xenophon's *Oeconomicus* no doubt Ischomachus entrusts his wife with the task of looking after their domestic goods. 'What a fine sight it is, to see shoes of all kinds neatly aligned; how beautiful are bronze vases, table ware, even the cooking pots, all nicely arranged! All these kinds of things form a chorus, and the space all round them is so lovely to see when it is cleared in this way!'[35] There would have been a row, all the same, if that perfectly-organized housewife, whose name moreover Xenophon neglects to give, had put her mark on the household crockery. Without wanting to draw too ambitious conclusions from this, let us remember that Etruscan women in the golden era had the right to possess their own amphorae made by Nicosthenes, and that they were sometimes highly cultivated. Did the same thing not occur at other periods? For example, at the end of the Empire, was it not the great ladies of the Roman aristocracy, whose semi-barbarian husbands were occupied on the frontiers, who were the most brilliant recruits to Christianity, and whom Saint Jerome found his most sensitive audience?

But there is even more to be deduced from our observations of the cemeteries of Caere. At some date a little posterior to the days of *Culni* and *Ati*, we found set up everywhere at the entrance to tombs innumerable little columns fitted into the flagstones next to little stone coffers in the form of sarcophagi or houses with a double slope to the roof. Provided with a painted or engraved inscription, first in Etruscan, then in Latin, these *cippi* inform the passer-by of the presence of a nearby tomb, and of the identity of the dead person. Now these columns, whose phallic significance is unquestionable, were put up for men, while the houses were for the women, perhaps because it was in the house that their activity was felt and because they spent the greater part of their lives there.[36] 'In Rome,' one historian remarks, 'it was the *pater familias* who was the centre of the home; in Etruria, it was the wife.'[37]

In Caere the distinction was clear; all the columnar *cippi* are marked with men's names: *A(vles) Campanes L(arthal) clan* or *L(ucius) Magilius L(ucii) l(ibertus) Pilemo* (Philemon). All the house-shaped *cippi* bear the names of women: *Thanchvil Pustinia L(arthal) s(ec)* or *Magilia L(ucii) l(iberta) Celido* (Chelido, a swallow). Nevertheless the rule does not seem to have been rigorously applied outside Caere, for at Tarquinii, where in any case the use of funerary *cippi* is much more limited, M. Pallottino has taken a mischievous delight in discovering one in the form of a house, dedicated to a man.[38] This was because in their funerary rites as in everything else, each Etruscan town had its own particular habits.

In Caere itself, the use of the *cippus* is not known until the beginning of the fourth century, when the development of funerary epigraphy lends them a very definite significance. But the tradition they seem to refer to had certainly more ancient origins, as is proved by another fact, less commented on, more mysterious, more important also, which one can notice in those tombs built from the end of the seventh century to the middle of the fifth century.

THEIR PRIVILEGES BEYOND THE GRAVE

Mengarelli, in 1927,[39] had distinguished in these tombs two sorts of funerary couches hewn from the rock and on which the dead were laid. Some of them reproduced faithfully the image of an Etruscan bed, or a Greek one (*klinè*), with its four round feet freely sculpted: where the head came, a semi-circular hollow was made to contain the pillow. The others, wider and longer, had the appearance of big sarcophagi of the Greek type, without a lid but with a triangular fronton at each extremity; inside, the semi-circular mark for the pillow can often be seen.

Let us consider the plan of a fine tomb from the second half of the sixth century, the tomb of the Capitals.[40] The anterior chambers contained only seats for the servants. In the central hall, eight *klinai* were aligned along the walls. But in the three chambers which open out from the back wall, and which, corresponding to the main rooms of the house, sheltered the remains of its masters, we find, each time, a bed on the left and a sarcophagus on the right. It becomes clear that we are here in the presence of conjugal tombs, those of the *pater familias* and of the *mater familias* in the centre, those of their children and step-children here and there; and we see that just as a *cippus* in the form of a house indicated a female sepulchre, so in these funerary chambers the sarcophagus was also destined for the mother of the family. Mengarelli thus was led to formulate a new law: in Etruscan tombs the body of the man, on the left, was disposed on a *klinè*, that of the woman, always on the right, in a sarcophagus.

And naturally, as always happens when a rule is formulated in an absolute way, objections came to light, and there were large numbers of exceptions. For example, there are funerary chambers in which we find side by side two beds with carved feet. Were these the last resting-places of two brothers united in death?

One tomb, called the Tomb of the Tablinum, contains two beds and eight sarcophagi, which would seem to indicate a family in which the girls predominated in an abnormal fashion over the boys.[41] But all things considered, we would consider that Mengarelli was right and so do the majority of etruscologists. His observation is too often borne out, even as late as 1951 during diggings carried out at Caere by the University of Rome,[42] for it to be called a coincidence or for us to interpret otherwise the disposition which he had the distinction of noticing first. There are even touching cases where the sarcophagus on the right carries a semi-circular design to fit two pillows instead of one, and one pillow is smaller than the other: a dead child had been entombed with his mother. Sometimes again a smaller *klinè*, for a little boy, was placed in the chamber, on the right, just beside the maternal sarcophagus.[43]

The exceptions to the rule can easily be explained if we consider that the distinction it enunciates is an historical fact that had its beginning, its apogee and its decline. Its beginning? It has been observed, for example, that in the very ancient Tomb of the Painted Lions, from about 650, right in the orientalizing period, a funeral bed had been transformed into a sarcophagus by the clumsy insertion of two small triangular frontons.[44] Its decline? About 450 – which is about the date of the Tablinum tomb – the specific significance of beds and sarcophagi seems to have lost its primal clarity. Between these two dates, the custom was observed in the majority of tombs though in the case of female inhumations the bed was not everywhere replaced by the sarcophagus. Some obscure purpose nevertheless is borne out in this persistent tendency.

We may perhaps see more clearly the profound significance of it if we turn our attention to a detail which escaped Mengarelli.[45] It is not quite exact to say that there are two sorts of funeral couches: a bed with carved feet and a sarcophagus. The sarcophagi, we have noted, were wider and had deeper sides. It is to be observed that masculine beds were generally eighty centimetres and the sarcophagi one metre ten centimetres wide: the difference in width corresponds to the thickness of the walls of the sarcophagus. Inside this, there was, in fact, for the woman also, a *klinè*, of which one may see the rounded extremity and whose carved feet were covered. In other words, the alternative is not one bed or one sarcophagus, but one funeral couch or bed, alone and unadorned, or one bed *inside* a sarcophagus, a bed covered by a sarcophagus. It does seem that the purpose of such additions and transformations was to make sure that a certain category of the dead, particularly women, would have a more sacred character; to preserve the remains better and to increase the inviolability of the funeral couch. The sarcophagus, if we may use here an anachronistic expression, functioned as a kind of reliquary, protecting particularly precious remains. It is as if, between 650 and 450, the Etruscans, or at least those of Caere, had considered women to be of a superior essence and more susceptible of divinization than men.

Here we are touching very superficially on impenetrable problems, whose solution, if we could reach it in the present state of our knowledge, would require a long examination. Let us simply indicate here that there was a special use of sarcophagi and funerary *cippi* in the form of houses in a certain Etruscan funerary ritual which is connected with a complex web of traditions stretching over all the ancient world from Asia Minor to occidental Europe and which could only be studied in relation to the use of hut-urns in the pre-Etruscan necropolises of Etruria and Latium and to those of the region of the Elbe as well as to the house-shaped steles in the Celtic cemeteries of Roman Gaul. The Etruscans seem to have taken over a widely diffused practice in order to load it with a significance which apparently was close to their hearts. Let us also note that scholars still cannot decide whether these sarcophagi represent houses or temples, for the temple, like the tomb, is conceived after the image of a human dwelling; and perhaps there is no way of making a definite distinction between what belongs to the domain of complaisant imprecision and deliberate ambiguity. Finally, in the universe of Etruscan religion, dominated by the all-powerful female divinity, the Earth Mother whom Veii and Caere worshipped under the name of Hera or Juno, Mater Matuta or Leucothea, it is possible that a dead woman the more readily inspired a religious cult in survivors if she appeared to merge, beyond the grave, with the great goddess; and that woman in general was considered by her very nature as participating in that of the divinity who reigned in the temples and necropolises.

The latter, in any case, furnish us with fresh reasons for attributing to the Etruscan woman, in a society where we see her mingling with such brilliance in the business and the pleasures of men, her character torn to pieces by envious outsiders but invested in her country with an authority that was almost sovereign; artistic, cultivated, interested in hellenic refinements and the bringer of civilization to her home; finally venerated in the tomb as an emanation of divine power, a privileged position which perhaps recalled that of Phaedra or Ariadne in Minoan Crete, and which Cornelia, mother of the Gracchi, would never have dared aspire to in Rome.

CHAPTER FIVE

THE ETRUSCAN COUNTRYSIDE AND PATTERNS OF RURAL LIFE

Fertility of the land – The problem of malaria – The successes of Etruscan hydraulics – The right of property – The cereals – Vines and trees – Agricultural implements – Etruscan agronomists – The raising of stock – Hunting – Fishing – The timber industry – The mines – The roads – The vehicles

FERTILITY OF THE LAND

It has been remarked above with what lyrical enthusiasm the ancients celebrated the fecundity of Etruscan soil. If we believe what they write, all Nature's gifts were assembled there, all the fruits of the earth there responded perfectly to the cultivators' care, and it was finally the very abundance of harvests of corn and wine that had sapped the energies of the race and contributed to its decadence. But if we take literally this evocation of an *Etruria Felix*, that is, fertile, in the sense in which one talked of the *Campania Felix* and *Arabia Felix*, and imagine a sort of idyllic landscape of vineyards and elm-groves and murmuring waters, we cannot help thinking that things have changed there considerably during the last two and a half thousand years.

Tourists who have followed the via Aurelia from Pisa to Rome hardly recognize 'these plains covered with cornfields that are separated by hills with cultivated slopes'[1] in the low, stony, marshy lands of an unhealthy Maremma whose centuries-old desolation has in recent years only partially been changed by the agrarian developments in the region. Nor do those idyllic descriptions correspond to what veterans of the Italian Campaign of June 1944 remember as they trudged along the via Clodia – a meridional Etruria of arid steppes and thorny thickets, of escarpments eroded into labyrinthine canyons in the middle of which rose the remains of ramparts, or carved by the sandy watercourses of the Fiora, the Orcia, the Ombrone. Today at any rate the classical descriptions are true only – and then they are marvellously exact – of the Etrurian interior, beyond the lake of Bolsena and the slopes of the Amiata, where one enters, in the shade of chestnut-trees, a new world where firmer horizons, rolling hills and deep-running waterways herald the real Tuscany. One receives then as one enters the valleys of the Paglia, the Chiana and the upper Tiber, towards Chiusi, Cortona and Perugia, the same impression that the Romans must have received about the end of the fourth century when, leaving behind the Ciminian forest they discovered, displayed before them, 'the opulent fields of Etruria', *opulenta arva Etruriae*.[2]

It was indeed of Tuscany, in the modern sense of the name, that our authors were thinking when they lauded the fertility of Etruria; and especially of a country known under the name of *Etrusci campi*, 'the Etruscan plains',[3] which extended from Fiesole to Arezzo, 'rich in corn, in cattle and everything'.

Would you care for a fine word-picture of it? We are indebted to Pliny the Younger for one: he had had built for himself, in the vicinity of Tifernum Tiberinum (Città di Castello), one of his country villas:[4]

'The aspect of the country is the most beautiful possible; picture to yourself an immense amphitheatre, such as the hand of nature alone could form. Before you lies a vast extended plain bounded by a range of mountains, whose summits are crowned with lofty and venerable woods, which supply abundance and variety of game; from thence as the mountains decline, they are adorned with underwoods. Intermixed with these are little hills of so loamy and fat a soil, that it would be difficult to find a single stone upon them; their fertility is nothing inferior to the lowest grounds; and though their harvest indeed is something later, their heavy crops are as well matured. At the foot of these hills the eye is presented, wherever it turns, with one unbroken view of numberless vineyards, which are terminated below by a border, as it were, of shrubs. From thence extend meadows and fields. The soil of the latter is so extremely stiff, upon the first ploughing it rises in such vast clods, that it is necessary to go over it nine times with the largest oxen and the strongest ploughs, before they can be thoroughly broken.

The flower-enamelled meadows produce trefoil and other kinds of herbage as fine and tender as if it were but just sprung up, being everywhere refreshed by never-failing rills. But though the country abounds with great plenty of water, there are no marshes; for as the ground is sloping, whatever water it receives without absorbing, runs off into the Tiber. This river, which winds through the middle of the meadows, is navigable only in the winter and spring, when it transports the produce of the lands to Rome; but its contracted channel is so extremely low in summer, that it resigns the name of a *great river* which, however, it resumes in autumn.

You would be most agreeably entertained by taking a view of the face of this country from the mountains: you would imagine that not a real, but some painted landscape lay before you, drawn with the most exquisite beauty and exactness; such a harmonious and regular variety charms the eye whichsoever way it throws itself.'

Very different, at all times, must have been maritime Etruria. Since the Roman era, it seems to have presented the aspect of a wild and pestilential scrubland infested with savage boars and serpents, which Dante paints in his *Inferno*,[5] and whose picturesque romanticism was sung by so many nineteenth-century travellers. Thus it had appeared, as we have said, to Tiberius Gracchus when he noted 'the desolation of the country, where there lived, in the fields and pastures, only foreign and barbarian slaves'.[6] At the beginning of the Empire, Veii was a site abandoned to a luxuriant vegetation amid cascades, and on what had once been its forum the shepherds pastured their flocks.[7] Caere was only the shadow of her former self, and Strabo assures us that a little nearby watering-place, the Aquae Caeretanae, was much more populous because of the crowds of people coming to take the baths.[8] There was no mention of Vulci, Vetulonia or Rusellae. At the beginning of the fifth century, the Gaulish poet Rutilius Namatianus, returning to his province by sea, described the Etruscan coast he was sailing along; everywhere the towns and villages of yore had given way to large farms; at Cosa, near Orbetello, he could make out 'ancient ruins and horrid walls that no one guarded'.[9]

THE PROBLEM OF MALARIA

Several causes could be attributed to the devastation and depopulation of this coast where the Tyrrhenians had once perhaps disembarked, and where their principal metropoles had been built: the silting-up, for example, of a port like Vetulonia, in ruins since the end of the sixth century; war, which had utterly destroyed Veii and Volsinii; the political régime, as Tiberius Gracchus referred to the extension of the *latifundia*: but also the ravages of malaria, a problem we must briefly discuss.

The impaludism which raged in the Maremma and sometimes in certain inland valleys brought upon the whole of Etruria, by unjust generalization, a disagreeable reputation for insalubrity. From his native Auvergne, Sidonius Apollinaris was to condemn it utterly in this respect: *pestilens regio Tuscorum*.[10] But one is astonished to see a cultured Roman of the end of the first century AD, Domitius Apollinaris, an admirer of Martial and a correspondent of Pliny the Younger,[11] expressing disquiet on learning that the latter is going, in summer, to his villa in Tuscany. And Pliny was to reassure him by pointing out that it is far from the sea, 'and at the foot of the Apennine range, so much esteemed for salubrity'. But he recognized that 'the air of that part of Tuscany, which lies towards the sea coast, is thick and unwholesome': *Est sane gravis et pestilens ora Tuscorum, quae per litus extenditur*.[12]

The most ancient testimony we have on this subject is from Cato, and, in its laconicism, this fragment summarizes an important historical event. In 181, Rome had founded, at the foot of the plateau on which Tarquinii was built, right at the edge of the sea, at the place called formerly *Graviscae* and now Porto Clementino, a colony destined probably to intimidate that proud city, which remained obstinately faithful to its traditions. But the enterprise was disastrous: the site proved unsuitable to the prosperity of a great urban centre, and the fevers which decimated the new colonists left the Romans with the bitterest memories.[13] Virgil and Rutilius Namatianus recalled this.[14] But Cato, who had lived through this disappointment, had already declared that

Graviscae drew its name from *gravis*, 'heavy', 'unwholesome', because the ground exhaled *gravem aerem*, 'an unwholesome air' – malaria.[15]

Let us try to go back a little further in time. A celebrated document, to which we shall have to return, places us in 205, towards the end of the Second Punic War.[16] That year, Scipio, who was preparing for his landing in Africa, called on the allies to arm a fleet for whose outfitting the State had refused to pay. Etruria, Livy tells us, distinguished herself by the speed with which she replied to the appeal, and the detailed enumeration of goods promised by each people tells us much about the special cultures and industries to which each was devoted. Caere was to deliver wheat and supplies of all kinds, Populonia iron, Tarquinii linen-cloth for the sails, Volterra timber for the keel and framework of the ships, as well as wheat, Arezzo three thousand bucklers, as many helmets, and javelins, *gaesa*, long lances (a total of fifty thousand items of each article); axes, spades, scythes, earth baskets and millstones to equip forty warships, and part of the provisions for the voyage to be used by the rowers and their officers, without counting one hundred and twenty thousand bushels of wheat; Perugia, Chiusi, Rusellae gave pine trees for the construction of the ships, and a great quantity of corn.

What strikes us at once in this list is that the centres of Etruscan prosperity had moved inland, and that to judge by the importance of both its metallurgical and agricultural contributions Arezzo really appears to have become the economic capital of Etruria. But if one considers the contribution from the towns in the coastal area, we notice, chiefly in between Tarquinii and Rusellae, which, upstream from modern Grosseto, had formerly taken the place of Vetulonia, a wide gap of about a hundred kilometres. In this cradle of Etruscan grandeur, where so many sites had brought themselves honour by signal gifts to civilization, Telamon, Ansedonia-Cosa, Sovana, Saturnia, Vulci, not one quintal of wheat could be collected. Vulci particularly, Vulci on the Fiora, is conspicuous here by its absence, not that life had altogether left it: it still had, at that period, its *zilath* who were preceded by lictors in solemn processions. Later, it would recapture its old enchantment in the glorious memory of Aulus and Caelius Vibennae in the François tomb. But the fact that it could not be taxed proved that it was ruined. And even Tarquinii, that boasted having seen the divine dwarf Tages[17] spring out of one of its field-furrows, had been able to produce only a bundle of cloth from its depleted stores. It is clear that some sort of calamity had overtaken all the region, and how could it be anything else but malaria?

Yet it is an obscure point, and it has caused much ink to flow. Scholars have wondered, and wonder still, exactly when maritime Etruria became insalubrious. No one denies that it had always been bordered by lagoons. But not all lagoons are malarial: Ravenna, though built entirely on piles in the middle of marshes, enjoyed such a tonic climate that a school for gladiators had been set up there.[18] The anopheles are dangerous only when they transmit a virus which they do not secrete themselves. If they propagate impaludism by stinging healthy men, they must first have stung infected men. So there must have been a moment when the malaria microbe was introduced – as it had been already in the plain of Sybaris in Magna Graecia – into Etruria. And as impaludism has its best breeding-places in tropical or sub-tropical regions, the foreigners who imported it are looked for in Africa or Asia. Nello Toscanelli gave those partisans of Herodotus' theory of the oriental origin of the Etruscans a nasty knock by telling us that it was the companions of Tyrrhenus who, after landing at Vetulonia, had contaminated the anopheles of Lake Prilius (Lago di Castiglione), and, as the sickness spread, had finally caused the loss of a people who until then had led wholesome and innocent lives.[19] Rejecting these audacious views, we tend today to believe that the scourge did not break out till fairly late, and those who believe that colonization had come from Asia point out that if the Maremma had already been in the grip of fever when the immigrants landed there, they would soon have left those inhospitable shores; or, if they had persisted in remaining, they would never have succeeded in creating the powerful civilization which flourished there for several centuries.[20]

It seems to us that this underestimates the resources of human energy, and the Etruscans were by no means lacking in it. We see today in Tuscany itself that there are means of purifying a malarial zone; there, after a long struggle, the improvement of the land and agrarian reform have eliminated the last tracts of marshland. The French are perhaps better informed on the history of the great Algerian plain known as the Mitidja, which, despite its natural fertility, indolence and the insecurity brought about by Turkish domination had turned into 'an immense sewer', and which, reclaimed after a hundred and thirty years of labour from fever-breeding swamps, now displays, as far as the eye can see, all round Boufarik, its fields, its vineyards, its splendid orchards.[21] And yet, at first, the ravages of malaria, in the army and among the colonists, had been terrible. We can translate into Etruscan terms what Toussenel, civil commissioner at Boufarik, wrote:

'In 1842, Boufarik was the most deadly place in Algeria. The faces of those rare inhabitants who had escaped from the pernicious fever were green and puffy. Although the parish had changed priests three times in one year, the church was closed; the justice of the peace had died; the entire civilian administrative and military personnel had had to be renewed, and the district officer, the one man left alive, had been invested with all kinds of functions through the decease or sickness of all other office-holders.'

Certainly the Etruscans did not know about quinine. They had had no Laveran to discover the microbe of impaludism for them. But it is not impossible that they may have put into practice the essential principles of anti-anophelean action which is aimed at depriving the larvae of the stagnant waters where they breed: this can be done by so shaping the ground that water cannot stand still, and draining away water when it gets bogged down – in other words, the warping and drainage of the marches.

It was no small surprise to us to discover in that fine work by Drs Edmond and Etienne Sergent, *Story of an Algerian Marsh*, from which we have borrowed the citations above, that there exists among the manuscripts of Leonardo da Vinci, preserved at the Institut de France, a note accompanied by a drawing, which shows 'how one should conduct, with running waters, the soil of mountains into marshy valleys, and make them fertile, and purify the surrounding air'.[22]

The learned doctors conclude: 'The practice of warping land was born in Tuscany, the native country of Leonardo da Vinci.'

Was born there? Possibly. Unless it is a question of a skill surviving and being transmitted across the ages to the unexpected heir of the Etruscan engineers.

THE SUCCESSES OF ETRUSCAN HYDRAULICS

It is a fact that, very early in its history, this people showed an exceptional talent for solving problems in hydraulics, and displayed a relentless determination to harness the waters of the earth. The recent re-emergence of Spina and Adria, of which we shall speak further on, has made intelligible the testimony of Pliny the Elder, who, describing the mouth of the Po and the great works that had made its course more regular, declares: 'All these diversions and canals, from Sagis (Porto di Magnavacca) onwards, had as their first authors the Etruscans: with the help of trenches they conducted the greater part of the river into the marshes of Adria.'[23] But without going so far, we recall that it was to the Tarquins that the annalists attributed, as one of the greatest services they had performed for Rome, the construction of draining-trenches and sewers that had purified a forum until then covered with stagnant waters.

Of Tarquinius the Elder (616–579) Livy writes: 'There were low quarters round the forum and in the valleys between the hills in which the lack of slope made it difficult for waters to run away; he drained them by using a system of draining-trenches running from high places down into the Tiber.'[24] Of Tarquinius Superbus (534–510) he writes: 'He caused to be constructed, despite the protestations of the people who found this labour very trying, a great subterranean sewer intended to receive all the filth of the city, a work which our modern magnificence found hard to equal.'[25] One can still see today, where it enters the Tiber, the arches of that famous *Cloaca Maxima*, since restored several times. Under the forum have been discovered several other subterranean galleries which were used as sewers, or aqueducts, or main-sewers collecting the waters under the Capitol; and all recent diggings confirm the capital rôle the Etruscans played in making Rome the city *in regione pestilenti salubrem*, 'salubrious in the midst of a pestilential region', which Romulus founded,[26] and in allowing the forum, once drained, to assume its historic rôle as the political centre of the city.

Yet there were still – when the Etruscans had left – frequent *pestilentiae* or outbreaks of malaria which made the region round the Tiber a dangerous place: many sanctuaries were consecrated to the goddess Fever, and Apollo, whose temple rose in the Campus Martius about the middle of the fifth century, was first of all invoked as a healing god, *Medicus*.[27]

How could this zeal fail to improve the sanitary conditions of their colonies by draining away stagnant or polluted waters – which recalls one of the most constant preoccupations of nine-teenth-century Europeans in their Asian or African possessions – how could it fail to inspire the Etruscans to do the same for their own territory? Even today one can still admire traces of their work. Though at Cosa the *Tagliata* which they were thought to have excavated in the rock to serve as an outlet to the Burano lagoon has been shown to be a canal from the Roman port whose silting-up it helped to prevent,[28] no one denies that they con-structed, near Veii, the tremendous covered trench, eighty metres long, four metres wide and ten metres deep, which they had laid out at the Ponte Sodo for the passage of the Cremera.[29] It has long been known that the soil of meridional Etruria, notably in the *ager Tarquiniensis* at Bieda, was mined with an internal network of *cuniculi* whose purpose was to 'withdraw the water underneath the absorbent layer of earth and make it run underground', thus 'removing the humidity without eroding the surface of the soil'.[30] Although one is probably wrong in attribut-ing all the merit for this vast system of cunicular drainage to the Etruscans – (it continues into Latium, and it is obvious that Rome did not entirely abandon it) – it is certain that they started it. Moreover, the science of the *haruspices*, indirectly reflecting the technical problems that the engineers had to solve, prescribed special rites for making water flow. When, at the time of the siege of Veii, it was reported to Camillus that the Alban Lake, by some unprecedented miracle, had overflowed, an Etruscan diviner was not caught napping and fluently described *quae sollemnis derivatio esset* or 'the ritual method of draining it'.[31] Etruscan hydraulics had a place in the most ancient foundations of religion.

Another small incident confirms their competence in this domain. Having carried out a study in depth of everything concerning the drainage of water, they were no less skilful in discovering and harnessing waters to irrigate arid terrain. Not for nothing did Varro call the *aquilex, Tuscus*:[32] Etruria was where the best water-diviners were found, and these were not common water-diviners; they knew for example how to find lakes of sub-terranean water by examining peculiarities of vegetation, and how to bore what are known today as artesian wells.[33]

So we are entitled to believe that impaludism, far from having made a late appearance among the Etruscans, then bringing about their downfall existed always in an endemic state on certain parts of the coast. A vigilant policy of action against the unhealthy conditions of the marshes, practised in their provinces when they were at the peak of their power, and whose prescriptions were registered in deep-rooted religious traditions shows them from the first conscious of a menace which they were very soon able to circumscribe and keep in check and which perhaps was partly responsible for making them what they were. But a drainage canal, if it is not looked after, becomes just as dangerous a place as a marsh.[34] From the third century at least, political and economic circumstances, the insecurity of wars and the destruction of certain cities, the shrinking of arable land and the encroachment of useless pasture resulted in a return and a spread of the evil; and, undermining Etruscan vitality, precipitated the decadence which had allowed the evil to declare itself. All the same, it was not a total and definitive decline. If the malaria at Graviscae decimated the first Roman colonists, Lake Prilius on the verge of the Maremma of Grosseto was not, at the end of the Republic, so insalubrious that it did not stimulate the greed of the tribune Clodius:[35] according to Cicero, he wanted to build himself a villa there on ground stolen from a local land-owner. Even at the worst times, the fever did not spread its virulence everywhere. Even around Graviscae, 'the verdure of dense forests'[36] and 'the shade of pine-groves undulating along the edge of the sea' were mentioned by Rutilius Namatianus.

THE RIGHT OF PROPERTY

Those naturally fertile plains, those low lands reclaimed from the sea, those methodically irrigated steppes were – and this is a second trait that ought to be noted in our description of the

Etruscan countryside – composed of measured and marked-off fields. The Etruscans never seem to have indulged in nostalgia for an age of gold in which the fruits of the earth flourished spontaneously in an undivided earth, in which Saturn governed peace-loving men who knew nothing of the desire to possess things: *amor habendi*.[37] Their earliest memories were of the coming of Jupiter, the law of work, the reign of property. Theirs was the hard and active world which Virgil, though he softens it with a note of universal tenderness, sings in the *Georgics*: 'Before Jove's day no tillers subdued the land. Even to mark the field or divide it with bounds was unlawful. Men made gain for the common store.'[38] This is what had also been proclaimed by an Etruscan prophetess, the nymph Vegoia, in a prophecy that has been preserved, in Latin, in a collection of texts about land-measuring, the *Corpus* of the *Agrimensores*. After an abbreviated fragment of cosmogony, in which she evokes the separation of sea and sky, she introduced all at once, as if Etruria had never existed before his advent, Jupiter, creator of property and protector of its laws:[39]

'Know that the sea was separated from the sky. Now, when Jupiter had claimed back his rights over the land of Etruria, he established and ordained that the plains should be measured and the fields marked. Knowing human greed and the desire to possess lands, he wished that everything should be marked by boundaries.' *Scias mare ex aethera remotum. Cum autem Juppiter terram Aetruriae sibi vindicavit, constituit iussitque metiri campos signarique agros. Sciens hominum avaritiam vel terrenum cupidinem, terminis omnia scita esse voluit.*

The Etruscan Jupiter, Tinia, is especially a Jupiter Terminus, to whom boundaries were consecrated – in Latin *termini* and in Etruscan *tular*. *Tular*, 'limits', 'confines', is in fact one of those words (the inflexion indicates a plural) the interpretation of which, definitely established in the course of recent years, has given us the best insights into the sociology of the Etruscan world.[40]

The nine inscriptions in which it figures, generally on stone cippi, have been cleverly replaced where they were found, and it has been demonstrated that they were meant to demarcate either the *pomerium**** of a town like Perugia,[41] or the territorial confines of a city like Fiesole,[42] with the name of the magistrates who had mapped them; they could also be either the bounds of a private property,[43] or those of a concession in a cemetery,[44] or finally the frontiers of the Etruscan league at Cortona.[45]

But this desire of the Etruscans to indicate clearly with incontestable marks that certain places belonged to the State, to a commune or to a private person was felt in their provinces and even among neighbouring peoples before it was taken up by Rome and conquered the world. Thus the place called *Tullare*, today Tollara, in the toponymy of the Apennine near Placentia as it is revealed to us in the Alimentary Tale of Veleia, tells us that even under Trajan there were still traces of an ancient Etruscan *limitatio*. And the Umbrians adopted the idea and the vocable, from which is derived their *tuder*, attested in the Tables of Gubbio, and better still in the name of the frontier town between Umbria and Etruria, *Tuder*, modern Todi.[46]

We should like very much to understand thoroughly these epigraphic documents about boundaries which encourage us to think of Etruria as a land governed by a rudimentary form of cadastral survey. Our knowledge of Etruscan law and of the laws of the ancients in general will be greatly enriched when the inscription on the *cippus* from Perugia[47] is elucidated; this sets out, on two sides, in some forty-six lines, the contract entered into by the *Velthina* and the *Afula* in settlement of a joint-property case which had brought them into opposition.

Another term, on a sepuchral boundary-stone from Montepulciano, excites our impatience: it is *claruchies*, which could only be the genitive of an adjective formed on the Greek *klèrouchos* and which the Etruscan tongue seems to have borrowed very late from the vocabulary of Ptolemaic Egypt, applying it to those colonists who were beneficiaries in the apportionment of lands.[48] This one, called curiously enough *Au. Latini*, that is, Aulus Latinius, was he not one of the followers of Sylla whom the dictator set up on the territory of Chiusi?

The great movement of colonization which the Gracchi had started in 133 BC and which was aimed at distributing lands

---

*The *pomerium* was a consecrated space outside the town, where it was not permissible to build or plough. (Cf. Chapter VI, i.)

among the poor citizens of Rome caused the most violent storms in the Etruscan world and even provoked in 91 a march on Rome. This wave of colonization struck both at the interests of landed proprietors and at the age-old feeling the Etruscans had for the inviolability of boundaries. The same maledictions fell upon law-breakers who shifted them clandestinely and upon the promoters of agrarian reforms. It was Jupiter who had planted the boundary marks and who gave them their sacred character. At Chiusi people claimed that Jupiter, assisted by the goddess Justitia, had revealed to the *lucumo Arruns*, using the nymph Vegoia as interpreter, the principles of Property.[49] At Tarquinii this revelation was attributed to Tages who, rising from the soil to the great surprise of the ploughmen, had made known to Tarchon the precepts of *limitatio*:[50] he was credited with a book whose title, in Latin, sounds strangely: *liber qui inscribitur terrae iuris Etruriae* – on 'the law relating to the land of Etruria', or 'the law of Etruria relating to the land'.[51] *Terrae ius Etruriae* was the literal translation (hence the gaucherie) of an expression which S. Mazzarino succeeded in deciphering in the inscription on the cippus at Perugia:[52] an agreement had finally been reached between the parties *helu tesne rasne* (in which *hil-helu* signifies 'land', *tesan-tesne* 'law' and *rasna-rasne* 'Etruscan'), consequently *e terrae iure Etruriae*, 'according to the law of Etruscan land'.

Such was the law that Jupiter had imposed upon Etruria when he took over its government: he made of it the ideal country for private property – large-scale property and also farms of small and moderate importance. This is what has notably emerged from researches undertaken in meridional Etruria during the last years by J. B. Ward Perkins and the British School at Rome:[53] before the bulldozers took over in an improvement plan and completely wiped out all vestiges of the past, it became urgent, and proved very instructive, to attempt to retrace, step by step, the ancient road-network: it was noticed that the whole of the Veii region and the western part of the *ager Faliscus* had, in the second and first centuries BC, been the scenes of intense repopulation which can still be seen in the density of the ruins of rural undertakings which denote a certain ease of life. As we go further back into the past we are reduced to conjecture. But the numerous indications offered by local epigraphy lead us to believe that if the territory of independent Etruria was generally in the hands of an aristocracy of landlords exploiting extensive domains, there also existed, or had been created, round the fertile valleys of the Paglia and the Chiana, from Chiusi to Arezzo and Cortona, small properties cultivated directly by peasant families. In this respect history has still not been able to modify radically the appearance of the Etruscan countryside.

THE CEREALS

A fertile country, well cultivated, abundant in resources and products of all kinds . . . Livy, discussing the contributions made by the various Etruscan peoples to Scipio's expedition, has given us, as we saw above, the elements of a regional economy already marked by signs of decadence. At the time of former prosperity we can imagine that all round the towns there was a chequerboard of fields and orchards in which a polyculture was practised that met all local needs. 'In a fat soil, as in Etruria,' writes Varro, who points out the difference between these and certain poor lands in the region of Tusculum and Tivoli, 'one sees fertile fields that are never fallow, fine straight trees and no moss anywhere.'[54]

Etruria grew sufficient cereals to be able on occasion to export them to her neighbours. In the fifth century, during periods of famine, Rome several times had recourse to stocks available in the granaries of maritime Etruria and Tiberine Etruria,[55] and texts bring before our mind's eye great convoys descending the river.[56] The 205 list also mentions supplies of wheat from Caere, Rusellae, Volterra and especially from Chiusi, Perugia and Arezzo. And in the classical period it was again in the interior, at Chiusi and Arezzo, that Etruria's richest granaries were situated. People praised to the skies the miraculous harvests of these *Tusci campi*, giving fifteen bags for one;[57] they praised the weight of Chiusi spelt (*far Clusinum*) that reached twenty-six pounds to the bushel,[58] and the whiteness of its flour (*candoris nitidi*[59]) with which Ovid was to advise his readers to powder their cheeks,[60] but which meanwhile was used by the common people to make that mash (*Clusinae pultes*[61]) which long constituted the basis of Etruscan and Italian food. But Clusium and Arezzo were also famous for their wheat, a fine variety known as *siligo*, which was used in confectionery.[62] This first-class wheat also made Pisa's reputation;[63] this city was no less famous for what we could call its *pasta*,[64] which was made with a sort of semolina (*alica*), mixed with honeyed wine. As for Cisalpine Gaul, it was particularly suited to the cultivation of millet.[65]

VINES AND TREES

We are also very well informed under the chapter on wines. Since the days of Alexander, the wines of Etruria had been known in Greece,[66] and Dionysius of Halicarnassus recommends them along with Falernian and the wines of the Colli Romani.[67] The Spaniard Martial acknowledges that they equal those of Tarragona.[68] Other writers state that the best wine was that of Luni on the borders of Liguria.[69] The wines of Graviscae, despite the malaria exhaled by the surrounding marshes, and those of Statonia on the slopes of the upper Fiora produced excellent vintages.[70] But the territory round Veii only produced (alas for the stomachs of Horace, Persius Flaccus and Martial!) a thin, sour wine with thick sediment which could please the stingy purses of only the most miserly hosts.[71] In Cisalpine Gaul there were the wines of Adria, of Cesena, and a *Maecenatianum* which probably came from a vineyard of Maecenas.[72] These wines were universally esteemed.

Of even more interest to us is the fact that the Etruscans preferred types of muscatels whose sugary taste, it is said, pleased the bees and so earned them the appellation of *Apianae*:[73] a fanciful etymology, for the name was probably derived from that of a wine-grower (*Appius*, with Etruscan simplification of the occlusive: we know of a Florentine, one *Aviles Apianas = Aulus Appianus*).[74] In any case, this sweet wine, very heavy, is the one the banqueters in Etruscan wall-paintings got drunk on. Other local vines hint at future Chianti and Orvietos: at Todi, on the frontier of Umbria, there was the *Tudernis*; at Arezzo the *Talpona* (which recalls the name *Talpius, Talponius*).[75] All these varieties indicate a long experience of viticultural techniques; grafting had long been practised in the creation of hybrids and there was a methodical arrangement of the vineyards so that different plants could be juxtaposed. Pliny tells us of a vine called *Murgentina*, introduced from Sicily into the Campania where it took the name of *Pompeiana* and which prospered particularly in the rich soil of the Chiusi hills.[76] But since this plant was imported at a relatively recent date, we dare hardly assume that it was the taste of its wine which inspired the Gauls to invade Italy.[77]

We have seen that the speciality of Tarquinii, at the end of the third century, was the cultivation of flax and the weaving of sails for ships: there is no longer any mention of this in Pliny. The textile industry also seems to have been a tradition of the Faliscan territory: the poets clothe their legendary heroes in flowing robes of fine linen which the Romans denounced as a symptom of degeneracy,[78] and even under Augustus the Faliscans were first in the manufacture of Etruscan hunting-nets, which were 'so strong that they could not be cut, so fine that they could pass through a ring, and so light that one man could easily carry slung over his shoulder enough net to cover a whole wood'.[79]

A curious fact is that the olive, whose silvery-green foliage seems to give modern Tuscany its typical colouring, must have been less common in ancient Etruria. The cultivated olive was still unknown in Italy in the days of Tarquinius the Elder,[80] and though in the second century Cato lovingly describes an olive-plantation in the region of Venafro, on the north-western edge of the Campania,[81] as far as we know there is no allusion in the ancient authors to any comparable cultivation in Etruria. It is not that the Etruscans did not make abundant use of oil. They borrowed the name for it at a very early date from the Greeks, as the Latins did, and one of the most ancient Etruscan inscriptions, engraved on a clay phial, refers to it under the name of *aska eleivana*, which means vase (*askos*) for oil (*elaion*).[82] But this oil had long since been imported by them from Attica in the innumerable amphorae that are scattered over the cemeteries of Caere and Spina.

At the time when, in an enthusiastic eulogy of Italy, Varro declared that it was 'everywhere planted with trees so that it looked like one enormous orchard',[83] we must indeed assume that Etruscan territory was no exception to the rule. But we must not forget that the majority of our fruits – and vegetables – were unknown in primitive Italy and were only brought there through the ages along with other refinements from the Orient. Not for nothing does Virgil entrust the garden of his dreams, in the fourth book of the Georgics, to a horticulturist just landed from Cilicia.[84] It was a time when cherries were considered an exotic fruit; they were brought from the Pontus by Lucullus[85] after his victory over Mithridates, and when the lemon, in the country 'wo die Zitronen blühn' (where the citrons grow) was still only a medicament used as an antidote or a breath-sweetener.[86] The connexions the Etruscans had with the Carthaginians, who brought the art of tree-culture to perfection,[87] as well as the great number of eastern slaves who entered their *familiae* had perhaps allowed them to steal a march on the Romans. It is sufficient to browse through M. Jacques André's *Lexicon of Latin Botanical Terms* to see that the citron or *cédrat* derives its name through Etruscan[88] from a non-Indo-European language, and that among the varieties of cherries there was one, the ruddiest kind, the *cerasum Apronianum*, whose inventor, one Apronius, must have been born in the region of Perugia.[89] Nevertheless, when the ancient agronomists enumerated the peninsula's most succulent fruits they cited the apples of Ameria, the pears of Tarentum, the figs of Herculanum and the almonds of Praeneste:[90] Etruria is absent from the catalogue, and Ovid simply says that the Faliscan region was rich in orchards.[91]

It is the same for vegetables; everyone praised the leeks of Aricia, the turnips of Nursia and Amiternum, the onions of Tusculum and the asparagus of Ravenna: a strange silence reigns over Etruscan vegetable-plots. Even the humble cabbage, which inspired Cato to an extraordinary dithyramb,[92] the cabbage, delight of gastronomes and universal panacea; the cabbage, the medicine for ulcers and melancholy that was cultivated by all the towns of Italy – Aricia, Ardea, Tivoli, Signia, Capua, Caudium and so on[93] – apparently even the cabbage left the Etruscans indifferent. A sign that the coastal *latifundia* had not encouraged the development of fruit and vegetable cultivation and that the interior plains were devoted to cereals and vines.

For information about earlier times we are compelled to study very closely the floral decorations on funerary paintings and works of art, which show – but these may be motifs borrowed from the ornamental repertoire of the Orient – the artichoke, bindweed, ivy, the dwarf palm and the oak, which belong to the indigenous flora; and the crocus, acanthus, laurel, cypress, lily, poppy, pomegranate and so on, which were importations.[94] The pomegranate appears on painted plaques at Caere of the sixth century: 'Punic apple', *malum punicum* in Latin, the discovery of which was claimed by the Carthaginians.[95] We can imagine what the lovely gardens of Tarquinii looked like from the frescoes in the Tomb of the Baron and the Tomb of the Triclinium:[96] palms, laurels, pomegranates, various shrubs whose branches bend under the weight of big blue bell-flowers compose for the dancers a setting which perhaps is related to the age-old tradition of the 'paradises' of ancient Persia.[97] Among the Etruscan texts which have come down to us in translation, one refers to trees of ill-omen: 'buckthorn, dogwood, fern, black fig, holly, wild pear, butcher's broom, eglantine, bramble'[98] – an infernal and fatal flora whose growth warned the *haruspices* to expect the direst calamities; but these trees and bushes also composed the rough scrubland which the farmer's tools had to be ceaselessly weeding and clearing.

AGRICULTURAL IMPLEMENTS

The Etruscans' agricultural implements are abundantly represented in the display-cases in the museum at Florence in the shape of iron instruments coming from Luni and Telamon, to which has been added a votive deposit unearthed on this last site and which was consecrated in 225 on the occasion of the victory won that year by the Romans and Etruscans over the Gauls.[99] The latter objects are in bronze, because of their religious character: Tages had ordained that the furrow which originally marked the boundaries of cities should be ploughed with a bronze ploughshare.[100] Here we have a complete collection of hoes and spades and picks, of bill-hooks for pruning and weeding, of sickles for cutting hay and corn; above all, there are two swing-ploughs which clearly illustrate our knowledge of ploughing among the Etruscans. Need we recall that our plough, with its fore-part borne on two wheels, saw the light in the northern plains, and that it is mentioned by the ancients in the first century of our era only as a recent invention of the Rhaetian Gauls?[101] Further on we shall see that the Celtic peoples were very much in advance of everyone else in the matter of carriages and chariots. The Mediterraneans for a long time contented themselves with light swing-ploughs, better adapted to the nature of their soil and the shape of their land.[102] One of the swing-ploughs from Telamon is the typical form; it is of the most primitive type: a long handle terminated by a hook. It figures thus in contemporary bas-reliefs, brandished like a weapon by a legendary warrior who, it is said, had fought at Marathon with nothing but a plough to defend himself with.[103]

We also have, in the same collection, a flat ploughshare in the shape of a spoon, which fitted on to the framework. The other swing-plough, of a composite type, was formed mainly of a pointed ploughshare, a long tail with a handle, a long beam at the end of which the yoke was fixed, with in the middle three pro-tuberances to guide the team's harness. A similar swing-plough is found, after the end of the sixth century, on the friezes in the *situla* of the Certosa at Bologna, where a ploughman on his way to the fields carries it over his shoulder while driving his oxen before him,[104] and, in a rather more perfected state, on a bronze from Arezzo dating from the beginning of the fourth century and which shows the ploughman at work behind his swing-plough and his placid oxen.[105] It is still not the plough of Virgil and Pliny with its coulter which, in front of the ploughshare, plots the furrow, and the mould-board that turns over the furrow-slice.

ETRUSCAN AGRONOMISTS

The great interest the Etruscans had in exploiting their land had inspired some agricultural treatises. It was perhaps not by accident that the Vegoia fragment was coupled, in the collection of ancient land-surveyors, with a text by the celebrated Car-thaginian agronomist Mago: *ex libris Magonis et Vegoiae auctorum* – by Mago whose twenty-eight books were translated after the Punic War and summarized several times in Greek and in Latin, and to which, apparently, the centuries-old bonds between the Carthaginians and the Etruscans had already attracted the attention of the latter.

In any case, judging by his name among other things, Saserna must have been Etruscan: his work, written at the end of the second century, and continued by his son, is often mentioned by Varro, Columella and Pliny in tones of mingled praise and mockery. In it he took as his model a domain he possessed in Gaul – that is, in Cisalpine Gaul where the Etruscan colonist had preceded the Roman ones, and probably in the region of Placentia or Veleia whose Varro contrasted the easy plains and moderate hills with the steep slopes of neighbouring Liguria.[106] And the Romans of the end of the Republic did not fail to jeer at the choice absurdity of his precepts. For Saserna brought all kinds of things into agriculture – medicine, hygiene and beauty-treatments. He evolved an infallible recipe for killing bugs:[107] 'Take a root of serpentaria and let it soak in water, then pour the water over the place you wish to disinfect: no bug will come near it. Or else mix ox's gall with vinegar, and rub the bed with this.' In order to depilate one's skin, one simply had to throw into boiling water a yellow tree-frog, and when its bulk had been reduced by two-thirds, to anoint one's body with it. Again, if one gave a cooked frog to a dog, this was the best way to teach him to follow one. But above all he had discovered a magical formula to cure gout: Varro got the recipe from a third person, a certain Tarquenna, who was also obviously Etruscan: when one began to feel pains in the feet, one had to repeat twenty-seven times, before breakfast, after having spat, and touching the ground, 'I think of thee, cure my feet, let the earth keep my pain, let health remain in my feet'.

These wise women's remedies, it must be said, have their echoes in the folk-lore of all countries: Cato also knew a charm against dislocations, and even the resorting to contact with Mother Earth has nothing specifically Etruscan about it. It is more interesting to observe that the very wide interpretation which Saserna gave to the word 'agriculture' shows that the rural property-owner usually made on the spot everything he needed for the storage and sale of his harvests. Saserna's world was a small, self-contained world. Though he greatly scandalized the Romans of the end of the Republic by devoting a chapter to the question of clay quarries (*figilinae*),[108] it was natural that he should do so, as he was exploiting those on his own land to supply the potters' kilns which were producing his corn-bins, his amphorae for wine and oil. The big estates had their own doctors, their fullers and their specialized craftsmen, which deprived rural labourers of any pretext for 'walking out in their best clothes on working days'.

Saserna, heir to long experience of agricultural labouring

problems, insisted with even greater force than Cato on the fact that the *familia rustica* must be strictly disciplined. 'No one is allowed to go outside, with the exception of the steward or of the man he sends on an errand. If anyone else absents himself, he must be punished; otherwise the steward is responsible.'[109] There were also, regarding the number of hands required to do certain tasks, precise directions: one man, working for forty-five days, was sufficient for eight *jugera* or about one hectare (2·471 acres); in fact, he could dig one *jugerum* (25 acres) in four days, but one had to reckon with thirteen days lost through ill health, bad weather and slacking.[110] Two teams of oxen were necessary for a ploughed area of two hundred *jugera* or about fifty hectares,[111] which gives us the dimensions of a typical farm, mid-way between the Roman colonists' small-holdings (one to two hectares at Modena and Parma) and the later big estates such as that of Pliny the Younger, reckoned at seven hundred and fifty hectares.[112] Even in the days of Martial, the richest land-owner in Caere, one Hilarus, the heir of an old local family, had his farmers cultivate small plots of land, one of which, as the poet describes it, measured scarcely three and a half hectares.[113] We must correct a few rather too facile generalizations about the *latifundia*.

THE RAISING OF STOCK

The pastures of the *latifundia* on the coast and the wooded valleys of the interior were the raising-grounds of fine cattle; the oxen of Etruria were heavy-shouldered and strong workers, and the heifers of the Faliscan region were white as snow and much in demand for sacrifices to the gods.[114] This does not add much new detail to our picture. But there was also the great reputation of the *pecorino*, the cheese made from the milk of ewes at Luni on the borders of Liguria: it was of an enormous size and could weigh up to a thousand pounds, 327 kilos. The trade-mark, in Roman times, was naturally a crescent moon. Martial, among the small presents he made to his friends, describes a *caseus Lunensis* big enough to provide a thousand dinners for the slaves in one *familia*.[115]

Another detail is interesting when we consider pig-breeding, which the Etruscans, like the Cisalpine Gauls, practised on a large scale: tripe in the Faliscan mode – *venter Faliscus* – was greatly renowned. As the Etruscans did everything to music they had trained their flocks and herds to follow the sound of the trumpet, unlike the practice noted in Greece by Polybius, where the swineherds drove them along in front of them. And the Greek historian describes immense herds proceeding along the beaches of the Tyrrhenian Sea, with the swineherds walking some distance in front of their charges and from time to time sounding a trumpet whose note and peculiar timbre the beasts knew well enough to keep following; thus they ran no risk of losing themselves and mixing with a neighbour's flocks. Varro also says that young pigs ought to be brought up by the farmer in such a way that from a very early age they are accustomed *omnia ut faciant ad bucinam*.[116]

HUNTING

The forests and marshes were stocked with abundant and varied game. When Rutilius Namatianus was returning to his native Gaul, he was held up by a storm in the port of Pisa, which has been replaced by Livorno or Leghorn, and profited from this enforced halt by organizing a hunting expedition:

'The farmer, our host, found us hunting-pieces and dogs trained to discover animal lairs by smell. Into our traps, into the large and perfidious mesh of our nets a wild boar fell and fought; it was a beast redoubtable indeed in its vigour and pugnacity, one which the arms of Meleager, nay, even the grip of Hercules could not have restrained. Then the horn sounded across the hills that re-echoed its notes; and our songs made the prey less heavy as we bore it home.'[117]

This description comes from the year AD 417, but though recorded ten centuries later, all the details agree with what we see represented on the figured monuments of the Etruscans living in the days of the mythical Lausus, son of Mezentius and *debellator ferarum*:[118] the weapons, spears, javelins and axes, the bloodhounds on the trail, the nets of Falerii in which the wild beast (the *Tuscus aper* of Statius)[119] is trapped, the call of the horn deep in the woods and the return from the hunt with the boar suspended from a pole borne by two farm-lads; even the evocations of the boar hunts of Calydon and Erymanthus that enchanted the imagination of the *lucumones* – there is nothing which is not illustrated in the friezes of the bronze *situla* of the Certosa and in the paintings at Tarquinii in the Tomb of the Querciola or the Scrofa Nera.[120] Boar hunts, deer hunts, the hunting of the hare . . .

At the end of the Republic – but that is merely when we begin to have texts, and there is nothing to prove that it was a recent innovation – there existed in the region of Tarquinii a game reserve of ten hectares, where the proprietor, Q. Fulvius Lippinus, not only raised hares (which earned these reserves the name of *leporarium*), deer and hind but also wild sheep. And Varro knew of even bigger reserves in the region of Statonia.[121] The feudal structure of their society, their country's great game resources are enough to explain the cynegetic vocation of the Etruscans. But perhaps other things were mixed up in it: obscure and incomprehensible ethnic traditions, familiarity of a religious nature with the world of beasts which perhaps had very remote origins. Later on we shall quote on this subject an extraordinary text by Aelianus about the rôle played by music in their legendary huntsmen's capturing of wild animals.[122]

Etruscan art retained, from the foreign influences under which it came to birth, a taste for certain animal representations which were used as decorative subjects. Those panthers on either side of a column, those lions jumping on gazelles compose a conventional bestiary and, together with the griffins and sphinxes of fable, hold up a screen of illusion in front of reality, in which real wolves roamed.[123] Sometimes the influence is a puzzle, for example in the case of the monkeys.

In fact, a whole simian menagerie has been discovered on Villanovan fibulae, on the amber amulets and necklaces of Vetulonia and Marsiliana d'Albegna, on the amphora of Tragliatella, from the end of the seventh century, where a horseman rides with a little monkey behind him; but there is not much difficulty in discovering, at Samos among other places, the oriental sources of the motif.[124] Later, a well-known tomb at Chiusi, from the first half of the fifth century, shows, taking part in funeral games which include all the attractions of a popular circus, a *wistiti* or little striated monkey tied by a chain next to the troupe's dwarf and equilibrist.[125] The monkey figures again in the paintings of the Tomb of the Sette Camini near Orvieto, which belongs to the following century.

We can hardly suppose that these animals were captured in the neighbouring mountains. They were little luxury pets such as the Greek world had made popular everywhere. A domesticated monkey plays a part at the beginning of the *Miles Gloriosus* or 'The Braggart Warrior' which takes place at Ephesus. But it was North Africa above all which was the principal market for them.[126] The Numidian Masinissa was one day to tell some pet-lovers who wanted to buy a large number: 'But gentlemen, in your country don't the women give you children?'[127] We see in the *Poenulus* of Plautus that in the best homes in Carthage there were tame monkeys capable of biting, in play, a little boy, leaving on his hand a mark whose timely recognition brings the comedy to a happy end.[128] The ones we see in Etruria are probably memories of some mercenary of Chiusi who had fought in an African campaign, or presents from a Punic businessman to his clients in Orvieto. They go to prove the lively relationship that existed between the two countries.

Yes . . . but perhaps things are not quite so simple. There are two disturbing features. The island of Ischia, where the first Chalcidian colonists disembarked in the eighth century, was named by them Pithecussae, from *pithekos* meaning 'monkey', and this expressive toponymic reappears in the Greek authors to designate various places in Africa where monkeys abounded. But it so happens that the old lexicographers have handed down to us quite unmistakably the Etruscan word for monkey, *arim-*, and if this gloss is exact the river Ariminus, at the mouth of which the Etruscans founded the town of Ariminum, modern Rimini, was a sort of 'Stream of the Monkeys' such as exists in the gorges of the Chiffa, near Blida.

It was perhaps the same word which lay at the root of the indigenous name for Ischia, *Inarime*, which the Greeks translated into their own tongue and which reappears, deformed, in its classical name *Aenaria*. This was a problem which exercised Strabo and has still not lost its fascination for modern scholars.[129] It has been suggested that *arim-* is a borrowing from the Etruscan or Punic *harim-*, 'flat-nosed', an epithet which the Carthaginians applied to their monkeys. It is supposed that it was the

Carthaginians who gave *Inarime* its name, but neither they nor the Phoenicians ventured into the region of Ariminum. What then? There were monkeys in Italy from the dawn of time; they seem to have left fossilized remains in Tuscany and they had also left traces in a very ancient toponymy. Moreover it is curious that Homer, Hesiod and Pindar knew the country of the *Arimnoi*, which they located in the region of Syria. The word *arim-* perhaps belongs to the Mediterranean substratum of language. But with regard to the period that interests us here, this does not alter what we have been saying: the amber necklaces of the seventh century were junk from some bazaar, the Tomb *della Scimmia* merely illustrates the friendship between Carthage and the Etruscans.

The skies of Etruria were flocked by birds which the *haruspices* had carefully studied. Their 'omen books' or *Ostentaria* were illustrated with pictures representing, against the accompanying text, those species whose augural significance they defined.[130] These included birds, Pliny stated, that no one had ever seen. But it is to these treatises that we owe our knowledge of the Etruscan word for eagle, *antar*, for hawk, *arac* and for falcon, *capu*.[131] We see a woodpecker about to fly away in a scene denoting observation of the flight of birds (*auspicium*) in the François tomb. There are indeed many enchanting birds in Etruscan paintings, caught in full flight or pecking about in the trees. The Tomb of the Triclinium is a veritable aviary in which, not counting the cock and hen watched by a cat under the banqueting couches, the dancers move surrounded by blackbirds and thrushes perched in the branches. The fights and bloody games depicted in the Tomb of the Augurs are dominated by the passage, on wide-spread wings, of great red palmipeds which have been identified as cormorants.[132] Moreover Strabo remarks that water-fowl were one of the attractions of Etruscan lakes and marshes. In the celebrated tomb *della Caccia e Pesca*, hunters standing on the cliff are trying to reach with their slings a multicoloured flight of wild duck.[133]

FISHING

Here the scene takes place at the seaside, and the fowling is accompanied by a fishing expedition. Boats guided from the rear by a tiller-oar sail on green and violet waves in which dolphins disport themselves. In the prow decorated with a huge, luck-bringing eye, a fisherman throws his harpoon or retrieves his net. There are even swimmers climbing up a rock in order to dive in among the boats. M. Pallottino has admirably characterized the originality of the artist who conceived this painting, 'unique in the productions of archaic and classical eras', which shows an extreme liberty in the interpretation of the most varied human attitudes and disposes them in an exuberant nature.

Texts, by comparison, are scanty. They hardly speak of anything but tunny-fishing; there existed on the promontories of Populonia and Monte Argentario, above Orbetello, two of those *thynnoscopoi* or look-outs from which the arrival of fresh shoals was observed. Pyrgi, the port of Caere, was famous also for its fisheries which, under the Empire, supplied the fishmongers of Rome. And we also know that the Etruscans had stocked the lakes of Bracciano, Bolsena and Vico with carp and sea-dace and with all kinds of salt-water fish that acclimatized themselves to fresh water.[134]

THE TIMBER INDUSTRY

An examination of the natural resources of Etruria now brings us to her forests. Of course, deforestation had its effects. Even in the days of Livy the impenetrable Ciminian Forest which right to the end of the fourth century had inspired in travelling merchants and Roman soldiers a sort of awe, had lost all its mystery; today it is no more than sparse clumps of weedy trees rising above bushes.[135] The slopes up which one climbs to Volterra are also denuded, so that one wonders where the oaks and beech-trees grew that were used in 205 to build the *interamenta navium*, that is, the interior parts, the hold and the keel of boats, whilst the fir trees of Rusellae, Perugia and Chiusi were used for the masts and bulwarks.[136] Well before Scipio, the Etruscan navy had long exploited, around Caere, the fir and pine woods described by Virgil, for whom the pine is an Etruscan tree (*Etrusca pinus*). Theophrastus, in the fourth century, spoke of beech-trees whose trunks, thirty or so metres long, formed the keels of 'Tyrrhenian ships'; but Pisa in particular, with its forests whose timber was especially suited to naval construction, had become the principal arsenal in Etruria; it was Pisa that had thought of providing the vessels of war with *rostra* for boarding-parties. But the day was to come when the decadence of the Etruscan navy and the increase of luxury in houses resulted in the timber of Etruria being used for beams and planks and for the ornamenting of palaces.[137]

Let us pass over the exploitation of quarries as the Etruscans did not know of the marble of Luni, today called Carrara, the discovery of which dates from the very end of the Roman Republic. Concerning the stone they did quarry, we have some indications in Pliny, for example about the white limestone of the *ager Tarquiniensis*, near the Lake of Bolsena, from which stone they carved the fine sarcophagi in the Tomb of the Partunu.[138] But we must hasten to consider one of the most ancient sources of Etruscan wealth – mines and metallurgy.

THE MINES

We have in fact seen that Etruria's mineral resources were the basis of her strength. When about 770 the Chalcidians founded on the island of Pithecussae (Ischia) a first advance post which would soon serve as a base for their establishment in Campania, they came perhaps counting on the tin and certainly on the copper and ingots of bronze offered them by central Italy.[139] The contrast between the abundance of bronze in the Villanovan tombs and the poverty of metal in the Greek tombs of the geometric period (ninth to eighth centuries BC), the beginnings of Greek colonization in the west coinciding with the upsurge of Etruscan civilization in the eighth century are the fundamental data which explain the prodigious enrichment displayed by the orientalizing tombs of Praeneste, Caere, Vetulonia and Populonia. But Populonia in particular, close to the present-day Piombino facing the Isle of Elba, 'generous in mines of iron' as Virgil says, was the centre of a mining and metallurgical industry which has earned it the name of the Pittsburgh of antiquity.[140]

The whole southern part of the province of Livorno, all the region comprised between Volterra to the north and Massa Marittima to the south are still full of traces of that centuries-old activity, largely extinct at the beginning of our era when Strabo saw, in the country round Populonia, many abandoned mines,[141] but which sometimes was preserved elsewhere, as at Massa

Marittima on the road to Siena: Massa whose marvellous Roman-esque cathedral, soaring up suddenly with its thirteenth-century palaces in the fold of a hill scarred with the red earth of excava-tions, speaks volumes for its continuing prosperity. Since 1830 the working of the mines has gone on where the ancients left off.

In particular the region of Campiglia Marittima, about ten kilometres as the crow flies to the north-east of Populonia, still shows visible traces of shafts dug as early as the Etruscan period in the search not only for copper and iron but also for argentiferous lead and for tin. It is well known – and the splendid researches of M. Roger Dion and M. Jérôme Carcopino[142] have been most illuminating in this respect – that the tin necessary to the ancient bronzesmiths came mostly from the far-off Cassiterides, islands off the Atlantic shores of Armorica and Cornwall, where the Phoenician galleys went to obtain a monopoly whose secret they jealously guarded but which the Celts, for their part, imported right into their own territory along a continental route probably opened up at the request of Marseilles and which made the fortune of those living along it: witness, in a princely tomb on the borders of Burgundy, the celebrated *kratér* or wine-bowl, a masterpiece of Greek toreutics, and the other priceless objects discovered in 1953 at Vix, near Châtillon-sur-Seine.[143] Yet this tin, together with the copper it was alloyed with in the normal proportion of eight to fifteen per cent,[144] existed in Etruria itself, in mines which for a long time were able to supply its industry, as is proved by the slag found near Campiglia, in places with evocative names like *Campo delle Buche*, the *Cento Camerelle*, the *Cavina*, and also on the island of Elba.

Here and there the extraction of copper preceded that of iron: this had already happened in the eastern Mediterranean, where iron, before the discovery of tempering, was at first used only as a meteoric substance miraculously fallen from the sky. Then, when its use had been extended, it was bronze that took on the sacred character which we find in numerous ritual pre-scriptions: almost all instruments used in rituals were of bronze, as Macrobius tells us; the Sabine priests, like the flamen or priest of the god in Rome had their hair cut with bronze scissors. Among the Etruscans, as we said above, the cult of the legendary dwarf Tages observed the same taboos, and they traced the boundary furrow of their towns with a ploughshare made of bronze. Antonio Minto, moreover, has noted that chariots discovered at Populonia in the necropolis of San Cerbone were covered with ornaments of bronze and iron, in which iron *lamellae* cut in open-work designs were incrusted in the bronze in the manner of marquetry:[145] the precious metal in those days was iron. There was a time at the end of the orientalizing period, that is, the end of the seventh century, when siderurgy was still a rare luxury.

In the case of Elba, the authors testify to copper coming before iron, and in the Campigliese this fact is confirmed by archaeology; there have been brought to light, notably in a valley which significantly bears the name of *Val di Fucinaia*, or Valley of the Forge, numerous mines with deep cavities open to the sky, with shafts, communicating galleries, supply trenches and lines of furnaces: the whole, judging from fragments of ceramics and bronze objects found in the vicinity, going back to the eighth century.

Some of the furnaces are fairly well preserved[146]: they have the form of a truncated cone, about one metre eighty cms. in diameter, the interiors lined with refractory bricks and divided into two chambers one above the other by a partition pierced with holes. This partition was supported by a column of local porphyry. A square door opened in the base to ventilate the furnace and regulate combustion. The upper chamber was filled with copper pyrites and charcoal. A fire was lighted in the lower chamber: the oxide of iron collected above while the copper was released through the holes: these have been found to be incrusted with carbonate of copper.

As can be imagined, it is a problem to determine the origin of this type of furnace; it presents affinities with certain examples discovered among the Philistines, metallurgists of renown, in Palestine (twelfth to eleventh centuries), or in the more recent Celtic civilization of La Tène; here again we must be hesitant of choosing between the influences, oriental or occidental, which may have had their effect. Let us content ourselves with remarking that the output was very low, as an examination of residues has shown: these have been used again by modern industry. We should like to know more about the activity of the workers in this district: but there has been one find which illustrates it in a concrete way – the miners' lamps, made of clay, sturdy in shape, with two holes at the back for a cord.[147]

But as we have seen iron finally triumphed over bronze. The extraction of copper and tin ceased in the Campigliese and on the island of Elba, perhaps because of the competition from the mines of Spain and Brittany which became more and more accessible to Mediterranean trade; perhaps also because the workings ran out. This was the case on the island of Elba, where, so the Pseudo-Aristotle tells us, no further copper could be found in his day (third century); however, in its place, and, he makes clear, in the same workings, iron was found in abundance.[148] This time the resources were boundless: people even believed that the iron mines on the island of Elba kept filling up again like the quarries of Paros from which the famous marble was extracted.[149]

The mineral rock was originally treated on the spot, in a multitude of furnaces which covered the Mediterranean heavens with a sombre smoke; hence, the etymologists assured us, the name of *Aithaleia* given it by the Greeks and which signified 'black with soot'.[150] But at some date which could not be anterior to the fifth century, it was seen that the mineral-bearing substance could not be smelted adequately in the island's furnaces, and it became the custom to transport it immediately to Populonia, where it was treated in more highly perfected installations. We can picture the convoys of great barges crossing the ten kilometres of the channel. The port, on whose quaysides ingots of bronze from the Campigliese had been stacked long before the cast iron of the island of Elba, became from then on the great siderurgical centre of Italy.[151] The Pseudo-Aristotle, Varro and Strabo were all agreed that the work was divided up thus, a consequence of technical progress which had separated the mine from the forge. Today Populonia lies beneath an enormous mass of iron slag which, having engulfed its necropolis and its archaic monuments, eloquently proclaims the intensity of its industrial production. For the last forty years metallurgical concerns have been working these pyrites, which still contain thirty per cent of iron, and archaeological diggings profit from this industrial intervention. But it was all known beforehand, in any case. Populonia, judging by its name, was the city of Fufluns, an Etruscan god who was assimilated with Bacchus, but who, in the Etruscan religion, was very close to the solar deity, Catha. Vulcan, with his tongs and hammer figures on the coins of the third century. And when in 205 Scipio levied specific goods from Etruscan cities, he asked Populonia for only one thing, iron.[152]

Some insights into the technique of smelting, at least in the period of decadence, have been left us by Posidonius of Apamea, who had long been familiar with the mines of Spain and had not neglected those of Etruria.

We read this in Diodorus Siculus:

'The island of Elba possesses a great amount of iron-rock, which they quarry in order to melt and cast and thus secure the iron, and they possess a great abundance of this ore. For those who are engaged in the working of the ore crush the rock and burn the lumps which have thus been broken in certain ingenious furnaces; and in these they smelt the lumps by means of a great fire and form them into pieces of moderate size which are in their appearance like large sponges. These are purchased by merchants in exchange either for money or for goods and are then taken to Dicaearcheia (Puteoli, modern Pozzuoli) or the other trading stations, where there are men who purchase such cargoes and who, with the aid of a multitude of artisans in metal whom they have collected, work it further and manufacture iron objects of every description. Some of these are ingeniously fabricated into shapes well suited for various arms, two-pronged forks and sickles and other such tools; and these are then carried by merchants to every region and thus many parts of the inhabited world have a share in the usefulness which accrues from them.'[153]

This is a very interesting text, not merely as regards its final passage in which, as the historian quotes it, a Stoic philosopher celebrates with wondering praise that trade by virtue of which the benefits of civilization are spread throughout human society. This dates the passage: far from describing, as has been thought, the most ancient phase of Elba's iron industry, he is showing us the final stages, when Pozzuoli had become in the second century BC – though it was still no more, according to Lucilius, than a

'little Delos' – the great *emporium* of Italy, enjoying close relationships with all the markets of Greece and the Orient.[154] An interesting text, but one in which, perhaps through some fault of the
abridger, one suspects an omission or an error: that Pozzuoli
should have forged agricultural implements is quite in keeping
with what we know of its workshops in the days of Cato;[155] and
that it should manufacture arms for the use of mercenaries or
Samnite gladiators is something less well known but which should
not surprise us.[156] But Diodorus must have jumped one of
Posidonius' phrases in which he mentioned the rôle played by
Populonia between the extraction of the ore on Elba and its
manufacture, in Pozzuoli, into commercial goods. Unless Elba
and Populonia were comprehended in the same vague expression.

In any case, some hundred years later, at the beginning of
our era, Strabo was still able to say: 'From the height of the city,
where I had climbed for that express purpose, I saw in the distance
Sardinia, Corsica, and, nearer, the island of Elba. I also saw the
forges where they work the iron brought from that island.'
Therefore the tall furnaces of Populonia were still not extinguished
and were continuing to receive, as soon as it had been extracted,
the raw iron ore. So let us put in the name which was omitted –
Populonienses – in the place where, according to the Pseudo-
Aristotle, Varro and Strabo, it had to come, in close connexion
with those words it defined, or ought to have defined: 'those who
are engaged in the working.' Moreover it was at Populonia that
the 'ingenious furnaces' of which Diodorus speaks must have
been found, and not on Elba, where all other authors agree that
they must have been inadequate.

Nevertheless from this uncertain account we can extract a
few precious indications concerning the imperfections in Populonia's foundry-work: this amounted to no more than a simple
initial torrefaction. The fact that the ingots produced had the
appearance of great sponges reminds us of a remark by Pliny the
Elder, who notes with astonishment that 'when a vein of ore is
fused the iron becomes liquid like water and afterwards acquires
a spongy and brittle texture: *in spongeas frangi*'.[157] Was Populonia
at this period able to carry out the operation itself? It seems to
have given up also the manufacture of trade articles. It had
certainly declined from its former prosperity. Its furnaces were

still working, but, as Strabo said in a few evocative phrases, 'today this township, with the exception of her temples and a few houses, is absolutely deserted. The quarter where the arsenal lies, with its little port at the foot of the hill and its two wet-docks, offers a less desolate prospect'. Another four centuries pass: when Rutilius Namatianus lands there on November 4, 417, on his way home to his native Gaul, he finds only 'a line of ramparts broken down here and there, and the roofs buried under vast piles of rubbish'.[158] The tides of history had turned away from the place that in its heyday had been the industrial capital of the Etruscan world, another Vulcan's Forge, a Pittsburgh of antiquity, whose tall furnaces blackened its walls with smoke: it had no need, then, of help from Pozzuoli in putting the finishing touches to its metal products, in forging the plough of Tages or the two-headed axe of Macstarna.

THE ROADS

It was indeed a great, busy land, with its lands reclaimed from the marshes, its forests and scrublands, its naval dockyards and its mining areas, and its chequerboards of wheatfields and vine-yards round its towns. We must now, before entering these, which give the land its meaning, attempt to retrace the network of roads that were the nervous system of that vast body and kept up the circulation between the various regions.

It is a difficult problem, this question of the roads in Etruria: upon this point at least the victory of Rome marked a considerable and brutal break with the past. The great routes of antiquity that crossed Etruria and whose traces are still followed by modern traffic all date from after the conquest and all lead to Rome, as is only natural: the via Aurelia, constructed in 241 BC, along the coast from Rome to Pisa; inland the via Clodia (225) crossing the plateau by way of Bieda, Tuscania, Maternum (Farnese) and Saturnia; the via Cassia (154 or 125), further to the east, running from Rome to Florence by way of Volsinii, Chiusi and Arezzo; the via Amerina (241) which followed the right bank of the Tiber as far as Amerinia. These four routes leave Rome, the centre of the world, exclusively preoccupied with Roman interests which were not necessarily those of the Etruscans and even at times ran counter to them: for example there was an old road running from

Caere to Veii and thence to Praeneste, in order to reach the Campania without passing through Rome; it crossed the Tiber at Fidenae (Castel Giubileo), eight kilometres upstream, and it really does seem that the legendary expedition of the three hundred Fabii against Veii had as its aim the capture of this line of communication.[159] The Romans never bothered to keep up that road, but they sent out into Etruria the four we have mentioned, like so many probing knives into conquered territory, using them to transport their legions as quickly as possible to the north of Italy where they were called by the Gaulish menace and prospects of further expansion. So that though the Romans sometimes took over already existing roads, for example from the *ager Tarquiniensis* where the via Clodia still serves Bieda, Norchia and Tuscania, their roads often passed in an undeviating straight line some distance from the ancient centres: the same via Clodia, after leaving Tuscania, goes on to Saturnia, a Roman colony, but Vulci and Sovana are not accessible excepting by side-roads, which contributed not a little to their decadence.[160]

We must beware of representing Etruscan roads as if they were like the Roman highways, with the fine slabs grooved with cart and chariot wheels of the via Appia. In any case, the via Appia itself did not begin to be paved until 293.[161] In Etruria the only paving we see on the roads is in the immediate vicinity of towns, for example at the north-west gate of Tarquinii.[162] Generally they appear as tracks cut into the rock and deeply pitted by the weight of carts and the action of water. And certain of these, at Veii, Bieda and Sovana with their high, precipitous sides with tombs opening off them half-way up, with the luxuriant vegetation carpeting the bottom, have a wild picturesqueness that recommend them to tourists. But an Etruscan origin must not be attributed to all the *Cave* nor to all the *Cavoni* mentioned by the guides. 'It is impossible to tell a road abandoned only a century ago from a road belonging to the Etruscan era.'[163]

The sole criteria are the tombs which sometimes border the latter and rock inscriptions. J. B. Ward Perkins' recent researches in the Faliscan territory[164] successfully brought to light numerous segments of pre-Roman road along the via Amerina and elsewhere. We must admire the boldness with which, in order to avoid over-steep slopes, the road was dug to a depth of fifteen metres; running parallel to one of the sides, a *cuniculus*, sometimes covered, provided for the running-away of water. Certain of these road-works are signed by the engineer: thus *Larth Vel Arnies*, near Corchiano.[165] All these facts allow us to build up a picture of fairly intense traffic between towns like Veii for example and Nepete (Nepi) and Falerii (Civitacastellana). They allow us glimpses, unlike the imperious simplicity of the Roman road system, of tangled side-paths and of a regional particularism which confirm what we knew already, the absence of centralization in the Etruscan world. At the *fanum Voltumnae*, near Volsinii, there was a site for an annual concourse. If we knew the Etrurian road-map better, would we look upon this as a fine star with twelve radiating branches? We doubt it. At the end of the Roman Empire the Umbrians of Spello ventured to ask Constantine to excuse them from having to undertake that journey across mountain escarpments and along difficult roads, *ardua montium et difficultates itinerum*.[166] Some ten centuries earlier, Tarchon must have received many similar requests.

THE VEHICLES

But there was a good deal of short-distance travel, from town to town. A history of Etruscan vehicles begins with the war chariots which were unearthed at Populonia, Vetulonia, Marsiliana and Caere in tombs dating from the seventh century:[167] chariots with two wheels reinforced with metal tyres and felloes and carrying a wooden body open at the back and rounded at the front; a long pole was fixed to it over which the driver leaned to guide his team. They are similar to those we see on Grecian vases ever since the days of the Dipylon, and bring to mind the battles in Homeric poems. But it is hardly likely that they ever were used, in Etruria, by some new Achilles, or in actual battles. Their panels adorned with more and more richly decorated bronze laminae prove that they were ceremonial chariots which perhaps were used only in solemn processions in honour of the leader who rode in them after a victory: in Rome they survive in the form of the quadriga with the four white horses of the triumphers.

This ceremonial character is even more marked in the chariots of Monteleone and of Castel San Mariano,[168] from the middle of the sixth century, with their bronze casing ornamented with repoussé masks of Gorgons and mythological figures – incomparable masterpieces of Etruscan toreutics but which have nothing in common with the arts of war. Moreover at that period war had changed its methods and its arms: the chariot, an archaic instrument for displaying individual prowess, gave way to cavalry manoeuvring in serried formations. It served only for parade or in the races at the games, like those for which the Tomb of the Bigae at Tarquinii shows preparations being made.[169] But the chariot is found again, in the third century, on steles from Bologna and urns from Volterra representing the infernal voyage of the dead who are being dragged after demon psychopomps.[170] As once happened on the roads of Etruria, the dead man goes on foot or rides a horse with Charon holding the bridle, or is borne in a chariot; and the latter, as is natural in an heroic scene, is often no other than the biga or quadriga of the archaic age whose galloping horses dash off into immortality.[171] But sometimes, too, Etruscan realism gives it the prosaic aspect of a contemporary cart or trap: a vehicle with two wheels, covered by a cradle-like hood which seems to be made of a tilt ornamented with fringes and embroideries and stretched over hoops; it is open at the front to show, comfortably seated and driving two peaceful mules, the traveller and his wife who look as if they are off to the local market.[172]

It was in this sort of vehicle that Tarquinius and Tanaquil, having left their native Tarquinii, had once arrived in Rome; in such a cart, which Livy properly calls a *carpentum*, they had piled their luggage (*sublatis rebus*) and journeyed to the summit of the Janiculum. And there, as Tarquinius was 'seated in his cart with his wife', *carpento sedente cum uxore*, an eagle had descended from the sky to prove to him that the gods were in agreement with his ambition.[173]

These *carpenta* often appear in the history of primitive Rome; in particular in the history of Roman feminism where they appear in the long fights the matrons had to wage in order to obtain, like their Etruscan sisters, permission to leave their houses. For at first, according to Ovid, the Italian ladies circulated freely in *carpenta*:

Nam prius Ausonias matres carpenta vehebant.[174]

(For of old Ausonian matrons drove in carts.)

But the Catos of Rome had ceaselessly contested, accorded, withdrawn, given back and bargained over this right, on the pretext that it caused traffic-jams in the narrow streets of the city, and, above all, offended against morals. A woman had to be brazen indeed – and an Etruscan! – like Tullia, daughter of Servius Tullius, to venture to expose herself to the gaze of men at the forum, where she had herself driven in her *carpentum (carpento in forum inuecta)*:[175] on her return, moreover, she had done even worse and gone so far as to crush beneath the wheels of her *carpentum* her old and dying father (*per patris corpus carpentum egisse fertur*). One had to be a shameless hussy like Propertius' Cynthia in order to ride to Lanuvium in the silk-upholstered *carpentum* of a boy-friend, especially when we are told that she sat 'near the pole, with her legs dangling'.[176]

In 395, after the capture of Veii, the dictator Camillus, in order to recompense the Roman matrons for having placed all their jewels at his disposal for the war-effort authorized them to ride in the *pilentum* – this was a ceremonial vehicle with four wheels – on the occasion of sacrifices and games, and in the *carpentum* every day, whether holidays or not.[177] In 213, during the darkest days of the Punic War, a *lex Oppia* had been passed again, forbidding women the use of horse-drawn vehicles, in Rome and in the other cities and in an area measuring one thousand paces all round them, excepting for religious purposes. When peace returned in 195, Cato had launched a diatribe against those who wanted to abrogate this law and succeeded in doing so.[178] With the passing years, however, in stables where they were joined by all kinds of other vehicles, tumbrils, charabancs, cabriolets, the *carpenta* had taken on the patina of ancient objects and the prestige of the ceremonies for which their use had been reserved. That is why, under the Empire, Messalina and Agrippina could think of nothing more gratifying to their pride than to have themselves borne to the Capitol in a *carpentum (carpento Capitolium ingredi)*, 'formerly the privilege of priests and sacred objects'.[179] At the death of his mother, Agrippina the Elder, Caligula had already started the circus and its games, in the course of which his statue would solemnly be borne in procession on a *carpentum*.[180] We can see the venerable equipage, promoted to the rank of carriage, on the medal struck on that occasion *memoriae Agrippinae*: the arched roof seems to be held up by four small statues. 'This type of covering is very probably of Etruscan origin.'[181]

In fact there is nothing to disprove that Rome had borrowed the *carpentum* from the Etruscans, among whom we first see it portrayed. Yet it is well known that Rome owed to the Gauls, in the final analysis, the majority of the types of vehicle she used at the same time as the vocabulary by which they were designated. 'The Romans,' it has been well said,[182] 'a sedentary people, proprietors cultivating their own land, did not possess the large chariots with four wheels in which bands of conquerors from Gaul transported their belongings and which served to encircle their camps at night.' The Romans borrowed the name from the Gauls whose activity in Italy contributed to their deliverance from Etruscan domination. This is also true of the *carrus*, a four-wheeled chariot, a word which was substituted in Romance languages for the Latin *currus*; as well as of the *petorritum*, the *benna*, the *covinnus*, the *rheda*, the *cisium*, the *essedum*, as well as of the *carpentum*, whose origin is attested by Livy (*carpentis Gallicis*) and Florus (*carpenta Gallorum*).[183] But it is evident that the Etruscans themselves had been the first to submit to this influence when we think of their proximity, fruitful not only in battles but also in commercial and cultural exchanges of every kind, with the Cisalpine Gauls, whose heavy chariots and light carriages rutted the vast plain of the Po. 'All Roman vehicles, models and names, were imitated from the Gauls.'[184] Quite probably, though, this was done through the Etruscans, who were better placed than anyone for discovering their secrets, among others those of these *carpenta*, however they called it in their own tongue, which we see depicted on their third-century urns in Northern Etruria, at Volterra and Fiesole.

CHAPTER SIX

THE TOWNS AND THE SETTING OF URBAN ACTIVITIES

Though the Etruscans showed themselves to be good agronomists and vigorously imposed their will on Nature, it was above all as builders of towns that they revealed their true genius. At the very beginning of Italian history they were the promoters of the idea and the first to realize it.[1] It has often been demonstrated that the Italians or rather the Italics did not spontaneously conceive the notion of city in the sense that the Latins gave to the word *urbs*, that is to say in the sense not of a more or less fortuitous agglomeration of buildings but of an entity at once material and spiritual, governed according to its own laws, its boundaries limited by strict rules and consecrated by foundation rites.[2] It is well known that it was the Etruscans who, from scattered villages on the hills around Rome made a true city, dominated by its Capitol above a forum that had already been drained. In all the places governed by them, where the natural tendency of the indigenous tribes was to spread out in rural districts scattered here and there with farms and hamlets, they concentrated in the cities the reserves of their strength, the organs of their governments and the ceremonies of their religion.

FOUNDATION RITES

No one in antiquity denies them this merit, and the finest praise one could give to a city was that it had been founded *Etrusco ritu*, according to the Etruscan rite. It was known that they possessed 'ritual books' in which was prescribed 'by what rite towns are founded, altars and temples consecrated; what made walls inviolable and gates permissible'.[3]

These foundation rites were carried on by the Romans who introduced them into all their colonies in the peninsula and in their provinces. After having consulted the omens, the augurer would orient the future city by taking the direction of the sun with the help of an instrument called a *groma*, thus establishing the position, from east to west, of the *decumanus*, and, from north to south, of the *cardo*. Then would begin the ceremonies of *limitatio*, whose picturesque details caught the attention of the ancients more than anything. The founder, his head covered with a part of his toga, would cut the primal furrow with a bronze ploughshare harnessed to a bull and a heifer; he was careful to cast the soil of this boundary furrow (*sulcus primigenius*) inwards, and when he arrived at where the gates (*porta*) would stand, he would lift and carry (*portare*) his plough. While doing this he was not only surrounding the city with a symbolic moat and walls, but also consecrating a space called the *pomerium* in which it was forbidden to build within and plough without.[4]

Inside this perimeter, a system of streets, parallel to the decuman and cardinal ways and laid out like them by means of a cord, separated the city into *insulae*, all of regular shape and size, whose appearance was that of a large chequerboard. The width of the principal streets, of the secondary streets and of the *insulae* was always in the same proportions.

Finally the Roman etruscologists affirmed that the founders of Etruscan towns did not consider as regular or *justae* those towns which had not three gates, three streets and three temples consecrated to Jupiter, Juno and Minerva.[5]

Such was the theory of the *ritus Etruscus*: taken literally, it invites us to imagine the most ancient Etruscan cities as being like those camps and colonies of the Empire at the height of its power, and which, in North Africa among other places, display an almost perfect quartering of the ground; the Tarquinii of Tarchon and the Agylla of Mezentius are said to have been, eight centuries beforehand, like Lambaesis and Timgad extending their chequered carpet down a gentle slope. No one will believe this: first of all because the shape of the ground in Etruria – as in Numidia – for the most part was not suited to the strict application of foundation principles, and because Nature often rebelled against this intransigent wish to dominate it in this rational way. 'If the ground allows of it,' wrote a Roman geometrist, 'we should follow out the calculations; if not, we should depart from them as little as possible.'[6] Very great departures had to be made in order to perch Orvieto on its pedestal surrounded by abysses, to plant Volterra on the rolling hills which are surmounted by its vertiginous pyramid. It needs the sharp eyes of the archaeologist to detect in the irregular contour of Arezzo, fan-shaped, or of Perugia, star-shaped, the design of an *urbs justa*.

We must add here that recent studies have rightly contested the claim that the Etruscans were the first to invent and the original conceivers of the marvels of antique town-planning. The little we know of the most ancient cities makes it difficult for us to see a symmetrical plan related to the two axes. Vetulonia, which disappeared at the beginning of the sixth century, is on the contrary characterized by the irregularity and the sinuosity of her streets which cross in various ways but never at right angles.[7] It is possible that Veii or Sovana presented an attempt at axial arrangement which went back to their foundation.[8] But the true orthogonal system and the chequerboard plan which is its logical development did not appear until fairly late, in the sixth to fifth centuries, and simultaneously throughout the whole of the Mediterranean basin, under the influence of the needs and the progress of Greek colonization, from Miletus to Agrigentum and Metapontum. The discovery is traditionally attributed to the architect Hippodamus of Miletus, who lived in the first half of the fifth century, and who must simply have codified and brought to their full expression the tendencies of the preceding generations.[9] All the same in this perspective the originality of the Etruscans seems less brilliant, though it was no small distinction to be the ones who introduced into Italy, giving it their own personal accent, Greek civilization.

The history of the language presents a confirmation and a symbol of this derivation in urban matters: the word for the apparatus used by the Roman surveyor, *groma*, is a borrowing from the Greek *gnômôn* or *gnôma*, but reveals a dissimilation of the nasal (gn/gr) which conforms to the rules of Etruscan phonetics and indicates the necessary intermediary.[10] Moreover the bonds which linked the Etruscans to Ionia are so numerous and so obvious that one seizes with satisfaction the opportunity to increase their debt towards the country of Hippodamus of Miletus.

But then new Etruscan foundations immediately adopted the type of plan given by Greek colonies. The Etruscans, too, from the beginning of the fifth century,[11] had colonies which they implanted like bridge-heads at the entrance to their Cisalpine and Campanian provinces, Marzabotto and Capua. Here it so happened that the configuration of the ground lent itself more easily to the demands of the rite known henceforward as Etruscan: in the former, on a terrace above the Reno near where it flows into Aemilia; in the latter, on the plain which, according to a mistaken etymology (but a classic one) had given its name to Capua, *a campo dicta*.[12] The fact is that Capua would always inspire in the Romans an admiration mixed with envy because of its privileged situation which allowed it to expand freely, on wide, flat ground, the intelligible harmony of its town-planning. Whereas their own city, 'placed', as Cicero says, 'in a setting of mountains and valleys, as though suspended in the air with its many-storeyed houses, divided by mediocre roads and very narrow little streets',[13] irremediably evoked the ancient cities of Etruria proper before the Hippodamian reform.

MARZABOTTO

The continuity of life at Capua for twenty-five hundred years has tended a little to efface or confuse its features. Those of Marzabotto, which an invasion by the Gauls destroyed in the fourth century, have been brought to light, during diggings made in the course of the last century and resumed after the war, with a clarity that has caused people to speak of an Etruscan Pompeii.[14]

Let us ignore, to the north-west, the acropolis of Misanello, which was the town's sacred centre: there the basements of five religious edifices, temples and altars have been found. At the foot of the Capitol, on the plateau of Misano, the town proper extended: a regular gridiron of streets separating rectangular blocks of houses formed a site of about one hundred hectares, half of which has long since crumbled away into the river. The two great axes have survived, very exactly orientated: they were two wide roads measuring fifteen metres across (a figure never equalled elsewhere) and divided into three parts, a roadway between two pavements of three metres each; they even had channels for carrying away rain-water such as were never seen in later Roman towns, like Ostia or Pompeii. The *decumanus maximus* was doubled, in the south, by other *decumani* which were not so wide (twelve metres) and which were linked by streets five metres wide running parallel to the *cardo*. This gridiron pattern restricted the spread of the blocks of houses of which only remain rough foundations of dry stones and whose walls must have been made of crude bricks.

The length of these *insulae* was unvarying, 165 metres, and their width, thirty-five, forty and sixty-eight metres. On them there were grouped without order round often very vast court-yards, more like farmyards or the yards of works than the *atrium* of the Roman house, small living-rooms, shops, workshops: heaps of iron slag examined in 1952 have shown the existence of a metallurgical laboratory. All this was decidedly much more modest than the setting – those big, well-designed arteries, those broad pavements, those hydraulic installations – had led us to expect. It may be that the founders of Marzabotto, in the creative intoxication of colonization, were too ambitious, and that the mediocrity of the place's resources and of its destiny betrayed the hopes that were placed in it: it left no trace on history, and we do not know even what it was called in ancient times – perhaps Misa. Doubtless it was never scarcely more than a small town. Nevertheless its tombs contained rich funerary furniture, which the 1944 bombardments partially destroyed, golden ornaments and Attic vases. The last diggings brought to light a very fine little head of an ephebe in Parian marble. At Marzabotto one was not very far – some eighty kilometres at the most – from the great Graeco-Etruscan city of Spina through which flowed Greek ceramics and all the refinements of Hellenism.

SPINA

In the archaeological research going on today, Spina[15] is very much at the forefront. It still lies submerged by water but its fascinating enigma begins to be unfolded. In the fifth century it had been the greatest port of the Adriatic, a sort of Venice built three kilometres from the open sea among the lagoons formed by one of the mouths of the Po, where Comacchio now stands. It was a cosmopolitan town where the indigenous Veneti, the new masters the Etruscans and the Greek merchants rubbed shoulders; the latter claimed they had settled there after Diomedes, the Homeric son of Tydeus, and their wealth and piety were proclaimed in a monument erected in their name at Delphi. It was a centre of international trade, where the Athenian fleet perhaps came to seek the amber of the Baltic and the tin of the Cassiterides, but above all the wheat that the plain of the Po, energetically irrigated and canalized by Etruscan engineers, produced in abundance. In exchange, Spina imported along with the products of the Orient the most beautiful Attic vases: these, unearthed in the course of thirty years of excavation in the mud of its necropolises, are today the pride of the museum of Ferrara. Many more have been found at Bologna and Marzabotto. Still others a little farther north, on the site of Atria, twin sister of Spina, that gave her name to the Adriatic and the exploration of which is also promised for the future.[16]

Special economic circumstances, which have just been made apparent with singular force, had built up the fortunes of Spina and Atria: in 474 the defeat inflicted at Cumae by the Syracusan navy marked the decadence of the Etruscan fleet and its expulsion from the Tyrrhenian Sea. This is what gave immediate importance to the Adriatic route, which enabled the Athenians to renew and intensify their relations with the Etruscans. It has been proved, from the dates on Attic vases discovered at Spina and also at Atria, Bologna and Marzabotto that the import figure rose swiftly after 470: sixty-three for the last quarter of the sixth century, 110 for the first quarter of the fifth century, but 309 for the second quarter.[17]

Twelve hundred tombs had been excavated before the war: today more than three thousand are known. Agrarian reform, drainage and improvement projects have offered archaeologists fresh opportunities; on the sand-banks which rose from the water further necropolises have been recognized; sunk in the slime, metal caissons have brought up a vast harvest of voluted bowls and panathenaic amphorae. This provoked some clandestine activity among the eel-fishers of Comacchio, but appropriate steps were promptly taken to halt the flow abroad of their miraculous draughts. After finding the city of the dead it remained to find the city of the living.

This has been accomplished since October 1956. A study of aerial photographs revealed what the eye could not distinguish – the outline of a city buried in the sands. A city of lagoons, where, as at Venice, traffic was confined to waterways: a Grand Canal thirty metres wide crossed it from one end to another in a straight line: this was the River Po whose course had been canalized and here was the port of Spina: it was cut at equal intervals by minor canals which, being today covered with taller grass, appear darker from the air, and which bounded the geometrical *insulae*. Helped by photography, the digger's pick at once began to look for remains of the edifices swallowed up by the marshes and unearthed lines of piles on which, as was to be expected, lay the buildings' foundations. A lacustrine city, Spina, in its own way obeyed the laws of the Etruscan rite, unless, as has recently been suggested, it was through Spina that the Hippodamian plans were imposed on Marzabotto and spread throughout the Etruscan world.[18]

The plan of Capua, the ruins of Marzabotto, the aerial photographs of Spina afford us only an illusory image of what the ancient metropolises of Etruria proper must have been. Quite different was the appearance of Tarquinii when Tanaquil left the palace of her fathers, or of precipitous Volsinii when the princes of all the nation climbed its steep flanks on the occasion of the concourse of the twelve peoples. The *urbs justa* was originally only a forbidden ideal about which one dreamed as one did about the perfections of the Greek world and which in any case was only partially realizable if a tyrant, Porsenna at Chiusi and perhaps already Tarquinius Superbus at Rome, invested as they were with vast edilitarian powers, decided one fine day to thrust dead-straight avenues through the archaic labyrinth of streets. We shall find later on in the cemeteries themselves, at Caere, from the beginning of the fifth century, at a time when the Greek vases are entering the country in large numbers, unexpected alignments of façades on small squares symmetrical in shape which certainly reflected what was happening at the same time in the city of the living.

Of the latter, we know still very little in general, despite the determined efforts of archaeologists to bring more to light. Since before the war P. Romanelli had explored, not just the tombs, but also the city of Tarquinii;[19] since the war the diggings carried out by the École Française at Bolsena, led by Raymond Bloch, have laid bare for us the city of Volsinii.[20] The surrounding walls have been excavated, the acropolises located, and fruitful soundings have been made in the interior; at Tarquinii there has been brought to light the temple known as the Ara della Regina, with a magnificent group of horses in terracotta; at Volsinii, the temple of the goddess Nortia has emerged. Yet despite all these fine results, the greater part of the two cities – their streets, their squares and their houses are still hidden from us, buried under vineyards and olive groves whose expropriation could not be countenanced; perhaps they will always be hidden from us in the higher parts where the action of running water over the centuries has carried away all surface works.

So it was with joy that we greeted in 1955 the news that the urban site of Vulci, whose tombs, ever since the days of Lucien Bonaparte, had enriched all the museums of Europe, was to be the object of a complete excavation under the direction of R. Bartoccini, superintendent of antiquities in meridional Etruria.[21]

This first of all required a meticulous preliminary investigation in which the most modern technical resources were employed: topographic studies, aerial photographs, geochemical prospecting and electrical and phonic investigations carried out in accordance with the methods perfected by the engineer Lerici, so that the desolate plateau on the banks of the Fiora on which the Etruscan habitat stood and where no trace of former edifices is visible today was able to be converted into a sort of instructional diagram permitting the archaeologists to work with great precision. The desire to avoid costly and futile exploratory work and to get in before the bulldozers of modern improvement schemes and the raids of clandestine diggers is here combined with a determination not to allow any indication contributing to the resuscitation of Vulci's past to escape.

THE FORTIFICATIONS

Meanwhile we have to content ourselves with what we can learn, for example, from the surrounding walls – those powerful fortifications made of enormous blocks, more or less roughly squared and uncemented which formerly were attributed to the fabulous days of the Pelasgians and the Cyclops.[22] In reality the Etruscan cities, naturally protected by their escarpmented position, had long done without fortifications. It was the threat of invasions by the Gauls, in the sixth and fifth centuries, which made them put up defensive walls. What particularly interests us here is the great extent of the fortifications: about ten kilometres of them at Tarquinii, nine at Volterra, six or seven at Volsinii. At Volsinii, the perimeter of the city embraces four hills. At Volterra, the ramparts, roughly rectilinear on the south front, send out to the north, right into the country, far-reaching extensions intended to enclose, with thoughts of a siege in mind, all the resources of the area. It becomes more and more apparent that these immense urban areas – 150 hectares for Caere, 135 for Tarquinii – were not built over altogether, but comprised gardens, pasture land for beasts and undefined territories. At Capua itself, all the eastern half of the city, though enclosed within the walls, is empty of all trace of building.

PREDOMINANCE OF PRIVATE DWELLINGS

A sentence from the Posidonius-Diodorus account provides us with a detail about the character of the Etruscan home. 'Among them, not only the slaves but also the majority of the freed men have all kinds of private dwellings.' At first this seems rather surprising: one might think it was some kind of disgrace which, instead of striking at the slaves only, affected even freed men. Now it is a question of what seems to us a very precious privilege: the enjoyment of individual homes.

In fact, the sequence of ideas is more complicated. In what

went before, the author had given examples of the luxury of Etruscan life, mentioned sumptuous repasts, embroidered carpets, silver plate, the number, beauty and splendid robes of the slaves: costumes, he said, which were far above the wearers' station. Here he brings in 'they have separate dwellings'. This is not a punishment, far from it: it is a fresh sign of magnificence or, if one wishes, of the indolence and softness of their masters. In making this remark, Posidonius is thinking of the usual condition of slaves, not only of those who, undergoing punishment, with their feet shackled, were packed into the *ergastula*, but also in general of the slaves of town and country who, one conjectures, despite the lack of information in the texts, occupied common apartments in the *villa urbana* or *rustica*. This is what has been noticed in rural areas round Pompeii, where they were accommodated near the stables in lines of cells.[23] Only it was not a question of the same slaves here. We have seen above that under this generic term the Etruscans understood a lower class whose more advanced or more favoured elements, freed men or clients, enjoyed a fairly liberal way of life.

Diodorus, having noted this privilege granted to the Etruscan 'slaves', abridging Posidonius, awkwardly perhaps, adds that this privilege is extended also to freed men. He would be more readily understood if he had said, 'Besides the private dwellings are also intended for freed men'. Only the first part of his sentence fits in with his description of the Etruscan *tryphè*. But even as he considers this kind of habitation it inspires him at once with another idea, to wit, that it is common among the non-servile population. As he thought this was worth mentioning, it is evident that Etruria in this respect was distinguished from the Roman world: it remained faithful to the idea of *domus*; it remained rebellious to the principle, already triumphant in the capital, of the *insula*.

M. Carcopino, in some fine pages in his *Daily Life in Ancient Rome*,[24] has described the creation of those tenement houses which, at the end of the Republic, became more and more common, accommodating a ceaselessly growing population and imposing on the city development 'in a vertical direction'. He recalls that 'already in the third century BC *insulae* of three storeys had become so numerous that no one thought them unusual at all'. There are many instructive texts which recount, in 218, the extraordinary tale of a bull which climbed to the third storey of one of the skyscrapers in the Forum Boarium, which was the cattle-market, and, confused by the spectators' cries, jumped into space; in 153, we read of the home found in Rome by an Egyptian king in exile, Ptolmy Philometor, at the house of the painter Demetrios who gave him the use of his garret on the top floor because the rents were so high; in 99, the case which cost T. Claudius Centumalus a house he possessed on Mt. Caelius and which he had to pull down because it was preventing the augurs from making their prognostications from the top of the Capitol. 'The Rome of Cicero,' according to the orator, 'would appear to be suspended in the air on the tiers of tenements.' One knows that the troubles of M. Caelius, Cicero's young friend, came from his having rented a lodging in the house of the tribune P. Clodius which from the landing or the garden made him a neighbour of Clodia, the beautiful Lesbia of Catullus. But at the gates of Rome the port of Ostia was soon, in its industrial centres, to have large blocks of towering tenements. Rome at that time was an example of overcrowding. In the light of this concentration of living quarters, Posidonius' remark reveals that in Etruria people were clinging to more dispersed modes of life: one *domus* to each person or to each family. But perhaps this was just a fleeting impression hastily noted by the traveller. It might in a certain measure be contradicted by what we learn from the chamber tombs which, from the end of the fifth century, no longer shelter the remains of one couple but are opened to accommodate more and more populous *familiae*, as well as from what is suggested by the *columbaria* of Sovana, Bieda and Veii with their two hundred or so *loculi*:[25] these seem to indicate human hives rather ill-adapted for individual privacy. But let us retain for the moment as an indication of a special feature – the one becoming archaic – the image of the physiognomy of an Etruscan city with its private houses, its individual dwellings, which naturally took up a good deal of space within the fortifications.

THE POPULATION OF THE CITIES

The extent of the urban perimeter is no less important and poses the problem of the numbers of the population. Here the historians, we must admit, have very little to go on. They do not possess those precious details which Beloch used as the basis of his *Bevölkerungsgeschichte Italiens* in the Middle Ages and in modern times:[26] recruitment lists in which Pisa and Siena after the end of the twelfth century inscribed the names of men who were of an age to carry arms; lists of households; lists of *bocche che mangiano pan* (mouths that eat bread); parish registers and so on. Thanks to these documents we know that Florence, just before she was decimated by the Black Death in 1348, had fifty-one thousand inhabitants, but that Corneto, formerly Tarquinii, had in 1503 only 6,810, Orvieto 9,190, Soriano (Sovana) 1,140.

One can only make conjectures about the days of antiquity. About thirty years ago, B. Nogara proposed that the figure for the population of Caere, on the basis of its area of one hundred and fifty hectares, should be fixed at twenty-five thousand.[27] And by analogy he attributed to Tarquinii, Volterra, Populonia, Veii, Chiusi, Perugia at the time of their prosperity an approximately equal number of inhabitants. The etruscologists of today tend to make this figure lower. At the recent Ciba Foundation conference, certain scholars refused to accept the idea that an Etruscan town could have contained twenty or thirty thousand inhabitants.[26] Yet they acknowledge that the demographic aspect of sixth-century Etruria could not have been very different from that presented in the Middle Ages, when new capitals like Florence with an urban population of fifty-one thousand inhabitants had replaced the Etruscan metropolises. 'Let's say five thousand,' suggested one. 'I'd go as far as ten thousand,' replied another. 'I cannot believe that a city like Tarquinii did not have more than five thousand inhabitants,' J. B. Ward Perkins quite rightly protested. Indeed these contradictory estimates and this haphazard bartering of round figures are not, perhaps, the last word in this branch of Etruscan research. G. Foti observed that we might attempt to estimate the population of an Etruscan town by studying the evidence of its cemeteries, but that such an approach had not been made.

Here is how we might proceed in such a case. Naturally we could not aim at absolute precision. The necropolises of Caere extended over four hundred hectares,[28] and had been used continuously from the beginning of the seventh century to the middle of the first. One of them in particular, the Banditaccia, has been the object since 1911 of systematic diggings whose definitive findings began to be published in 1955 by the Accademia dei Lincei in the *Monumenti Antichi*.[28] Here we find detailed descriptions and very clear plans.

Let us take, in zone A called the Recinto (enclosure), the sector E called the Tumulus della Quercia because of an oak that had grown over one of the tombs:[29] the northern part of this sector constitutes a rectangle of 74 by 47 metres or 34·78 ares, which has been almost completely explored. Here we find a huddle of one hundred and seventy tombs of all kinds and periods, tumulus tombs, chamber tombs, grave tombs, and even two or three incinerary tombs. Some are filled with the most lovely Corinthian or Attic vases, others contain Arezzo ceramics, others bucchero ware, others rough terracotta ware. Altogether we can reckon 354 depositions, which gives a figure of 8·8 per are. A second rectangle of 40 by 42 metres or 16·80 ares, in the neighbouring D sector, called the Tumuli *della Cornice*,[30] gives us 184 depositions or 9·1 per are. Taking into account the 'blanks' in the other sectors, it looks as if they would produce equivalent results. Consequently, if we suppose, as aerial photography leads us to, that the four hundred hectares of the Caere necropolises were just as well filled everywhere, we are brought to the conclusion that in the course of the six and a half centuries (700–50 BC) in which they had been used some four hundred thousand persons had died in the city.

Now we recall that life-expectancy at birth, according to the calculations we presented above, was a little more than forty years (40·88).[31] Probably Caere was not so densely populated in the second century as it had been at the height of its prosperity. We cannot assume that its population had been constant. But with this reservation we can agree that the six hundred and fifty years of its history must have renewed sixteen times (15·90 times) these periods of normal life-expectancy. Which means that the number of inhabitants in Caere at any given time must have risen to four hundred thousand divided by 15·90, or 25, 157. This is the lowest figure, for the 184 and 354 depositions in our rectangles from the sectors D and E, the four hundred hectares containing the necropolises of Caere, are low figures, and we do not forget that Caere, in the course of the centuries, gradually lost its population. But all we have attempted to do is to establish a scale, and in this perspective the result we have arrived at, and which agrees exactly with the suppositions of Bartolomeo Nogara, twenty-five thousand inhabitants, may serve to give us a fairly precise view of the situation.

II

WHAT THE TOMBS OF THE DEAD TELL US ABOUT THE ABODES OF THE LIVING

Despite the praiseworthy efforts of contemporary archaeology to discover the secrets of the Etruscan city's appearance from the cities of the living, we must again descend to the infernal regions of the necropolises which are better able to provide us with more precise details. And probably the best-known burial-ground is that of Tarquinii, because of the frescoes which make it the art museum of Etruscan painting. But no less moving in the grandiose severity of their naked stone, and even more instructive for the solution of the problem which occupies our attention, are the burial-grounds of Caere, with their rows of tumuli here and there along the sepulchral road, and, below, tombs whose beauty often is confined simply to their architecture.

We have already had an opportunity to visit one of them, the Tomb of the Grecian Vases,[32] and to discover in it unexpected information about the woman's place in Etruscan society. And in preceding pages we have pointed out the riches of the recent publication of excavation results between 1911 and 1933.[33] Moreover, considerably enlarging the domain explored, the aerial photographs of J. Bradford have just revealed, deep under the vegetation, the outlines of more than a thousand unknown tumuli which we see like innumerable air-bubbles on the surface of his pictures, showing even the entry to the tomb and, here and there, traces of streets and squares that led to them.[34]

The necropolises of Caere, from the seventh century onwards, must have spread out all round the city, principally on two elevated sites, the Banditaccia and Mount Abetone which extend parallel to the city in the north-west and the south-east, beyond

The engraving on this mirror case shows one of the main Etruscan gods, Tinia, who corresponds to the Greek god Zeus

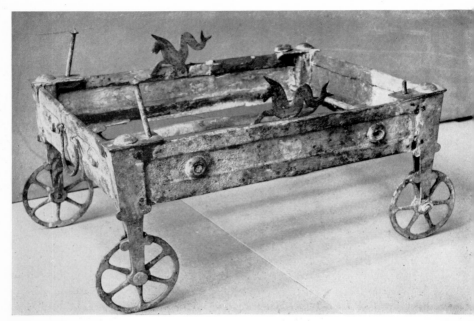

2 A bronze brazier, 11¾ ins. high, from Chiusi. Sixth century BC

3 A household colander made of bronze. On the handle is a figure of Acheloös. Length 10½ ins. 520 BC

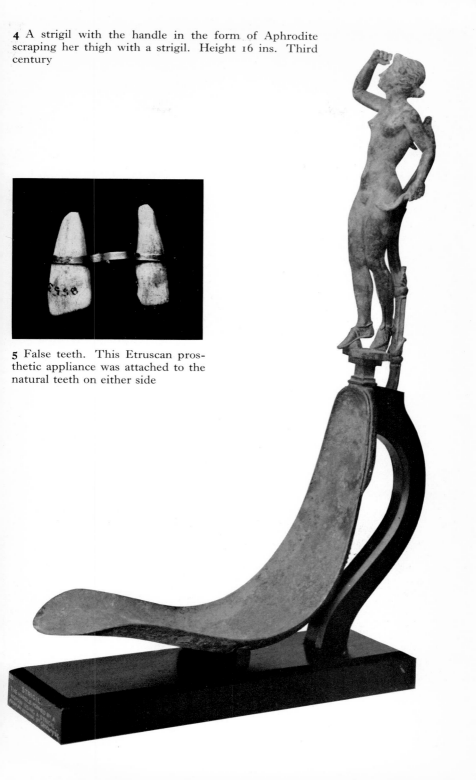

4 A strigil with the handle in the form of Aphrodite scraping her thigh with a strigil. Height 16 ins. Third century

5 False teeth. This Etruscan prosthetic appliance was attached to the natural teeth on either side

6 Fourth-century Etruscan coins

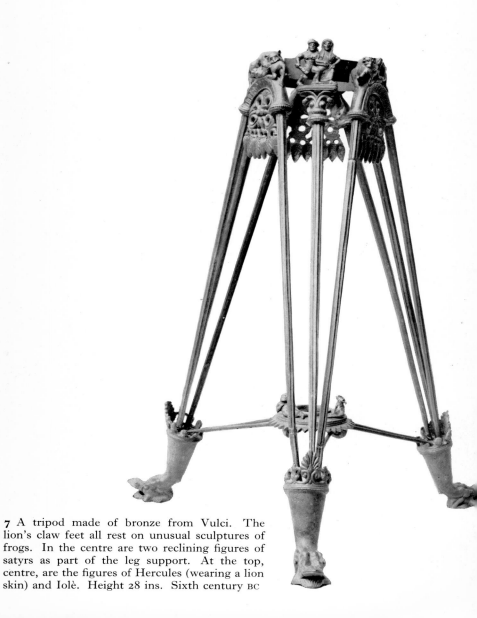

7 A tripod made of bronze from Vulci. The
lion's claw feet all rest on unusual sculptures of
frogs. In the centre are two reclining figures of
satyrs as part of the leg support. At the top,
centre, are the figures of Hercules (wearing a lion
skin) and Iolè. Height 28 ins. Sixth century BC

8 A stone seat now in the Galleria Corsini, Rome

9 A bronze
mirror stand with
the figure of
Aphrodite from
Naples. Early
fifth century

10 A wall-painting from the Tomb of Hunting and Fishing. The boat is of the small type used for fishing and has a 'lucky eye' in front of it. The painting is a most unusual funerary subject. 520–510 BC

11 A sculptured relief of Ulysses and the Sirens in alabaster from the front of an urn used for cremation burial. The relief, which was painted, shows a larger type of sea-going vessel. Ulysses is being tied to the mast by the sailors. The ship has a ram's head figurehead, is steered by a paddle and rowed by ten oars which emerge through five leathers on each side. The sirens from left to right are playing a lyre, Pan's pipes and the double flute. From Volterra. Second century BC

12 A chariot and driver with three horses riding over the body of a man. This is the foot of a cista from Palestrina. About fifth century

13 Heracles subduing the horses of Diomede. This small bronze statue from the lid of a cista from Palestrina shows the horses wearing collars with bullae. Heracles is wearing a lion skin over his head, which is tied in front, continues down his back as a ridge of plaited hair. Height 6⅜ ins. Tenth to third centuries BC

14 A bronze ceremonial chariot from Monteleone. 550–540 BC

15 A small bronze statue of Demeter in a rustic cart. From Amelia.
About fifth century

16 A panel from the Tomb of the Triclinium. The youth, playing the double pipes, has short, curly hair then in fashion, and a short transparent Chlamys. The mural, of very high quality, was probably worked from sketches as there are no incised lines and a great sense of cohesion compared to similar works. 470 BC

17 A terracotta figure of an actor. The figure probably represents a parasite. He is holding a small covered pot in his right hand and a ham at his side. The figure is wearing a mask and a short chitôn with the himation over the left shoulder. The hands, feet and face are painted red and traces of white slip can also be seen on the terracotta

18 This painting from the Tomb of the Seven Chimneys at Orvieto shows the typical horn instruments and dress of the fourth century

19 A copy of the wall painting in the Tomb of the Monkeys at Chiusi showing wrestling and riding at funerary games. The severe style represents the period of political and cultural prosperity that this interior Etruscan city was enjoying in the fifth century

20 A bronze statue of Mars showing the type of tunic and cuirass worn in the third century. The figure is holding in its left hand a shield with a central handle only and a broken sword and the right hand has held a spear. The helmet has cheek-pieces turned-up and a high hair crest reaching to the waist. The chitôn is short and has an elaborate cuirass with overlapping plates and a double row of flaps over the hips. The arms and shield were cast separately and added later. Height $12\frac{5}{8}$ ins.

21 A plate with the design of an archer. The archer carries a bow and quiver at his side and is blowing a trumpet through a phorbeia. From Vulci. Late style. Diameter $7\frac{1}{2}$ ins. Sixth century

22 This bronze statue of a warrior has elements of the primitive Etruscan art. Height 11⅛ ins.

23 This detail from a lid of an urn shows four female archers on horseback using bows. Two of the archers have exceptionally large crests in the shape of swans. 480 BC

Costume and Jewellery

24 The man on the left is wearing the vestment of an Etruscan priest and is in the act of welcoming a man carrying a sceptre or military emblem. The woman on the right is carrying a lance and wreath. This and **25** and **26** are paintings done on white slabs. Sixth century

25 & 26 These two paintings of three women very clearly show the costume of the period. **24, 25** and **26** are rare survivals of nonfunerary Etruscan painting. All three are painted in marvellous shades of deep purple-brown, black and yellowochre

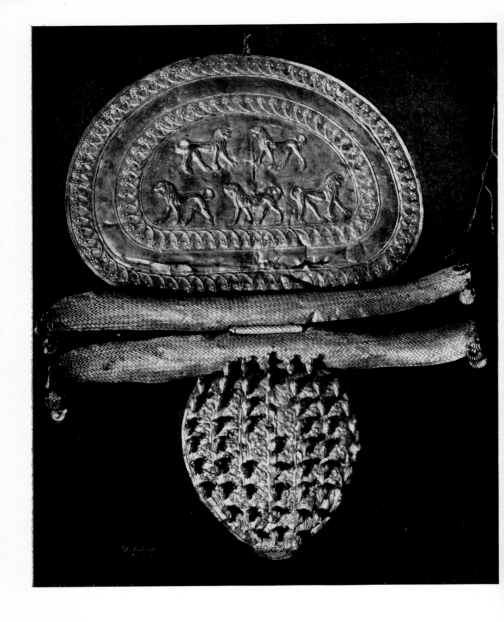

27 This gold fibula and pendaglio is a particularly fine example of Etruscan jeweller's craft. It was found in the Regolini-Galassi Tomb at Cerveteri. Seventh century

8 A pair of gold votive bracelets from a tomb at Praeneste. Seventh century

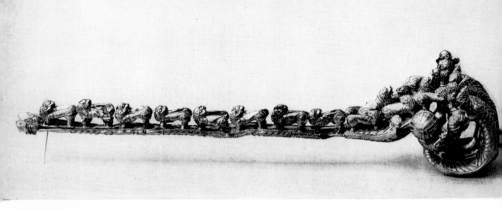

29 A gold fibula from Vulci. Two rows
carefully worked lions face four sphinxe

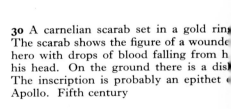

30 A carnelian scarab set in a gold rin
The scarab shows the figure of a wounde
hero with drops of blood falling from h
his head. On the ground there is a dis
The inscription is probably an epithet
Apollo. Fifth century

31 A large, beautifully worked gold rin
with a sard centre. Fifth century

32 A bronze sistula or bucket from Offida, Picenum. Just below the handle there is a
relief of a winged goddess and above the foot there is Heracles strangling the Nemean
lion. Late fifth or fourth centuries.

33 The Tomb of the Reliefs. This large family tomb is of special interest because common household tools and personal possessions, such as spades, spoons, game, bed linen, have been carved in realistic detail

34 A funerary couch from Caere now in the Louvre. Late sixth century

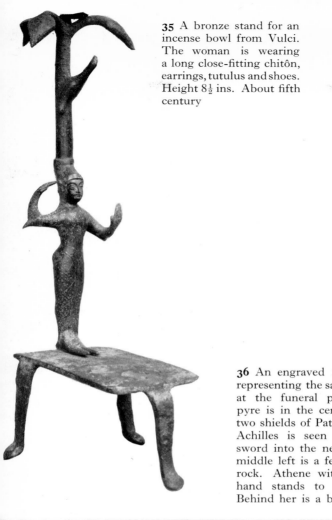

35 A bronze stand for an incense bowl from Vulci. The woman is wearing a long close-fitting chitôn, earrings, tutulus and shoes. Height 8½ ins. About fifth century

36 An engraved frieze on a bronze cista representing the sacrifice of Trajon captives at the funeral pyre of Patroclus. The pyre is in the centre and the cuirass and two shields of Patroclus are placed on top. Achilles is seen on the left plunging a sword into the neck of a captive. In the middle left is a female deity leaning on a rock. Athene with a spear in her right hand stands to the left of the deity. Behind her is a beautifully drawn owl

37 This banqueting scene from the Tomb of the Leopards has the usual *graffito* preparation. The style and costumes show the influence of the Greeks but the brilliant colour and movement are more Etruscan. The men have black hair and reddish faces and the women fair hair and white faces. 480–470 BC

38 A limestone sepulchral chest from Chiusi. The side shown depicts the banquet scenes from the funeral and includes many details: coverlets, pillows, ducks picking up crumbs from under the table. To the left a boy is serving fruit; to the right a boy is playing the flute. There are still remains of the red paint that must have covered the relief. Height 45 ins. Late sixth century

the ravine formed by two torrents, the Manganello and the Mola. However, at the other two extremities, and especially to the south-west in the angle formed by the confluence of these two rivers, more ancient cemeteries, in which were crowded grave tombs and shaft tombs provided with very poor funerary furnishings go back to the pre-Etruscan phase in the history of the site. This necropolis of the Sorbo is particularly important because it allows us to grasp, as at Tarquinii and Volsinii, the uninterrupted continuity that, ever since the iron age, united the Villanovan and the Etruscan civilizations. We must remember that it was on the Sorbo, and not in the Banditaccia or the Abetone that was discovered, in 1836, the Regolini-Galassi tomb whose golden ornaments, silver plate and ivory plaques had been placed next to the mysterious figure of Larthia. Now this tomb is situated in immediate proximity to the city, at the foot of its cliff, and dominates the Villanovan cemetery to the south like a lord surveying his vassals.

But after this period the Etruscan tombs invaded the hills to the north-west and the south-east, and it was there, on the Banditaccia in particular, that one can best follow their gradual evolution. Aerial photography, as we have said, shows that round the tumuli of larger size there are hundreds of tiny blisters representing smaller tumuli of a diameter ranging from ten to fifteen metres. This was the size of the most ancient (*tumuletti arcaici*), and it remained the normal size until the end of the fifth century, though meanwhile it had in certain cases increased to thirty, forty and even fifty metres. This was because, unlike the *tumuletti arcaici*, these greater tumuli covered several tombs: they had been built over precious tumuli which in all probability belonged to members of the same family; the descendants, when constructing their own tomb, wanted to have their ancestors sheltered under the same hemispherical mound of earth and grass.

THE EXPLORATION OF A TUMULUS

One sees this clearly when one considers the large tumulus II, whose base has a diameter of forty metres.[35] It contains four distinct tombs, the most recent being without doubt the tomb called after the Grecian vases, more than one hundred and fifty in number, and often very fine, of Attic ceramics decorated in the severe style with black and red figures, which were scattered on the ground and the seats. They testify to the cultural refinement of the occupants, particularly the women, and also allow us to date this tomb from the end of the sixth century. Moreover one notices that the entrance passage's position corresponds to a radius of the tumulus' circle, showing a passion for symmetry which is related to the taste evidenced by those Hellenized Etruscans we have spoken of previously: without doubt it was they who had the great tumulus II built, comprising three former tombs.

Let us visit these in turn. As we go along we shall be witnessing the development of the chamber tomb from the seventh to the fifth century, a development which naturally obeyed its own laws of logic but which was also constantly influenced by the houses of the living. As soon as the Etruscan tomb ceased to be just an oblong grave dug in the rock, it grew to the dimensions of an actual room provided with annexes, and which one reached, often after a stairway, by means of a passage built on a gentle slope (Greek *dromos*). But in order to solve the roofing problem the interior imitated a real two-sloped roof with exposed ridge-beam (*columen*),[36] One descends into it along a wide *dromos* which has at its end two alcoves to right and left; it leads into a trapezoid chamber surrounded by benches, then into another, smaller one. This tomb was dubbed the Tomb *della Capanna* because its two chambers are both surmounted by a sort of arris vault suspended from the relievo representation of a thin beam, and the sides of which extend right down to the ground: it reproduces the thatch roof of archaic houses before the introduction of tiled roofs. Likewise the door at the bottom is a rustic opening with inclined jambs joined at the top by an arch-shaped beam. All this recalls very clearly the primitive huts such as we know them from the cinerary urns made in their image and which are very frequent in the cemeteries of Latium and southern Etruria, and from the traces their foundations left in the rock of the Palatine and at Bolsena.[37]

The funerary furnishings, particularly the cups and plates of that rough ceramic, black and reddish-brown, known as *impasto* ceramic, with the local imitations of Protocorinthian vases,

confirm the dating of this tomb to the middle of the seventh
century. But shall we ever know the meaning of the *grafitto*
engraved on the handle of an amphora, *henphathn*, which Nogara
read as *Heli Phathn*, translating it into Latin as Helia Fatinia,
presuming that it was the owner's name?

We have only to pass to the two next tombs to see how, in
half a century, the plan, proceeding from that primitive outline,
became enriched and regularized. The first tomb[38] has two
names: in its anterior sector, formed from two lateral chambers
which open up at the extremity of the entrance passage, it is
called the Tomb of the Andirons (*degli Alari*), because, among the
abundant kitchen utensils in the left-hand chamber were found
two iron andirons. The back of the tomb, consisting of two big
rectangular chambers linked by a passage, is called the Tomb of
the *Doli*, because of several enormous *impasto* jars attaining a
height of ninety centimetres: they are still in place with the rest
of the furniture – great wine amphorae of local make, Protocorinthian and Corinthian vases – all of which date from around
600.

The chamber on the left of the Tomb of the Andirons had
always escaped attention, and its discovery caused a sensation.
Mengarelli's notes[39] bring to life again the excitement felt by all
when, on April 10, 1910, in the presence of Prince and Princess
Ruspoli, ambassador Titoni and other Roman personalities,
the door was solemnly loosened – a door which had not been
opened since, two and a half thousand years earlier, the remains
of an aristocratic Etruscan lady had been borne across its
threshold.

'When we had lifted away the upper blocks, we saw on the
black, wet ground several objects of gleaming gold and a
quantity of vases and objects arranged in groups together with
little Protocorinthian vases and Egyptian figurines surrounding
a funeral couch of small splinters of decomposed wood, the
wretched remains of the sarcophagus or of the bed on which
the dead woman had been placed. Yet nothing remained of
her skeleton because, as always, the acidity of Caere rock had
destroyed, over the centuries, the bones and all organic matter.
A few small Protocorinthian vases were still hanging on the

walls, suspended from oxydized nails. As we looked more closely, without entering it, at the interior of the tomb with the help of portable lamps, we realized the complexity of the rich furnishings that had been placed there: gold ornaments, little toilet vases for oil and perfumes, *pyxides* imitating wooden coffers for keeping small objects in: all things which could only have been dedicated to a woman for her life beyond the tomb. But together with these objects were indispensable kitchen utensils: andirons and spits, a cauldron with a tripod to support it; finally a whole dinner service, the very one which had been used for the funeral feast in honour of the deceased: jugs, wine amphorae, vases for drawing water or for mixing liquids, drinking cups and dinner-plates. In all one hundred and nine objects.'

And Mengarelli concludes: 'The woman who was buried in this tomb must have been a mother dearly beloved by all her family.'

The tomb, lower down and on the left, known as the Tomb of the Beds and Sarcophagi,[40] is almost contemporaneous with the other, perhaps a little more recent. We only possess, out of funerary furnishings pillaged by antiquity, a late Protocorinthian *olpè* (630–610), with this *grafitto* under the base: *mi L . . . ia Apicus*, the meaning of which, despite mutilation, is clear: 'I belong to Larthia, wife of Apicius.'

But this tomb is interesting to us particularly because of certain details of its architecture. Here again the *dromos* leads to two lateral chambers, then debouches into a principal chamber, 4·30 metres by 3·70 metres, which gives on a smaller chamber of 3·20 metres by 2·70 metres. In these two rooms the roof is two-sloped with a wide median beam; but the two slopes come down at a very gentle incline and rest two metres above the floor on the lateral walls.

Communication between the *dromos* and the lateral chambers, between the *dromos* and the principal chamber and finally between the latter and the farthest chamber is made through two doors with inclined jambs supporting a tympanum entirely filling a curved arch. It is the same arched doorway as the one in the Tomb *della Capanna* but has here become the trapezoidal type of door. But in the third case the door is flanked by two narrow windows surmounted by blind arches. What were these windows used for? The architect simply wanted to give the posterior wall of the main chamber the familiar appearance of the front of a house. A similar arrangement may be seen in the contemporaneous Tomb of the Casetta (or Little House).[41] The rear chamber was bordered, on three of its sides, by benches, but the principal chamber and the entrance chambers were provided, against the walls, with beds and sarcophagi which gave the tomb its name. We have already indicated that the beds contained the remains of men and that the sarcophagi were reserved for women.

Next comes the Tomb of the Grecian Vases, from which we started.[42] The plan at once makes clear that the elongation of the previous tombs had given way to a general disposition of all the chambers in a sort of square whose sides measured about nine metres. The central chamber was considerably widened (8·70 metres) without being made any deeper; consequently the beam of the *columen* is perpendicular to the entry. This widening has caused it to go slightly beyond the right and left limits of the two lateral chambers. But in addition, at the back, not one but three chambers open on it, so that here again the total development in width is almost equal to that of the central room. A similar ground-plan, characteristic of the end of the sixth century, can be found in some of the finest tombs of Caere, the Tomb of the Seats and Shields, the Tomb of the Capitals, and the Tomb of the Cornice.

The posterior chambers were furnished only with benches, but the lateral chambers and the central chamber contained beds: in the latter, on the sides, two feminine sarcophagi with triangular frontons were preceded, near the entrance, by two masculine beds with, at the corners, hollows in which the feet of the actual beds were set. The door jambs of the posterior chambers had been cut away to allow the passage of funerary beds which had been too big to get through.

When we compare it with the one we have described in the Tomb of Beds and Sarcophagi, we can appreciate the fine architectonic décor provided by the wall at the back of the central room. Of the three doors, the one in the middle is often a little higher: it obviously gives on the chamber of the masters. All three are trapezoidal, with their uprights and lintel framed in

projecting beading, originally painted green. But in the Tomb
of the Cornice the little windows with arc-shaped tympana still
survive: one on either side of the central door, and one on each
of the interior flanks of the lateral doors. In the Tomb of
the Seats and Shields[43] and in the Tomb of the Capitals[44]
these windows have become rectangular, and there are only
two: new decorative elements have taken their place. But we
still recognize the façade of a house, giving on a courtyard or a
peristyle.

We shall not repeat what we have said about the particular
cultural refinement, especially of the women, revealed by the
profusion of Grecian vases that gave the name to one of these
tombs. The same refinement is reflected also in the harmonious
arrangement of the palaces of which these fine funerary abodes
were the replicas.

THE ATRIUM

We have until now prudently avoided any other term but 'central
chamber' in speaking of the huge room round which, in the Tombs
of the Grecian Vases, of the Capitals, of the Cornice, etc., the
whole edifice was organized. But why not give it the name of
atrium, which is the one we must employ to describe the large
room or hall at the centre of the Roman house where the crowd
of clients came every morning to greet their patron and ask for
sportulae? Those familiar with Pompeii will have already made
the comparison when reading the above description. The comparison is even plainer when we consider a tomb like the *Tomba
della Ripa*,[45] which is a little more recent, well on into the fifth
century, and which shows, opening on the *atrium* not by a
narrow door but across its entire width, the *tablinum* or salon
of later houses: despite the relative irregularity of the plan,
we cannot fail to recognize in it an anticipation of the house
called Livia's on the Palatine[46] or that of M. Lucretius Fronto
at Pompeii.[47] In the wall at the rear of the *tablinum* everything,
even a false door with arched top, suggests the existence, behind,
of a back exit to the *hortus* or vegetable plot. And this arrangement
persisted in more recent tombs, even in the tombs of the Volumnii
at Perugia[48] and the François at Vulci,[49] tombs which, at the
height of the Roman era, also reflect the architecture of real

houses and help us to realize once again the great debt that Rome owed to Etruscan civilization.

Moreover, the Romans were conscious of this debt; there was a variety of *atrium* which they called *tuscanicum*, 'Tuscan', in honour of the fact, as Varro says,[50] that they 'had begun to imitate the interior courtyards of the Etruscans'. Moreover, among the etymologies they proposed, Varro and his disciple Verrius Flaccus preferred the one which linked the word with Atria in Etruria, for 'it was among the inhabitants of Atria that the model had been copied'.[51] We have already had occasion to mention this city at the mouth of the Po, which, from the middle of the sixth century, must have contributed a great deal to the hellenization of Etruria.[52] In confirmation of this etymology, we note that the word *athre* appears in fact in the inscription on the Mummy of Zagreb, though in a somewhat obscure context.[53]

Nevertheless the definition which the ancients gave of the *atrium* is very much more precise than the one we have contented ourselves with until now; the problem deserves to be studied a little closer.

'The *atrium*,' we read in Festus' compendium,[54] 'is a sort of construction situated in front of the house and containing in the centre a space where the rain, collected from all parts of the roof, pours itself down.'

'In front of the house', *ante aedem*, which means that the *atrium* did not properly speaking form part of it. The heart of the dwelling was the *tablinum*, the master's reception-room where his bed and the chapel of his ancestors were placed. Such at any rate was the feeling which prevailed at the end of the Roman Republic; it is a question debated by archaeologists, whether it had always been so, or whether the subordination of the *atrium* to the *tablinum* was the result of a long evolution. Some imagine that the primitive Roman house, and therefore also the Etruscan house from which it derived, had its true heart in the main body of buildings with one, two or three chambers, such as we have described as existing in the posterior sections of our tombs, and which was originally comprised between the *atrium*, courtyard or vestibule, and the *hortus*, the vegetable garden.[55] Here they see a connexion with the Mycenean house, where the *mégaron* is similarly preceded by an *aulé*. But other scholars – and perhaps they are right – believe that the *atrium* came first, that the house only contained one central room where the fire was kept lighted in the hearth and where, against the wall facing the entrance, the nuptial bed was placed: the alcove wherein it was ensconced is claimed to have become the principal bedroom, transformed thereafter into a ceremonial chamber.[56] In the majority of the tombs we have studied – before the Tomb *della Ripa*, also called *del Tablino* – we are still at the point where the future tablinum is only the master's sleeping-chamber, flanked by those of the children: it has been said that this displays 'the primacy of the parents over the rest of the *familia* which was grouped in the adjoining rooms'.[57] It is not by chance that the rooms which, at the entrance, give on the *dromos*, contain only – for example in the Tomb of the Capitals – instead of ornamented beds, simple benches: these chambers correspond, in dwellings above ground, to the servants' quarters. Ever since the sixth century, consequently, what we have read in Posidonius could be verified, namely, that the *atrium* of the Etruscan houses served to isolate the masters from the noise made by the swarms of servants.

Moreover, among the Romans the *atrium* of necessity admitted of an opening made in the roof (*compluvium*) through which the rain-water poured into a basin placed just underneath (*impluvium*). In reality, here again it is a question of a refinement which was only introduced fairly late: the tombs, faithful mirrors of domestic architecture, offer us no examples of this, while the oldest houses in Pompeii, in their first state, were covered with a roof and had no *compluvium*.[58] The tombs of Caere show no trace of any opening to the sky at the centre of the roof, though all the details of the ridge-beam, rafters, laths, cofferings are rendered with the greatest care. Their *atria*, or their *cavaedia* – one and the same thing – were, to employ the terminology of Vitruvius in his description of the various forms of interior courtyards,[59] of the type known as *testudinatum*, because their roof resembled the *testudo* or carapace of a tortoise. One tomb however at Tarquinii, called the *Mercareccia*[60], and an urn in the form of a house, found at Poggio a Gaiella near Chiusi[61] mark a new stage: they are lit by a rectangular orifice in the place of a *compluvium*. But neither is anterior to the fourth century, and their four-sloped roof, like a truncated pyramid, is inclined towards the outside, making the rain-water run away to the exterior of the house: it is what Vitruvius calls a *cavaedium displuviatum*. The *compluvium-impluvium* system implies on the contrary that the four triangular planes of the roof incline inwards towards the central opening, and the rain-water flows along these convergent slopes. But on this subject we do not possess any archaeological document; we have to turn again to Vitruvius, who distinguishes between the Tuscan *atrium*, the terastyle *atrium* and the Corinthian *atrium*.

'In the first,' he says, 'the beams were placed across the width of the *atrium*, with other transversal beams, and gutters that descended from the corners of the walls to the corners of the framework, the rafters forming the roof's eaves being all inclined towards the *compluvium*.' The essential thing is that the latter was formed by the intersection of four beams set in the walls, and that the whole was suspended from these beams. In order to widen the *atrium*, columns had to be used, four at first (tetrastyle *atrium*) or an even greater number (Corinthian *atrium*) on which the roof rested.

COLUMNS AND PERISTYLES

The name of *cavaedium tuscanicum* had remained attached to this relatively archaic form of *atrium*, whose roof with the *compluvium* was supported only by horizontal beams without the assistance of columns. The expression indicates on the part of the Romans a recognition of their debt and gives the borrowing a fairly ancient date. Under the Empire, Pliny the Younger was to mention with pride the existence in his villa near Ostia of 'an *atrium*, simple but not without elegance' (*atrium frugi nec tamen sordidum*[62]), and in the villa he had had built in Tuscany at Tifernum Tiberium (Città di Castello) – where the spirit of the place had perhaps inspired him to this return to Etruscan traditions – he writes of his '*atrium* of an old-fashioned style' (*atrium ex more veterum*): by this he probably meant a Tuscan *atrium*, without columns, whose bare severity provided a refreshing contrast for his sensibility surfeited with the baroque luxury of marble colonnades.[63] But this does not mean that the Etruscans themselves, abjuring the prestige of Hellenistic colonnades, remained eternally faithful to the formula which they were the first to illustrate. The proof is that when Posidonius wished to speak of the Etruscan *atrium* he used the word *peristôion*, which in Greek is synonymous with 'peristyle'.[64]

Vitruvius[65] defined a Tuscan order, distinct from the Ionic, Doric and Corinthian orders, and comprising a very slender column: the thickness of the shaft was a seventh of the height; but such a column has not been discovered in any monument which has survived to the present day. Here again it was the result of a long evolutionary process, for the Etruscan architects, in the course of several centuries of obscurity, had worked hard. We know this order only in its very first stages: already in the tombs of the sixth century which owe their name to them, columns supported the ceiling of the atrium: there were two of them in the Tomb of the Doric Columns[66] and in the Tomb of the Capitals at Caere;[67] there was one in the tomb at Vignanello in Faliscan territory.[68] These columns, remarkably stocky, rest on a circular base, the shaft being smooth or fluted; they are derived from a very ancient type of Grecian column which took on a surprising development on Etruscan soil: witness the astonishing capitals which, in the tomb of this name, display on two opposed faces a double row of volutes between which is a palm-leaf ornament; the sides of the capital only present vertical sections of the volutes, repeated ten times and packed close together as volumes on a bookshelf. It must be noted that the faces are parallel with the dimensions in depth of the tomb; they decorate a sort of central avenue which, prolonging the *dromos*, leads ceremoniously to the principal chamber at the rear. These capitals have been called Aeolic, and antecedents have been found for them, with a marked oriental flavour, in Assyrian art.

We may form the idea of the sometimes exuberant taste for colonnades that seized the Etruscans when we consider, a little later (fourth–third centuries) the rock tombs hewn in the cliffs of several small towns, perched like eagles' eyries in the region of Tarquinii and Vulci, San Giuliano, Bieda, Norchia, Sovana.[69] Outside they have a portico of two, four or six Doric or Corinthian columns; sometimes the porticoes even have two storeys, the second one recessed. Such must have been, about 200 BC, the loggias of the Etruscan houses overlooking the valley. They also suggest the façade of a temple, but the domestic architecture and the religious architecture are inseparable. These rupestral tombs are entered by a trapezoidal doorway, and it is interesting to note in this the new forms that the Etruscan door took on since the days of the archaic tomb: the frame was really wooden, and the carpenter's chisel took pleasure in carving into volutes the overhanging lintel.[70]

TRACES OF A REGULAR PLAN

But to return to the Banditaccia necropolis. It can still teach us something about the life of the Caere inhabitants: for example, about the streets and squares of their city. The first tombs from what we can tell, were dug haphazardly, without the slightest concern about orientation, without any reference to a concerted plan. The funeral processions slowly, as it were, bashed out their own track when proceeding to the most ancient tombs in the area of the great tumulus II: a track which, despite its windings, was eventually oriented in a vaguely east-west direction like a *decumanus*. But no *cardo* ever crossed it. The city of the dead never looked like those orthogonal cities, an ideal which the Etruscans, as we have seen, dreamed ever since the end of the sixth century of making rebellious nature conform to. And yet it is interesting to see, in certain parts of the diggings and of those areas made familiar to us by aerial photography, the slow emergence of a new tendency towards regularity: constructing small rectangular or triangular spaces, closed-in like those public squares in so many present-day Italian cities; the sort of square that Mengarelli calls the *Piazzetta incassata*, 'the little enclosed place',[71] or those that appear as miniscule black squares on Bradford's photographs; and also, along many streets, fine long lines of identical tombs. The via XIII, called the Street of the Grecian Vases because abundant examples of Attic pottery are still found there, deserves to be considered rather closely in this respect.[72] It is a modern part of the necropolis: the whole was built at a later date, about a generation later than the princely tombs of the Capitals or of the Shields which, under their tumulus, expressed the desire for symmetry and majesty in their great *atrium* which informed the palaces of the second half of the sixth century. We arrive at this date from an analysis of the furnishings, composed for the most part of Attic vases with black figures, but often, among many others in the form of the *lecythus* (tall, slender-necked vases of elegant form), of a very shoddy style: they are recent or late 'black figures' whose production can be dated between 515 and 480. Some 'red figures', for example, in tomb 355, and a cup by Skythes go back to about 520; or, in tomb 343, there is an *oenochoè* or 'wine-pourer' from the beginning of the fifth century. Beside this there were some examples of *bucchero*** and fragments of Etruscan vases qualified as 'late'. Such is the common character of all the tombs of the via XIII: they must have been constructed in the first half of that fifth century, and are all visibly contemporaneous.

The data furnished by pottery can be supplemented by those which can be inferred from the adoption of a new type of funerary monument which was henceforward to have no rival. These were the *a caditoia* tombs, so called because of a sort of 'chimney' which, piercing the roof of the entrance passage, rose vertically to the surface: we hardly know what they were for, unless perhaps, to let in a little daylight, once the slabs that obstructed them had been cleared away. But the main thing to notice is that there is no *atrium*, no more funeral couches. There are one or two chambers surrounded by benches, on which the places for the bodies are marked by rectangles terminated by the semi-circle reserved for the head. They are no longer sepulchres made for one household or family in the restricted sense of that word. The authority of the parents over their children and over the rest of the *familia* is no longer evident in this simple arrangement of chambers and beds. It is quite certain that these unexpected arrangements correspond to innovations which we know nothing of in the religious rites – perhaps a reform with a puritan flavour had taken place? – and in social and political institutions. Let us not forget that the beginning of the fifth century, when these *a caditoia* tombs first appear, as well as those with multiple resting-places, coincides throughout central Italy, and not only in Rome,

---

*This is the name given to an often very fine type of pottery, of a very lively and brilliant black. It was an Etruscan secret, and, ornamented with incisions and reliefs, was from the seventh to the fifth centuries one of their specialities.

with the end of the monarchy and the coming of the Republic; and that Etruscan decadence is about to begin.

Something also changed in the necropolis at Caere. Let us consider the plan. While the left-hand side, that is, west of the street, shows complete disorder in the grouping of the tombs, the right-hand side, to the east, presents on the contrary a perfect alignment of five tombs, one after the other. The first three must certainly have been constructed at the same period, and we cannot help wondering what the relationship was between the various occupants. The fifth, whose dimensions are smaller, has been carefully brought into line with the rest. There are mason's signs on this tomb's blocks and on the door jambs. The steps which separate the third from the fourth, and the fourth from the fifth seem to have had no other purpose than to mark property divisions. Of course we are lost in conjecture when we try to imagine the modalities affecting the sepulchral rights determining certain arrangements, and the comparison with a better-known and more recent necropolis, the Roman one on the Isola Sacra at Ostia, would provide us with much interesting information on this subject. At any rate, it is curious to see that dead-straight wall, those identical tombs, that obscure attempt to make a plan according to set rules: in the *via dei Vasi Greci* and in other parts of the Banditaccia they betray the influence of a feeling for space which, at the same period, must have been shared no less strongly by the living in Caere.

III

DOMESTIC INTERIORS

These more and more clearly defined streets and more and more regular squares which the necropolises allow our imaginations to restore in busy and noisy towns must also be re-populated by all the coming and going of Mediterranean life – running slaves from some comedy of Plautus, cattle being led to market by the sound of trumpets, a magistrate's procession preceded by his lictors, *Culni* riding in a *carpentum* to visit the Greek who sold the Attic vases. And in addition there were the 'traffic jams' like those Juvenal deplored in Rome, long before Boileau in Paris; although, according to the former, there was no fear, 'at Volsinii amid its wooded slopes' of tottering tenements which endangered the lives of passers-by in the Eternal City.[73]

But what have the interiors of the tombs revealed to us about these houses themselves, which, as we have seen, were principally 'private residences'? Only bare walls pierced by trapezoidal doors and symmetrical windows: we must try to complete the picture of domestic life by trying to give them, as far as we can, some items of furniture.

ETRUSCAN FURNITURE

In fact, Etruscan furniture would appear to have been very simple, like the Greek furniture it was largely patterned on.[74] We have already described, and shall find again, those beds with turned feet on which one lay not only to sleep but also to eat, when low, rectangular, two-tiered tables were placed beside them: as in Greece, these tables had three feet.[75] There were the seats: we shall return to those. There were linen-chests, but no wardrobes, no chests of drawers, no shelves: this also recalls ancient Greece.[76] There were *trapezai*, tables with four feet shaped like horses' legs, on which the plate was kept.[77] The principal luxury in the furnishings seems to have been those bronzes which the Etruscans exported even to Greece, and whose unequalled perfection was celebrated by Critias the Tyrant – who had his moments as an elegiac poet – at the end of the fifth century. He praised 'all the bronzes of Etruria which are the ornament of the house, whatever use is made of them'[78] – candelabra, tripods, incense-burners and braziers mounted on wheels, for protection against the winter cold.

What about the seats? If one did not sit on the edge of the bed there were light seats, stools and folding chairs which we are well familiar with from Attic vases. In a painting in the Tomb of the Augurs we can see one being carried on his shoulder by a boy slave who is taking it to one of the referees in a boxing-match.[79] When covered with ivory plaques, the seat became the ceremonial chair of kings and judges, the curule chair of the Roman magistracy.

More peculiar to Etruria proper seems to have been a type of armchair, squat in shape, of which the Tomb of the Seats and

Shields, from the sixth century, affords us two fine examples hewn in the rock, their backs to the rear wall of the *atrium* and standing in the spaces between the doors which give on the main rooms. The seat itself is made of a large drum of stone surmounted by a rounded back and open in the front on a small bench for resting the feet on. These stone armchairs perhaps reproduced wicker-work chairs, and indeed they do remind us, as well as of certain types of our own garden-chairs, of those basket-work armchairs we see in bas-reliefs from the Roman Rhineland.[80] But they are not placed there for the repose of visitors anxious to enter the beyond. We find them again, at Chiusi, made of terra-cotta and of bronze, used as supports for those human-faced ossuaries which are called *canopi*.[81] At Caere too they must have borne images of the defunct in all his glory. They were really thrones of an old indigenous model (they appear on the *situlae* or bronze pails of the Bologna area which are so rich in piquant details of local costumes and customs).[82] They were superseded by the Greek thrones with high, straight back and moulded arm-rests. The Barberini Tomb at Praeneste contained one, covered with bronze plating; but at the same period there was another in the Regolini-Galassi Tomb, one of classical shape.[83] We even know of one in marble, from the fourth to third centuries, the Corsini throne in Rome, which, in its archaistic setting, shows plainly the sort of seat that had been retained as ritual furniture.[84] Displaced by the Greek fashion, they disappeared fairly early from secular furnishings.

THE TOMB OF THE RELIEFS

If we wish to recapture the real atmosphere of an Etruscan interior, we must inspect carefully a tomb which through the enthusiasm of its finders was named by them, in the nineteenth century, as if it were some great opera singer, *la tomba bella*, and which we today call the Tomb of the Reliefs.[85] This because it shows, suspended from the walls on nails, all the utensils necessary for a comfortably distinguished life, or after-life. But all these objects are phantom objects, modelled in stucco and painted with fine colours – rose-pink, red, maroon, yellow, blue; these pick out the details and, sometimes, reveal the nature of the objects.

This tomb, a little more recent than those we have examined so far (third century), is composed of a single room whose ceiling is supported by two square pillars; the walls are hollowed out into long niches in which the dead were placed as it were in alcoves. There are thirteen altogether, reserved for the most important members of the family, while a much larger number, about thirty, of less important dead were laid on the ground in rectangular spaces marked by a slight ridge.

This was the family of the *Matuna*, a name whose first attempted latinization is given the form *Maduius* (*Lartia Maduia*)[86] before it was definitely translated into *Matonius, Mathonius*:[87] doubtless a considerable family, one branch of which is known in another tomb at Caere, to the north-west of the Banditaccia, near the tomb named after the Tarquins.[88] In other towns, like Tarquinii, inscriptions tell us the *curriculum vitae* of its dead: we know what offices and priestly positions they held. Caere's epigraphy does not give these details, for various reasons, among others because, at that time, it was still no more than a Roman prefecture and probably no longer had its own magistracies. All we read at Caere in the funerary epigraphs are names of parents and relatives, which of course is extremely interesting.[89]

An inscribed *cippus* found near the door acquaints us with the man who had the tomb constructed: *Vel Matunas Larisalisa ancn suthi cerichunce*, '*Vel Matunas*, son of *Laris*, had this tomb constructed'.[90] Besides this, nine *graffiti* in various niches furnish us with the elements of a genealogy.[91]

Vel Matunas had apparently married one *Canatnei*, whose name was transmitted to their son and daughter:

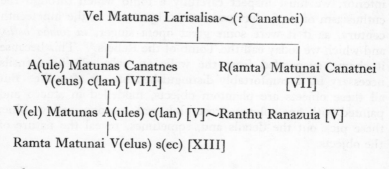

Vel Matunas Larisalisa〜(? Canatnei)

A(ule) Matunas Canatnes   R(amta) Matunai Canatnei
V(elus) c(lan) [VIII]   [VII]

V(el) Matunas A(ules) c(lan) [V]〜Ranthu Ranazuia [V]

Ramta Matunai V(elus) s(ec) [XIII]

At this point there is a gap in the filiation; but it takes up again in the following generations:

(?Matunas~?Clatei)
|
M(arce) Matunas Clate [II]~Ranthus Plavti
V(elus) s(ec) [IV]
|
M(arce) Matunas M(arces) c(lan) [XIII]

There remains one *La(rth) Matunas* (II) whose connexion with the family is also uncertain.

The name of *Ramta Matunai Canatnei* is engraved in the central alcove of the rear wall: and everything, in the arrangement and the decoration of the tomb, was conceived in such a way as to give this alcove the place of honour. Right from the entrance the eye is led, one might almost say ceremoniously conducted, between the two pillars whose interior and internal faces are the only ones decorated to that specially favoured niche where there is everything to suggest the bedroom of a young lady fallen asleep. The bed is represented, a bed with carved feet and legs, between which are depicted in bas-relief infernal monsters. But the two pillows, one on top of the other, at the right, are still awaiting the deceased girl's head. In front, a very low footstool bears her sandals, as in Carpaccio's *Dream of Saint Ursula*. On the left, a chest with a well-rendered lock, opened by dropping the side: it is carrying a pile of carefully folded linen. On the pillars framing the alcove vases are hung, as well as a necklace, a feather fan and a long stick. Above these, on either pillar, is a bust, both unfortunately mutilated; the left-hand one seems to be that of a man, the right-hand one that of a woman, and they are turned slightly towards the bed. Surely these would be the parents, *Vel Matunas* and *Canatnei*, watching over the daughter who had been snatched away from them?

But this is only one of the possible interpretations. It is usually thought that this niche, the object of so much care and attention, was made for the father and mother of the family, and that the busts on the lateral pillars were their portraits. An impressive argument in favour of this conclusion is that the skeleton of a man was found there. A feminine epitaph but a male skeleton: here is one of those irritating contradictions which too often stand in the historian's way: so one would have to imagine that *Vel Matunas*, son of *Laris*, constructed this tomb for his daughter (*Ramta*) and her husband. We still believe however that the single pair of superimposed pillows, the single pair of sandals on the foot-stool and the particularly feminine nature of the objects surround-ing it (does the stick, or sceptre, necessarily indicate a man?) prove that this funeral couch was intended only for *Ramta*. Her brother *Aule* lay in the niche immediately to her left (VIII). The parents must have been placed in a tomb preceding this. In principle, each niche in the Tomb of the Reliefs was intended for one body. But after the second generation a married couple was placed side by side in niche V and even later two members of the family (two men) were placed in niche II and in niche XIII were placed a man and a woman, cousins perhaps, but not nec-essarily married. The proven use of the tomb over several centuries, the increasing clutter and disorder too must have brought about the re-utilization of the niches, and in the most beautiful, previously emptied of the legitimate occupant's re-mains, the intrusion of the male skeleton which was the only one to be discovered.

The Tomb of the Matuna had therefore been opened on the occasion of a young girl's decease, a girl whose tranquil dis-position is sufficiently apparent from the ornaments and the fan attributed to her. But it was also the tomb of a family of soldiers, and the general theme of the decoration that runs like a frieze above the niches and along the beam holding up the roof clearly shows, perhaps more than any other tomb in Caere, its warlike vocation. We see helmets and greaves, circular shields, swords in their sheaths, *phalerae* for horses' necks and great horns for sounding the signal to attack.

Nevertheless the strange and charming bric-à-brac that covers two adjacent faces of each of the pillars in the middle of the chamber is something quite different. We have altogether four rectangular panels about two metres high and fifty and seventy centimetres across, on which are arranged, as in a panoply, a collection of mainly household implements: all that was needed for a happy home in the life beyond. They have been arbitrarily selected, and the choice has been determined more by a sense of pictorial balance and by a horror of empty space than by a desire to provide the present study with a methodically classified documentation. Indeed several objects are hard to identify and have long excited, and will continue to do so, like so many picture-puzzles, the sagacity of archaeologists who here require the specialized knowledge of carpenters, harness-makers and ironmongers.

First, the familiar animals at the bottom of three of these panels, as in the banquet scenes of the Tarquinii frescoes, arch their backs in sinuous curves according to the oriental tradition. Here are the marten that has caught a mole, the goose pecking at the ground, the sleeping duck with his head tucked back over his wing, and the wild cat holding a lizard in its claws. Above these are essential items from any well-stocked kitchen. A bronze wine-jug or *oenochoè*, a terracotta bowl with handles and decorated with laurel leaves, a complete set of ladles and spoons and above the basin on its tripod and to the left its pestle, a very practical knife-rack: two knives are stuck in it, with grey-green, that is, iron blades and light-coloured therefore wooden handles. Immediately to the right is a bunch of spits for roasting meat. There are also a pickaxe between a cutlass and a big coil of rope, and tongs and pincers made for extracting those large-headed and hooked nails from which the objects are hung. But some of these objects require more detailed investigation.

The upper half of a panel is occupied by a light yellow (therefore perhaps wooden) rectangular tray with a moulded border and two handles, one on the long side, the other on the short side; this is the one which suspends the tray from the nail, from which there also hangs a leather pouch. Eleven horizontal lines are traced on the surface of the tray.

Some scholars have taken this to be a table with a bronze top ruled to receive some inscription; others, an abacus with its divisions for counting. Recently an ingenious attempt was made to prove that the tray was a board for kneading macaroni.[92] For this purpose were used the roller attached by a string, on the left of another panel, and the little saw-toothed (?) wheel which figures on the first panel between the duck and the tongs, and which may have been used to give the paste the required form – *fettucine* or *tagliatelle*. The pouch itself would be a flour-bag.

And the author of this interpretation seemed to think it all the more likely as he felt that the master buried here and so obviously concerned with arms and kitchen equipment could only be a dealer in army supplies!

Without wishing to deny that the ancients were familiar with macaroni (the old humanists believed the word was derived from the Greek *makar*, 'happy', because of the felicity it procured its adepts), the solution of the problem must be sought elsewhere.[93] We are here in the presence of a *tabula lusoria*, a sort of chessboard across whose twelve compartments two players would advance the pawns probably contained in the pouch. We know that the ancients were passionately fond of dice and backgammon or trictrac, or at any rate games which strongly resembled them: the rules of these games are not known to us, but the material evidence is supplied by figured monuments. Grecian vases and Etruscan mirrors show Achilles and Ajax thus engaged in alleviating the tedium of the siege of Troy: seated facing each other, they have placed on their knees a board divided into a variable number of zones by seven or twelve parallel lines and on which we can make out two dice or pawns. The game of dice is one known to have been played by the Etruscans; there is that famous pair of dice found at Tuscania and now in the Louvre, and which, the numbers being inscribed in letters on their six faces, provide the chief source of our knowledge of the first six Etruscan names of numbers. But there were more than two dice in the pouch or purse accompanying this *tabula lusoria*, and we may suppose that the *Matuna* preferred to play a game requiring numerous pawns, for example the game called *latrunculi* or little robbers of which Varro speaks:[94] at Venafro in Campania, in a tomb from the heyday of the Empire, a whole collection of figured pieces was discovered, carved from bone, something to exercise the imagination of a modern chess-player, and which was destined to amuse the dead.

Another problem which is not insoluble is that posed by a strange object in panel 2, on its left (plate 33): it might be thought at first glance to be a rudder with a stern-post, if we did not know that such a device was uknonwn to antiquity, when ships were steered by oars. It appears as two long, thin rectangles joined together, of unequal length: the longer one is yellowish-white and a third of its width is covered by a band of red colour which seems to be fixed on with a series of white studs or nails; the other rectangle, the shorter, is violet, and its ends are cased in white iron bindings which are extended laterally by two round rods, each of which ends in a pair of disks.

Again in this case the most diverse hypotheses have been put forward: a rudder, as we have already mentioned; a surveying apparatus worthy of the most advanced geometricians – this suggestion was hazarded by the same scholars who, rightly filled with respect for Etruscan science, see the games table as an abacus. But many have thought that the object would only be in its normal position if it was unhooked and placed on the ground; then, when the two rectangles were horizontal, the disks would be seen to be wheels. It appears to lack depth because it is being viewed from the side, and the two wheels in front are thought to be partially masking two behind.

It has recently been suggested that the object is . . . a cradle:[95] the stuff or the red leather which is nailed to the upper part of the frame would then dip down inside to receive the child's body. The thick wheels whose axle-cases seem to have touched the ground could scarcely have revolved: the whole thing was meant to be rocked, not rolled.

All very plausible, and we should ask for nothing better than that this ingenious explanation should be accepted if the idea of a cradle in a tomb did not militate against it. Certainly children were buried with their dolls. But in a tomb like this, whose bas-reliefs are obviously designed for the comfort and satisfaction of grown-ups, it is difficult to admit that their belief in the future life included the possibility of procreation.

So we are compelled to turn to a less dazzling solution but one which can be supported by comparisons of this 'trolley table' with well-known objects in the Etruscan world: at the museums in Orvieto and Chiusi, small bronze trolleys, of a more ancient date, ornamented at the four corners of the upper tray with carvings in the shape of horses' heads, offer a remarkable resemblance to this mysterious object (plate 2).[96] These are usually taken to be mobile braziers, and in the case of our own object this use seems to be excluded by the covering of red cloth or leather; but the same contraption may have been used to transport other things, foodstuffs for example, and this would be in conformity with the general tone of the reliefs.

There are other elements in the decoration of the pillars that could claim our attention. For instance there are two pairs of strange vertical rods. Each is composed of a cylindrical stem which, about two-thirds up, divides into three branches forming an ellipse with its axis: this part of the object seems to be made of a small cord or of a twisted rush. The whole thing, slung on a hook that passes through the hole, seems to be rigid, and, extending beyond the normal framework of the panels, crosses the capital and touches the ceiling.

It has been thought that these represented distaffs or the sort of *caduceus* which apparitors carried on their shoulders in magistrates' processions on certain frescoes. But the simplest explanation is also the likeliest one: they are slings, similar to those used by the huntsmen in the painting in the *Tomba della Caccia*.

There are also two long sticks with curved ends in the form of a shepherd's crook. Must these be identified with those *litui* which Rome, borrowing them from the Etruscans, had made the characteristic attribute of her augurs and which they used to trace out in the heavens the sacred region within which the flight of birds was to be observed? But the true *lituus* is generally shorter: we suggest that we have here simply shepherds' crooks, with which, in the blessed pastures, the dead man would continue to watch over his flocks.

At all events, he liked cheese: witness the yellowish disk hung from the top of the fourth panel, obliquely, perhaps because it is shoved slightly to one side by the neighbouring slings. The concentric striations on its surface have made some savants see in it a wicker-work object, a sieve, a basket, a *fiscina* – a sort of withy mould for straining cheeses in. But its circumference shows notches that have not come there by chance: we share the opinion of those who see in it a cheese, a little gnawed round the edges by mice.

Finally, do not let us forget, between the wheels of our trolley, the haversack to which a *patera* and a scent-bottle are attached by interlacing straps. This *mantica* had to supply the necessities for the voyage, the great voyage – the requirements for the toilet en route, for who knows what sacrificial ritual at some mysterious crossroads.

Such was the house of death belonging to the *Matuna* family. It evokes, as we have seen, with a detail worthy of a Flemish master, the mode of life of an Etruscan family in the third century, in a city now incorporated into the Roman State. There was no doubt of the family's military traditions. But the arms which, hung round the chamber walls, recall the glorious memories of fights against the Gauls and against Rome herself, belong to a vanished past; the warlike trumpets are silent. Perhaps the *Matuna* did not break their swords for good; perhaps they served again in the legions or in special cohorts under the skies of Sicily and Africa, wherever the Punic Wars and the Roman Conquest took them. Nevertheless their essential interests were still of another order: making the best of the truncated territory of Caere, they must have cultivated their domain to assure themselves substantial revenues and become absorbed in the enjoyment of a material prosperity within limited horizons. These gentlemen-farmers had their flocks grazing on the surrounding hills, hunted the wild duck with their slings, pruned the trees in their orchards, raised all kinds of domestic stock, made plump cheeses from the milk of their ewes. They were great handymen, always with a pair of pliers in their hands. They sometimes played trictrac. And their homes were full of the aroma of roasting meats and the hissing of boiling liquids. They indeed waxed fat.

IV

ETRUSCAN COSTUME

Meanwhile the daughter of the house, surrounded by women servants who fanned her with a feather fan or took clothes out of the chest at the foot of the bed, was getting ready to go out. We shall have much to say about Etruscan costume.

The one worn by *Ramta Matunai* in the Caere of the third century scarcely distinguished her from those elegant young ladies whose long, draped robes, secured by a shoulder-brooch, and light shawls worn loosely round the shoulders are familiar to us from the pages of Theocritus' *Syracusans*[97] and the terracottas of Myrrhina. The tyranny of Greek fashion had been imposed upon all the Hellenistic cities, and Caere, we imagine, was not the last to surrender to it. Nor Tarquinii: in the paintings in the Tomb of the Shields,[98] which are contemporaneous, *Ravnthu Aprthnai* and *Velia Seitithi*, both seated at the foot of their husbands' bed, are both wearing an undergarment, the short-sleeved linen tunic (*chitôn*) and on top of that a white cloak (*himation*) with black or red border. Moreover the musicians beside the latter are already wearing, as if they were Romans, a toga that is more or less classical in style, as does also the famous *Arringatore* ('The Orator') whose bronze statue, discovered near Lake Trasimene, is that of a Cicero of Chiusi or Cortona at the end of the second or the beginning of the first century.[99]

But before this uniformity appeared in male and female garments the archaic monuments present us with other images. We know those marvellous dancers from the Tomb of the Lionesses, from the Tomb of the Leopards, from that of the Triclinium and that of Francesca Giustiniani, the lively and fresh colours of their cloaks, the infinitely varied cut, sometimes quite modern in style, of their robes. Naturally we must beware of reading too much into these. The disappearance of great Greek painting, of which we see only an almost monochrome reflection in the pottery with black or red figures, and the disappearance of the primitive polychrome on their sculptures makes us peculiarly sensitive to all that was most colourful in the Etruscan world. On the other hand, the costumes with which these dancers and musicians are clothed for those banquets and games that were given such animation by their grace and talent, are stage costumes and belong to a décor whose other side we must not neglect. Later, Posidonius was to be struck by the magnificence of these clothes, 'more beautiful than is fitting for slaves': here he was of the same opinion as miserly and prosaic Cato, who wanted them to be given once every two years a shirt one metre in length and a *sagum*; when they were given new ones, the old were to be given back to be made into rags.[100] What we are admiring here is the *lucumo's* corps de ballet.

But this makes it all the more interesting: in the wardrobes of our theatres there are preserved the armour of the knights and the gala costumes of days long since vanished. The Etruscans, when designing the costumes of their '*histrions*' sometimes had recourse, not to contemporary models, but to the enchantment of a very distant past.

Indeed how else can we explain, for example, in the Tomb of Francesca Giustiniani[101] the extraordinary trio composed of a young man in a blue mantle and two women whose sumptuous garments seem to be those of some magnificent Renaissance court?; then we think again, and connect them, more reasonably, with those worn by the princesses of Minoan Crete. One of the women is playing the double flute and has short hair: we assume she is a servant; but in the centre there is a truly regal figure: she has her left hand on her hip, and the other arm is raised; she wears a diadem, a necklace, bracelets and a long robe, very 'waisted', over which she has a thick jacket. What is remarkable is not so much the richness of the costume (in which the dominating feature is the strong contrast between the dark red of the upper part, which would seem to be of velvet, and the orange-pink of the fine material of the robe scattered with little dots and stars) as its fundamental difference from the Grecian 'line', characterized by the vertical drapery of *chitôn* and *himation*. Here, on the contrary, we have the hour-glass form of the bell-shaped skirt, perhaps puffed out by a stiff underskirt or bustle, and those broad horizontal stripes which, below the belt and along the lower edge, echo the colour of the bodice, and the division, also in horizontal bands, of the embroidery motifs; and we have also the effect of kimono sleeves which broaden the shoulders and diminish the waist.

But as Gustave Glotz rightly observed in his *Aegean Civilization*,[102] 'never, in the continual variations of fashion, did the Minoans display the noble posture which the folds of floating veils and the natural hang of soft draperies gave to the Greeks and Romans', and he insisted upon the forms which were taken by the two essential parts of Minoan clothing, the bodice and the skirt, analysing the brilliant use of colours in the materials, the profusion of pleatings and puffings, the starching or the whalebones that stiffened the crinolines or the skirts with fly-away panels. He even went so far as to explain the modernity of these models by writing that the Aegeans had, 'in the space of two thousand years, made modifications to feminine costume which northern peoples, retarded by the long predominance of Greek and Roman modes, took three thousand years longer to reproduce'. This is what we meant when we spoke earlier on of the modern cut of certain Etruscan dresses which appear modern in a para- doxical way, through the archaistic conservatism which we have pointed out several times, and through an indefectible loyalty to the forms of Mediterranean civilization, with its conception of woman which had reigned triumphant long before the advent of the Indo-Europeans. So we are justified in believing that some obscure ancestral memory of former queens sometimes, at least as far as costume is concerned, came to life again in the games of Tarquinii. Let us imagine that the scene in the Francesca Giustiniani tomb represents the meeting between Ariadne and Theseus or that of Phaedra and Hippolytus, while Oenone plays the flute; but nothing will stop the young hero from mounting the fatal chariot.

What we have just been saying scarcely applies to the women's costumes. Only Ariadne is dressed in the ancient mode. The flimsy mantle that barely veils the bronzed torsos of Theseus, Hippolytus and the other male dancers in the Tombs of the Leopards and of the Triclinium has not such a remote origin.

Moreover, it is more often[103] a sort of scarf rather than a mantle, and cut so as to present in front a very low-plunging, rounded neckline, with broad panels falling freely behind. Of a vivid colour – orange, pale green or royal blue – it is bordered, inside and out, with an embroidered band of another colour – yellow or blue, pale yellow with a maroon saw-tooth motif, or white with red polka-dots. The material is thick and the folds are heavy. We do not hesitate to give this garment the Latin name *lacerna*, which is derived from Etruscan, meaning an under-mantle, the short and narrow woollen surtout (*breves laenae, angusta lacerna*) of which the poets speak.[104] The warriors of Homer already knew it and called it *chlaina*, which passed into Latin, doubtless through the intermediary of Etruscan, under the form *laena*, the French *laine* or wool.

The women wore over their tunics very ample cloaks: witness on the left of the rear wall in the chamber of the Lionesses, a female dancer 'immobile, with feet widespread':[105] over her orange-pink *chitôn* embroidered with little flowers she has cast a cloak of dark red wool provided with what appear to be broad revers or facings of blue that fall in front like the straps of a tippet. We see other details like these on the dancers' cloaks in the tombs at Chiusi.[106]

The Etruscans must have borrowed these *chlainai* or *lacernae* with their brilliant colours and embroidery from Ionia. We have already had occasion to emphasize the fact that in the west there was a great vogue for the fine dyed woollens of Miletus which were so appreciated at Sybaris that historians saw in them the main reason for the friendship between the two peoples, and even for the friendship between Sybaris and the Etruscans.[107] There was no more famous garment in antiquity than the *himation* of the Sybarite Alcisthenes which was to pass into the possession of Dionysius of Syracuse before he went to Carthage: from the start it was a museum piece and an inexhaustible theme for the moral philosophers.[108] Our Etruscan mantles would not claim so much. All the same they are in exquisite taste, and prove in Tarquinii, even as late as the middle of the fifth century, the persistence of Ionian modes after the destruction of Sybaris (510) and Miletus (494). The Etruscan costume grafted on to Mediterranean traditions which it had not entirely abandoned certain orientalizing and Ionian features to which it has still remained faithful.

FROM THE TEBENNA TO THE TOGA

Another type of Etruscan cloak was to have a much longer history, and a more glorious one, than this fugitive-coloured stuff which after all soon wore out: this other type was known as the *tebenna*.[109] The word, which appears in the Greek authors (though only, unless we are mistaken, from Polybius[110] onwards and therefore belongs to a strongly Romanized Greek who may have adopted it in Italy) disconcerted Dionysius of Halicarnassus:[111] where could it have come from? It did not have a Greek look about it. For modern scholars there is no doubt about its derivation: unless it goes as far back as the pre-Indo-European substratum, it has every likelihood of being Etruscan.[112] And as it happens the Pollux *Onomasticon* gives us the following explanation: '*tebenna*, cloak or chlamys worn by the Etruscans.'[113] Only Dionysius of Halicarnassus, at the beginning of the Empire, was not quite sure whether the *tebenna* was the short cloak worn by Roman knights and also called *trabea*, or the toga in which Roman citizens draped their bodies.[114] The fact is that both *trabea* and *toga* are derived from the primitive Etruscan cloak, the former being more or less fixed in its archaic form, the other being longer and, in the course of time, freed from the rigid simplicity characterizing its primitive state.

The painted terracotta plaques from Caere which are now in the Louvre and the Campana plaques from the middle of the sixth century show the image of a king armed with a sceptre and seated on a curule chair before the effigy of a goddess.[115] Over a short white tunic bordered with a red embroidered galloon he has cast over his left shoulder an even shorter mantle, purple in colour and bordered with a decorative motif and which leaves the right shoulder bare. This *tebenna* was to go down in history as the sign of the patrician class: with slight variations, it kept its original form, preserving its background colour or bands of purple or scarlet and in general its exiguous dimensions (*parva trabea*): this cloak, at once sacerdotal and military, was to become, in Rome, the *trabea* of the Salii and other religious colleges, the *paludamentum* (longer) of the general-in-chief and the parade uniform of the Roman knights in their ceremonial processions.

But in general, apart from these cases where ritual and tradition preserved its character of a warrior's cloak, the *tebenna* was to take on other colours, modifying its shape until it became the long Roman toga. The most ancient and at the same time most classic example we have of this garment is that displayed by the *Arringatore's* bronze statue – that 'Orator' who, in the last century of the Republic, was a magistrate from Cortona or Chiusi. But we can follow the development of the *trabea* into the toga in figured monuments. In the Tomb of the Augurs,[116] which is only a few years more recent than the Campana plaques, four persons are wearing the *tebenna* – the two *tanasar*, who, on either side of the door, are making gestures of lamentation, and the two *tevarath* or organizers of the games who, on the neighbouring wall, are refereeing a contest between two wrestlers. Their cloak very closely resembles that of the king, excepting that in three cases it is black, which may be explained by the funeral significance of their rôle; it is also less well-arranged, and longer, and allows a hint of draping from the left shoulder, from which there falls, like the 'revers' on the cloak of the dancing girl in the Tomb of the Lionesses, a wide red band. But by the beginning of the fifth century it is dark in colour and decorated with a border (*toga praetexta*) and covers the knees of the noble spectators in the Tomb of the Bigae.[117] Even a legendary king, the Nestor in the François Tomb, is provided, over his red-bordered tunic, with a tebenna that comes down to his feet, while the dead man is also enveloped in a great blue embroidered cloak (*toga picta*[118]). Even the musicians in the Tomb of the Shields are draped in a true toga, pure white. In the various processions of magistrates at Tarquinii and Volterra we see the gradual lengthening of the Etruscan *tebenna*, and this could help us towards a more precise dating; at the same time the disposition of the folds becomes more and more marked until, with the *Arringatore*, it becomes the Roman toga.

This is why Dionysius of Halicarnassus, who called the *tebenna* the '*trabea*' of the Salii, uses the same word for the 'toga' with which he clothes his Tarquinius: when he was describing the latter's cloak, he could not help imagining it in the form he had seen in the Rome of his time – the ample purple toga with golden threads which Augustus and Tiberius displayed on their triumphal progresses, and the copious, flowing robes worn in theatrical performances by the kings of tragedies.[119] He could see only one difference between the two, which was that the flowered cloak of Darius was cut as a large square of stuff while the toga was cut in the form of a segment of a circle.[120] But it is very difficult for us to distinguish, in the paintings, whether the *tebennae* of the Campana plaques and of the Tomb of the Augurs already followed this pattern.

FOOTWEAR

The dancing girl in the Tomb of the Lionesses can teach us something more: the long, pointed shoes she wears were also a borrowing from Ionia, a region that was very generally admired in Etruria. We can see similar ones on the feet of men and women in the Tombs of the Augurs and of the Baron,[121] among others, and they seem to be long slippers of red, maroon or green cloth, opening widely at the front and reaching very high, in a point, on the calves. These are the *calcei repandi* (turned-up) which Cicero had noticed on the ancient statue of Juno Sospita at Lanuvium.[122] But there were different models, though always with turned-up pointed toes. Especially remarkable are the shoes of the 'king' and of the deities on the Campana plaques.[123] Still 'turned-up' and split down the front, they are provided with a long tongue and fastened, above the heel, by several horizontal straps; in addition the top of these shoes, which reaches mid-calf, is tied with another strap that passes through a big eyehole (plates 24–26). They are doubtless the same as those worn by the lady of the Caere sarcophagi whose shoes have crossed laces below the straps which are partly covered by the edge of the tunic (plate 24).[124]

Naturally the other dancers do not load their feet with such heavy buskins; they wear only low shoes, and mainly light sandals, made simply from a sole held on by crossed straps: the Tomb of the Triclinium shows various kinds of these. Etruscan sandals, *Tyrrhenica sandalia*,[125] were well known in Athens from the middle of the fifth century, for a predecessor of Aristophanes, Cratinus mentioned them, doubtless in one of his fiery diatribes against the inroads being made by foreign luxury articles. Lexicographers inform us that they had gilded straps and a wooden sole that was often very high, thus making them resemble the *cothurnus* of the Athenian tragic actor. At Bisenzio and Caere metal studs have been found which were used to preserve these soles.[126] The sandals at the foot of *Ramta Matunai's* bed, awaiting her re-awakening, are more modest: wooden soles, with semi-circular bands and a median cord passing between the great toe and the next.

But though the sandal became, as in Greece, the usual foot-wear, the Etruscans did not abandon buskins, though the domination of classical taste gradually did away with those provocative turned-up points. In the Tomb of the Shields, *Velia Seitithi* and the little girl slave with the cropped hair fanning her both wear high shoes, black, with a red strip down the middle; this seems to have been an opening, rather like that in modern snowboots.[127] But it was the strapped boots seen on the Campana plaques that enjoyed the greatest fame:[128] they were retained as a sign of nobility in the ceremonial dress of magistrates, and it is well established that they were the originals of the *calcei patricii* or *senatorii* shown on a great number of Roman statues: with their tongue (*lingula*), their four straps (*corrigiae*), their black tone and the suppleness of their leather which was treated with alum, they faithfully reproduce, with only slight modification, the essential features of Etruscan shoe-making. Meanwhile a transitional stage is shown us in the statue of the *Arringatore*, who, in his city on the shores of Lake Trasimene, was already wearing authentic *calcei senatorii*.[129] A continuous evolution of which the Ancients were fully conscious: Virgil describes the awakening of King Evander thus: 'The old man rises, puts on his tunic, and wraps his feet in Tyrrhenian sandals',

... *Tyrrhena pedum circumdat uincula plantis*,[130]

on which Servius comments in these terms: 'According to certain authors, these would be *calcei senatorii*, because this type of footwear was borrowed from the Etruscans.'

HEADGEAR

Finally the girl dancer in the Tomb of the Lionesses allows us to pass from cloaks and footwear to headgear. Her conical-shaped cap must also be attributed to an Ionian mode; it is apparently made of the same material as the *chitôn*, and it seems to cover a high chignon. It is related to all the turbans, mitres, foulards, kerchiefs and so on in which the women of Asia Minor bound their locks, and even to the Phrygian cap and the ancient *hennin* of the Aegeans. We have already seen it on the head of the deceased wife in the Caere group.[131] It is worn by female spectators depicted in the Tomb of the Bigae.[132] In particular, on archaic bronzes, it appears as the head-dress of goddesses like the *Turan* or Etruscan Venus of Perugia,[133] and even of gods, for example the Hercules from Este.[134] It is called a *tutulus*, for thus, according to Varro and Festus, was known the pyramidal woollen head-dress of the pontiffs and the flamines, as well as the mountains of tresses which the matrons piled up in a purple ribbon interwoven with their hair.[135] So that it was retained only for ritual purposes. Even the Etruscan ladies tired of it in the fifth century, and most often we see them with blonde or bleached hair covered only by a few head-ornaments.

JEWELLERY

We have noticed the great ear-rings, disk-shaped, which adorn our dancer in the *tutulus*: we could find the exact originals in the Campana collection at the Louvre; for example, as we look through E. Coche de la Ferté's beautiful work on *Antique jewellery*,[136] we see a disk of rose-shapes and palm-leaf ornament in granulations, diameter five centimetres, or another, ornamented with nodules and globules, only measuring two centimetres.

All the women whose portraits have been preserved – the enigmatic Mona Lisa who, in the Tomb of the Ogre, is known to us only by her first name, *Velia*,[137] the beautiful Persephone of the Golini tomb,[138] and even that young servant in the same tomb who is supervising the preparations for a banquet,[139] and all those who are represented on their sarcophagi, still paying attention to their appearance like *Larthia Seianti* of Chiusi[140] – have their hair, their necks, their wrists loaded with diadems, necklaces and bracelets. But though these reproductions of a more or less recent epoch reveal an unflagging taste for jewellery, they cannot be compared with the actual pieces of the most splendid period, pieces which, as it happens, we possess: brooches, clasps, pendants, pectorals, brassards, ear-rings, golden rings, all of which, discovered in the seventh and sixth century tombs at Caere, Palestrina, Populonia, Marsiliana d'Albegna, Vetulonia or Vulci, illustrate the sudden and extraordinary enrichment of the Etruscan people at that time.[141]

Who could forget the great brooches or clasps of the Regolini-Galassi and Barberini tombs, ornaments whose framework is masked by a plaque covered with a hundred or so double heads in serried rows, in which we can make out lions, horses and sirens? (plates 27–29).[142] Or the exquisite Corsini fibula, on which there is a procession of a dozen ducks,[143] or again, turning from such baroque exuberance, the pure *skyphos* from the Barberini tomb whose great worth is in the quality of the metal, the elegance of its lines and – sole ornament – the two slight figurines of sphinxes seated on the handles?[144]

They reveal, besides skill in the elementary processes of the jeweller's craft – hammering, repoussé, stamping – a peculiar mastery in the handling of filigree and granulation. The Greeks and the Etruscans knew how to scatter on the surface to be decorated thousands of minute granules of gold, fixing them with a secret solder which did not detract from the delicacy of the work. Research going on at present will no doubt soon re-discover that secret, jealously guarded by a small number of initiates and which was lost with the fall of the Empire. It seems that the origin of this secret, like that of all those devices Etruscan jewellers used in their art, must be sought in the Orient, in the region of the Caucasus, land of the legendary Chalybes, celebrated for their immemorial experience in the arts of metal, or in Mesopotamia, in Syria, Crete and Egypt.[145] Nevertheless, as far as granulation is concerned, the Etruscan jewellery bears away the palm for its regularity and the delicacy of the golden balls, whose diameter sometimes attains the unbelievably tiny figure of two-tenths of a millimetre. And the artists used this exceptional skill to work with the greatest freedom: after having used the granulation to represent their motifs on a base of plain, flat gold, they proceeded to fill in the scene with figures:[146] an artistic revolution which reminds us of that which took place about the same time in Attic ceramics when the black figures gave way to red ones. One of the most magnificent products of this Etruscan style is the pendant in the Louvre with its image of the river-god Acheloös: the beard and part of the hair are in granulation, the face done in repoussé.[147] It is as well to remember, when looking at the photographs of this masterpiece, that the head is only four centimetres high. But it is one of the last masterpieces of Etruscan jewellery, which, with the decline of Etruscan power, also suffered a swift decadence.

And here we find ourselves in the presence of the insoluble mystery: we have been speaking of Etruscan jewellers, assuming, as is more and more the case among scholars today, that these jewels were not imported from the Orient. E. Coche de la Ferté writes:

'Like some spontaneous creation springing from the darkness in which the beginnings of Etruscan civilization are lost, this jewellery appears at the dawn of that civilization, radiant with skill of a high quality and with a wealth of decoration. We have said what its origins may be. Nevertheless it is remarkable to see in the tombs of central and septentrional Italy, the emergence of ornaments that have no resemblance to these immediate antecedents: about the year 700 BC, they begin to take the place of the bronze ornaments which are so abundant in the Villanovan tombs.'[148]

Yet in the same tombs where, at the beginning of the seventh century, Etruscan jewellery, suddenly in full possession of all its techniques, blazes out of the dark, the other arts, statuary for example, are just beginning, as if they were starting from scratch, to invent their forms and their tools. It is difficult to understand that the technical virtuosity which produced, in the tumulus of La Pietrera, at Vetulonia, a 'necklace formed of twenty pendants, each decorated with two human heads with curly hair,[149] could have existed alongside the laborious skills displayed in the sculptures that decorate the tomb.[150] Nor do we know from which Italian mines so much gold could have been mined. But let us consider one hypothesis. It was the attraction of Etruscan copper and iron, we have seen, which brought about the Greek colonization of Italy and the Chalcidian founding of Cumae in the eighth century. 'But what did the Greeks bring in return?' it has been asked.[151] Would not the reply to this be: gold . . . golden jewellery?

CHAPTER SEVEN

SOME ETRUSCAN DIVERSIONS: BANQUETS AND GAMES

I *The divisions of time*
II *Table delicacies – A quick look at the kitchens – Banquets – Silver plate*
III *Games – Music – Dancing – Bacchic dance – Sport – Racing – Athletics – The tribunes and the public – Gladiatorial combats – The game of Phersu*

I

THE DIVISIONS OF TIME

The temporal framework of Etruscan life was in general the same as that of the Romans, who borrowed it for the most part from the Etruscans, or elaborated it together with them. Our authors are generally silent about this, because, finding in the Etruscan calendar a system identical with their own, they assumed that it went without saying. The rare indications they give us are inspired by etymological inquiry or by astonishment at seeing the Etruscans sometimes departing from the common usage.

Thus they did not count their days from midnight to midnight, as did the Romans; nor did they follow the Babylonians who counted them from dawn to dawn – their word for 'dawn' was *thesan*[1] – nor the Athenians and the Germans who reckoned them from sunset to sunset. No, the Etruscans measured their days from noon to noon.[2] This curious importance given to the moment when the sun is at its zenith is perhaps justified by the fact that it does not depend on the seasons nor on the unequal length of days: in Rome too, noon was always noon, and also the end of the sixth hour, whether the sun rose early in June or late in December. But Varro thought it absurd; a child born at the sixth hour, at noon, on the day of the calends, would have a birthday containing half the calends and the following day up to noon. But this tradition spread from the Etruscans to many of their neighbours in Umbria.[3]

As in primitive Rome, they had a lunar month, that is, one measured by the interval between two consecutive new moons. The proof of this is in the word for month itself, which was 'luna'. *Tiv* was the goddess of the night, but her name reappears as an appellative, in the genitive plural, on epitaphs: *Vel Vipinanas*, at Tuscania, died *avils XX tivrs sas*, 'aged twenty years and six (or four) months'.[4]

At the full moon in the middle of the month the Etruscans celebrated the day of the Ides, and it was from them that the Romans borrowed the name, *idus*, or as it was formerly written with a mute dental, *itus*. Certain scholars[5] gave the word a bizarre interpretation: *itis*, they claimed, meant 'confidence in Jupiter', or in light – the same thing – because on that day the light did not die with the setting of the sun, for the daylight was prolonged thanks to the radiance of the full moon. At any rate, the Etruscan ides, like the Roman ones, became consecrated to Jupiter.

We shall say nothing of the calends (*Kalendae*) as the name is not Etruscan. In Etruria there were nones (ninth day before the ides), and, as in Rome, weeks consisting of eight full days (*nundinae*): the ninth day, market day, was the one on which the Etruscan kings held audience, and everyone had the right to go and consult them about their personal affairs.[6]

A series of eight names of the months, in Latinized Etruscan, has been preserved by glossarists: *Velcitanus* (March), *Cabreas* (April), *Ampiles* (May), *Aclus* (June), *Traneus* (July), *Hermius* (August), *Celius* (September), *Xosfer* (October).[7] We see that they proceed in sequence from the month of March, which doubtless opened the year, as in primitive Rome. Several of these names are to be found in inscriptions: *acale* (= *acle*, *Aclus*) and *celi* (*Celius*) in the Zagreb ritual,[8] where the date of the three ceremonies, counted backwards, as in Latin, from the end of the month, shows that the latter was of thirty days. Certain other names are those of deities: *Traneus* (*t(u)rane*) was the month of Turan (Venus) and Hermius that of Hermes. *Xosfer* (*chosfer*, *cesfer*) was perhaps formed on the name of number *cezp-* (eight?), and, like *October*, designated the eighth month of the year.[9] Finally it is probable that the names of the months had local variants. *Aprilis* in Latin has been cleverly interpreted as being derived from the Etruscan name of Aphrodite-Aphrô.[10] Elsewhere people said *Cabreas*.

Every year (*avil*), at Volsinii, the Etruscans hammered a nail into the wall of the temple of the goddess Nortia,[11] and this ceremony, which symbolized the irrevocable fulfilment of destiny, was adopted by the Romans and applied by them in the temple of Jupiter Capitolinus; this formed a basis for chronological computations used by the first historians.

Finally, there were the centuries, whose variable duration, corresponding to the duration *maxima* of a human life, generally was more than a hundred years and sometimes reached 119 or even 123 years. The completion of each century was announced by miracles known to the *haruspices*; they taught that the Etruscan nation would last for ten centuries, an epoch that had begun in 968 BC.[12]

II

TABLE DELICACIES

The Etruscan day is not known to us, unfortunately, in all its details. Innumerable texts allow us to reconstruct in our imaginations the day of the Greek or the Roman; but no one has told us at what hour a *lucumo* left his bed or whether he received his clients in the morning or enjoyed a siesta and a bath in the afternoon. The only precise piece of information we have about his timetable concerns his food: he had two meals a day.

This is something noted by a rather scandalized Posidonius as one consequence of the fecundity of the soil and the weakness of their character: 'Twice a day the Etruscans have their tables sumptuously laid with everything that contributes to delicate living; they have prepared for them bed-coverings embroidered with flowers, and they are served from quantities of silver plate; they have also at their beck and call a considerable number of slaves.'[13]

They sat down to a meal twice a day. The remark takes on its full meaning only when we remember that the Greeks and the

Romans had in theory three meals a day: the Greeks had their *akratismos*, *ariston* and *deipnon*, while the Romans had their *jentaculum*, *prandium* and *cena*, corresponding to our breakfast, lunch and dinner. But custom had gradually reduced the first two meals to the very simplest of repasts: on rising, one partook of a crust of bread rubbed with a clove of garlic or dipped in a little wine; between eleven and noon there was a light collation consisting of the left-overs from the evening before. Only the dinner, after two or three o'clock, really deserved to be called a meal.[14] One had to be a pig like Vitellius to demand three (or even four) repasts.[15] Seneca and Pliny the Elder required very little for their breakfast: the philosopher a bit of dry bread; the naturalist, a few mouthfuls (*gustabat*[16]).

Though these testimonies only go back as far as the Empire in its heyday, it is clear that the Romans of the Republic were equally fastidious. Cicero, in his second *Philippic*, rails against Antonius, who, after the Civil War, had confiscated the learned Varro's villa at Cassino and converted that sanctuary of learning into a house of debauchery: from the third hour (nine a.m.) 'they drank and vomited'.[17] The expressions *convivium tempestivum* and *cenare de die* used to describe a banquet that started too early and a dinner that began in the middle of the day characterized the delights of Capua and the excesses of gormandizers. But already in Greece the comic poets had been hounding with their sarcasms 'those who were not satisfied with a single meal and even dined twice in one day'.[18] Unaware of universal reprobation, the Etruscans 'dined twice a day', and not only for their *cena* but also for the *prandium*, which Seneca turned into a light snack eaten standing *sine mensa*, they had tables laid, before which couches were set for them to lie on.

A QUICK LOOK AT THE KITCHENS

The Golini tomb at Orvieto, built at the end of the fourth century for the *Leinie* (*Laenii*) family, not only shows us in its paintings the funeral banquet of two brothers in the presence of Hades and Persephone, but also takes us into the kitchens where eleven servants are busy with the preparations for the feast.[19] They are the same as those kitchen-hands who, in an inscription of Falerii in archaic dialectal Latin, lauded the merits of their profession:

quei soueis argutiais opidque Volcani
condecorant saipisume comvivia loidosque.

'By their own skills and with the aid of Vulcan, they give banquets and games all their lustre.'[20]

The Sybarites wove laurel wreaths for their cooks. The Etruscans must have held them in at least equal honour. In this tomb, each one is identified by two words engraved underneath him, the first being probably a personal name, the second a title indicating his function: they are mostly inexplicable, but some day their significance will be revealed, and this will be a great step forward in our knowledge of the language.

On the entrance wall, to the left, are painted carcasses of beasts and fowls: two small trees place this *carnarium* in the open air. From a round beam there is hung, by its hind legs, a whole ox; its chopped-off head, with large eyes worthy of a Juno, is laid on the ground nearby. Further on, under a lean-to roof, a hare and a hind are hung between two pairs of fowls.

The adjoining wall shows the butcher-boy slave who, with an apron slung round his naked hips, is chopping meat with a hatchet in front of a fire on which he will cook it.

At the other end of the fresco, *pazu mulu(.)ane* who is also naked except for a brief pair of drawers, is bending over a mortar in which he is pounding something with two short pestles. This object, dark yellow, is probably made of bronze: standing on three legs, it consists of a circular dish whose edge is provided with a lip for pouring. He is perhaps the household's baker-boy, kneading his dough. But the instruments in his hands remind one of a boxer's gloves and seem to indicate that he is crushing rather than kneading something. He is busy confectioning one of those mixed dishes the ancients found so tasty and in which there were all sorts of well-ground ingredients and enough hot spices to wake the dead.

In the *Moretum* attributed to Virgil, a peasant prepares in his mortar, with a small pestle, a cake composed of herbs, garlic, cheese and wine.[21] The *satura*, before giving its name to a poetic form, the satires of Horace and Boileau, was a sort of macedoine or hotchpotch made of barley mash, dried raisins, pine kernels, pomegranate pipes, the whole laced with honeyed wine.[22] And

187

Rome's Brillat-Savarin in the days of Tiberius, Apicius, whose name we have already encountered in a Caere tomb, has left us a collection of recipes whose secret lay in the 'pounding' (*terere*).[23] To season a jugged hare, pound together pepper, lovage, chopped celery, *nuoc-mam*,[24] silphium, wine and a little oil. To bring out the flavour of a boiled chicken one places in the mortar some chopped fennel, dried mint, silphium root; sprinkle these with vinegar, add date honey, pour in a few drops of garum, a little mustard, oil and boiled wine for sweetening; serve straight from the pot. Between the rustic simplicity of the Virgilian *moretum* and the imperial refinement of the Apician sauces was the cuisine of the *lucumones* of Orvieto, which also demanded the pounding of pestle in mortar, and this is what, in the painting, *pazu mulu(.)ane* is doing. Let us mention in passing that his title perhaps contains the Indo-European root which is found in the Latin *molo*, 'grind'. He is Paccius, in charge of grinding.

Standing behind him to give his movements the necessary rhythm is one *tibicen* playing for his benefit: he is *Tr. thun. suplu*. The abbreviation *Tr.* is apparently his name, *trepu*, *Trebius*; *thun* is connected with the name for the number 'one', and perhaps signifies *primus*; but *suplu* is certainly the same word as *subulo*, which Varro tells us is the Etruscan word for flautist.[25] Moreover we shall see further on that the Etruscans did their cooking to music.

Also on the rear wall, is depicted a stonework oven with two half-naked servants. One brandishes with great authority in his left hand a casserole: he is the *tesinth tamiathuras*, which means, according to an almost certainly correct interpretation, the *curator* or foreman over the vassals, in other words the kitchen superintendent or head cook.[26] Under his directions *klumie parliu* who is in charge of the *parla*, in Latin *patella*,[27] is carefully inserting into the blazing oven – or taking out – a frying-pan.

Especially appetizing are the four tables in a row between the butcher-boy and the pounder-and-grinder, in the centre of the painting on the lateral wall. A woman servant on the left is running towards them; she is *thrama mlithuns* and is wearing a yellow bodice and a skirt embroidered in the ancient fashion; she is bringing two receptacles. Behind the tables are a slave and another woman, whose name is illegible; she is very elegant: she wears a bandeau, dangling ear-rings, a necklace, a white cloak bordered with a purple fringe. She is gesturing to *thresu f(.) sithrals*, who has placed his arms round one of the tables, to carry it before the guest couch.

These tables are rectangular with three legs (here in the form of horses' legs) as was the fashion in Greece and Etruria. They are already laden with three layers of pancakes, among which can be seen two 'portions' for the two banqueters on each couch. Everyone will have his individual cake, probably round, the usual shape of bread and pastry in Rome and Pompeii, then indistinct piles of victuals among which there are perhaps eggs; finally, topping the lot, a bunch of black grapes for each guest. But also between the two cakes is a pomegranate flanked by two small pyramids which must be sweetmeats.

Finally the partition wall which divides the tomb into two parts. Next to the picture of the oven this contains a very mutilated painting of three servants behind a wooden table on which are various receptacles: all sorts of little violet-coloured bowls (perhaps the painter was trying to suggest the metallic shine of black varnish), drinking-cups, goblets, etc., which seem to be filled with yellow or reddish liquids or substances. The figures right at the end, *aklchis muifu* and *thresu penznas*, exist only as two fine profiles turned to the left; in the middle *runchlvis papnas*, with his little pointed beard and his naked chest, has not suffered so much damage: with his right arm raised to balance him, he is carrying in his other hand a heavy bronze decanter of unusual form; one might call it a *kylix* with large handles surmounted by a lipped cover; it recalls certain vases of Apulian style to which the name *lépastè* perhaps belongs;[28] its bearer is apparently about to pour the contents into the drinkers' cups.

BANQUETS

The pictures of kitchens given us by the Golini tomb are quite exceptional. Representations of banquets are much more frequent, painted as frescoes in the tombs at Tarquinii, modelled in bas-relief on the architectonic terracottas of Velletri, or sculpted on the urns and *cippi* of Chiusi which we have already met (plates 37 and 38). They are inspired by Greek traditions whose prototypes are formed by the friezes of Larisa in Aeolis[29] and the drinking-cups of Attic dandies:[30] here we find already the couch or bed with two guests on it, the low table in front of the couch, the cock or the dog scavenging under the table, the musician playing the double flute, the cup-bearer filling the cups. Within this conventional framework it is difficult for any unusual aspects of Etruscan life to make themselves felt.

We can tell nothing about where or at what time these banquets were held. They take place in an imaginary setting: often small trees with feathery leaves and a bright, diffused lighting suggest the open air, a park. Elsewhere crowns and garlands and ribbons, fans and arms hung on an invisible backcloth invite us to place the scene within some idealized *triclinium*. But in the Golini tomb the banquet of the two brothers, *Arnth Lecates* and *Vel Leinies*, whose preparations we have just been observing, takes place in the light of six candles on two lofty candelabra.

Usually a man and a woman are reclining on each couch – man and wife, we may be sure. We have already noted that this participation of the Etruscan woman in banquets was a freedom not granted to Greek women; in Athens it was only courtesans who lay beside young men on banqueting couches. Even when at home, the Greek wife did not keep her husband company while he was dining though she might sit beside the couch on which he took his lordly ease. This good breeding finally made itself felt, under the Grecian influence, even among the Etruscans, and in the Tomb of the Shields in Tarquinii, which dates from the third and perhaps from the second century, *Velia Seitithi* is seated modestly at the foot of the bed beside *Larth Velcha*, who is reclining.[31] All the same, she is giving her husband's shoulder an affectionate pat while with her other hand she is offering him a fruit which she has taken from a basket on the table. She shows the same melancholy tenderness which, three centuries earlier, in the Tomb of the Painted Vases, informed the delicately pathetic gesture of the man: taking his spouse's chin in his hand he turns her face towards him in order to look into her eyes for the last time.[32] But we must admit that in other cases, as in the Tomb of the Leopards, the young banqueters crowned with myrtle are giving themselves in the most carefree manner to the pleasures of wine and dalliance: the men have black hair and the women are blondes; they are wearing splendid multi-coloured cloaks. One of the young men is holding a ring between his thumb and first finger and flashing it in front of a young woman who gazes at it in fascination: the neighbouring pair both turn at the same moment to stare at a Ganymede, naked, who is passing by with his wine-jug. It is a scene of teasing, prattling, and sudden gusts of desire.[33]

Among the luxurious appurtenances of their banquets, Posidonius particularly admired the coverings, embroidered with gay colours, which adorned the beds.[34] These were doubtless the same Milesian woollen stuffs which we described above round the shoulders of dancers. Cicero was to accuse the embezzling praetor Verres – whose name, by the way, reveals an Etruscan origin in its inflexion – of having stolen wool from the Milesians[35] and of having turned all the Sicilian noblemen's palaces into workshops turning out purple cloth, 'as if, for each of his dining-rooms, in Rome and in all his country villas, he wanted to have three hundred beds covered with the stuff in every room, and not just three: covering them with magnificent materials (*stragula vestis*) and with all the other stuffs that are used to decorate banquets'.[36] Posidonius talks of *strômnai antheinai*, but we shall not take the adjective in its etymological sense (*anthos*) by translating it as 'covered with flowers'. The Etruscan paintings often show materials ornamented with little flowers, but *antheinos*, like its synonym *poikilos*, signifies in a more general sense 'embroidered with various colours', and indeed that is how we see the bed-coverings in the Tomb of the Leopards, with their fine red check and blue lines.[37] Such was the fashion at the beginning of the fifth century. Later, in the Tomb of the Shields, purple was to predominate everywhere in decorative schemes that were always geometrical.[38]

SILVER PLATE

Finally Posidonius tells us that the guests used abundant and varied silver plate. We have already quoted the verses of Critias the Tyrant, who celebrated, at the same time as their bronzes, 'the Tyrrhenians' gold-plated phials'[39] – phials means the little shallow cups, with a raised piece in the centre, which were used in libations. We have also mentioned several times all the buckets, basins, amphorae, jugs, pitchers and cups, in silver or in silver-gilt, sometimes with an engraved or repoussé design, which adorned the princely tombs of the seventh century in Vetulonia, Caere or Praeneste. Moreover the silverware in the Regolini-Galassi tomb, at least the goblets and cups, is marked with the proprietor's name, for she seemed to attach particular value to it.

Posidonius' observation nevertheless refers to a much more recent period, and we must acknowledge that it is not confirmed by archaeological evidence. Neither the paintings nor the funerary furnishings after the seventh century show this 'quantity of silver vases of all sorts' which the philosopher saw on Etruscan tables. In one of the frescoes of the Tomb of the Painted Vases in Tarquinii at the end of the sixth century, it is just possible that the white colour of a big *kylix* in a banqueter's hand might be taken to indicate that it was made of silver.[40] Usually all we see in the way of vases are bronze and pottery ones. The study of the furnishings of a necropolis like the one at Caere leads to the same conclusion: though it is incomparably rich in Attic pottery, it is extremely poor in metal objects. At that time silverware seemed to have disappeared from the Etruscan household. Must we look for the cause of this in the people's growing poverty, in the decadence that had cut it off from the centres of silver production, Spain in particular? Must we believe that avarice prevented them from sacrificing to the cult of the dead objects of great value? Or again that their passion for ceramics, nourished at first by Greek imports, and which had then developed in their own workshops, from the archaic *bucchero* with its black glaze to the late Arezzo red-glazed pottery, an uninterrupted manufacture of terracotta occupied them exclusively? All these things may have contributed to it. But we must note that the taste for silver vases had not died out so completely, for they invented, in the fourth to third centuries, in southern Etrurian centres, especially at Orvieto and Bolsena, a silver-glazed pottery in which there was the illusion of silver-plating.[41]

From the third century onwards, Etruria, incorporated in the Roman world, began to enjoy some of the benefits of conquest and reserved for its own use a little of the enormous quantities of luxury plate which from then on began to flow into Italy. The comedies of Plautus, shortly after the Second Punic War, show us sumptuous silver plate displayed on the sideboards of the rich. 'Those who have their houses filled with treasures', said the slave Stichus, 'drink out of embossed beakers and tankards and fancy goblets, while we drink out of our Samian jug. But we drink just the same.'[42] The Etruscan *lucumones* began drinking out of 'embossed beakers' again, out of tankards and fancy goblets made of silver and Alexandrian gold, and from those which their gold- and silversmiths, roused from their torpor or seized with a spirit of emulation, had begun producing again.

In 206, P. Scipio Africanus brought back from Spain more than fourteen thousand pounds of silver, not counting silver coin.[43] In 189, his brother Lucius displayed at his triumph over Antiochus 1,023 pounds of gold plate and 1,423 pounds of silver plate.[44] In 161 a sumptuary law forbade leading citizens attending the banquets at the Ludi Megalenses to bring more than one hundred pounds of silverware.[45] Therefore one is not surprised that one of the rare Etruscan tombs in which one glimpses a pale reflection of what the silver plate of ancient times must have been, the Tomb of *Larthia Seianti* at Chiusi, should be dated by the presence of a Roman uncial as bearing the head of Janus from the first half of the second century – at the earliest. We find there, mixed up with various toilet articles, hairpins, comb, depilatory tweezers, a few *vasa argentea*, a small *kratèr*, a casserole and plates.[46] Those who entertained Posidonius in their own homes were doubtless much richer: it was Rome that restored to their banquets this essential part of their splendour.

III

GAMES

Whatever we are best acquainted with in the manners and customs of the Etruscans comes from their games, because, in the special form of funeral games, they loved to depict these on the walls of their tombs or sculpt them on their *cippi* and sarcophagi. No one has disproved that the institution went back to a very early date: it is attested by tradition from the days following the battle of Alalia (*c* 535): the Caerites, having captured a great number of Phocaean prisoners there, had led them out of the town and stoned them; the Delphic oracle, when consulted, 'ordered them to do what they are still doing today'. (Here it is Herodotus speaking, in the middle of the fifth century.[47]) 'They offer rich sacrifices to the shades of the Phocaeans and institute in their honour gymnic and equestrian games.'

Moreover it is fairly certain that these manifestations of strength and vitality which the Etruscans, like the other peoples of antiquity, displayed at their funerals to exorcize the omnipotence of death were not different from those which, in country festivals, were used to excite magically the energies of Nature, or, in urban ceremonies, to assure the gods' protection of their Capitols. Whether they were dedicated to the shades of the dead or to the gods made no change in their programme. Thus, later on, in a Rome which was only following the example of the Etruscans, the comedies of Terence would be played at the Roman Games, the Ludi Megalenses or the Funeral Games of Aemilius Paulus (when the *Adelphi* of Terence was first staged). We may be sure that the dances and races we witness in the tombs at Tarquinii are reflections, perhaps embellished and stylized, of those which were held not only in the necropolises but also in all the sanctuaries – among others the Temple of Vertumnus, *fanum Voltumnae*, when the federal assembly of the nation met there every spring.[48] It was then that were celebrated the solemn games in which, along with the artists in their personal troupes, the *lucumones* of the twelve peoples participated; we remember the anecdote about the king of Veii,[49] who, beaten in the elections, at once left for home with his histrions and pugilists, just like those depicted in the Tomb of the Augurs and the Tomb of the Leopards.

Again, these paintings not only bring back to us the great public gatherings, with the noisy and brightly coloured activity of the nearby fairground, but also the political intrigues which began in the shadows of the sacred woods; these festivals were simply an opportunity, returning at regular intervals, to live out more intensely the gestures of everyday life. These spectacles reflected, like a magnifying but not a distorting mirror, the various activities of common reality. Just as the funeral banquets introduced us into the intimacy of their two daily meals, the games make us see what music, dancing, sport – and also, naturally, the theatre – meant to the Etruscans.

MUSIC

The enormous place occupied by music in the lives of the
Etruscans is certainly one of the most striking features of their
civilization. Here our intention is not to diminish in any way the
superiority of the Greeks, who made music – and not only in the
sense of a cult of the Muses and of intellectual culture, but in the
strict acceptance of the terms 'instrumental' and 'vocal music' –
the foundation of their cities and the nourishment of the soul.[50]
Certainly it is to the Greeks we owe the myth of Orpheus
charming the animals, the rocks and even the gods with the sound
of his lyre. The whole fable is full of names of legendary cithern
and flute-players, disciples or rivals of Apollo, Orpheus, Linos,
Amphion and Marsyas who, by the power of music, raised the
fortifications of cities and tamed savage beasts. And in effect
Athenian and even Spartan education placed first on their
syllabus 'the lyre, light dancing and singing'.[51] Concerts are a
favourite subject for the painters of fifth century vases. 'There
was no feature of any importance in urban or rural existence –
marriages, funerals, harvests, grape-gatherings – which did not
have a more or less well-developed musical accompaniment.'[52]

In this as in everything else the Etruscans were pupils of the
Greeks. But they found ways of extending the empire of music
to domains where it had never before penetrated. It was indispensable at the games, where it regulated the movements of the
dancers; it was natural that it should contribute to the drunkenness
of guests at banquets; that it should come into the liturgy of
religious ceremonies was quite a normal thing; and it had always
been used to excite the ardour of troops in battle. But we share
the astonishment of Aristotle who noted as a significant indication
of moral weakness that the Etruscans conducted boxing-matches,
whipped their slaves and even cooked to the sound of the flute.[53]
Thus all their occupations, even the most banal, were accompanied
by music. One thing that must have been difficult to find in an
Etruscan city was silence. One must imagine their activity
against a continuous background of noise: not just *il lieto rumore*,
'the happy murmur' of Leopardi which fills Italian villages on
Saturday evenings, but rather the sort of thing we hear strolling
home through the outskirts of Florence, after dinner – the ever-
lasting radio, turned on at full volume, transmitting from *villino*

195

to *villino*, through thousands of wide-flung windows, the entire *Norma* of Bellini.

Italian music was already triumphant and played everywhere in the days of the Etruscans, but whatever Aristotle says, it was quite the reverse of anything effete and languorous. For in his enumeration of these three apparently incongruous uses of the flute, the philosopher does not seem to understand that their object was to regulate three types of violent movement. In Greece, too, the *auletes* or flute-player helped the rowers to keep a concerted rhythm; armed with a megaphone, he can still be found in our boat-races. The blows of Etruscan pugilists were also scanned in this way, but this custom, which turned boxing into a sort of measured dance, was by no means intended to soften the blows. The swish of the vibrant rod on the bare flesh of a slave had also to be administered according to certain rhythmical laws, but despite what Plutarch says in his treatise *On the art of restraining anger*,[54] music in this case was not intended to soften the feelings either of master or of slave. As for cooking, we are better able to understand what Aristotle meant thanks to an indication given us by the Sicilian historian Alcimos:[55] the latter does in effect speak of 'kneading bread', a labour which must have been performed in a rhythmical manner. We have noticed, in the paintings in the Golini tomb, the flute-player, *suplu* or *subulo*, who is helping *pazu mulu(.)ane*, bent half-naked over the ingredients he is energetically kneading or grinding, and here the music is not provided to slow up his movements or to make his sauce turn out badly.

Then there was hunting, in which music played a considerable part. Not only were there horns and trumpets to encourage the hounds. The *Characteristics of Animals* composed in the third century AD by Aelian alludes to an Etruscan tradition according to which music brought the game into the nets.[56]

'There is an Etruscan story current which says that the wild boars and the stags in that country are caught by using nets and hounds, as is the usual means of hunting, but that music plays a part, and even the larger part, in the struggle. And how this happens I will now relate. They set the nets and other hunting gear that ensnare the animals in a circle, and a man proficient on the pipes stands there and tries his utmost to play a rather soft tune, avoiding any shriller note, but playing the sweetest melodies possible. The quiet and the stillness easily carry the sound abroad; and the music streams up to the heights and into ravines and thickets – in a word into every lair and resting-place of these animals. Now at first when the sound penetrates to their ears it strikes them with terror and fills them with dread, and then an unalloyed and irresistible delight in the music takes hold of them, and they are so beguiled as to forget about their offspring and their homes. And yet wild beasts do not care to wander away from their native haunts. But little by little these creatures in Etruria are attracted as though by some persuasive spell, and beneath the wizardry of the music they come and fall into the snares, overpowered by the melody.'

It is difficult to tell where Aelian, who was from Praeneste and knew well the circumstances of Italic life, could have found the material for this passage still quick with a mysterious feeling for the life of wild creatures and for the magic power that music has over them. Aristotle knew of this curious kind of trap, but he only mentioned it in connexion with the hunting of the deer, an animal whose musical sensitivity had struck the ancients: the boar seems to be a casual addition from the Etruscan source.[57] However such a method of hunting is not entirely imaginary. It is reported that on the Ivory Coast the hunters 'attract the antelopes by playing a long flute, and the inquisitive beasts, charmed by the sounds, approach unsuspectingly and are soon slain with a lance or an arrow'.[58] But perhaps the origin of the distant echo which we find in Aelian resides in some poem where a hunting prince, a Gilgamesh or some unknown Cyrus of the epics of Vulci or Chiusi hunted the deer and the wild boar accompanied by a marvellous Etruscan Orpheus who turned his musical gifts to cruelly utilitarian ends. But unlike the legendary player on the lyre, the Etruscan Orpheus would have drawn his irresistible notes from a flute.

All through their history the flute remained the favourite instrument of the Etruscans. The paintings and the *cippi* of the sixth and fifth centuries show, throbbing under the fingers of their players, lyres and citherns of seven strings and more, according to whatever new refinements the Greek lute-players had brought to the instruments at that period. And the flute-players are inseparable from these players of stringed instruments, at least in the early days. But then the duet between the Apollonian lyre and the Dionysiac flute was interrupted, but in different ways, in Greece and Etruria. In the former, the flute which Pericles had played like a virtuoso fell under the disapproval of Plato and Aristotle.[59] In the latter, only the flute was heard at public and private concerts. Authors and monuments have made us familiar with many varieties of flute, which modern musicians would prefer to call clarinets or oboes. According to Virgil, the ones used at sacrifices were made of ivory; Pliny says they were made of box-wood.[60] In archaic times small, short ones were preferred;[61] on a late urn from the Tomb of the Volumii at Perugia a 'German' flute – that is, one held sideways – is depicted.[62] But on the whole Etruria remained faithful to the double flute, which is composed of two pipes, and Rome followed her, hardly ever using anything but *tibiae*, in the plural.

So it was the song of the flute that constituted the background of the sounds we imagined we could hear in the Etruscan street. We should like to know more about it, but the music of the Greeks is very little known: even less so that of the Etruscans. Was it perhaps more chromatic than the Grecian modes? We must suppose that, conservative as they were, and obstinately attached to the flute and the tradition of wind instruments that had favoured the emergence of the enharmonic mode and the taste for the nuances of fractional tones, they cultivated those musical fashions of Asia Minor which perhaps stirred atavistic memories in them: the Phrygian mode, for example, and that Hypolydian mode whose character, according to the musicologists of antiquity, was 'dissolute, relaxed and voluptuous'. But the rhythm of it must sometimes have been fairly brisk, to keep the baker pounding his dough.

In any case, the reputation of Etruscan flautists conquered the world: an Athenian philosopher at the beginning of the third century, who was too fond of the flute was saddled with the mocking nickname of 'Tyrrhenos'.[63] Rome in particular soon got into the way of bringing from Etruria the *subulones* who were indispensable at the ritual celebration of sacrifices, which they would prelude with an air on the flute. In the Eternal City they formed a college that was very jealous of its rights, and that reserved for itself the monopoly in this art. One day, at the end of the fourth century, they went on strike, and, because they had not been given their traditional banquet at the Capitol, moved away to *Tibur* (Tivoli). The Senate was obliged to give way, and, in order to get them back, had to have recourse to a ruse: various families in Tivoli, having announced that they would be holding banquets, invited the musicians for dinner (the anecdote could be illustrated by a fresco from Tarquinii) and made them drunk – for as Livy says (but it is a Roman speaking), 'these people have a taste for drink'. Carried off in chariots, they did not wake up until they were at the Forum, where their privileges were restored to them.[64] We shall see further on that the Etruscan dancers were one day to join their flute-playing countrymen in Rome, where they collaborated in the creation of the Latin drama.

As well as its sacred music, Rome borrowed Etruria's military bands. Ever since Aeschylus the ancients praised the excellence of the Etruscan trumpet. *Tyrsénikè salpinx, Tyrrhenica tuba*[65] – the straight trumpet whose horn swells out in the form of a bell. Another type of trumpet with a curved end, like the *lituus* of the augurs, is represented in official processions, as are the semi-circular trumpets which resemble our hunting-horns. But whether straight, curved or semi-circular, *tubae, litui* and *cornua* sounded the attack for the Etruscan armies and the fanfares for their official parades; it was they that sounded the attacks at Sentinum and Philippi, and even the haruspices thought they could hear them in the sky, proclaiming the end of a century or announcing the will of the gods:

Tyrrhenusque tubae mugire per aethera clangor.[66]
(The Tyrrhenian trumpet-blast rang through the heavens.)

DANCING

There were dances both sacred and profane in Etruria – the distinction between the two is however rather uncertain – and we must mention first the warrior dances, similar to those which the Salii – their name, etymologically speaking, means 'dancers' – practised in Rome, clashing together their sacred *ancilia* or shields fallen from the sky. 'They chanted hymns accompanied by rhythmical leaps and ritual dances.'[67]

This armed dance was held in great honour throughout the whole of Central Italy, and a small votive buckler, bilobate like those of the Salii, and which R. Bloch found in a Villanovan tomb at Bolsena,[68] shows definitely that it came before the full flowering of Etruscan culture which adopted it into its ceremonies: an *intaglio* in the archaeological museum at Florence and dating from the fourth–third centuries represents two Salii carrying *ancilia*. Moreover, in Greece itself, many religious festivals included a mock battle which, danced to the sound of the flute, was called Pyrrhic. We find echoes of these in the Tomb of the Bigae and on the cippi of Chiusi.

In the festivals of the Salii, there was a *coryphaeus*, a leading dancer, the *praesul*, meaning 'he who dances in front'. He executed dance steps which the rest of the dancers did after him. Two old Latin verbs which rapidly became obscure characterized these two movements of the dance: *amptruare* and *redamptruare*.[69] The prefix *amp-* indicates a circular movement: the leader first made a turning jump (*amptruabat*) which was repeated by the ensemble (*redamptruabat*). The radical *-truare* is unknown: apparently it had a meaning in Etruscan.

At the time of Augustus, Rome witnessed the resumption of an ancient parade on the Campus Martius, in which three armed squadrons of young horsemen of high birth took part. This display was called the *troia*; the expression was *troiam ludere*, 'to celebrate the *troia*', and *lusus troiae*, 'the game of the *troia*'; and there was no doubt among scholars that, by virtue of a convenient etymology, the institution of this game went back to the legendary origins – *Trojan* origins – of Rome; it was the 'game of Troy'. Virgil had encouraged this delusion, by giving the *troia* a place among the funeral ceremonies in honour of Anchises which he describes in Book V of the *Aeneid*. There he depicted first of all, in celebrated verses, the parade of the *Troiae juventus*, 'the youth of Troy', then the horsemen's evolutions, whose twistings and turnings reminded him of the Cretan Labyrinth.[70]

'They galloped apart in equal ranks, and the three companies, parting their bands, broke up the columns; then recalled, they wheeled about and charged with levelled lances. Next they enter on other marches and other countermarches in opposing groups, interweaving circle with alternate circle, and making an armed mimicry of battle.'

Now an *oenochoè* discovered at Tragliatella, near Bracciano, about ten kilometres from Caere, and whose style, of Protocorinthian influence, reveals an Etruscan work of the late seventh century, presents, roughly engraved on its flanks, a labyrinth from which are emerging two armed horsemen preceded by seven foot-soldiers performing a warrior dance.[71] Within the labyrinth, we can clearly read, in Etruscan characters, the word *truia*. It is generally admitted that this word meant either a sort of armed dance or the place or arena, perhaps a fortified camp, in which it took place, and that it was perpetuated in Latin in the ritual vocabulary of the Salii (*amptruare*) and that the *lusus troiae* also owes its name to this.[72] From the seventh to the first centuries, the *troia* survived in obscure forms throughout the whole history of Etruscan orchestics, finally conquering Rome herself where it provoked mythographists to draw the most fanciful etymological conclusions.

BACCHIC DANCE

But it was Dionysos rather than Mars who seems to have brought self-awareness to Etruscan dancing and given it a permanent style. Everywhere in Graeco-Etruscan Italy we see Sileni and Maenads dancing mad farandoles across the cornices of temples, on the covers of *lebes* or funerary cauldrons, ornamenting candelabra and tripods and decorating vases and drinking-cups. Using various dissociated examples, an attempt has been made to recreate the successive steps of a whole choreographic sequence.[73] The first movement, an invitation to the dance, is represented by a handle which shows Silenus leaping joyfully towards a Maenas who, startled, is attempting to escape. Proceeding to the delightful antefixes of Falerii, Lanuvium and Satricum, the Silenus and the Maenas are progressing with their arms around each other, 'as if they were dancing parallel steps'. Finally, the last figure of the dance – shown on a bronze in the Metropolitan Museum of New York – the Maenas is hoisted on the shoulder of the triumphant Silenus 'as if on to a living pedestal'. So this dance also seemed to have a mimed significance, a dramatic subject: it was the ballet of the Abduction.[74]

The Bacchic inspiration behind Etruscan dancing persisted, with all the paraphernalia of masks and disguises it implied, right up to the time of the procession that was held in Rome on the occasion of the games at the Circus Maximus: this procession consisted, after the serious dances were over, of burlesque dances of Sileni and Satyrs, the former wearing shaggy tights and flowered cloaks, the latter goatskins with an upstanding mane on their heads.[75] Dionysius of Halicarnassus adds that he had seen, at the funerals of illustrious persons, troupes of dancers disguised as Satyrs proceeding in front of the coffin. All this was probably a very ancient and persistent tradition imitated from the Etruscans.

The funerary paintings omit the accessories of the *thiasus*, but the dances they represent still preserve, with different costumes, the character of orgiastic folly that is peculiar to the Bacchic dance. This can be seen in the Tomb of the Lionesses and in the one which is actually named *dei Baccanti*, circa 520; and in the Tomb of the Triclinium, dating from about 470, are several pictures which allow us to follow the evolution of the dance over the fifty years during which the tomb was used.

In the Tomb of the Lionesses, on the rear wall, on either side of a big *kratèr*, are, crowned with the ivy of Dionysos, a flute-player and a cithern-player. To the right and left there are dancers.[76] On the right: a couple.[77] The male dancer's naked body is brick-red; both he and the female dancer, who is clad in a transparent tunic, with castanets in her right hand, and is facing him, are driven, as M. Pallottino very rightly notes, 'by the agitated rhythms of the *tripudium*'. *Tripudium* is an old Latin word which designated a dance in three-four time in which one stamped three times on the ground; more generally it indicated, whether in three-four time or not, a dance composed of leaps. Here our dancers are doing both things, and performing the same gestures: stamping one foot on the ground, raising the other leg. Is it a dance in three-four time? We cannot tell. The important thing is the leap which lifts them from the ground and the position of the arms, one lowered, the other in the air, which prolongs their flight. What is very remarkable is that the dancer is at the same time raising his right arm and right leg, the female dancer her left arm and left leg, without any consideration for the law of opposites which governs and balances regularly-composed dances, but not Bacchic ones.

On the other side, a single female dancer, heavily coiffed, shod and clad, in complete contrast to her lightly-garbed partners, is making a long, sliding step to the left, but it is also a turning step, as can be seen from her cloak which is still giving a front view of its folds. Of her two arms, one is raised, the other lowered from the elbow, and both hands are bent back in opposite directions. This *cheironomia* plays a great part in Etruscan dancing, which is done with the hands more than with the legs. The famous ceramologist, Sir John Beazley, who makes a study of it in his *Etruscan Vase Painting*, has a profound admiration for this 'Etruscan dancer's hand' when he sees it on the wine-cups and *stamnoi* of Chiusi. 'I know an Italian family,' he declares, 'a mother and two daughters, who can make Etruscan-dancer gestures with their hands, but judge the faculty to be uncommon even in Italy.'[78]

As we proceed from tomb to tomb, leaps and gesticulations become more and more free, until we arrive at the marvellous figures in the Tomb of the Triclinium (plate 16), where the players of flute and cithern themselves enter into the dance among the bushes of an enchanted garden. Perhaps their leaps are more restrained, their gestures more sober, their heads inclined a little more gently. But the classicism resides in the painter; the dionysiac intoxication still informs the dancing figures absolutely.

Rome, which had already had recourse to Etruscan flute-players, called upon these dancers (tradition has it, in 364). Livy, in a charming litotes, said the Romans much appreciated their 'not ungraceful evolutions': *motus haud indecoros*.[79] At the same time he tells us their Etruscan name, *ister*, which was latinized into *histrio*, giving us our 'histrion'. In Latin they were also called 'ludions' (*ludii*). Now the essential feature of their art still lay in the leaps of the *tripudium*. Ovid, in his *Art of Love*,[80] evokes anachronistically the games of Romulus' day at which the Sabine women were abducted because they were distracted by the spectacle of the dance and unaware of danger, 'while to the

Tuscan flute-player's rude strains the dancer struck thrice with his foot the levelled floor, in the midst of the applause . . . the king gave the people the expected sign of rape'.

But already in Plautus' *Curculio* we find a lover playing a serenade outside his loved one's house: he addresses himself to the bolts on the door, that they may burst and let him in:

> Bolts, ah, bolts, I greet you gladly:
> Take my love and hear my plea,
> Hear my prayer, my supplication,
> Fairest bolts, ah, favour me.
> Change to foreign dancers for me,
> Spring, I pray you, spring on high,
> Send a wretched man his dear love,
> Love that drains his life-blood dry . . .[81]

(Trans. Paul Nixon.)

When they arrived in Rome, the Etruscan ballets must have produced something like the same impression as the Russian Ballet did on Paris in 1911, and their leaps did not seem to have been any less vertiginous than Nijinsky's.

SPORT

Sport was also consecrated in the games celebrated in honour of the gods and at funerals: here again the Etruscans, disciples of the Greeks, were the educators of the Romans. The tradition was long-established: Tarquinius the Elder had scarcely ascended the throne before he gave, after his first victory, the most magnificent games, better organized than those of any of his predecessors.

'It was then that the ground was first marked out for the circus now called Maximus. Places were divided amongst the Fathers and the knights where they might each make seats for themselves; these were called "rows". They got their view from seats raised on props to a height of twelve feet from the ground. The entertainment was furnished by horses and boxers, imported for the most part from Etruria. From that time the Games continued to be a regular annual show, and were called indifferently the Roman and the Great Games.'[82] (Trans. B. O. Foster.)

The event is believed to have been as early as the end of the seventh century. In the days of Cicero the Etruscan nobles still had their racing stables: Aulus Caecina, heir of one of the greatest equestrian families in Volterra, raced his *quadrigae* at the Circus Maximus; when he went to Rome he would take with him swallows which he would release to announce the result to his friends in Etruria; they would return to their nests dyed with the colour of the victorious team.[83]

RACING

The figured monuments abundantly illustrate the place which the gymnasium, the stadium and the hippodrome occupied in Etruscan life. Quite recently – on March 26, 1958 – there was unearthed in Tarquinii a new tomb with frescoes, and it immediately received the appellation of 'Tomb of the Olympic Games' after the games which were later to take place at Rome, and whose success this magnificent discovery, due to the photographic soundings of the engineer Lerici, seemed to portend.[84] There had been painted on its walls, about 525–520, the principal gymnic and equestrian contests that figured in the programme of ancient games: these included the discus, high-jump, boxing and especially racing, both human and equestrian. On the right-hand lateral wall is depicted a foot-race between three athletes who have almost reached the tape: all three are naked, save for a skimpy loincloth; all three are swinging their arms to the rhythm of their racing feet; but they are diversified by the curious pointed beard sported by the first and the third runners, and even more so, in a very subtle way, by the different expressions on their faces, corresponding, in their confidence, determination and hopelessness, to the order of their arrival at the end of the race.

Even more remarkable, on the left, is the race between four *bigae* or chariots drawn by two horses; these, too, are in sight of the post; they are out in the open country and not in the level arena of a circus. Each auriga wears a jockey's jacket, either blue or red; but the horses' and the chariots' colours are also blue or red, alternately, which perhaps is due to the artist's taste, though possibly we can see in this arrangement an indication – as during the Roman Empire and even, as we have seen, in the days of Caecina – of the faction to which they belonged. One detail that was previously unknown: the two reins are tied behind the charioteer's back, forming an immense knot. Each one is belabouring his horses furiously. The first, already almost the winner, is turning round to see how far ahead he is; the third is on the point of overtaking the second on the left; the fourth chariot has just overturned, one of its horses is on its back with all four feet in the air while the other is rearing and the charioteer is being thrown backwards: three women watching the event have put their hands to their heads and are screaming with fright. There is more elegance, more talent in other paintings at Tarquinii. The value of this one derives from the extraordinary dynamic quality that animates it, and the lively humour, the narrative ingenuity with which the Etruscan painter, in rendering the things he has seen, interprets the Greek tradition.

If this unfortunate charioteer in the overturned chariot had been driving, instead of a *biga*, a *quadriga*, we might well have called him Ratumenna, the name of an Etruscan *auriga* whose wonderful story is told us by Plutarch and Festus;[85] he lived at about the same time as the Tomb of the Olympic Games was constructed. He was of illustrious birth: which goes to prove that, as in archaic and classical Greece, sports – the noble sports in any case – were practised by amateurs and not by professionals, by men of high condition and not by slaves. At that time there was a difference between Rome and Veii about a *quadriga* made of terra-cotta which Tarquinius Superbus had ordered from a workshop in the Etruscan town; it was to crown the temple of Jupiter Capitolinus; but the authorities at Veii did not wish to deliver this masterpiece, because of an omen that had revealed it would give Rome the supremacy. Ratumenna, at the end of a race he had won at Veii, had just received the victor's crown and was driving his chariot at a walking-pace out of the race-course when his horses took fright and ran away; he could not restrain them, and they set off at a gallop for Rome, where they did not halt until they had reached the Capitol, having thrown to the ground their driver whose name was given to the Ratumenna Gate.

ATHLETICS

Of the various representations of gymnic and equestrian games which figure in the tombs of Tarquinii and on the *cippi* of Chiusi, we have chosen those, more recent, of the Tomb of the Olympic Games. But we can learn much from other tombs. The Tomb of the Augurs, dating from about 530, shows a subject whose origin was in Asia Minor, two wrestlers, completely naked;[86] not only have they been given splendid muscular development but also a well-defined oriental type of features: ebony-black hair and beard, very long eyelashes, thick lips and a receding forehead; one would think they had been picked up in some Levantine slave-market, but it was probably an Ionian model, caricatural himself, who inspired the painter. The latter, in any case, gave them Etruscan names, *Teitu*, *Latithe*; the first of these is not known, but the second was borne by honourable families of Cortona and Chiusi. Again, two important personages, wrapped in their cloaks, are standing near the wrestlers; one of them, who lifts in his right hand a curved stick (*lituus*), carefully referees the holds. Both of them are, as can be seen from the inscription repeated above their heads, *tevarath*, that is, *agonothetes* or organizers of the games, referees. Between the wrestlers three great vases of bronze stand waiting to be awarded to the victor.

Another tomb, the Tomb of the Bigae (beginning of fifth century), has a painting right at the top of its walls, a little frieze which does not seem to omit any of the sporting tests included in the Games.[87] The taste for slim silhouettes and the assured finesse of the drawing prove that in this new stage of its evolution Etruscan painting followed the progress made by its Grecian masters, as it was reflected in the Attic ceramics of that period. Here we have the procession of the *bigae* before the starting signal, and also the preparations for a horse-race with jockeys; we see wrestlers, with pugilists fighting bare-fisted or wearing boxing-gloves; there is discus-throwing and javelin-throwing, high-jump and armed dancing. Athletes resting converse before entering the arena. *Agonothetes* carrying the *lituus* wander among the groups.

THE TRIBUNES AND THE PUBLIC

But we would draw particular attention to the tribunes or stands reserved for the public.[88] They are placed two by two at the extremities of each part of the frieze, facing each other and turned towards the spectacle taking place at the centre. We wonder perhaps if it does not represent – but nothing in the style of ancient painting authorizes this hypothesis – a cross-section of an amphitheatre, showing only sections of stands which actually went right round an arena in the form of an ellipse or a circle. Whatever the explanation, they recall very precisely, though they are less high, the 'seats raised on props' which Tarquinius the Elder had set up in the Circus Maximus for the Roman senators and knights.[89] The ones found in paintings comprise beams at least three feet high supporting a wooden platform over which is stretched a *velum* which protects the spectators from the sun. They are crowded eight or ten to a platform, seated one behind the other on a single bench; it is impossible to say whether this is shown from the front or the side. But here we recognize, in the liberal promiscuity we have mentioned, older men, youths and women wearing the *tutulus* – all the high society of Tarquinii. In the rather confined space between the platform and the ground, crouch or recline as best they can a host of turbulent slaves: those who can see anything appear to be watching and sometimes applauding; those crowded to the back pass the time in a way that proclaims their liberal spirit but is not always innocent.

A similar stand appears again on a *cippus* from Chiusi,[90] but this time it is the jury sitting there for the distribution of awards. Two magistrates who seem to think they are gods and imitate the attitude of Olympians in the frieze round the treasury of the Siphnians turn towards each other, sceptre or *lituus* in hand, and deliberate. Behind them, an *apparitor*, evidently belonging to the police, points with the end of his stick underneath the platform, where are assembled the vases offered as prizes. On the edge of the stand, a secretary with a diptych open on his knees is writing down the names of the victors: the first of these, wearing a crested helmet and holding a lance and a buckler has just been dancing the pyrrhic; he is followed by a whirling female dancer wearing a helmet and a skirt which recall the costume of the women in the Francesca Giustiniani tomb; a flautist accompanies her; finally we see a discobolist and his trainer.

This scene, taken as a whole, and despite the *lituus* of one of the judges and the costume of the female dancer, could be Greek and situated for example in Sicily, not far from that Palermo where the fate governing collections caused the *cippus* from Chiusi to be preserved. But at the same period, still at the beginning of the fifth century, and in the same city of Chiusi, the Tomb of the Monkey mingled with the common themes of Hellenic civilization – wrestlers, pugilists, armed dancers, equestrian virtuosi – more particular subjects which have a popular and local accent.[91] It has been said: 'The Greek taste for palaestra and stadium here seems to give way to an air of peasant festivity.' It is not just the presence of the monkey and the bearded dwarf that gives it this character: enveloped in a huge black cloak which covers her neck and hair, and from which her face emerges as from a cowl, is a lady in deep mourning seated on the edge of a chair or a bed, her feet placed on a stool; she is sitting in the shade of a parasol whose handle she is holding upright in front of her with both hands.

This is certainly the dead woman whose tomb it is, gracing with her presence the games given in her honour. During these some strange mountebanks have made their entry: a female dancer and her flautist . . . but the dancer is also a juggler; as she dances she carries on her head a sort of candelabrum, and one could almost swear that its candle is lighted; she does not hold it with her hands which, brought forward over her chest, are playing castanets. She is wearing very modern clothes – or very archaic: a chemisette or bodice, crossed-over at the front, and, falling from an embroidered belt, a real skirt, all black. The musician's costume is even more bizarre: very tight tights, of a light flesh-tint, coming right up to his neck, contrasting with the brick-red colour of his arms that are three-quarters bare, and with his face, as well as with the broad belt round his waist from which there hang in front, over his thighs, three flaps. In addition he wears a broad-brimmed hat which does not have its like in all antiquity, unless perhaps it is the hats on the *situla* of the Certosa and on Bolognese bronzes,[92] or again that worn by the warrior of Capestrano.[93] It is an odd garment, which we might expect to have seen in the wardrobe of the Commedia dell' Arte. We shall see, in fact, that certain masks worn in Etruscan revelries are forerunners of those familiar faces, Harlequin and Punch. But rather than an anticipation it was a survival from a very distant past; these things were brought out of chests to clothe this pair of mountebanks when, at the funeral of a great lady of Chiusi, obscure indigenous traditions claimed their rightful place despite the overwhelming influence of the Grecian style, and provided, among more modish contests, an unforeseen intermission in the country's taste.

GLADIATORIAL COMBATS

These games were sometimes bloody ones. It appears that the Etruscans long remained faithful to the barbarous custom of sacrificing prisoners to the shades of their dead warriors. Before the opening of the funeral games in honour of his friend Patroclus, Achilles had immolated on the funeral pyre 'four noble mares, two of his hounds and twelve noble sons of the magnanimous Trojans'.[94] This vision of the funeral of Patroclus never ceased to haunt the imagination of the Etruscans. The ceremony was reproduced everywhere: on vases from Falerii and Chiusi, on a *cista* from Praeneste, a sarcophagus from Orvieto, an urn from Orvieto, an urn from Volterra, paintings at Tarquinii and above all at Vulci in the famous François tomb. Sir John Beazley counted seven of these monuments, stretching in time from the fourth to the first centuries, and all of which are derived from the same lost original.[95] And without any doubt the representations of massacres no longer corresponded to any actual massacre; they were not carried out any more, much as at Rome in the Argeian festivities twenty-four wicker-work dummies were thrown into the Tiber instead of living victims. It enabled the families of dead persons to enhance their mourning by raising it to the level of the Greek legend, and to console themselves for the mortal condition of humanity through the enchantments of poetry. Yet the history of the Etruscans sometimes gives glimpses of sudden returns – and not token ones either – to a furious lust for blood. In the middle of the sixth century, the Caerites had stoned the prisoners they captured at the battle of Alalia.[96] In 358, during a war between Rome and Tarquinii, 307 soldiers, Romans, were immolated in the Forum of that city.[97] During the civil wars, when Octavius captured Perugia, he sacrificed three hundred of her nobles to the shades of the Julii, cynically claiming that he was giving his enemies a taste of their own rites; perhaps the Etruscans in his camp had inspired them.[98]

So we cannot ignore certain testimonies and certain facts which attribute to the Etruscans the institution of the gladiatorial games, which the ancients regarded as progressive because, instead of killing prisoners on the tomb, they were made to fight in front of it, which gave them a chance. Nicolaus of Damascus, who wrote under Augustus, stated that Rome had borrowed this custom from them, probably in the first half of the third century.[99] Again, the word *lanista*, which means 'superintendent of the gladiators', was, according to those grammarians of antiquity approved by modern scholarship, of Etruscan origin.[100] Finally the Fathers of the Church, indignantly denouncing the sanguinary madness of the amphitheatres, witnessed there, between combats, a clown whose task was to carry away the corpses: he used to wear – significant survival – the costume and the attributes of the Etruscan Charon with his mallet.[101]

Yet it was not in Etruria but in Campania and in Lucania that the gladiatorial games must have come to their full development and taken on their classic form. From the fourth century, in the paintings of Capua and Paestum, we see pairs of gladiators fighting it out, in their aigretted helmets, carrying buckler and lance, covered with wounds and dripping with blood.[102] In southern Italy, the Samnites of the mountains provided abundant material for these games: among the various classes in which the gladiators had to arrange themselves, those called after the 'Samnites' were the most ancient, and the only kind that was known before Sylla added the 'Thracian' and Caesar the 'Gaulish' kinds. *Samnis* was for a long time a generic term, and the Campania always remained the main area for the recruitment of gladiators, the centre for their schools and the theatre of their revolts.[103]

Nothing like this is known to have existed in Etruria. We search in vain in bas-reliefs and paintings for examples of these duels between two gladiators, sword in hand.[104] But we do find something else, which is more ancient, more mysterious and richer: though the gladiatorial games reached their full development elsewhere, they were based on a principle whose ancient manifestations can be followed, from the sixth century, in the frescoes at Tarquinii.

THE GAME OF PHERSU

Two tombs from the second half of this century show, among the scenes of funeral games which decorate their walls, a strange combat which is at the same time an example of corporal punishment which proclaims from afar the future martyrdoms of the Roman amphitheatres. In a painting from the Tomb of the Augurs,[105] a man condemned to death is being subjected to the attacks of a savage dog which has planted its fangs in the man's left leg. His body is completely naked except for a loin-cloth, and is already bleeding in many places. For it is in vain he tries to defend himself with the club he holds in his right hand: his head is covered with a sack or bag which prevents him from seeing anything and forces him to strike out like a blind man. The chances of this ludicrous Hercules saving his life are very small.

Now the same picture, formerly quite unique, has since been found to have a double, which proves that it represented not some unusual fantasy but a consecrated rite. In the Tomb of the Olympic Games we find, among the equestrian and gymnic games we have described, the same desperate duel between a blinded man and the wild beast tearing him to pieces.[106]

Of course, the Imperial amphitheatres also knew combats against lions and bears. 'The pleasure of these festivities was not complete,' Tertullian was to write, 'unless the human bodies were torn to pieces by savage beasts.'[107] But at least the *bestiarii* were armed, and though for most of the time they apparently fought naked or very scantily clothed, at least they could keep their eyes on their adversary's approach and try to counter it; besides, they could move about freely.

Now behind the figure of our gladiator with the bag over his head there stands, in the attitude of the referees in the adjoining boxing-match, the man in charge of this cruel game. He seems both attentive and remote; he is not merely there to observe the outcome of the combat: he holds up delicately in his left hand a leash which perhaps is attached to the dog's collar, but which is also tangled round the neck, arms and leg of the gladiator, whose movements it impedes.

He wears an extraordinary assortment of clothes which helps us to recognize him elsewhere and in other situations, on the opposite wall of the Tomb of the Augurs, where he is running as fast as he can from an adversary who is now invisible;[108] in the Tomb of the Olympic Games, where he appears at the end of a track along which chariots are dashing, and his superhuman size seems that of a god; finally, in a third tomb, contemporaneous with the preceding two, and called, for reasons we shall see later, the Tomb of Pulcinella, despite small differences of costume, we see him again, unmistakably, walking with a light step and waving his arms.[109]

And at first he is, incontestably, masked; for his head disappears beneath a mock bonnet imitating a helmet – a Phrygian helmet with raised visor, lateral head-pieces and ear-covers; below is a mask of some dark colour to which is attached a long black beard. In the Tomb of Pulcinella the head-dress resembles more a magician's pointed hat, with a pompom at the top.

His clothes are no less singular: a short jacket and, generally, short breeches; but in one of the paintings in the Tomb of the Augurs the red of the jacket is sewn with tiny scraps of light-coloured stuff, and in the Tomb of Pulcinella it is chequered with alternate black and white squares. We understand why it reminded the Italian archaeologists of the Neapolitan Pulcinella. One might also have said: Harlequin.

Finally, completing our astonishment, Pulcinella, in the Tomb of the Augurs, reveals to us his real name, twice: it is *Phersu*. Now Phersu, with the omission of the familiar Tuscan aspiration and with the addition of a diminutive suffix, is no other than the word that survives in the Latin *persona*, which properly signifies 'mask', then 'dramatic rôle', then 'person'; the point of departure for an extraordinary semantic evolution which, reaching as far as our modern 'personality' and its derivatives, marks out one of the main roads through the history of civilization.[110]

So at the beginning it was the Mask, an infernal demon whose name is connected with that of Persephone (*Phersipnai*), who reigns over the dead by the side of Hades (*Eita*). He is the most ancient of those Hieronymus Bosch devils of the Etruscans, devils that later, under the names of Tuchulcha, Charon or Orcus, with their hooked noses, hair made of writhing snakes, vengeful mallets and fatidic scrolls, were to populate the tombs on frescoes and urns. It is interesting to note that, from the sixth century onwards, Phersu plays the rôle of a nonchalant organizer of tortures but that he sometimes takes to his heels when the spectators start stamping in the stands during funeral games in which elements of comedy and horror are mixed. We should not be surprised at this; there is an age-old association between the nervous release of laughter and the dread of death, against which laughter is a powerful defence. For example, Terence's *Adelphi* was on the programme of the funeral games in honour of Aemilius Paulus. The popular spectacles of early Rome in which the Etruscan influence was not unknown were full of hallucinating and grotesquely scarifying creatures, *formidines*, ogres and bogies, worthy imps, not of Satan, but of someone almost as bad, Phersu, and brought out to affright and delight children of all ages. At the end of the procession which annually paraded round the Circus Maximus on the occasion of the *ludi maximi*, the crowd awaited the entrance of laughable and terrifying figures, *ridiculae formidolosaeque*, in a state of delicious apprehension that drove away the spleen; among these figures were a drunken old woman and a screeching gossip, but the one they applauded most was Manducus (from *mandere*, 'to chew') who would open wide his fearsome chops, making a sound of horribly grinding teeth.[111]

Through all later manifestations of the Italian comic spirit there runs a tenuous but solid thread linking them with Phersu. Apuleius, enumerating the accessories of a theatre in his days, describes the tunic worn by the mimes and calls it *centunculus* – a garment made of various patches sewn together.[112] But even before that an *Atellana* by Pomponius was entitled *Pannuceati*,[113] from *pannus*, a piece of stuff, and this recalls the jacket of Phersu. These *Pannuceati* were not so much 'the Tatterdemalions' (as it is usually translated) as 'the Harlequins'.

We have just mentioned the *Atellana*: this was a kind of popular farce which had enjoyed its first success in Atella, a small town near Naples, in a thoroughly etruscanized Campania, before being transferred to Rome. Now one of the essential features of the *Atellana* performers was that they should be masked. It was the poet Naevius, from Capua, who at the end of the third century first produced a Latin *Atellana: fabula personata*, a masked comedy which was played by actors called *Atellani, qui proprie vocantur personati*, 'who are properly called the Masks (or Maskers)'.[114]

These masks are fairly well known to us:[115] they were Maccus the glutton with his fat chops, Bucco the fool, gossip and gormand-izer, Pappus the grandfather, Dossenus (Punch) the hunchback. The latter's name is generally recognized to be Etruscan. The plays that they presented in a lively manner were often of an impudent tartness and had such titles as Maccus the Tavern Keeper, Maccus in Exile, Maccus the Soldier, Maccus the Virgin. Sometimes, following the classic pattern of the Menaechmi, there were two of them, twins, twin Macci and twin Dosseni. Bucco was a gladiator and adopted son, Pappus a farmer and an unfortunate candidate. Despite the vexing lack of authorities, we can recognize in these figures the ancestors of Harlequin, Scapin, Brighella, of Capitan Spavento and Capitan Matamore who later, during the Renaissance, would set off from Naples to conquer London and Paris. The *Commedia dell'Arte* knew all about this, for its Pulcinella's birthplace was given out to be the Campanian town of Acerra.

We shall not go so far as to attribute the *Commedia dell'Arte* to the Etruscans. Even without Phersu, the Italian *vis comica* could not have failed to produce its own Pulcinella. But it was not without interest and profit to follow right to its end this guiding clue and to note that the paradoxically religious tradition of which Phersu is the origin persisted right through the pranks of Maccus and Harlequin and established quite definitely the masks, the costumes and to a great extent the form of broad farce. On the other hand there is no reason why we should not imagine, in Etruria proper, the existence of comic games similar to the Oscan games[116] of one of its provinces, echoes of which are preserved in the *Atellanae*. Perhaps it was not altogether due to chance that the greatest comic genius of Rome, the Umbrian Plautus, was born at Sarsina on the Etruscan frontier and had begun in the theatre, like Molière, as an actor and director, playing at fairs in small towns lost in the country the rôle of Maccus, the clown with the fat chops.

CHAPTER EIGHT

ETRUSCAN LITERATURE

I *Alphabets and spelling books – Tablets and scrolls – The wrappings from the Mummy of Zagreb*
II *The books of fate – The Etruscan religion and its prophets – The haruspices*
III *Did the Etruscans have a profane literature? – Fescennine hymns and songs – Dramatic spectacles – Historical literature – The traditions of the great families – Geneaological trees – Maecenas – The writings of Maecenas*

I

ALPHABETS AND SPELLING BOOKS

We should like to know to which of their national heroes the Etruscans attributed the invention of writing, which the Greeks attributed to Cadmus or Palamedes, and the Romans to the ancient king Evander. In any case the part they played in spreading through northern and central Italy, from Campania to the Alps, an alphabet derived from the Greek one is one of the most important aspects of the Etruscans' civilizing influence. The Umbrians of Gubbio, the Veneti of Este, the Osci of Capua, the Latins of Praeneste and the Romans themselves learnt to perpetuate their first texts by writing them down in Etruscan characters, more or less adapted or rearranged according to the needs of their various dialects and languages.[1] But dating from the earliest times are monuments whose authenticity allows us to imagine how the little Etruscans learnt their *a b c*.

A little town in maritime Etruria behind the lagoon of Orbetello, Marsiliana d'Albegna, had known, in the seventh century, a prosperity equalling that of Vetulonia and Caere; then about 600 it had declined, doubtless due to the progress made by its rival upriver, Saturnia. Now its tombs have given us, besides a celebrated golden fibula adorned with a delightful line of ducks, numerous orientalizing ivory objects, among which is a little writing-tablet, nine centimetres by five, still containing remains of the wax on which a schoolboy, using a stylus, had practised his pothooks: on one of the long sides of the frame there was an alphabet of twenty-six letters which he used as a model.[2]

The same alphabet, a little later in the course of this seventh century, is found at the base of a bottle (*leguncula*) in bucchero ware from the Regolini-Galassi tomb at Caere:[3] moreover a syllabary is inscribed on the side: *ci ca cu ce vi va vu ve zi za zu ze*, etc.

In imitation of the Etruscans, who themselves imitated the Greeks in this respect, the whole peninsula began to learn its letters. We have several alphabets like this on the wine-cups from Nola in Campania,[4] and at Este, at the mouth of the Po, numerous bronze tablets show, set out in squares, lists of letters to be used in the teaching of writing and even particular rules of punctuation which were current among the Veneti.[5]

Yet it would be inexact, just because these model tablets conjure up in an innocent light the primary schools of all times and all lands, to think that their use was entirely pedagogic. M. Lejeune has rightly remarked in one of his fine studies of Venete philology: the alphabetic tablets of Este were part of a collection of votive objects offered to the goddess of the place, Reitia, and it cannot be doubted that their didactic nature also had a magical or sacred significance. 'This teaching, originating in the sanctuary, for a long time kept a sacerdotal character.'[6]

Those who, having mastered the secrets of writing, were able to seize words on the wing suddenly found themselves in possession of a redoubtable weapon, an admirable, powerful and disturbing one proper to the subjugation of primitive imaginations. The Greeks themselves were never to be free of the 'religious respect' with which they regarded the letters of the alphabet, *stoicheia* or *elementa*, from which their philosophers were to create the primordial elements of things.[7] Then what about the Veneti? The Etruscans, always deeply involved in the supernatural, were also unable to regard their alphabets and syllabaries simply in the light of their didactic utility: the tablet from Marsiliana d'Albegna is not so very different from other *tabulae ceratae* which have been preserved at Pompeii and elsewhere because instead of being in wood it is of ivory because this luxury object was found in a tomb.[8] The same applies to the vase from Caere and the other alphabets. We even know of some that had never been used for didactic purposes by the living before accompanying them in death: a chamber tomb, at Colle near Siena, shows, painted on one of its walls, a fine example of *a b c d* . . . and of *ma me mi mu*.[9] Writing, liberating men from the domination of the moment and from the fatality of oblivion, was obstinately bound up with the idea of permanence, if not of eternity or immortality.

It so happens that the act of writing is one for which we know the word in Etruscan. According to a bilingual epitaph at Chiusi, *Vel Zicu* was called in Latin Q. Scribonius C.f.,[10] which suggested the idea that the root *zic-* or *zich-* was equivalent to the root *scrib-* and this key has opened every door we have been able to try it on. A verb in the preterite *zichuche*, *zichunce*, at the end of the ritual of Capua and of the convention of setting the bounds of Perugia concludes the inscription: 'So-and-so wrote this.'[11] It is even possible that this word, inscribed on vases, might have had the meaning of the Greek *egrapsen*, and introduced the signature of the painter.[12] Moreover *Larth Vetes zichu*, on an ossuary,[13] was probably *Lars Vettius scriba*, that is, a secretary or a registrar. Finally the *volumen* which the supposed magistrate of the tomb at Tarquinii unrolls before him and which recalls his career has at the opening of the inscription the words *ancn zich*, 'this writing,' which gives us the name of the book in Etruscan.[14]

TABLETS AND SCROLLS

The writing material at the disposal of the Etruscans was no different from that used by the other Mediterranean peoples: what we know of it comes almost entirely from the evidence provided by funerary monuments, confirming what we have just said about the sacred and magical character attached to all written things. The Books of Death which, in the form of a diptych or a scroll, appear in the tombs in the hands of the dead person or of infernal divinities conjure up the irrevocable sentences of the *fatum*.

A diptych, consisting of two tablets joined together on one of their long sides, is depicted clearly in one of the paintings of the *tomba degli Scudi* (Tomb of the Shields) at Tarquinii.[15] A young demon with naked body and large red wings is seated cross-legged before a large diptych, one of whose tablets rests on his knees, while the other hangs down in front. Two black marks in the space between the two tablets indicate the hinges by which they were attached. On the tablet hanging down three lines are written along the rectangle, beginning from the inner edge. The banker Caecilius Jucundus, at Pompeii, uses his tablets in the same way. On the other tablet, the demon is writing with an invisible stylus the next part of his text: he has reached the end of the second line. We are able to read: *zilci Velus Hulchniesi Larth Velchas Velthurs Aprthnalc clan sacnisa thui eith suthith acazr*, meaning: 'Under the magistracy of Vel Hulchnie [= Fulcinius] (in Rome we would have a consular date), Larth Velcha [Lars Volcius], son of Velthur and of Aprthni [Aburtennia], received in this tomb the funeral honours.' Only two of the words – *sacnisa acazr* – cannot be fully explained, but the meaning is certainly very close to what we have written.

Another diptych can be seen on a mirror from Bolsena[16] of which we have already spoken: on it we can see Aulus and Caelius Vibennae attacking the augur Cacus in his sacred wood; he is singing, accompanying himself on the lyre; crouching at his feet, a young listener, *Artile* (*Ar(n)tile*), little Arruns of Clusium, is also singing as he reads from a diptych open on his knees. He reminds us of the musical angels of Piero della Francesca and of Luca della Robbia. But in the absence of any other profane representation of educational scenes, this picture is of particular interest to us, offering as it does, in a legendary setting, the image of an Etruscan schoolboy reciting his lessons.

Much more frequent, in decorations on urns and in paintings, is the representation of the *volumen* or scroll: whatever signs may be traced on it, the name of a Fury or the epitaph to the dead person, it is a symbol of the imprescriptible decrees of fate. This is why it is held by, among others, Charon, no less redoubtable than the mallet which the guardian of Hell brandishes in the other hand. Lying on the lid of their sarcophagus, the dead often hold one in their hands.[17]

What material was this scroll made of? It is very unlikely that it was papyrus, though Strabo names papyrus among the aquatic plants which grew on the edge of Lake Trasimeno and Lake Bolsena, and he adds that whole shipments of it were sent down the Tiber to Rome: it would seem that all kinds of reeds and rushes, not suitable for paper-making, were called by this generic name in Italy.[18] Perhaps there existed, even before the spread of parchment to the west, 'books of skin', if that is really the meaning, in the inscription at Tarquinii, of the *zich nethsrac* of *Laris Pulenas*.[19] But the majority of the scrolls were doubtless of cloth, and similar to those *libri lintei* which, so the historians tell us, were preserved in the temple of Juno Moneta at Rome and which contained lists of magistrates going back to the fifth century.[20]

THE WRAPPINGS FROM THE MUMMY OF ZAGREB

An extraordinary stroke of luck has made one of these books available to us, not in the form of a painting or of a relief but in the shape of an actual book.[21] In the middle of the nineteenth century, a Croatian tourist brought back from Egypt a female mummy which, after having adorned his collection in Vienna, went, on his death, to the museum at Zagreb. But when, after having unrolled and somewhat torn the wrappings in which she was encased, someone gave them a closer look, it was seen that they bore writings which at first were taken to be Arabic or Ethiopian, until J. Krall recognized them for Etruscan.

It had needed an unusual concatenation of circumstances to bring us into possession of an outstanding monument to the sacred literature of this people about whom we know so little. Théophile Gautier's *Tale of the Mummy* seems very ordinary when we consider the fantastic history of this *volumen*, which came, judging from the characteristics of the language, from northern Etruria, from Chiusi or Perugia therefore; this *volumen* which was intended to shroud the remains of a woman somewhere (we do not know exactly where it was found) in the Delta or the Faiyum where the arid climate assured its preservation, and which a last migration was to bring to Europe, finally coming to rest in a museum in Jugoslavia. We are lost in conjecture about how it could have got to Egypt, at a date – a fairly late one – which it appears could be fixed between 150 and 30 BC. The physical type of the dead woman tells us nothing about her race: she measured 1 m. 62, and though her hair today has a reddish tinge, this may be due to the discoloration brought about by time or by the chemical preparations used in embalming her. Whether she came from Etruria proper or was born on the banks of the Nile, she was certainly the wife or daughter of an Etruscan who had settled in Egypt and who, converted to the funerary rites of the country of his adoption, had all the same wrapped her in the folds of a relic he had brought with him and which reminded him of the religion of his fathers. It has been thought that he might have been a mercenary in the service of the Ptolemies – we know of some of these, of Etruscan origin, from the third century onwards – and installed as a *cleruch* or soldier-peasant in a home in central Egypt. It is quite possible. Except that we can hardly see how – though religious life was intense in the Hellenistic armies – our *Miles Gloriosus* could have possibly carried round in his luggage so precious and fragile a document. But there were *haruspices* in the entourages of Roman generals like Gabinius, Caesar, Antony and Cornelius Gallus who stayed in Egypt at various times. Above all, the Hellenistic world brought priests, magicians and soothsayers into close contact with each other; Egypt, land renowned for its mysteries, where, in the Hellenistic period, there came about a syncretism of all religions, was such a powerful centre of attraction that one can see many reasons why an adept of the *Etrusca disciplina* should go to compare its tenets with the teachings of the Alexandrian clergy or the traditions of the scribes of Memphis; we have already seen that there were *zarapiu*, Serapion, in Etruscan families.[22]

The text itself did not concern personally the woman whose shroud it was; it did not even contain, as did the Egyptian Books of the Dead, prescriptions drawn up to assure her happiness in the beyond: it appears that no matter what sacred book, whatever its contents, could express as well as any other the omnipotence of fate. The document under discussion, whose general meaning we are able to grasp thanks to the labours of Krall and Torp and later of Herbig, Runes and Cortsen, Pallottino, Vetter and Olzscha, was a ritual in the form of a calendar indicating at their dates in the year (June 18, September 26, etc.) the ceremonies to be held in honour of Jupiter, Neptune and other gods.[23] Here again, the etruscologists know much more than is generally supposed, though naturally much less than they would like.

Meanwhile the wrappings of the mummy of Zagreb form a unique example of an antique *volumen*. It was a 'book of linen', and this, in an Egypt where papyrus was used, is sure confirmation of its foreign origin. What is left of it – about one half – is formed of twelve strips of varying lengths (from 17 cm. to 3m. 24) and of a fairly constant width (from 6 to 7 cm.). Fortunately several could be joined up with others to form the elements of a reconstituted whole. This was originally a scroll whose total length was 13 m. 75 (papyrus scrolls were usually much shorter: twenty sheets placed end to end, or about 5 m.).[24] But the width cannot be reckoned, though it was more than 33 cm. This band was divided longitudinally into twelve columns separated by perpendicular lines; each column was 25 cm. wide and, in the best-preserved parts (four superimposed fragments), containing twenty-three or twenty-four lines: there must have been about thirty all told. The text was read, as was normal in Etruscan, from right to left, and, also reading from right to left, the columns are numbered XII, XI, X, IX, . . . III, II, I. The whole thing – letters and dividing lines – is done in red ink with a neatness and care which go to show the value attached to this book by the *haruspex* who had transcribed it.

Indeed there is no doubt that the *volumen* of Zagreb is one of the famous *Etrusci libri* of which Latin authors frequently speak, particularly at the end of the Republic, when, in order to obtain a more precise knowledge of them, they could make use of Romanized Etruscans who were still proud of their native traditions, Aulus Caecina of Volterra, friend of Cicero, or Lucius Tarquitius Priscus, friend of Varro. Moreover, they were beginning to be more widely known by the general public: the misfortunes of the times and people's disturbed consciences encouraged a demand for esoteric writings and especially for these old black-books with their certainties and consolations that were frowned upon by official religion and the schools of philosophy. Lucretius vainly put forward rationalist theories for natural phenomena; more and more people preferred to interpret them by having recourse to the 'Etruscan books'.

'This is to understand the true nature of the fiery thunderbolt, and to see by what power it plays its part; not by unrolling backwards the scrolls of Tyrrhenian charms, vainly to search for signs of the hidden purpose of the gods.'

> *non Tyrrhena retro volventem carmina frustra*
> *indicia occultae divum perquirre mentis.*[25]

Usually the words *retro volventem* are translated as 'reading and re-reading', as if *retro* meant nothing more than 'once again'. But the historian Niebuhr, at the beginning of the nineteenth century, was correct in assuming here a reference to 'retrograde' writing, or rather, to the succession of columns, read backwards, from right to left, in an Etruscan book which, like that encasing the mummy of Zagreb, must have unrolled from left to right, in a contrary direction to that to which the Romans were accustomed. 'Rolling Tyrrhenian songs backwards' must have appeared as strange to Lucretius as leafing through the Koran would to a Christian. This proves that he had seen and handled some of these Etruscan books. (It has sometimes been suggested that he was Etruscan by birth, and that his protests against belief in the tortures of Hell were directly inspired by a properly Etruscan anguish at the prospect of death.) There is proof also of the attraction this strange literature had for the contemporaries of Cicero; the orator himself, quoting in his *De Divinatione* some verses which he had devoted to his consulate of the year 63 and to the strange natural events which two years earlier, at a moment when Catiline was weaving the web of his conspiracy, had disturbed superstitious Romans, states that the She-wolf of the Capitol was struck by lightning that destroyed the Twins she was suckling: 'Then what diviner, in turning the records and tomes of the augurs, failed to relate the mournful forecasts the Etruscans had written?' (trans. William Armisted Falconer).[26]

II

THE BOOKS OF FATE

The ancient authors make many references to these books and even make some borrowings which supply us with many details about them. It was usual to class them in three categories:[27] the *libri haruspicini* first of all, in which were registered and recorded the secular experiences of the Etruscan people in the scrutiny of the entrails of victims (*exta*), and this was the real domain of the *haruspices*; then there were the *libri fulgurales*, which handled the interpretation of thunder and lightning, and of which one part is known to us, among others, through Seneca's *Naturales Quaestiones*; finally, the *libri rituales*, whose contents covered much wider ground, for they embraced 'prescriptions concerning the founding of cities, the consecration of altars and temples, the inviolability of ramparts, the laws relating to city gates, the division into tribes, curiae and centuriae, the constitution and the organization of armies, and all other things of this nature concerning war and peace'.[28] We may therefore say that there was nothing either in public or private life whose course had not been foreseen and fixed by the 'ritual books'. It is among these that we must place the ritual in the form of a calendar from the mummy of Zagreb. They also included in particular certain 'Acherontic Books', which were intended to guide the dead along the paths of the beyond, and the *libri fatales* which gave knowledge of the workings of destiny: herein were preserved all conceivable forms of prodigy (*ostenta*) through which the experts claimed to see the hidden will of the gods.

Thus the whole surroundings of Etruscan life could suddenly reveal, in the innocent plants and the familiar animals, unexpected threats or promises.[29] One had to beware, in an orchard, of all kinds of trees which were presumed to be maleficent, and to burn at once, as soon as they showed above the earth, the eglantine, the fern, the wild pear, the dogwood whose branches are coloured red, the black fig and those plants which gave black fruits and berries, for they were protected by the infernal powers. On the other hand, the laurel could bring good fortune to ambitious people: if by chance one grew on the stern of your trireme, you could be sure of a victory at sea. A laurel in a garden grew up beside a peach tree (*persicum*) and in less than a year overtopped it: an omen which no one doubted meant the defeat of the Persians . . . The habits of bees deserved close attention: despite the favourable things said about them in legends, for example, that they had settled on Plato's mouth when he was in his cradle 'thus foretelling the sweetness of his discourse', the Etruscans considered omens coming from bees to be sinister, as when a swarm settled right in the Forum at Cassino. It is true that at the same time, at Cumae, mice had gnawed the gold deposited in the temple of Jupiter. If a huge lion happened to leap upon an army on the march and succumbed to its arrows, the haruspices who even as late as the fourth century AD accompanied the emperor Julian concluded that a king was about to die. But who? Julian, or his adversary Sapor? They did not say. Serpents often intervene in Etruscan divination, bringing ambivalent omens. And the same with birds: one day a woodpecker perched so tamely on the head of the praetor Aelius Tubero, who was sitting in judgement in his tribunal in the Forum, that it was easily seized; the haruspices said that if it was released, the Empire, and if it was killed, the praetor would be threatened with dire catastrophe. The praetor at once killed the bird, and there was the defeat of Cannes, from which Rome recovered, but at which seventeen members of the *gens Aelia* perished.

We have already recalled how Tarquinius the Elder, on his arrival in Rome, saw an eagle steal his cap, carry it off and then put it gently back on his head, whereupon Tanaquil did not hesitate to entertain the highest hopes of the future. Again it was told how the future Augustus, while still a child, was picnicking in a wood just off the highway when an eagle suddenly swooped down, snatched his piece of bread, only to restore it to him a few moments later. But particularly remarkable is that text which was translated, almost literally, it would seem, from Etruscan into Latin and which Virgil remembers in his Fourth Eclogue: ' "If the fleece of a ram or of a sheep be specked with purple or gold, it forebodes for the prince a great happiness and prosperity in his order and lineage, a growth of glory and prolificness in his lineage and offspring." In the world regenerated by the mysterious child's birth, of himself the ram in the meadows shall change his fleece, now to sweetly blushing purple, now to saffron yellow; of its own will shall scarlet clothe the grazinglambs.' (Trans. Rushton Fairclough.)

We may imagine with what close attention the Etruscans investigated the nightmares of pregnant women: premature births, androgynes, two-headed daughters, boys with elephant heads, and that calf born – in the reign of Nero – by the wayside in the region of Placentia, which had its head on its hindquarters. The haruspices concluded from the latter that preparations were being made to give the Empire a new head, but that it would not be very secure; nor would the plot be well concealed, because the animal's head had been like that when it was still in its mother's belly and had been brought into the world by the roadside.

Above all, celestial phenomena excited the ingenuity of the interpreters of omens. Not only the flight of birds but the course of the stars and in particular the appearance of comets, were generally considered as a bad omen, as well as storms and rains – rains of milk, of blood, of iron, of wool or of brick, all announcing public disasters; but a rain of white chalk, in 98, was interpreted as an earnest of a good harvest and fine weather. The great civil convulsions at the close of the Republic were preceded by sudden earthquakes, mysterious trumpet-blasts and inexplicable sounds of arms clashing in the sky.

We possess a speech of Cicero from 56 which illustrates the authority that ancient Etruscan civilization exercised over the Roman mind.[30] Violent, dull grumblings had one day terrified a whole quarter at the gates of Rome. The haruspices were appealed to; they consulted their books and pronounced that it was the sign that consecrated places had been profaned. Publius Clodius, the sworn enemy of Cicero, declared it was the ground that the latter was rebuilding his house on that was being defiled; his house had been destroyed during his exile and the land had been confiscated and dedicated to the goddess of Liberty. Not at all, retorted the orator, it was the neighbouring house, the one belonging to Clodius, that the gods were referring to: despite the sanctuary and the altars inside it, he had made it a place of debauchery. Then, developing his counterblast, Cicero proved that if the *libri fulgurales* were more deeply studied, it appeared that other offences, for which Clodius was responsible, had also been committed: public games neglected or degraded, ambassadors murdered, solemn oaths violated, ancient mysteries not celebrated, and finally a state of mortal danger created in the Senate and among the chiefs of State by discord in the Conservative party. It has been noted that in diagnosing these evils the haruspices were not so much defining Roman society as Etruscan society which had consigned to their sacred books its religious obsessions and its aristocratic institutions.

This also emerges from the examination of another *liber fulguralis* which M. Piganiol discovered in a Greek translation by a Byzantine author;[31] the text, some six centuries earlier, had been translated from the Etruscan into Latin by a contemporary of Cicero, Nigidius Figulus. It is a 'brontoscopic' calendar, that is to say, indicating the significance of thunder-claps for every day of the year: if it thunders on September 11, the clients of noble houses will foment a political revolution; if it thunders on October 24, the people will overthrow their masters because of the disagreements among the latter; if it thunders on December 3, a dearth of fish will cause men to eat the flesh of their flocks; if it thunders on March 26, convoys of slaves will enter the port; if it thunders on July 14, power will return to the hands of a single man, who will wield it unjustly; if it thunders on August 19, women and slaves will carry out assassinations.

THE ETRUSCAN RELIGION AND ITS PROPHETS

The Etruscan religion, unlike the Greek and Roman religions, but like the Jewish and Christian religions, was a revealed religion.[32] All the books we have just been talking about were held to contain the teaching of a few inspired people, semi-divine, who had made known to men the secrets of the universe. The most celebrated of the prophets, Tages,[33] was particularly venerated in the religion of Tarquinii. It was said that one day a ploughman had dug his ploughshare too deeply into the earth, and that Tages had at once sprung from the furrow. He had the appearance of a child, but the wisdom of an old man. The whole of Etruria had soon gathered together to listen to him and to take down his words in writing. A mirror from Tuscania shows Tages teaching Tarchon the art of foretelling the future from the entrails of victims. A number of sacred books were ascribed to him: the brontoscopic calendar translated by Nigidius Figulus, for example, was attributed to him. The *libri Tagetici*, as they were called, enjoyed great favour even in Rome, and particularly from the second century AD were tirelessly read and re-read and commented by the philosophers who extracted from them an esoteric doctrine capable of rivalling Christianity: Apuleius, author of the *Metamorphoses* (or *The Golden Ass*) had devoted a book to the elucidation of Tages' poems.

Elsewhere the prophet took the name Cacus from an old Italic divinity who, in Latium, appears under quite a different light as a frightful brigand who stole the oxen from Hercules.[34] On the contrary, several urns and a mirror from Etruria make Cacus appear as an inspired Apollo prophesying while accompanying himself on the lyre; at his feet *Artile* or *Ar(n)tile*, little *Arnth* or Arruns, hero of Clusium, sings the responses to his song.[35] But Caelius and Aulus Vibennae make a sudden appearance in the wood and endeavour to seize the lyrist. This theme of the capture of the diviner, from whom ordinary men try to wrest by violence the secrets he tells only to initiates has other examples in Etruscan religion, but it was also widespread in Mediterranean folklore. The old man of the sea, Proteus, is well known: the Menelaus of Homer and the Aristaeus of Virgil laid hold of him so well that he tried to escape them by metamorphosing himself into a lion, a serpent and running water; only then did he speak.[36] And Silenus, in the sixth Bucolic, only very unwillingly consented to sing the creation of the world, the loves of Gallus and the works of Apollo after two young shepherds had surprised him in drunken sleep.

Again sometimes it is a 'nymph' who is entrusted with the divine message. And just as in Rome that pious king, Numa Pompilius, conversed nightly with the nymph Egeria who gave him instruction in the forms of worship, so at Clusium, Arruns, in certain forms of the legend, learnt from the nymph Vegoia 'the decisions of Jupiter and of Justice'.[37] Tarquitius Priscus, in the days of Cicero, transcribed into Latin the *libri Vegoici*, which were preserved in the temple of Apollo Palatinus, and, by extraordinary good luck, a fragment of this has come down to us under the title: *Extract from the books of Vegoia to Arruns Velthumnus* of which we have already quoted the beginning; here is the complete translation:

'Know that the sea was separated from the sky. Now when Jupiter had claimed back the land of Etruria, he established and commanded that the plains should be surveyed and the fields limited. Knowing well what human avarice and passions are excited by land, he desired that everything should be defined by boundary-marks. One day, when moved by the avarice of the end of the eighth century someone will treat these bounds with contempt, men, by fraudulent means will violate them, lay hands upon them or displace them. But whoever shall touch and displace them in order to extend his property and diminish that of others shall for this crime be condemned by the gods. If such men be slaves, they shall be brought into an even lower state of servitude. But if there be complicity on the part of the master, soon the house of the latter shall be extirpated and his race shall perish utterly. Those who displace the bounds shall be stricken by worse sicknesses and worse wounds, and their weakened limbs shall be afflicted. Then shall the earth often be shaken by tempests and whirlwinds that shall make it tremble. The harvest shall frequently be spoiled and laid flat by rain and hail, shall wither beneath the canicular heat and shall be destroyed by mildew. There shall be numerous dissensions among the people. Know that such punishments shall take place when such crimes occur. Therefore be not of bad faith, nor speak deceitfully. Plant our teachings in your hearts.'

We shall not comment here on the details of this prophecy: it inserts into an account of the creation of the world, which at times reminds us of certain verses in Genesis, a vengeful imprecation against those who break the laws, pronounced by Jupiter himself, of landed property. The Etruscan Jupiter – we have already had occasion to demonstrate this – is a Jupiter of boundaries, whose inviolability he guarantees, and Etruscan civilization defines itself here, among all Italic civilizations, as a civilization of peasant farmers passionately attached to the 'right of Etruscan land', *ius terrae Etruriae*. They proudly defended the sanctity of their boundaries, and this attitude went right back to the origins of their race, when Jupiter had established his reign; our fragment is probably of very ancient inspiration. But it did not appear in this form until the moment when Etruscan soil was undergoing mortal difficulties, when the agrarian reforms of the Gracchi and their successors threatened, by planting new colonies in Etruria, the age-old security given by the boundaries. Usurping the legendary name of Vegoia, taking upon himself the style and the formulae of traditional divination, a *haruspex* at the end of the eighth Etruscan century, that is to say in the years before 88 BC renewed the malediction of the sacred books addressed to those who interfered with the boundaries. We have recently shown that the date of this can be precisely stated: it was in 91 that Vegoia's prophecy first saw the light of day in the form of a popular propaganda pamphlet, an expression of Etruscan revolt against the programme of the tribune Livius Drusus, who is referred to in the text only in an anonymous fashion which befitted oracular language, as 'someone'; but we know that his policy provoked a march on Rome by Etruscans who had sprung to arms at the call of the consul Philippus, and that he perished in the uprising. It is the fevered atmosphere of that year which gives this fragment its frantic tone, but its general feeling is authentically Etruscan: a final wave from the ocean of time coming to expire on the shores of the classical era. 91 was also the year in which Cicero sets the serene and learned conversations, held in a villa in Tusculum, of his *De Oratore*: what a difference between that stormy, lightning-struck evening and those pure summer mornings!

The truths revealed by Tages, Cacus and Vegoia and consigned to the sacred books constitute a body of doctrine, a tradition, a teaching to which the Etruscans gave a name we are still ignorant of, but which perhaps is hidden, according to a hypothesis recently put forward by S. Mazzarino, in the inscription on the *cippus* from Perugia: *tesns rasnes*.[38] In any case, it was what the Romans called the *Etrusca disciplina*. The expression recurs often in our texts, and Latinists will not fail to notice that in this stereotyped formula the adjective always precedes the substantive: an emphatic position, clearly indicating opposition of this tradition foreign to the national tradition.[39]

The Etruscan discipline, whose birth had been presided over by the most famous *lucumones* of legend, one Tarchon at Tarquinii and one Arruns at Clusium, remained for a long time the common patrimony of the great aristocratic houses. But we are not informed of their fidelity to it until the moment when the aristocracy was in decline and on the point of escheating this patrimony. Cicero in his *De Divinatione*[40] mentions an assembly of the Senate which passed an edict that must date from the second century; it prescribed that in each of the twelve peoples of the confederation the noble families should give the State six of their sons to study religion: this remarkable course brought about the official organization of the Etruscan discipline under the protection of the Senate which thus proclaimed its interest in a science it had so often had recourse to, and would so often have recourse to again. Cicero retained this decree among the laws of his ideal constitution: 'Let Etruria teach princes the discipline': *Etruria principes disciplinam doceto*.[41] In fact, the formula was not very clear, Cicero's text quickly became corrupted, so that a rather muddled thinker like Valerius Maximus at the beginning of the Empire was capable of believing that it was young men from the *Roman* nobility who were to be sent, *ten* at a time, to each of the Etruscan peoples to learn their discipline. But the interpretation we have given, and which conforms with the views of nearly all historians, is confirmed by the allusion made by the emperor Claudius in one of his speeches on the college of haruspices: he showed then, in AD 47, his determination to struggle for the preservation, in face of the waves of foreign superstitions, of 'the most ancient discipline in Italy', and he founded his policy on the example of the past, the days when 'the great in Etruria, either by their own accord, or by the instigation of the Senate, had maintained and propagated this knowledge in the families'.[42]

THE HARUSPICES

The assembly of the Senate in the second century had expressly aimed at reacting against the indifference to their national traditions which had been brought about by the decline of the *lucumones* 'so that so great an art, in consequence of the humble condition of those who devoted themselves to it, might not be deprived of the dignity proper to a religion and reduced to the level of daily toil for gain'. The crisis in the recruitment of *haruspices* which reigned among the upper classes is in fact attested by the contempt into which they had fallen: a sacerdotal vocation had become a sordid job. As the number of qualified *haruspices* diminished, there arose a host of village soothsayers, *haruspices vicani*, who, under a name that took no one in except the naïve, exploited the latter's credulity.[43] Plautus and Pomponius have nothing but sarcasm for these charlatans, and Cato, anxious to keep good order in his rural domain, forbade the entry of '*haruspices*, augurs, fortune-tellers and astrologers'. The same Cato felt astonishment that a *haruspex* could look at another without bursting into laughter.[44] Still later, at Gubbio, L. Veturius Rufio, *avispex*, *extispicus*, an expert in the observation of the flight of birds and in the scrutiny of victims' entrails, called himself *sacerdos publicus et privatus*, public and private priest; apart from his official functions, he gave individuals private consultations, evidently well paid.[45] There was a worse danger to be feared: Augustus passed a law forbidding *haruspices* to receive private visits and to deliver prognostications concerning the decease of individuals.[46]

Nevertheless the Senate's effort to resuscitate religious vocations among the aristocracy does not seem to have been in vain. Thanks to superstition, there were still as many, if not more, unofficial *haruspices*. Under the Empire, *haruspices* are found everywhere, practising their art in the municipalities and the legions, in the houses of provincial governors and at the court of emperors.[47] We know that as late as 408, at the moment when the approach of the Goths of Alaric constituted a mortal threat to Rome, there were in the city Etruscan *haruspices* whom the invasion had driven out of Tuscany and whom the prefect of the city and Pope Innocent the First did not disdain to consult.[48] But among these more or less accredited functionaries we note, mainly after the beginning of Claudius' reign, the existence of an 'order of the LX *haruspices*', organized as a college and having its centre at Tarquinii and then in Rome, with a president elected for one year and funds administered by a treasurer: this *ordo* henceforward played the rôle of authorized guardian of the Etruscan discipline, and assured its long survival, right to the end of antiquity and even into the Byzantine epoch.[49]

From the last century of the Republic, the renewed loyalty of the *lucumones* to their traditions is shown by certain facts: first of all by the quality of the *haruspices* whom the great men of State engaged not only as technicians but also as trusted friends – Herennius Siculus, who, involved in 121 in the downfall of C. Gracchus, proudly committed suicide just as he was about to be imprisoned;

Postumius, who, through the sagacious interpretation of an omen, helped Sylla in 89 to capture the Samnite camp outside Nola; finally, Spurinna who warned Caesar, who right up to the last moment refused to believe him, of the ineluctable outcome of the Ides of March. All three were certainly of good Etruscan stock: the first, *Tuscus* despite his surname which merely expresses the fact that either he or his family had interests in Sicily; the second perhaps from Perugia; the third probably from Tarquinii.[50]

But above all among the contemporaries and friends of Cicero we see representatives of families from central Etruria in whom the 'discipline' is piously transmitted from father to son like something in a direct line of inheritance. We have already had the occasion to mention that Tarquitius Priscus[51] whom an epigram attributed to the youthful Virgil disrespectfully associates with Varro and other high-flown rhetors.[52] His fame lasted to the final years of antiquity as one of the masters of the arts of divination: he had translated into Latin collections of supernatural events (*Ostentaria Tusca*); Pliny cites him as one of the sources of this material, and the *libri Tarquitiani* were still being consulted in the fourth century. Now two inscriptions at Tarquinii,[53] made in the days of the emperor Claudius and which perhaps had been placed in the premises of the *ordo LX haruspicum*, inform us, despite their mutilations, about this person and his son. The first had published Latin translations of several Etruscan books, one of which concerned the ritual of public assemblies (*ritus comitialis*). Others, even more important, contained the legendary teachings of Arruns of Clusium, given after the revelation he had received of the will of Jupiter and of Justice through the medium of the prophetess Vegoia: *sacra quibus placare numina Arruns a magistra edoctus erat ex Jovis et Justitiae effatis*. And he had taught his art in Rome for over thirty years. The second, probably his son, had learnt from him the art of interpreting thunder, and, after his death, had succeeded him, without great distinction, in the same high office. But these two 'eulogies' of the Tarquitii Prisci at the end of the Republic had been drawn up at the beginning of the Empire, at the request of a third Tarquitius Etruscus by a fourth Tarquitius Priscus who in the middle of the first century of our era was the counsellor of the emperor Claudius in his policy of religious revival; he was hostile to the 'foreign superstitions' and to combat them relied on 'the most ancient Italian discipline', which was the Etruscan discipline. Thus the attachment to this discipline over four generations by a Tarquinii family whose membership of the equestrian order is sufficient to show its high local origins, was not relaxed.

Even better known, and no less proud, even in the days when it participated in the political life of Rome, of the memories of its race's grandeur, was the *gens* Caecina, of Volterra.[54] The theatre of its native town has recently been excavated, and is full of inscriptions bearing this name, reserving the seats of honour for the family in its hemicycle.[55] But long before its accession to the consulate under Claudius with C. Caecina Largus, the family had had its representatives in the clientela and in the intimate circle of friends of Cicero.[56] Aulus Caecina, in 69 or 68 BC, had been defended by the orator in a case concerning the land he had received from his wife Caesennia, a rich heiress of Tarquinii: for the Etruscan nobility rarely made misalliances with foreigners. At the time of the civil war between Caesar and Pompey, A. Caecina had fought against the former, and had been condemned to banishment. It was from then, in 46, that can be dated an epistolary exchange between him and Cicero – three letters from Cicero, one reply from Caecina – which show the esteem they had for each other and their intellectual affinities. Caecina was a good writer: he had the gift of eloquence. Apart from the very violent pamphlet he had written against Caesar, and the later plaintive retraction which earned him, to soften his exile, the privilege of residing in Sicily, he had left writings on Etruscan science, notably on the interpretation of thunder, which were used by Seneca in his *Naturales Quaestiones* and by Pliny in his Book II. He was an expert in divination, and an entire letter from Cicero contrasts amusingly the predictions he made from his own augural experiments and those which Caecina was able to base on the Etruscan discipline; and what he says is worth quoting here: *ratio quaedam mira Tuscae disciplinae, quam a patre, nobilissimo atque optimo uiro, acceperas*, 'the truly marvellous teaching in the Etruscan discipline which you received from your father, whose merit equalled his birth'.[57]

With Tarquitius Priscus, with Caecina, we find ourselves in an Etruria which, thanks to the efforts of the Senate in the second century, of Cicero at the end of the Republic, of Claudius at the beginning of the Empire, struggles obstinately to survive. Here it is permissible to go further back in time and quote an example at least of the piety with which the leading Etrurians spontaneously (*sponte*) upheld the 'discipline' in their families. Such indeed is the lesson to be learnt from the lengthy epitaph we have already referred to engraved on a sarcophagus at Tarquinii, known improperly as the sarcophagus of the Magistrate: it should more correctly be called 'of the Priest'.[58] The dead man, shown semirecumbent on the lid of the sarcophagus, is a little old man with a big head and weak features on whom the heroic accoutrements sit rather badly: his chest is bare, and he wears two wreaths, one round his neck, the other round his head – this one at first sight might be taken for a beret. Yet with his stern regard and his frowning brows he affects a vaguely Napoleonic authority.

He was an eminent local ecclesiastical personality. He unrolls before him a *volumen*, and we have already seen that the presence of a book was frequent in the decoration of funerary objects, suggesting as it did the laws of destiny. This book is in fact identified at the beginning of the inscription by three words *ancn zich nethsrac* which seems to signify 'this haruspicinal book',[59] and to designate one of those *libri fatales* in which the precepts of the Etruscan discipline were written down. But here the parents of the dead man have seized the opportunity to inscribe on it his *curriculum vitae*: nine lines of which only one part presents a clear and undisputed meaning, but of which the general gist is plain. *Lars Pulenas* – such was his name – had held numerous religious offices at Tarquinii; he had been, among other things, the equivalent of what was known in Rome as the *rex sacrorum*, and had instituted and practised certain rites; in particular he had played an important part in the celebration of the Dionysiac mysteries, which, introduced from Greece, had been greeted with fervour in Etruria and which were to spread from Etruria to Rome 'like some morbid pestilence' as Livy says, there to provoke, in 186, the famous disorders connected with the Bacchanalia. The epitaph can be dated from about 200.

But the onomastic formula with which it opens: *Laris Pulenas, Larces clan, Larthal papacs, Velthurus nefts, prumts Pules Larisal Creices* is no less informative; it proudly enumerates, going right back to the fourth generation, the ancestors of *Laris Pulenas*: his father, *Larce Pulenas*, then his paternal uncle, *Larth Pulenas*, then his grandfather, *Velthur Pulenas*, and finally his great grandfather, *Laris Pule Creice*, all of which reserve until the end, inverting the usual order of words, the really extraordinary surname the last one bears. Translated, we read: *Laris Pulenas*, son of *Larce*, nephew of *Larth*, grandson of *Velthur*, great grandson of *Laris Pule* the Greek.

So the founder of the *Pulena* family, whose name was to survive in Latin, during the Empire, in the *gens* of the Pollenii, was one *Laris Pule* or *Pules*, whose descendants liked to imagine that he had come from Greece in the fourth century. Whether this was so or not, there is nothing astonishing about such an attitude. The Romans liked to set the origins of their civilization in Greece, and many great families claimed Ulysses or Aeneas among their ancestors. But the Etruscans had got in before them and continued to out-do them in their Philhellenism. A priestly family of Tarquinii could not do less than the Aemilii of Rome, who boasted of having the blood of Pythagoras in their veins.[60]

Moreover, *Pule*, in Greek Polles, is in fact the name of an ancient Greek diviner who had no equal in divinatory talent except the celebrated Melampus, 'Black Foot', sung by Homer. A proverb, referring to an omen difficult of interpretation, says that it required the art of a Melampus or a Polles to unlock its secret.[61]

>   . . . *Polles, cui penna loquax dat nosse futura.*[62]

Or: 'Polles, whom the talkative plumage (of the birds) allows to know the future.' But we must not think that this mysterious Polles came from Lydia – where the name is particularly well known – about 350 BC to bring Tarquinii the benefits of the *Etrusca disciplina*, but simply that a rather far-fetched homonymic had allowed the *Pulena* to regard themselves as the depositaries of his art; having transmitted it without a break for four generations, they were to perpetuate the tradition for many more centuries, for under Marcus Aurelius we see one of their descendants, Pollenius Auspex, acceding to the consulate: his *cognomen* shows the continuance of an ability to predict the future by observing the flight of birds.

III

DID THE ETRUSCANS HAVE A PROFANE LITERATURE?
The preceding pages have perhaps made clearer what was one
part of Etruscan literature, the *Etrusca disciplina*, a collection of
holy scriptures such as were possessed by all oriental civilizations.
Greece had none at all, and Rome herself probably knew of them
only through the influence of the Etruscans from whom she had
received her Sibylline books. Did there exist, alongside this
sacred literature, a profane literature intended for amusement
and instruction and a heightening of life, like the poems of
Homer, the comedies of Plautus, the histories of Tacitus? This
seems to be the implication of a phrase by Posidonius in Diodorus:
'They cultivated the art of letters, natural sciences and theology.'[63]
Here we see that the humanities were scrupulously distinguished
from what was properly the Etruscan discipline.

This difficult problem has for long enough been answered in
the negative. Even as late as thirty years ago Pericle Ducati
maintained that 'the Etruscan people were not a literary people:
devoting their time to commercial activities, to industrial and
agricultural enterprises, producing many engineers, particularly
specialists in hydraulics, and many doctors whose practical
knowledge bordered on magic and superstition, the Etruscans
did not rise to the level of creating poems which reveal not only
the fires of the imagination or the passion of personal feelings but
also the sublime soaring of the spirit freed from the daily cares of
material existence'.[64] That is a big mouthful, and a rather rash
deduction confusing pell-mell statements of fact, value judgements and attempts at explanation. Already a great scholar like
Bartolomeo Nogara was attempting to break away from such
summary negations,[65] and new data have come along to prove
him right.

There are three points to be considered. First of all, we may
be sure that the genius of the Etruscans, as it is revealed in the
skill of their technicians as well as in the talent of their artists,
was in no way, *a priori*, incapable of literary expression. Secondly,
though their works have almost entirely perished, there remain
at least traces of them, and especially a memory and a considerable

impression in other literatures. Then as to whether their literature was good or bad, original in its inspiration or slavishly imitative, written in a noble style or in a coarse form, is a question we cannot answer here, though here again we are able to make certain guesses.

We owe to Livy an affirmation which at first sight is surprising but deserves our attention.[66] We are at the close of the fourth century, at a moment when Rome is undertaking the conquest of Etruria. Tradition always ascribed to this period a great military exploit, the march through the Ciminian forest which, in the region of present-day Viterbo, to the east of the Lake of Bolsena, seemed to place a redoubtable obstacle in the way of the Roman legions, one as terrifying as that which, at the time when Livy was writing, made them pause at the entrance of the wooded defiles of Germania. But a reconnaissance of its impenetrable ways was made, that year, in 310 by a member of the *gens* Fabia; according to the texts, the Claudii also claimed the merit for these operations. This person, Caeso Fabius according to some, C. Claudius according to others, the brother by the same father or only by the same mother of the consul Q. Fabius Rullianus, disguised himself as a peasant and accompanied by a single slave succeeded in slipping into enemy territory where without being discovered he established an itinerary that took him right to Chiusi in the Val di Chiana. What saved his life on this hazardous expedition was his perfect knowledge of the Etruscan language, so that he never for one moment aroused the suspicions of his interlocutors and guides.

How did he come to know Etruscan so well? He had been educated in Caere, in a family connected with his own by the bonds of hospitality, and there he had been instructed 'in Etruscan letters'. Livy adds, weighing his words, 'I have texts which prove that it was the usual custom in those days to instruct young Romans in Etruscan letters, just as today they are instructed in Greek letters: *Habeo auctores vulgo tum Romanos pueros, sicut nunc Graecis, ita Etruscis litteris erudiri solitos*'.

What does he mean by 'Etruscan letters'? It is clear that it did not mean simply learning to read and write on alphabet tablets and syllabary boards like those from Marsiliana and Caere. The word 'letters' is ambiguous: it not only means the letters of the alphabet but also, and indeed more so, grammar and literature. What literature could it be?

Livy is not here thinking of the Etruscan discipline properly speaking. The comparison he makes in this respect with the Greek education of young Romans of his time sends us off in quite another direction: 'just as today they are instructed in Greek letters.' He is evidently thinking of boys under seventeen (*pueri*) who, attending the school of a *grammaticus* (the word for 'grammarian' in Latin is Greek), learnt to read Homer, the Tragic Poets and Menander. It was in order to coach his sons in the *Odyssey* that Livius Salinator in the third century had brought from Tarentum the Greek poet Andronicus; it was to give the best grounding in Greek to young Scipio Aemilianus that Aemilius Paulus in the second century surrounded him, in the library of Perseus which he had brought from Macedonia, with a whole team of Greek professors, painters, sculptors, etc. And even in the days of Livy the study of the Latin poets in secondary education had scarcely overtaken that of the Greek poets. Cicero read and spoke Greek as well as his mother tongue. For many centuries Roman culture was bilingual.[67]

This is what Livy found in his sources, and it astonished him as much as it does us. But he insists: 'I have texts . . .' in the face of the sceptics. Texts in which *several* annalists are in agreement that before turning to Greece Rome had sought in Etruria a cultural initiation whose elements were lacking in her own background.

And is there anything very shocking in that? There is nothing so very unlikely in Caere, for example, at the end of the fourth century, having the attraction of an intellectual capital for youthful Fabii or Claudii; what its monuments and works of art tell us seems to make it very possible, despite what Pericle Ducati says, that Caere raised herself above 'the daily cares of material existence'. After Veii fell in 390, Caere was not only the nearest Etruscan metropolis to Rome, only about fifty kilometres away along the future via Aurelia. It was also the most active centre of Hellenism in central Italy – and Rome aspired towards Hellenism through Etruria. Did not Caere have its treasury at Delphi, as if it were an authentic Greek colony? The tombs have shown us with what passion the inhabitants collected the finest examples of black-figured and red-figured Attic vases. Greek artists had even come to the place in order to satisfy more easily an insatiable clientele. From the curved flanks of their vases, to say nothing of other imported articles, the Caerites had long since learnt to recognize the heroes of legend: the Trojan War, the voyages of Ulysses, the labours of Hercules, the crimes of the Atreids were no secrets to them.

Indeed the problem is not to know whether or not the Etruscans had a taste for literature. If there ever existed a Boeotian race, the *hydriae* or water-jars of Caere and the frescoes of Tarquinii were not made for its members. What is more to be feared is that the prestige of Greek might have been so great that it discouraged the Etruscans from using, in order to express their sense of the tragedy and joy of life, the uncertain resources of their own language. We can imagine the existence of a bilingual Etruscan aristocracy, similar to the Roman nobility, composing its first Greek essays and keeping its native tongue for the somewhat disdainful composition of its sacred books. In general, that is what must have happened. Yet certain facts seem to show that the Etruscans did more than that.

FESCENNINE HYMNS AND SONGS

The memory of oral poetry composed by the Etruscans had not entirely disappeared in the classical period. Dionysius of Halicarnassus knew that at the annual festival of Juno Curitis at Falerii a chorus of young girls used to sing in honour of the goddess 'hymns composed by their ancestors'.[68] But though Falerii was part of the Etruscan federation, it was ethnically and linguistically a double town in which were mingled Etruscan and Italic elements and the girls sang perhaps in a Faliscan dialect, one close to Latin and Sabine. With reference to the verses by Virgil in Book 8 of the *Aeneid*, in which he describes the dances and songs of the Salii who, he says, 'chant praises of Hercules and his lofty deeds', it was remarked that certain people attributed to the king of Veii, Morrius, perhaps Mamarrius, the institution of the Salian rites (the Salii were priest-dancers in Rome) in which the Salii must have celebrated the founder of his race, Halaesus, son of Neptune.[69] Here again, except for the mention of Veii, there is nothing specifically Etruscan. Halaesus was also the eponymous hero of Falerii; moreover we have shown already[70] in connexion with the double-indented buckler similar to the ancile or sacred shield of the Salii which Raymond Bloch discovered in a Villanovan tomb at Bolsena, that these warrior dances or armed dances had spread throughout the whole of central Italy since the first Iron Age. Finally we remember the 'Fescennine Verses', that sort of rustic poetry consisting of unbridled puns and obscene abuse which, it is said, the peasants formerly sang 'to a rude and clumsy metre'. They got their name from the small town of Fescennium, from where they had made their way to Rome. Here again we have an Etruscan town, though in Faliscan territory. All we can say is that the *fescennini versus* represented a spontaneous vein of popular comic doggerel, widespread in all the central part of Italy, and which, at Fescennium, under Etruscan influence, began to take on some artistic form: these first refinements led to a generalization of the name which thenceforward was applied to all similar manifestations of rustic mirth.[71]

These three testimonies, curiously localized in the same region, at the bottom of the southerly curve of the Tiber where some very ancient Etrusco-Latin osmoses took place, are far from being the works of literature, even oral ones, that we were hoping for. The last example however recalls another fact which the Etruscans played in the beginnings of Italic farce: we have already spoken of the place given in their funeral games to masked demons, the distant prototypes of the *Commedia dell' Arte*.[72]

DRAMATIC SPECTACLES

Yet with Phersu, however influential the impulse he provided for the Atellana, we are still in the domain of mime, still far removed from spoken drama, let alone written drama. But Varro mentions a certain Volnius who had 'written Etruscan tragedies'.[73] In order to appreciate the value of this testimony, we have to go back to the celebrated chapter, already quoted, in which Livy describes the arrival in Rome of the Etruscan dancers and the beginnings of the Latin theatre.[74] That year, 364 BC, a plague ravaged the city: with the failure of all medicaments, the people turned to religion. In order to appease the celestial ire, scenic games were started: this was a great novelty for a people that so far had only known the chariot-races at the circus. 'Without any singing, without imitating the action of singers, players who had been brought in from Etruria danced to the strains of the flautist and performed not ungraceful evolutions in the Tuscan fashion.' Roman youth, which had long been accustomed to exchanges of obscene and abusive verse-dialogues known as *Fescennini versus* got the idea of imitating the Etruscan players by adding to the choreography this spoken element, and by adapting the movements to the words. And the game became perfected with practice: there was a period when professional actors of Roman stock and 'called histrions because in Etruscan *ister* is the word corresponding to player', performed 'satires', properly speaking 'farcical plays', which resembled revues or farces in which there was a mimed dance, accompanied by singing, and a musical score containing all these elements. But we have to wait until the middle of the third century and the arrival in Rome of the Tarentine Livius Andronicus bringing in his luggage the whole repertoire of Greek tragedy and comedy before these improvisations were given a plot, a subject and a final text.

It was probably from Varro's *Antiquitates Rerum Humanarum et Divinarum* that Livy borrowed this erudite reconstruction of the origins of the Roman drama:[75] we see how it lays bare the various sources and note the successive intervention of each in a progressively unified ensemble. And at once the evident artificiality of the process, which tries to find in this evolution the stages which, according to Aristotle's *Poetics* had marked the emergence of the Greek theatre, invites us not to accept what we are told quite literally: facts are never as simple, nor as systematic as that. We have Livy stating, not without astonishment, that an art which was to have such a noble future had started very insignificantly, and even came from abroad, from Etruria. Moreover he gives us the Etruscan word for these artistes, *ister* or *hister*, a word which, latinized into *histrio*, was to have great fame. But the initial responsibility accorded to these is confined to the dance, a dance whose beauty he does not deny: *haud indecoros motus tusco more dabant*: 'they performed not ungraceful evolutions in the Etruscan manner.' And this *litotes* reminds us at once of the marvellous dancers in the archaic paintings at Tarquinii. But their dances were done to the flute only: they were not accompanied by any *carmen* or rhythmed speech. In fact, however hard we look, we can find no singer represented in the tombs;[76] nor do these dancers attempt to mime feelings like love or actions like fighting: it is so to speak pure dancing they perform – and that indeed is what the choreographic movements in the paintings on the walls of the Tomb of the Lionesses, of the Leopards and of the Triclinium appear to be.

Yet we may wonder if, in this analytical preoccupation with giving everyone his due, the patriotism of Varro and Livy had not tended to over-emphasize the part played by Rome. The Etruscan historians at the beginning of the fourth century had perhaps themselves, under a Greek influence which could not fail to make itself felt on a public as Hellenized as theirs, begun to realize that great theatrical possibilities lay within their dances. Above all, it is inconceivable that once the theatre had been born somewhere in central Italy the community of culture which as we have already said united Rome, Caere, Praeneste, Tarquinii and Chiusi should not have produced everywhere the same results, and that the development which Livy attributes to the games in the Circus Maximus should not at least have had repercussions on the games of the Etruscan federation at Volsinii.

Why should Etruria have deprived herself of dramatic spectacles when Sicily and southern Italy were full of them? Right from the first half of the fifth century, Syracuse had a magnificent theatre where Aeschylus saw his *Persians* performed and on whose stepped seats Pindar and Plato sat. Tarentum had two theatres in which Livius Andronicus applauded Euripides before introducing him to Rome; Apulian ceramic with its numerous scenes from tragedies painted on its vases offers definite proof of the splendour of their productions.[77] It is true that farther north Velia, Paestum and even Cumae have still not been found to possess a theatre in stone, that Pompeii did not have hers until the beginning of the second century, and Rome until 55. But we know that the theatres of stone were preceded, in Rome, by wooden trestle stages on which were played the tragedies of Ennius and the comedies of Plautus. If there were scenic games in Etruria, they must have used temporary installations which have disappeared.

Etruscan tragedy seems to be reflected, as far as the third and second centuries are concerned, on the sarcophagi and urns of Tarquinii, Chiusi and Volterra.[78] All the legends of the epic and tragic repertory of the Greeks are represented there, especially scenes of carnage, as if they were offering the defunct a modest equivalent, but raised to a higher level by the prestige of the legend, of the human sacrifices which he could not afford and which we hope the increasing mildness of custom had abolished. Thus a famous sarcophagus in the Vatican illustrates the classical themes of the *Oresteia*: here between two servants struck dumb with horror and behind Electra who is crouching down in a dreamy pose, is depicted an altar upon which lies, head thrown back, the half-naked corpse of Clytemnestra. To the right, Aegisthus is struck down by Orestes assisted by Pylades. To the left the Erinyes are already pursuing the murderer. The rear face represents the duel between Eteocles and Polynices, and other episodes from the tragedy of *Seven Against Thebes*. On one of the short sides, exactly as shown by Euripides in his *Telephus*, the hero of this name is seizing the boy Orestes and threatening to cut his throat. On the other short panel, just as the same poet had related in his *Hecuba*, Polyxena is being sacrificed by the Greeks on the tomb of Achilles.[79] Elsewhere, we see the sacrifice of Iphigenia, Philoctetes abandoned on Lemnos, Andromeda chained to her rock, Hippolytus dragged along by his chariot.[80]

M. André Piganiol, in his *Researches on the Roman Games*, remarks that the composition of these reliefs often imitates the décor of a theatre, the cave or the temple in front of which the actors performed, the port where they embarked, the tower or the ramparts of the besieged city, the door of the palace opened on the chamber where Agamemnon is expiring, together with altars and other ordinary accessories used in setting a scene.

On urns at Volterra Medea appears in a chariot drawn by dragons. It was in such an equipage that, in a lost tragedy of Euripides, she fled from Corinth after having slain her children. And doubtless the funerary symbolism could be interpreted as an earnest of immortality. But we also know that the Latin tragic writers of the second century were very fond of this complicated machinery: a fragment of Pacuvius describes the *angues ingentes alites iuncti iugo*, 'the enormous winged serpents harnessed to a yoke' of Medea. And the satirist Lucilius mocked those who, in order to inflame the imaginations of their spectators, had recourse to such puerile devices.[81]

Still other urns show a child attacked by a warrior on horseback, and here we recognize at once an episode from the legend of the king of Thessaly, Athamas who, during a hunt, was struck by madness and killed his son Learchus. This was the subject of a tragedy by Euripides, *Ino*, from which Ennius took his *Athamas*.[82]

The imagery on all Etruscan urns presents these kinds of correspondences, not only with Greek myth in general, but with adaptations which Latin tragedy from Livius Andronicus to Accius had made from the myths. We might wonder perhaps if the tragedies which inspired this imagery were not so much Etruscan as Latin tragedies which came into being from about 250 to 100 BC. But apart from the fact that it is difficult to believe that such performances could have influenced from a distance and in so tyrannical a way, the workshops of Volterra, we have reason to believe that the sculptors had a more direct and local knowledge, expressed in their own language, of the subjects they treated.

For these personages of Greek myth, on certain paintings and certain mirrors, are for the most part referred to by very deformed proper names:[83] Agamemnon becomes *Achmemrun* or *Achmenrun*; Achilles, in Greek *Achilleus*, becomes *Achile* or *Achle*; Clytemnestra (*Klutaimnèstra*) *Clutumsta*; Alexander (*Alexandros*), that is to say, Paris, is changed to *Alechsantre*, *Elachsantre* and even *Elcste*; Ganymede (Ganumèdès), the cup-bearer of the gods, is almost unrecognizable as *Catmite*, which insinuates itself even into Latin in the *Catamitus* of Plautus.[84] These deformations can perhaps be explained here and there because the borrowing from the Greek is from dialect sources; but they are generally in accordance with the tendencies of Etruscan phonetics: syncope, metathesis and aspirations which are well known to us from inscriptions where they have been studied and defined with precision. Some features of these phonetic peculiarities even seem to have been perpetuated through the centuries in certain characteristics of Tuscan pronunciation: in Florence, one always hears la *hasa*, not la *casa*.

What conclusion must we draw from this? It is that the painters who placed these proper names on their mirrors, paintings or vases were not docilely copying them letter for letter from Greek models; they were transcribing them as they sounded to their ears, and consequently Agamemnon, Achilles, Clytemnestra, Alexander and Ganymede had passed through Etruscan mouths before changing to *Achmemrun*, *Achle*, *Clutumsta*, *Elcste* and *Catmite*: in short, they had had in Etruria a long oral life which can only be explained by recitations of lyric, epic and especially of dramatic works.

It is certain that there must have existed Etruscan tragedies, at least during the third and second centuries which saw the parallel emergence of Latin tragedy, and it is in this perspective that the Volnius of Varro finds his right place. It is in speaking about the names of the three primitive tribes of Rome that the erudite author, in his *De lingua latina*, quotes this unknown writer. 'The Roman territory was divided originally into three regions, whence the names of the tribes – the *Titienses*, the *Ramnes* and the *Luceres*. These names, according to Ennius, were derived from: Tatius, in the case of the *Titienses*, Romulus in the case of the *Ramnes* and, according to Junius, from Lucumo in the case of the *Luceres*. But Volnius, who wrote tragedies in Etruscan, declared that all these words were Etruscan: *sed omnia haec vocabula Tusca, ut Volnius, qui tragoedias Tuscas scripsit, dicebat.*'[85]

We know nothing more about Volnius: his name, a very common *gentilicium* in the form of *Velna* or *Velina*, notably at Volterra, Siena, Chiusi, Perugia, Bologna, does not indicate exactly where he came from. Whatever Varro says, it does not follow that he had written a tragedy, as did Naevius at the end of the third century, on Romulus and the foundation of Rome. But he was, as well as a dramatic author, a scholar who, like Accius in the second half of the second century, combined his poetic vocation with the labours of a philologist. Accius had disagreed with Lucilius on the reform of orthography. Volnius, quoted here after M. Junius Gracchanus, friend of C. Gracchus and historian of common law, had intervened in the discussion, which had raged since the days of Ennius, on the etymology of the names of the three Roman tribes. Everything points to the fact that he too may have lived in the days of the Gracchi or a little later and that he was admitted into Roman literary circles. He divided his time between the capital and his homeland, to which he was evidently very attached. He claimed an Etruscan origin for the three disputed words, and in this he is supported by modern philologists.[86] He was proud of his native traditions, and it was perhaps in a spirit of despairing loyalty to a cherished and threatened cause that he wrote his Etruscan tragedies: erudite and archaistic works which perhaps were played on the last trestle-stages of Chiusi or Volterra and there revived *in extremis* a fire that was about to be extinguished. That Varro says *tragoedias Tuscas scripsit* does not mean that he was the only one to do so or that no one had done so before him. He simply means that this Volnius whom we have seen among us, such a cultured man, who spoke Latin so well, and who, after all, was a Roman like everybody else, had composed tragedies in his native language, a language very difficult to understand. But we can be sure today that Volnius was only the epigone of a long line of poets whose names we shall never know but whose productions were reflected in the decorations on funerary urns, whose verses echoed in the memory of workmen, whose tragic style finally imposed itself on Etruscan historiography and gave it its particular form.

HISTORICAL LITERATURE

The Etruscan certainly had an historical literature. But the problem it raises is no more easy of solution than that of the drama. For it, too, has entirely disappeared, and though its former existence is testified by two irreproachable witnesses, we cannot find it except partially translated and naturally deformed by the use that was made of it by Latin historiography.

The two authors who mention it can be trusted. First, there is Varro: his friends, the *haruspices*, either Tarquitius or Caecina, told him about the *Tuscae historiae*, and he had found in them, among other things, a general theory about the *saecula* which determined the destiny of the nation, the total number of centuries of existence it would have, the variable duration of each of the centuries and the specific omens that marked the passage from one century to the next. But Varro knew that these *Histories* had been composed during the eighth Etruscan century, and it has been calculated that this coincided with the second century BC.[87]

The emperor Claudius' knowledge of Etruscan things was, as we have shown above when referring to his historical works, derived from the best sources: in a famous speech delivered at Lyons in 48, the text of which is preserved on a bronze tablet and in which he spoke of the ancient legend of Servius Tullius, he was well qualified to discuss certain details of it as he had been able to compare the account given by the Latin annalists with the translation of it by men whom he expressly referred to as *auctores Tusci*.[88]

Already before Claudius, Verrius Flaccus in the reign of Augustus and Varro at the time of Caesar seem to be referring to these Etruscan authors; but they are not known to us now, excepting one who is no other but Aulus Caecina, Cicero's correspondent and expert in the art of divination; or, if it is not he, it is his father, who had instructed him in that science. In any case, we possess, in Caecina's name, a tiny fragment which attributes to Tarchon, the hero of Tarquinii, the conquest of the province of Padane Etruria. Crossing the Apennines with an army, he had founded the first city, which he called Mantua from the Etruscan name for the god of Death, then eleven others which were likewise dedicated to Mantus; thus there was formed in Cisalpine areas a confederation of twelve cities similar to those in Etruria proper. Caecina adds that Tarchon had consecrated the foundations according to the rites and had organized the 'year', that is, had divided up the year with calendar feasts. Only a few lines, but they define fairly well the historian's attitude, and the insistence with which he underlines the religious rather than the military character of Tarchon's work relates it closely to the general tone of the *Etrusca disciplina*. We also see that Caecina had written his history in Latin, evidently from Etruscan sources.[89]

The anonymous *Tuscae historiae* which we know of through Varro also enter into the category of sacred literature. Varro quotes from them a Latin phrase: either the entire work had been translated by an Etrusco-Latin *haruspex*, or else he had had translated for his own use the passage about the centuries, which interested him. But everything gives us to understand that the original text was in Etruscan, like the other *libri rituales*.

We are told that it dates from the second century BC, from some date between the years 206 and 88 BC, the years which cover the eighth Etruscan century. And this too is an interesting fact, for it shows the parallel development of the Latin and Etruscan literatures within a common culture. The second century is precisely when Latin historiography began. The annalists, who at first wrote in Greek, because it was the language of cultured men which Herodotus and Timaeus had imposed upon the historical genre, soon began trying to express themselves in their native tongue for the special benefit of their compatriots who had become deeply conscious of the significance of the Roman past. It is remarkable that a similar evolution should have brought into being, in Etruria, and at the same period, that collection of historical works (which is, it seems, the precise meaning of the plural *historiae*), in which the Etruscan people manifested the awareness that had come to them, a little late perhaps, of the importance of their destiny. The publication of the *Tuscae historiae* reminds us of the collection and publication of the old official chronicles of Rome known under the name of *Annales Maximi* about 123 during the pontificate of P. Mucius Scaevola. As we have said above, the Roman Senate had taken the initiative of reviving the teaching of the discipline in Etruscan families; this makes us wonder if similar counsels or spontaneous emulation could explain the awakening of an historical sense which conformed more to the Roman temperament than to the particular vocation of the Etruscans.

It has often been remarked[90] that the Roman genius for methodical and tenacious conquests of the world of reality never found better expression than in its representations, in paintings or bas-reliefs, of historical events. 'Love whatever one shall never see twice!' Alfred de Vigny's line defines fairly exactly one of its fundamental attitudes. But the Etruscans were perhaps less themselves in their worldly activities than in their other-worldly preoccupations with the will of the gods. They lived more naturally in the absolute, and, when the contemplation of celestial signs did not occupy their minds, they pondered the marvellous substitute given them by Greek mythology, through which for a long time they interpreted the vicissitudes of their personal fate. From the sixth century onwards, the quarrel of Apollo and Hercules over a sacred hind was what they displayed on top of a temple in Veii.[91] In their funerary monuments, they showed Achilles waiting to kill Troilus, or the Trojan prisoners sacrificed to the shades of Patroclus, which they felt expressed exactly their attitude to death.[92] It was not until very much later, and then very rarely, that Etruscan myths were introduced into this imagery.[93]

Hence the extraordinary interest of the paintings in the François tomb at Vulci, if we admit, as is right, the recent date – second century or even beginning of the first – which the best judges give them. We have already described a part of these, the one which, on the right-hand wall of the rear chamber, represents Mastarna cutting the bonds of Caelius Vibenna, while his companions massacre the enemy princes who held him captive. This epic battle, the account of which the emperor Claudius was to read later in his *auctores Tusci*, is borrowed from the purest native traditions of the Etruscans. But on the left-hand wall, facing it, the usual Greek subjects are displayed: Nestor, flanked by the owner of the tomb, Vel Saties, clad in his fine embroidered toga and scanning a flight of birds; Eteocles and Polynices, with the corresponding figures of Marce Camitlnas and Cneve Tarchunies; finally the sacrifice of the Trojan prisoners at the funeral of Patroclus, opposite the battle raging round Vulci.[94] This confrontation is full of significance; it is carried out symmetrically on the opposite walls of a single tomb that is contemporary with the awakening of Etruscan historiography – an episode from the *Iliad* against an episode from the Vulcian *gesta*, a Greek legend against an Etruscan legend; in short, a confrontation of what was mythological and what for the Etruscans was becoming historical.

The François tomb is one of the rare monuments of this people in which native tradition claims a place in a repertory reserved almost exclusively, until now, for foreign elements. We cannot help thinking of what was to happen in Latin literature at the end of the Republic, when Rome ventured to face up to Greece with a courteous and even admiring pride, when Virgil did not hesitate to claim that his *Aeneid* was equal to the dignity of the Homeric poems and to sing of the foundation, on Latin soil, of a new Troy whose emergence had not been prevented by the efforts of new Achilles and new Ulysses. 'Ye shall lack nothing,' his Sibyl prophesies, 'neither the Simois nor the Xanthus nor the Dorian camp. A second Achilles has been born for Latium.' Some hundred years earlier the Etruscan historians were basing a Vulcian cycle on the plan of the Trojan and Theban cycles: *non Simois tibi nec Xanthus . . . defuerint alius 'Etruriae' iam partus Achilles*, one might say, replacing, in Virgil's line, *Latio* with *Etruriae*.[95]

THE TRADITIONS OF THE GREAT FAMILIES

Such, it seems to us, were the characteristics and the influence of the *Tuscae historiae* which had come to the notice of Varro. Closely dependent on the *Etrusca disciplina*, in natural or intentional accord with the development of Latin annalistics they had brought together all kinds of disparate traditions into a systematic scheme dominated by the concept of the *saeculum* and by a determinism whose tendencies were confirmed by Chaldean preaching and the lessons of Stoicism. But though this consolidation saved from oblivion obscure local chronicles, revived in the decadent Etruscans the sense of its own historical importance and perhaps determined the upsurge of national pride which inspires the frescoes in the François tomb, it is quite obvious that it had not created all of a piece the elements it brought into play. It supposes, distinct from that current of sacred history, another current, ancient and diversified, which, in retracing the origins of cities and the deeds of heroes, was concerned less with the laws of fatality than with the variable nature of particular events and deeds. Claudius' speech at Lyons unconsciously reflects this different aspect of historical development: 'Mastarna, the most faithful friend of Caelius Vibenna, and his inseparable companion in all his adventures (*casus*), Mastarna, whom the vicissitudes of fate (*varia fortuna*) had driven from Etruria . . .' After all, the Etruscans were not altogether lacking in imagination and memory. Dedicated to the eternal as they were, they had been brought up in an Ionizing spiritual world and nourished on Hellenistic affabulations; the Clio of Herodotus and his successors had not completely abandoned them: before writing history, they had told stories.

Very ancient traces of these stories, dating to before the compilation of the *Tuscae historiae*, can still be glimpsed. There is one in the rather absurd romance of Arruns of Clusium who, according to Livy and Dionysius of Halicarnassus, was one of the immediate causes of the invasion by the Gauls at the beginning of the fourth century:[96] Arruns of Clusium was an old man to whom the *lucumo* of the town had confided, on his death-bed, the guardianship of his son: the ungrateful youth seduced Arruns' wife, and Arruns, seeking vengeance, had encouraged the Gauls to attack his country by acquainting them with the delights of the white wine of Montepulciano. Now this legend, evidently a composite one, and which we might be tempted to attribute to the disordered imagination of a late annalist, was already current and complete in 160 BC. The adulterous loves of Arruns' wife had already been recounted in detail by the austere Cato in Book II of his *Origines*.[97] Witness a short phrase which has come down to us, shorn of its context, but which finds its echo in the account by Dionysius of Halicarnassus. 'He was not content, says Cato, until he had publicly dishonoured the woman he had already corrupted in private. *Neque satis habuit, quod eam in occulto uitiauerat, quin eius famam prostitueret.*' But Dionysius, doubtless taking this titbit from the same source, adds: 'He not only sought to have commerce with her in private, but also in public.'

It was not Cato who invented such a tale: his indignant tone assures us of that. The adultery shocks him less than the scandal – and here we find again the characteristic astonishment of the Roman at a society which tolerated such promiscuity between men and women. He took it from one of those original documents, city chronicles (in this case Clusium), regional archives and even inscriptions which his curiosity had made good use of, unless a preceding annalist had already compiled the facts in a book of his own. In any case, it had already entered into the vulgate which Polybius had at his disposal; but the latter, too serious to report such imbecilities, only makes a disdainful reference to them which betrays the knowledge he had of them. 'The Gauls, on a very flimsy pretext, invaded Etruscan territory.'[98]

Before this, a good number of Etruscan traditions had already been incorporated into the growing works of the annalists. We know that the annals were first created during the Second Punic War by Fabius Pictor who was the first to give the history of Rome a continuity which his successors could develop, rectify or deform according to their temperament or interests but which he had fixed *ne varietur* as far as its chronology and essential facts were concerned. For example, everything Livy tells us about the reign of the Tarquins and the war waged by Porsenna, apart from the analytical and dramatic elements, was already to be found in Fabius Pictor.

An interest in Etruscan things was something this Fabius' ancestors had all enjoyed. Among the Roman families who, as we have seen, sent their sons to Caere at the end of the fourth century 'there to learn Etruscan letters' there had been a Fabius. The gentilitiary archives of the Fabii were full of accounts of battles waged in that Etruria which had in a way become their domain. One of their most illustrious members, Q. Fabius Maximus Rullianus, five times consul from 322 to 295, had opened the Ciminian forest to the Roman conquest, been the first to enter inner Etruria and with the *lucumones* of Chiusi, Arezzo and Perugia had formed bonds of hospitality and clientele which are confirmed by local epigraphy: a bilingual text from Clusium is inscribed in the name of *Au. Fapi. Larthial* – A. *Fabi(us) Iucnus*.[99] After that, his son (or grandson), Q. Fabius Maximus Gurges, was the victor at Volsinii in 265; but the surname he bears, and which the Latins were pleased to interpret as 'gulf or abyss' was in fact nothing more than the transcription of a proper name, *Curce(s)*, twice attested at Chiusi.[100] So it need not surprise us that Fabius Pictor, in writing of the Etruscans, displayed a familiarity with them which he got from his own relatives; he had at his disposal, when writing of the Etruscan centuries in the history of Rome, materials of a richness that, as soon as Tarquinius and Tanaquil appeared on the scene, garbed in brilliant colours, relegated to the shades the bloodless shapes of Romulus and Tullus Hostilius. This was because 'histories' of the Tarquins existed before he started to write; and the Fabii had assimilated in the course of their campaigns, at the same time as members of the *gentes* of Etruria established in Rome, the Volumnii, the Ogulnii, who enter the Fasti at the turn of the fourth and third centuries, these stories which they passed on to the Roman public.

It is possible, and even very likely, that, just as the *Annales* of Fabius Pictor were written in Greek, these stories too were put into Greek, either by Etruscans or by Greeks. The legends relating to the origins of Rome, and especially those which connected them with the arrival of Aeneas and his Trojans in Latium, furnished the third century with an outstanding theme developed with feverish ingenuity by a host of *Graeculi* of whom we know only the name: Diocles of Peparethos or Derkyllos.[101] Among them was 'a certain Promathiôn', as Plutarch says, author of a *History of Italy*, who interests us directly. This is how he recounts the miraculous birth of Romulus:[102]

'. . . they say that Tarchetius, king of the Albans, who was most lawless and cruel, was visited with a strange phantom in his house, namely, a phallus rising out of the hearth and remaining there many days. Now there was an oracle of Tethys in Tuscany, from which there was brought to Tarchetius a response that a virgin must have intercourse with this phantom, and she should bear a son most illustrious for his valour, and of surpassing good fortune and strength (*rômè*). Tarchetius, accordingly, told the prophecy to one of his daughters, and bade her consort with the phantom; but she disdained to do so, and sent a handmaid into it. When Tarchetius heard of this, he was wroth, and seized both the maidens, purposing to put them to death. But the goddess Vesta appeared to him in his sleep and forbade him the murder. He therefore imposed upon the maidens the weaving of a certain web in their imprisonment, assuring them that when they had finished the weaving of it, they should then be given in marriage. By day, then, these maidens wove, but by night other maidens, at the command of Tarchetius, unravelled their web. And when the handmaid became the mother of twin children by the phantom, Tarchetius gave them to a certain Teratius with orders to destroy them. This man, however, carried them to the river-side and laid them down there. Then a she-wolf visited the babes and gave them suck, while all sorts of birds brought morsels of food and put them into their mouths, until a cow-herd spied them, conquered his amazement, ventured to come to them, and took the children home with him. Thus they were saved, and when they were grown up, they set upon Tarchetius and overcame him. At any rate, this is what a certain Promathiôn says, who compiled a history of Italy.' (Trans. by Bernadotte Perrin.)

We recognize in this bizarre story a variant, or rather a first draft, which posterity cast aside, of the fable of the twins exposed on the banks of the Tiber by a tyrant, suckled by a she-wolf, taken in by a shepherd. Scholars have seen in it references to the web of Penelope and done etymological research into the meaning of the name of Rome in Greek (*rômè* = strength) which would reveal the author's Hellenic culture; as if *Promathiôn*, derived from *Prometheus* or in Dorian *Promatheus*, were not sufficient indication of his origins. But we also notice here that the rôle played by the phallus is exactly the same as that attributed to it in the birth of Servius Tullius,[103] in which there is expressed the cult, widespread among the Italics, of sexual energy. But above all we notice the Etruscan character of the denominations, and this would appear even more clearly if they had not been deformed by Plutarch's Greek: Tarchetius is obvious, for we know of Tarquitii at Veii, Chiusi, Sutri, Capena and Caere: here a tomb has given us numerous inscriptions in the name of the *Tarchna*; Teratius probably conceals a Terrasius, a Tarracius, or that Tarrutius who figures as 'a rich Etruscan' in the legend of Acca Larentia. These proper names indicate an effort to etruscanize the origins of Rome: it was an Etruscan king who ruled at Alba Longa; it was an Etruscan cow-herd who watered his beasts on the banks of the Tiber. What is more, it was an Etruscan oracle that Tarchetius consulted, an oracle by the sea, for it was Tethys, wife of Neptune, who reigned there, or perhaps the nereid Thetis, with whom she is frequently confused. The location is difficult, but if we modify a little Klausen's suggestion, who placed the oracle in a temple of Fortuna at Caere,[104] we believe that this Tethys or Thetis was no other than the nereid Leucothea venerated in the port of Caere, Pyrgi, where excavations now taking place will perhaps reveal her sanctuary.[105] Because of his Etruscomania, and even

more so because of the links he seems to have with Caere, it is
not impossible that Promathiôn was a Greek or a Hellenized
Etruscan of that city, and his story, scabrous as it is, one of those
products of Etruscan literature which the young Romans went
to Caere to study.

Fortunately a recent discovery has proved the reality and
clarified the nature of these native sources of Etruscan history
which until now we have only been able to sift from a host of
allusions, echoes and resemblances. In 1948, Pietro Romanelli,
publishing the result of diggings he made before the war on the
site of Tarquinii, has made known epigraphic fragments which
probably came from the forum of that city.[106] They are bits of
'eulogies' (*elogia*) which in Rome and Italy it was usual to engrave
under the bust or statue of a magistrate or general whose career
and victories they would relate.[107] A whole collection of them
was found, devoted to the great legendary or historical figures of
Rome – Aeneas, Appius Claudius, Marius, etc. – in the ruins of
the forum of Augustus, dedicated in the year 2 BC. Likewise the
public squares of certain colonies in the peninsula, notably
Pompeii and Arezzo, have furnished us with *elogia* singing the
exploits of Romulus, Fabius Cunctator or Aemilius Paulus.
Here we find a strange thing: Arezzo, one of the twelve Etruscan
capitals, where the ancestors of Maecenas ruled, forgot, at the
beginning of the first century BC, its own glories and concentrated
on the illustrious heroes of Roman history: this lapse of memory
makes us wonder; perhaps it is explained by the extinction of the
local aristocracy in the civil wars, from which only those nobles
had escaped who, like Maecenas, had dedicated themselves with
Augustus to the achieving of Italian unity. But the attitude
of Tarquinii must have been quite different; for the thing that
characterizes the *Elogia Tarquiniensia*, forming in fact its principal
interest for us, is that they celebrated only the heroes of Etruscan
tradition, heroes otherwise quite unknown to us: in Latin,
certainly, and according to formulae inspired by Roman eulogies.
But their contents have obviously been taken from native sources,
from those *auctores Tusci* mentioned, because he had used them,
by the emperor Claudius. So this ancient metropolis, this
religious centre of the Etruscan people that proudly claimed to
come right from the origins of its history, to have founded its

empire, to have revealed its religion, did not hold its glorious past so cheaply. Behind the severe, closed doors of its palaces were preserved the family archives guarded jealously with pride and piety. And it is these which came to light again fragmentarily when Tarquinii, inspired to emulation by the example of Rome, encouraged by the Etruscological sympathies of Claudius, decided about AD 40 to create a companion-piece, in its own forum, to the *Elogia* in the forum of Augustus.[108]

Just as in Rome the series opened with a eulogy of Aeneas, in Tarquinii it opened with one to the city's eponymous ancestor, Tarchon, though unfortunately the mutilation of the inscription does not allow us to add very much to his legend: we can only make out, under his name, that of Etruria, then Tarquinii, and then HAM . . . which remains unexplained.[109] Another *elogium*, more complete, related in eight lines the lofty deeds of a praetor, or *zilath*, who remains anonymous – the top part of the stone is broken – but who was the first of all the Etruscan captains to lead an army into Sicily and who, in reward for his meritorious conduct, had received the insignia of triumph – a sceptre surmounted by the eagle and the crown of gold.[110] There has been much discussion about which overseas expedition this referred to, though in any case it was in the very remote past; it has even been claimed that it referred to the immemorial migration which had carried the Etruscans from Asia Minor to Italy, with a call in Sicily.[111] The event has been placed at the beginning of the fifth century, for at that period the naval policy of the Etruscans, in the region of the Sicilian straits, seems to have been singularly active.[112] It has been dated to 414–413, a time when, responding to an appeal from the Athenians besieging Syracuse, the Etruscans sent to Sicily a contingent of land forces as well as three warships each with fifty rowers.[113] Again it was thought that the so-called praetor of Tarquinii was only one of the mercenary chiefs who often intervened, at the end of the fourth century, in the wars between the Greeks and Carthaginians in Sicily.[114] It is difficult to make the correct choice among these divers hypotheses.

The important thing for us here is that we glimpse a fragment of Etruscan history relating to facts of a high antiquity and totally independent of Roman or Greek history. In it things were related exclusively from the viewpoint of the Etruscan people, even when its armies formed a part of the coalitions in Mediterranean politics during the fifth and sixth centuries.

A third fragment,[115] no less remarkable, praised a person whose names are also unknown to us: one of his names, beginning with S, perhaps read *Saturius* or *Saturnius*; his origins are proved in the second line by the adjective *Orgolaniensis*: he came from that little town in Norchia known in the Middle Ages as *Orcle* or *Vicus Orclanus*, whose rock tombs, about twenty kilometres to the north-east of Tarquinii, we have already described.[116] This man had conquered a king of Caere, triumphed in the war at Arezzo and seized nine strongholds from the Latins (or the Aretines).

```
. . . . . . . . . . . . .VS.S. . . .VR. .
. . . . . . . . . . . .ORGOL(ani)ENSIs
. . . . .CAERITVM REGEM VI(cit
. . . . .ARRETIVM BELLO. . . . . .
De La)TINIS NOVEM O(ppida cepit
```

Here again the inscription brings us back to the heroic epoch when Tarquinii, without any sense of the solidarity which, one would think, united it with Caere and Arezzo, waged against other Etruscan cities inexpiable battles, somewhat similar to those which Rome, in the sixth and fifth centuries, waged against her neighbours. We recall once more the frescoes in the François tomb, where the princes of Vulci battle against the lords of Volsinii and Sovana, and not the least interest of this text is that it authenticates, to some extent, the tradition which inspired these paintings by showing that it, too, must be very ancient; later it would fall to the scholars like Varro and Claudius to try to reconcile these specific and heterogeneous facts with those of Roman historiography.

GENEALOGICAL TREES

Such are some of the *elogia* which a decree from the municipal council of Tarquinii brought into being round its forum. They were put up to show the Roman administration, which in any case was very sympathetic in the person of the emperor Claudius, that Tarquinii had lost nothing of her patriotic pride. Then the council had to requisition the archives that filled the *tablinum* of each house, and take down the ancient inscriptions that commented on the ancestral portraits at the top of the family trees which climbed the wall of the atrium.[117] For the Etruscan aristocracy had no less concern for its noble quarterings than the Ponticus of Juvenal who, 'armed with two rods tied end to end' strained to reach, in order to point them out to his visitors, the masks of wax, gnawed away by time and covered with smoke, of the dictators who had formerly made his name illustrious.[118] Already Persius of Volterra had taken to task one of his fellow citizens who was puffed up with pride because, 'on a Tuscan family tree, he was at the head of a branch, the thousandth . . .'

Stemmate quod Tusco ramum millesime ducis.[119]

There was no well-born Etruscan who did not have these *stemmata Tusca*. Maecenas himself, remote as he may seem from such vanities, had his own in the atrium of his villa on the Esquiline, and the poets he entertained there had often gazed reverently upon it. When Horace in his *Odes* and Propertius in his *Elegies* sang of the royal blood that flowed in his veins (*Tyrrhena regum progenies . . . Maecenas*[120]), it was no vague statement on their part: they had followed their patron's genealogy along the garlands that ran from one inscription to another, as far back as those Cilnii who, in the fourth century, had ruled at Arezzo; and they were all the more penetrated by the grandeur of his birth because he was not the sort of man to show off about it. Horace, son of a freed man, was grateful to him for not despising his common origin, 'though of all the Lydians that are settled in Tuscan lands none is of nobler birth than you, Maecenas, and though grandsires of yours, on your mother's and father's side alike, commanded mighty legions in days of old, . . .'

. . . avus tibi maternus fuit atque paternus
olim qui magnis legionibus imperitarent.[121]

Do not these two verses seem to embrace with one vast gesture the whole extent of Maecenas' family tree, and to condense into one general impression ('commanded mighty legions in days of old') all the detail of the wars which was made explicit in circumstantial *elogia*? And if we remember that it was through his maternal ancestors that Maecenas was linked to the royal dynasty of the Cilnii, even the precedence given these by Horace (*avus maternus*), whom he names before the paternal ancestors (*paternus*), seems to express a characteristic feature of the *stemma* – although, to tell the truth, it may be for metrical reasons (*a* is long in *maternus*) that the two adjectives were placed in this order.

MAECENAS

We have just referred to Maecenas, and perhaps it would be fitting, at the end of this inquiry into Etruscan culture, to pause at this eminent and complex personality whose political rôle and literary influence were so important, and whom the Romans found no less disconcerting than the strange people he had issued from. Indeed, it would appear that certain of his vices and virtues, or at least the majority of his 'little ways' can be explained as inheritances from his distant ancestors, the *lucumones* of Arezzo. Or rather we can imagine him as a very fine specimen of what could be produced *in extremis* by the Etruscan aristocracy at a time when, almost on the point of extinction, it was becoming the new Italian governing class without quite abandoning its distinctive characteristics and one might say its patina, without having its vitality undermined by the weight of the past and the consciousness of being the last of its kind. For it was a marvellous quirk of history to associate with Augustus, as his most dependable collaborators in the creation of the Empire, two men as different as the plebean Agrippa, a forceful soldier, perpetually frowning, 'more rustic', cries Pliny, 'than refined!' – and this prince of Tuscany.

What particularly astonished contemporaries of the man whom Augustus had made 'a general administrator of Rome and Italy'[122] was that, while exercising power, he disdained its outward show. Agrippa was consul several times, and even, having married Julia, daughter of Augustus, received the proconsular *imperium* and tribunitial power.[123] Maecenas never intrigued for public position, and lived quite satisfied with the purple-bordered toga and the gold ring of the knights of Rome. 'He was no less dear to the prince than Agrippa,' comments Velleius Paterculus,[124] 'but he had less honours and contented himself all his life with equestrian rank. He might easily have risen as high as the other, but he did not care to.'

This attitude has been compared[125] with that which Cicero had already attributed to the Roman knights in the days of the tribunate of Drusus (91), among them a certain C. Maecenas, who was probably the grandfather of Maecenas on his father's side: these knights had refused to enter the Senate, declaring that they preferred to remain in 'their own class and that of their parents; that they preferred to enjoy a quiet life far from the storms provoked by public animosities'.[126] This reserve on the part of the aristocracy of the Italian cities, whose fortunes placed them in the equestrian order and apart from any honour-seeking career, is connected with its hostility, in principle, to the policy of the Gracchi and their successors: we shall not enter into the problem here. But it is clear that this was the same attitude which, two generations later, Maecenas adopted when he pretended to show coolness towards the Roman magistracies. Propertius acclaimed it as a philosophical merit in him:[127] (*'parcis et in tenues humilem te colligis umbras'*); '. . . yet holdest thou back and dost withdraw in lowly wise to modest shades.' (Trans. H. E. Butler.) P. Boyancé has also detected in him that 'orgulous modesty' shown by those 'heirs of illustrious families' who, from the cradle onwards, appear so blasé about official positions and think themselves above 'all else they might henceforward be accorded'. There was something of all this in Maecenas.

Only if Maecenas announced he was going to devote himself to the administration of his immense patrimony, of his vineyards and gardens, these 'modest shades' were no sinecure. For thirty-five years he was Augustus' most faithful minister, the most vigilant, the most efficient, and the one to whom he confided the duty of replacing him when he was absent from Rome. Let us state briefly here his talents as a diplomat: he was one of those of whom Horace says that they are 'old hands at settling feuds between friends'.[128] (*aversos soliti componere amicos*); the rivalry between Antony and the future Augustus gave him many an opportunity to exercise his conciliatory gifts; his political realism, too, if it is true that in a memorable debate with Agrippa he advised the prince to create institutions better adapted to the dimensions of the Empire rather than to make a chimerical return to the past;[129] his sang-froid and his humanity, which more than once allowed him to bring an irritated Augustus round to clemency, as has been shown by Corneille;[130] the way he guided the domain of letters, helping poets like Virgil, Horace and Propertius to discover their true vocation and orientating this to fit in with the régime's ideal.[131]

In this considerable activity, we feel everywhere a superior intelligence; everything reveals an innate experience of business and an intuitive understanding of men. If the 'Roman revolution'[132] which carried Augustus to the principate was started by 'new men', Maecenas was only a 'new man' when he was in Rome: he had behind him several centuries of political culture.

But with what nonchalance, true or affected, he accomplished that overwhelming labour! We might almost say that he merely lent himself to the State, and Romans disapproved of anyone who did not pretend to throw himself into things whole-heartedly. His air of a distrait and condescending grand seigneur reminds us a little, if we may be permitted the comparison, of Count Mosca in *Charterhouse of Parma*, and when Horace introduced himself to him for the first time his feelings cannot have been very different from those of La Sanseverina when, in a box at the Scala, she first encountered His Excellency. 'The frankness, the *disinvoltura* with which this minister of so redoubtable a prince was speaking aroused the countess's curiosity; she had expected to find a pedant full of self-importance, but instead she saw a man who was ashamed of the gravity of his position.'[133]

Because he pretended to be interested only in pleasure, and the most refined pleasures at that, public opinion kept its eye on him. The Republican opposition seized every chance it could find to calumniate Augustus' grey eminence. The Stoic philosophers, who suspected in him an epicureanism not theoretical but practical, unleashed their fury after his death. And doubtless he had vices, those of his time. But the thing that Seneca, who loses no opportunity to defame him, finds most intolerable in his conduct is: *vitia sua latere noluit*, that 'he did not wish to hide them'.[134]

We must believe that Maecenas' hedonism at least had this advantage, that in apparently concentrating his attention on pleasure he allowed his virtues to retain their spontaneity and their modesty. A Stoic cannot credit a morality that requires no effort: for them, it is an exercise on the short rein: one must be able to hear the will puffing and panting. With Maecenas, pleasure is sometimes a little forced, but fine sentiments, cloaked in modesty and discretion, are naturally developed. He was most improbably faithful to his friends, but the word fidelity is never uttered.

He was especially criticized for wearing too-ample garments. For costume and morals are often linked. In the seventeenth century in England, the conflict between Puritans and Cavaliers was typified by the name Roundheads assigned to the former and the right not to cut their locks claimed by the latter. In Rome, the disagreement was about the dimensions of the toga. About the middle of the first century BC there had been a revolution in men's wear which today provides archaeologists with a means of dating bas-reliefs,[135] but which at the time divided society into two camps. Instead of the narrow toga, *toga exigua*, of ancient times, the dandies adopted a wider toga whose capacious folds shocked righteous conformists. Agrippa, the austere, remained faithful to the narrow toga, but the gilded youth that hovered round deliciously frivolous Julia displayed togas of gloriously vast proportions. Maecenas did even worse. He had replaced the Roman toga with the Greek *pallium* which foreign actors and professors had introduced into Rome, and this cloak, liberally draped over a loose tunic, seemed the symbol of every depravity. Seneca always calls Maecenas *discinctus*, 'without a belt'. He declared: 'Maecenas was indeed a man of noble and robust native gifts, but in prosperity he impaired these gifts by laxness.'[136] (Trans. Richard M. Gummere.) In fact, his vices would hardly have been noticed, if he had said he was a Stoic and had worn a narrow toga.

It is strange that in attacking the 'laxness' of Maecenas, in criticizing the purple stuffs he adored draping himself in, casting sour glances at the swansdown litters he had himself borne along in, as well as finding fault with his indolent demeanour in walking, the warmest baths in which he swam, the meat of ass's foals he had made fashionable, his passion for the actor Bathyllus and even the infidelities of his wife Terentia,[137] it is strange that his detractors never remembered his origins nor the traditional accusations made by Greeks and Romans against Etruscan ways. We said at the beginning of this study what we must think of this, but we must admit that Maecenas did have some of the characteristics of those *lucumones* of the decadence whose relaxed pose we have noted on the lids of sarcophagi in Tarquinii and Chiusi. From an epigram he addresses to his friend Horace, we may even conclude that he was not altogether lacking in a certain rotundity of figure.[138]

Dionysius of Halicarnassus says that the Etruscan way of life resembled that of no other people: this was true of Maecenas, whose eccentric behaviour deliberately cocked a snook at public opinion. Not only did he drape himself in a *pallium*, but it is claimed that in all the ceremonies in which he took part he had a way, seen in no other person, of covering his head so that only his ears appeared. Seneca says this made him look like those escaped slaves in mimed plays who try in this way to conceal their faces.[139] In fact, this is a caricature such as statesmen like Mazarin or Louis-Philippe have always had to put up with. Here a malicious pen has presented as habitual the grotesque appearance of Maecenas one day when illness forced him to show himself in public wrapped up in his *pallium* in order to protect himself against the cold or the heat of the sun. For – need we say it? – it will already have been guessed: Maecenas' health was very delicate; he suffered from perpetual fevers and during the last three years of his life Pliny assures us that he never slept for longer than an hour at a time.[140] In an admirable phrase which this time evokes Shakespeare rather than Stendhal, Seneca shows him to us 'drained by love and in despair at the rebuffs of a whimsical jade, imploring sleep to the soft harmonies of a distant music' (the Latin is more beautiful: *per symphoniarum cantum ex longinquo lene resonantium*).[141] And here we cannot fail to remember, prompted by these invisible harmonies which, played behind the shrubbery of his gardens on the Esquiline, soothed the raw nerves of an unhappy *lucumo*, the place held by music in the civilization whose heir Maecenas was.

Well, then, he was a nonconformist, a peculiar person; and it was as to a peculiar person, though a dearly loved one that Augustus addressed himself to him, for example in that letter in which he gently mocks his exquisiteness, his rarefied taste for precious stones and strange materials: 'Farewell, my ebony of Medullia, my ivory of Etruria, my silphium of Arezzo, my diamond of the Adriatic, my pearl of the Tiber, emerald of the Cilnii, jasper of the Iguvians, beryl of Porsenna, carbuncle of Italy, and, in fine, courtesans' mattress.'[142]

THE WRITINGS OF MAECENAS

But Maecenas' bizarre nature appears most resplendently in his literary works. For Maecenas was a writer. Probably he had no illusions about his talent. He surrounded himself with the greatest poets, whose classical genius, simple grandeur, natural tone and taste he perceived, encouraged and doubtless preferred to his own leanings. And the poets, who were not sparing of eulogies to the great man, the statesman, the benevolent and discreet friend, preserve a significant silence regarding the author. His writings were not a subject of conversation. Nevertheless Maecenas went on writing, in prose and verse, epigrams, dialogues, a symposium, a *Prometheus*, a *De Cultu suo*, a title we should like to translate as 'On the Cult of Oneself' but which means 'On my way of life'. In any case the fragments we have been left of it resemble nothing else that has come down to us from antiquity.[142]

It is not so much the inspiration behind all this which astonishes us: too little of it remains for us to judge properly. All the same we see in it an irrepressible love of life which comes out again and again. While all the philosophers from the most heroic to the most cynical, proclaimed that death is not a disaster, he insisted that even a glorious death, even one with the compensation of immortality, is the worst of all possible disasters, and that life, however low and degraded, however mutilated, is the only thing that counts. 'I shall have nothing to do with the tomb: *nec tumulum curo*.[143] I should not bother to attend my own funeral,' he declared. His best known lines are those burlesque and macabre ones, adorned with expressions at once rare and popular of which translation can give only an imperfect idea:

> Fashion me with a palsied hand,
> Weak of foot, and a cripple;
> Build upon me a crook-backed hump;
> Shake my teeth till they rattle;
> All is well, if my life remains.
> Save, oh save it, I pray you,
> Though impaled on a stake![144]

The scandal was caused by his mannerism. Augustus regarded it as the height of precociousness and bad taste and amused himself with pastiches of what he called the 'scented sweetmeats' of his darling Maecenas. Seneca recognized in it his way of life: 'Is his style not as lax as he himself, *discinctus*? Are not his words as infamous as his attire, his house, his wife?'[145] An attempt has been made recently to rehabilitate Maecenas the writer by calling him 'baroque'.[146] Let us say only that certain types of modern poetry would perhaps help us to a greater appreciation of his hermetism.

It is to Seneca we owe our knowledge of a few fragments of his *Prometheus* and his *De Culto suo*. And at once we see that this prose is really prose poetry, and that the 'intoxication of language' with which people reproached Maecenas is simply the result of taking to the extreme those liberties which poets are commonly allowed. There is certainly some injustice in reproaching him with this phrase in his *Prometheus*: 'It is their very elevation that thunderstrikes the peaks', claiming that what he should have written was: 'that draws down lightning on the peaks.'[147] These fragments seem to be composed of short bits of phrases using a hard, uncertain syntax that excludes all prepositions and in which there swarm images expressed by rare words which are only found in him or in vulgar Latin. In a piece written in satirical vein, if a lover winks at a woman 'he pleats (or wrinkles) his face with a wink': *cinno crispat*; if he snatches a kiss, 'he pecks at her with his lips as do doves': *labris columbatur*, a verb invented for the occasion. Maecenas likes to spin out his metaphors, a habit the Latins disapproved of. Describing a boat trip between banks wreathed in verdure, he describes the gardens mirrored in the water in this way: *alveum lintribus arent versoque vado remittant hortos* (the phrase is in the subjunctive); he takes the epic expression 'furrow the sea' (*aequor arare*) and applies it to the bed of the stream (the Tiber) by restoring its original sense of 'to plough': 'they plough with their barks the bed of the river', and prolongs the artifice with: 'and as they turn the waters, *verso vado* (because one says that a plough 'turns the earth', *terram vertit*), 'they reflect there', or 'they cause the gardens to be reflected there'.

We can understand how this metaphorical mania often resulted in proper conundrums. There is one, rather curious, which does not appear to have been understood: *Irremediabilis factio rimantur epulis lagonaque temptant domos et spe mortem exigunt*. What's he driving at? The key to the enigma is in the words *mortem exigunt*, which are inspired by the common locution *exigere vitam*, 'to spend one's life'. It is too banal to say the living spend their lives hoping. Here a play on words gives us to understand that people spend *their deaths* hoping, and these can only be the Shades.

A time-honoured belief was that at certain festivals, during the Athenian Anthesteria and the Roman *Lemuria*, the souls of the dead should be invited back to their former homes; then, after having tasted the offerings of food prepared for them, they had to be ritually expelled by the *Pater familias*.[148] But many people were convinced that the ghosts permanently haunted the outsides of houses, which they tried to enter at night in order to feed on the left-overs from meals. A type of mosaic very common in the days of Maecenas, called 'the unswept room' (*assarôtos oikos*), represents on the ground chicken-bones, fish skeletons, shells and fruits which the amphitryon, it is thought, had left on the floor to feed the revenants.[149] It is this maleficent and much-feared band of spirits that Augustus' Minister of the Interior calls here, with highly relished impropriety, by a name taken from political vocabulary, a faction, a party, a conspiracy, qualified by a neologism which perhaps gave him the long adjectives, *irremeabilis*, *inextricabilis*, employed by Virgil in his descriptions of the lower regions. It was certainly Virgil who gave Maecenas the expression *rimantur epulis*, 'seeking their food', which appears in the *Aeneid*[150] in a description of the eagle that tears at the liver of the chained Titan: *rimaturque epulis*. But what is astonishing is that Virgil's dative (*epulis = ad epulas*) has not been understood by his imitator who, thinking it an ablative, associates it with *lagona*. If we add that the collective singular *factio* could easily call forth a plural verb, and that the spirits were no less eager to drink than to eat, whence the vulgar little decanter (*lagona*) instead of the noble *cantharus* of the mosaics, we shall have no difficulty in translating thus: 'The irremediable faction on the look-out for food and drink haunts our dwellings and passes its death in hoping.'[151]

While we admit that he did not attach much importance to such trifles, all this corresponds very closely to the idea we have of Maecenas: a fine sensitivity, somewhat sickly, attentive to the reflections of leaves in water, appreciative of pastoral concerts of soft music, conscious of the omnipresence of the dead in everyday life, displaying a nonchalance that is pleased to treat serious

subjects in a mocking way – just as royal personages occasionally
like to stoop to the use of slang, and indeed Latin satire does like
to mingle the familiar and the sublime; we are aware also of his
subtle ability to seize the secret relationships between things,
which, joined to a curious scorn of classical syntax, drags him
into an obscurity in which he is rivalled only by one other poet –
simple coincidence? – the satiric poet Persius Flaccus, the most
difficult of the Latin poets, Etruscan by birth and education.

Then must we attribute all these singularities to an ethnic
atavism, to inherited culture and luxury, even to a morbid im-
poverishment of the blood? Perhaps. But we must not forget,
when analysing the defects and absurdities of Maecenas, to recall
his virtues: in this author, almost too refined for words, a true
knack of divining real literary value in others; in this self-indulging
and idle playboy, constancy and loyalty, and a very human
lucidity in his counsels. If, by way of conclusion, we were to
attempt a résumé in a single image of what counts most in him,
we could imagine him as an intelligent and devoted dilettante
who knew how to gird up his loins when occasion demanded it;
who travelled all the roads of Italy to reconcile divided friends;
we see him rudely shaken by the paving-blocks of the Appian
Way, escorted by all the great poets of the period riding and
capering round his carriage. Or if we moved to another century
we might well see him, with a few inevitable alterations, as a
Roman or Florentine prelate of the Counter-Reformation, as a
Scipio Broghese or an Antonio Barberini. He would have protected the artists of that time, would have caused many fine
baroque churches to be built; he would have composed very
precious mythological poems in the style of Marino. But above
all he would have brought to the resolution of human conflicts
that wise prudence, that art of not compromising the essentials
by an ignorant preoccupation with accessory factors, that genius
for *combinazioni* which has so long been one of the best of Italian
political traditions, and which often provides, in fact, the only
means of repairing the damage done to the world, through their
intransigence and violence, by men like Savonarola, by the Borgias,
by Brutus and Antony. In saying this, we are not so far removed
from the character of the Etruscans, for as we have already seen,
if we look for an Etruscan we find an Italian.

CONCLUSION

Our present study has confirmed us in the view we stated at the outset that Etruscan civilization, which we have attempted to bring to life again in its concrete form, to present in its characteristic attitudes and its daily life, is really only a moment, a long moment but one of the most ancient, most brilliant and most richly significant moments in the history of Italian civilization. Moreover, this was fundamentally the feeling of the Romans themselves. Despite the astonishment they felt, at the end of the Republic, in observing the manners and customs of this reputedly strange people, despite the legends in which its origins were lost, Livy for example never doubted that Tanaquil was of Italic stock;[1] Varro or Verrius Flaccus often attributed their Etruscan etymologies to those whom they simply called the *antiqui*, 'the ancients'.[2] A great feeling of filial gratitude gradually took the place of hostile prejudices originally copied from the Greeks.

Their strangeness seems to us due less to a difference of race than to a difference of chronology. We have described an archaic civilization, a sort of continent slowly submerging which, despite the onslaught of the waves, obstinately sticks to its traditional forms of life. The social structure, the relationships between the sexes, the insignia of power, certain items of clothing retained their immemorial aspect much longer than was usual in other peoples. For the Romans, to make the journey from Rome to Tarquinii or Chiusi must have been like entering a kind of vast natural reservation of Mediterranean antiquities. There they still flourished the bipennate axe of Minos, and *Phaedra* was played in the crinolines of that era. Political evolution and agrarian reforms were constantly held up by a natural, native conservatism.

And yet this fidelity to a very ancient past had nothing hidebound or sclerotic about it: it was on the contrary very active and lively. The Etruscans, as soon as an access of prodigious wealth had enlarged their horizons, were converted to Hellenism with an enthusiasm which made of them, in Italy, the most ardent propagandists of their faith: barbarians in the eyes of the Greeks and in the proper sense of the word (since they did not speak the language of Homer), they nevertheless established the most fervent of all Greek outposts in the western or the eastern world. Herodotus tells us the story of some princes in Scythia, Anacharsis or Scyles, who were sacrificing clandestinely to Cybele and Dionysos, and whose greatest pleasure was to visit a colony on the coast of the Black Sea, there to divest themselves of their national costume and to stroll about dressed as Greeks, until one day when they returned home they were betrayed and put to death.[3] But the Philhellenes of Etruria did not need to hide, quite the contrary. The entire nation could think of nothing finer than to live like Greeks: it was eager to possess everything that came from the workshops of Ionia or Athens, and to see the latest refinements in their techniques. Etruria was the best market for Attic ceramics and imitated its productions; it immediately adopted the orthogonal plans of Hellenic urbanists and gave the warmest welcome to missionaries bringing them the Grecian mysteries. So much so that often the daily life of the Etruscans resembles the daily life of the Athenians. But we have striven to show that part of the Etruscan temperament which resisted complete assimilation.

Heirs to a world that goes back beyond historical time, and passionate imitators of the Greeks, the Etruscans were also the educators of Rome and thus the creators of the future. We have demonstrated with the greatest possible precision all that the Eternal City owed them in the domain of institutions, religion, ceremonial and liturgy; owed not only to those who had reigned over her and really founded her, but also to those whom she later subjugated to her own laws and with whom in the course of many centuries of struggles and cultural exchange she had evolved her own civilization. But in tracing the course of these borrowings, we were not so much aiming at establishing the persistence of Etruria in the Roman world as defining at source the forms of an Etruscan State which are unknown to us. The Roman triumphs of the Republic tell us something because they are the reflections of Etruscan triumphs of which nothing, or almost nothing, is known to us directly.

Finally, we have given great importance to the intellectual life of the Etruscans, for since the fear of the gods and a passion for the arts occupied so much of their time, we should have neglected an important part of their daily life if we had not tried to form some idea of what their literature could have been. One of our predecessors assures us nothing is known of the daily life of the lower classes:[4] however, we have tried, thanks to epigraphical studies, to lighten a little the darkness that weighs upon them. Without wishing to disguise the insufficiencies and lacunae in this picture, we trust that it will perhaps help people towards a better understanding, in a context of the history of ancient Italy, of one of the fundamental manifestations of her genius which seemed beyond the common limitations of time and space.

CHRONOLOGICAL TABLE

I – THE ORIGINS:

Thirteenth Century BC	Legendary migration of the Lydians from Tyrrhenos.
Ninth to Eighth Centuries	Villanovan civilization. Beginning of Greek colonization in Italy and Sicily (about 770 Chalcidians settle on Ischia, then at Messina and Cumae).
Seventh Century	Orientalizing civilization: rise of the Etruscan cities.

II – THE HEYDAY OF ETRUSCAN POWER:

Sixth Century	Alliance of Etruscans and Carthaginians gives their navies control of the western Mediterranean.
About 535	Naval victory over the Phoceans off Aleria (Corsica).
616–509	Reign of the Tarquin Dynasty in Rome.

Second half of the century: Etruscan expansion in the valley of the Po and in Campania.

III – DECLINE OF THE ETRUSCAN EMPIRE:

End of Sixth Century – Beginning of Fifth Century	Liberation of Rome (509: expulsion of the Tarquins; 508: fighting come-back of Porsenna, king of Clusium, master of Rome; 504: victory of Aristodemus of Cumae and of the Latins at Aricia over a son of Porsenna; 499: victory of Rome over the Latins at Lake Regillus).
474	Naval battle at Cumae: the Etruscans, crushed by the Syracusan fleet, lose control of the Tyrrhenian Sea.

423	Capture of Capua by the Samnites.
About 400	Beginning of Gaulish invasions in Italy: the Etruscans suffer a set-back.

IV – THE ROMAN CONQUEST:

396	Capture of Veii by the Romans.
390	The Gauls reach Rome, which they besiege and set fire to.
386	Alliance between Rome and Caere.
384–383	Dionysius of Syracuse raids Caere.
358	Start of the war between Rome and the Etruscans.
353	Victory of Rome over Caere.
351	Victory of Rome over Tarquinii.
310	March through the Ciminian Forest; conquest of inner Etruria; victories over Arezzo, Cortona and Perugia.
308	Surrender of Tarquinii.
301	Uprising against the Cilnii at Arezzo.
295	Defeat of the Gauls and the Etruscans at Sentinum; surrender of Volsinii, Arezzo and Perugia.
280	Treaty of alliance with Volsinii, Arezzo, Perugia, Vulci, Rusellae, Vetulonia and Populonia.
273	Founding of the Latin colony of Cosa.
265	Capture and destruction of Volsinii.

V – ROMAN ETRURIA

	(264–241 – First Punic War)
245 (?)	Founding of the Roman colony of Pyrgi.
241	Destruction of Falerii; construction of the via Aurelia and the via Amerina.
225	Victory of the Romans and their Etruscan allies over the Gauls at Telamon; construction of the via Clodia.
	(218–201 – Second Punic War)

218	Founding of the Latin colony of Placentia.
205	The Etruscan cities contribute towards Scipio's expedition against Carthage.
196	Revolt of the slaves in Etruria.
189	Founding of the Latin colony of Bologna.
183	Founding of the Roman colonies of Parma and Modena.
181	Founding of the Roman colonies of Graviscae and Saturnia.
177	Founding of the Roman colony of Luni and the Latin colony of Lucca.
154 (or 125)	Construction of the via Cassia.

(133–121 – Agrarian reforms of the Gracchi, which do not affect Etruscan territory)

91	March on Rome by Etruscans hostile to the laws made by the tribune M. Livius Drusus.
90–88	Social war, after which the Etruscan cities receive the rights of Roman citizenship.
82	After the First Civil War, in which Etruria had fought on the side of Marius, Sylla takes the rights of suffrage from Arezzo and Volterra and confiscates part of their territory.
42	During the Second Civil War, Perugia, occupied by the troops of Mark Antony, is besieged and burnt by Octavius.

NOTES

The bibliography is vast. In the notes we have given the titles of the principal works and articles consulted, in addition to the references to texts.

We have also listed below a few general works which form the basis of our researches and the source of our illustrations, or where further reproductions of Etruscan sculpture not shown in this book may be found.

MUELLER, O., DEECKE, W.	*Die Etrusker*, Stuttgart, 1877 (M.D.)
MARTHA, J.	*L'Art étrusque*, Paris, 1889
DUCATI, P.	*Etruria Antica*, Turin, 1927; *Storia dell' Arte Etrusca*, Florence, 1927
SOLARI, A.	With an excellently illustrated appendix by A. Neppi Modona, Florence, 1931 (N.M.)
NOGARA, B.	*Gli Etruschi e la loro Civiltà*, Milan, 1933 (B.N.)
GIGLIOLI, G. Q.	*L'Arte etrusca*, Milan, 1935 (A.E.)
PALLOTTINO, M.	*Etruscologia*, Milan, 3ᵉ éd. 1955 (first edition revised, translated by R. Bloch, Paris, 1949); *La Peinture étrusque*, 1952 (P.E.); *Testimonia Linguae Etruscae*, Florence, 1954 (T.L.E.)
RIIS, P. J.	*Etruscan Art*, Copenhagen, 1953
BLOCH, R.	*L'Art étrusque*, Paris, 1959

INTRODUCTION

1 Dion. Hal: 1, 30, 2
2 Her.: 1, 94 (trans. Ph.-E. Le-Grand)
3 The thesis of Oriental origin has been strongly upheld by P. Ducati: *Le Problème étrusque*, 1938; more recently by A. Piganiol: *Les Etrusques, peuple d'Orient*, Cah. d'Hist. mondiale, 1, 1953, pp. 328–352. The chief criticism of this view has been made by M. Pallottino: *L'Origine degli Etruschi*, 1947
4 Cic.: *De Div.*, 11, 50
5 M. Pallottino: *ibid*, p. 152 *et seq*; F. Altheim: *Der Ursprung der Etrusker*, 1950, p. 34 *et seq*
6 R. Bloch: *Le Mystère étrusque*, 1956, p. 216–217
7 J. Bayet: St Etr., XXIV, 1955–1956, p. 5 *et seq*
8 G. Vallet: *Rhégion et Zancle*, 1958, p. 57
9 J. Heurgon: *Capoue préromaine*, 1942, p. 77
10 J. Heurgon: *L'État étrusque*, Hist. VI, 1957, p. 86 *et seq*
11 R. Bloch: *Les Origines de Rome*, 1959, p. 98 *et seq*

12 S. Mazzarino: *Dalla Monarchia allo Stato repubblicano*, 1946, p. 95 *et seq*

13 The *Elementi di Lingua Etrusca* of M. Pallottino remains after more than twenty years the clearest and most accurate exposition. The Etruscan texts are collected in *Corpus Inscriptionum Etruscarum* (abr. C.I.E.), in course of publication; the most important can be found in *Testimonia Linguae Etruscae* (abr.T.L.E.) by M. Pallottino, 1954, to which in most cases we shall refer

14 T.L.E., 142

15 T.L.E., 129

16 T.L.E., 136

17 E. Vetter: Gl., XXVIII, 1940, p. 168 *et seq*

18 S. Mazzarino: Hist. VI, 1957, p. 108 *et seq*

CHAPTER ONE, THE PHYSICAL TYPE

1 G. de Beer: *Sur l'origine des Étrusques*, Rev. des Arts, 1955, p. 139 *et seq*.

2 G. E. W. Wolfstenholme and C. M. O'Connor: A Ciba Foundation Symposium on Medical Biology and Etruscan Origins, 1959

3 M. Pallottino: *L'Origine degli Etruschi*, p. 130; A. Neppi Modona: *The Scientists' Contributions to Etruscology*, in A Ciba Foundation Symposium, p. 67, with bibliography

4 C. S. Coon: *The Races of Europe*, cited by G. de Beer; *ibid*, p. 143 *et seq*

5 A.E., pl. 116–119

6 Ch. Picard: *La Sculpture antique*, II, 1926, p. 325

7 E. Fischer: *Rassenfrage d. Etrusker*, Sitzungsber. d. Preuss. Akadem., Phys. Math. Kl., 1938

8 E. Bux: *Die Herkunft d. Etrusker*, Klio, XXXV, 1942, p. 17, *et seq*

9 Cat.: 39, 11; Virg.: Georg., II, 193

10 R. Herbig: *Die Jüngeretr. Steinsarkophage*, 1952, On the Sarcophagus of San Giuliano, Herbig, n° 90, pl. 23; cf. Arch. Anz., 1934, p. 516 *et seq*, fig. 6 et 7; Ch. Picard: R.E.L., XIV, 1936, p. 146; M. Pallottino: *Tarquinia*, *Mon. Ant.*, XXXVI, 1936, p. 462, fig. 118; on the sarcophagus at Partunu, Herbig, n° 107, pl. 26 a; on the sarcophagus at the Musée de Florence, Herbig, n° 21, pl. 60 a; cf. A.E., pl. 365

11 Gell.: N.A., VI, 22; Plut.: Cato Mai., 9

12 Lucil.: 75 M

13 Lucil: 1235 M

14 A. Oltramare: *Les Origines de la Diatribe romaine*, 1926, p. 50: 'Obesity is a sign of depravity'

15 T. Dohrn: Röm. Mitt. LII, 1937, p. 119 *et seq*; J. D. Beazley: *Etruscan Vase Painting*, 1947, p. 128

16 L. Cipriani: St Etr., III, 1929, p. 363 *et seq*

17 R. Étienne: *Démographie et Épigraphie*, Atti del III, Congresso Intern. di Epigrafia Greca e Latina, 1959, p. 415 *et seq*.

18 H. L. Stoltenberg: Gl., XXX, 1943, p. 234 *et seq*
19 T.L.E., 98
20 T.L.E., 324
21 C.I.E., 109; 5385; 54
22 C.I.E., 5421; cf. Pliny the Younger Ep., III, 1
23 C.I.E., 18 *et seq*
24 C.I.E., 159
25 J. Beaujeu-Garnier: *Géographie de la population*, 1956, p. 180 *et seq*

CHAPTER TWO, THE MORAL TEMPER

1 Hér.: 1, 167
2 Virg.: Aen., VIII, 483 *et seq*
3 Timaeus: in Ath., XII, 519 b
4 G. Vallet: *Rhégion et Zancle*, 1958, p. 166 *et seq*
5 Corn. Nep.: Alcib., 11; cf. A. Croiset: *Hist. de la Litt. gr.*, IV, p. 688
6 Ath.: 1, 23 d
7 F.H.G., II, 16, p. 217
8 Ath.: IV, 153 d; XII, 517 d
9 Ath.: XII, 517 d, *et seq*. We thank here *L'Association Guillaume Bude* for letting us use this hitherto unpublished chapter from the translation of Desrousseaux
10 Diod. Sic.: V, 40; sur Posidonius, source de Diodore, F. Jacoby: F. Gr. Hist., II, A, 87, 119 and C, 154 *et seq*
11 Virg.: Georg. II, 533
12 Liv.: V, 1, 6
13 Fest.: p. 486 L
14 Paul. Fest.: p. 38 L
15 P.E., p. 120; cf. Cat. de l'Expos. de 1955, p. 77
16 R. Bloch: L'Art étrusque, pl. 81

CHAPTER THREE, ETRUSCAN SOCIETY

1 A. Alföldi: Rom. u. der Latinerbund um 500 v. Chr., Gymnasium, LXVII, 1960, p. 193 *et seq*
2 Pl.: N. H., XXXVI, 91 *et seq*
3 *Infra*, p. 136
4 J. Heurgon: *Ver Sacrum*, 1957, p. 18 and n. 5
5 Liv.: IV, 20, 7
6 T.L.E., 36, 38
7 A. Degrassi: *Inscriptiones Latinae liberae Reipublicae*, I, n°s 64 and 237; St Weinstock: Gl., XXXIII, 1954, p. 307, does not acknowledge any connexion with Tolumnius-Tolonios
8 Paus.: V, 12
9 *Infra*, p. 318
10 Serv.: ad Aen., II, 178
11 Cic.: *De Rep.*, II, 14; Prop.: El., IV, 1, 29

12 Liv.: I, 34, 10
13 W. Schultze: *Zur Gesch. d. lat. Eigennamen*, p. 179
14 T.L.E., 131
15 T.L.E., I^{1x} (2): interpretation argued recently by K. Olzscha: Ægyptus, 1959, p. 351 *et seq*
16 Dion. Hal.: III, 61, 1
17 A.E., pl. 108, 1
18 B. Bilinski: *De Catone Silii in Italiae descriptione un solo fonte*, 1937, p. 42 *et seq*
19 Sil. Ital.: Pun., VIII, 483 *et seq*
20 Not. Sc., 1898, p. 156; A. M. Colini: *Il Fascio Littorio*, 1933
21 G. Glotz: *La Civilisation égéenne*, 1923, p. 268 *et seq*; Ch. Picard: *Les Religions préhelléniques*, 1948, p. 82, 102, 163, 190 *et seq*, 199 *et seq*
22 A.E., pl. 59, 1
23 T.L.E., 363; E. Vetter: St Etr., XXIV, 1955–1956, p. 301 *et seq*
24 T.L.E., 35; C.V.A., France, 16 (Musée Rodin), pl. 28–30; J. D. Beazley: *Etruscan Vase Painting*, p. 25 *et seq*; M. Pallottino: Etrusc., p. 104, pl. IX, 1
25 A.E., pl. 398, 1; 404, 3; F. Messerschmidt: Jahrb. d. Inst., 1930, p. 76 *et seq*
26 Varr.: De L. L., V, 46 *et seq*; Tac: Ann., IV, 65; Paul Fest.: p. 38 L
27 Fest.: p. 486 L
28 C.I.L., XIII, 1668; A. Momigliano: *L'Imperatore Claudio*, 1931, p. 35; J. Heurgon: C.R.A.I., 1953, p. 92 *et seq*
29 F. Messerschmidt: Jahrb. d. Inst., Erg. Heft, XII, 1930, A.E., pl. 266–270; R. Beoch: *L'Art étrusque*, pl. 80
30 F. Münzer: Rh. M., 1898, p. 607; G. de Sanctis: Klio, 1902, p. *et seq*
31 S. Mazzarino: *Dalla Monarchia allo Stato Repubblicano*, p. 136 *et seq*
32 J. Heurgon: *L'Etat étrusque*, Hist., VI, 1957, p. 66 *et seq*, with the previous bibliography
33 T.L.E., 324
34 T.L.E., 325
35 R. Lambrechts: *Essai sur les Magistratures des Républiques étrusques*, 1959, p. 117; T.L.E., 137
36 R. Lambrechts: *ibid*, p. 123 *et seq*
37 Cic.: De Rep., II, 55
38 P.E., p. 125; N.M., fig. 49
39 Diod. Sic.: V, 40; *supra*, p. 50
40 Sen.: Ep., 47, 2 *et seq* (trans. H. Noblot)
41 Diod. Sic.: V, 40; *supra*, p. 50
42 Liv.: V, 1
43 Plut.: Tib. Gracch., 8, 9
44 Liv.: IX, 36, 12
45 Liv.: II, 44, 7
46 Dion. Hal.: IX, 5, 4; J. Heurgon: *Les Pénestes étrusques chez Denys d'Halicarnasse*, Latomus, XVIII, 1959, p. 713 *et seq*

47 Cf. Scullard, *A History of the Roman World*, p. 39: 'Closely attached to the gens or family, were the dependants (clientes) who stood in a filial relationship to their patrons (patroni)'
48 Juv.: VIII, 180
49 Mart.: IX, 22, 4
50 Liv.: X, 3, 2
51 R. Bloch: *Volsinies étrusque*, M.E.F.R., LIX, 1947, p. 9 *et seq*
52 Ps. Arist.: De Mir. Ausc., 94 A; cf. Steph. Byz.: s.v.; A. Solari: *Topografia storica dell' Etruria*, II, p. 27 *et seq*
53 Val. Max.: IX, 1, Ext. 2; Flor.: I, 21; Zonar.: VIII, 7
54 Liv., Per.: XI; Acta Triumph. Capitol., C.I.L., I, p. 46
55 *En dernier lieu*, Th. Frankfort: *Les Classes serviles en Etrurie*, Latomus, XVIII, 1959, p. 3 *et seq*
56 Liv.: XXXIII, 36, 1
57 Oros.: Adv. Pagan. IV, 5; Aur. Vict.; De Vir. Illustr., 36
58 C.I.E., 3692: In what follows we are using chiefly the memoirs of S. P. Cortsen: *Die etruskischen Standesund Beamtentitel*, 1925; and E. Vetter: *Die etruskischen Personennamen lethe, lethi, und die Namen unfreier oder halbfreier Personen bei den Etruskern, Jahresh. des Oesterr.*, Arch. Inst., XXXVIII, 1948, p. 56 *et seq*
59 C.I.E., 3704; 3001
60 Ernout-Meillet: Dict. étym., s.v. famulus
61 Pl.: N.H., II, 199
62 C.I.E., 719–721, 1508, 1667–1675, 4700
63 C.I.E., 1671; T.L.E., 554
64 E. Vetter: *ibid*, p. 64, 87
65 S. P. Cortsen: *ibid*, p. 61
66 R. Mengarelli: Not. Sc., 1915, p. 347 *et seq*; 1937, p. 355 *et seq*
67 E. Vetter: *ibid*, p. 67 *et seq*
68 C.I.E., 4143
69 M. Lejeune: R.E.L., XXXI, 1953, pp. 130 and 152
70 C.I.E., 4379
71 C.I.E., 2013
72 C.I.E., 2422, 2426
73 C.I.E., 40; T.L.E., 387; cf. C.I.L., XIII, 6740 a; Dess., 7085; G. Dottin: *La Langue gauloise*, p. 273
74 C.I.E., 2383
75 C.I.E., 1601
76 C.I.E., 4046
77 C.I.E., 3088; E. Vetter: *ibid*, p. 86
78 C.I.E., 2096, 2934–2935; E. Vetter: *ibid*, p. 68
79 C.I.E., 4144; E. Vetter: *ibid*, p. 66
80 T.L.E., 169
81 J. Heurgon: Hist., VI, 1957, p. 96
82 Pol.: II, 17, 12
83 C.I.E., 4549
84 Liv.: XLIII, 16, 4

CHAPTER FOUR, THE ETRUSCAN FAMILY AND THE RÔLE OF WOMEN

1 Strab.: XVI, 4, 25
2 Caes.: B.G., V, 14
3 Her.: I, 173
4 T.L.E., 131
5 T.L.E., 586–587
6 *Supra*, p. 48
7 T.L.E., 136
8 C.I.E., 678–679, 802; B. Doer: *Die Röm. Namengebung*, 1937, p. 158 *et seq*; F. Slotty: *Zur Frage des Mutterrechtes bei den Etruskern, Archiv Orientalni*, XVIII, 1950, p. 262 *et seq*
9 C.I.L., XIV, 3607
10 *Supra*, p. 4
11 Pl.: Cist., 562–563
12 R. Flaceliere: *La Vie quotidienne en Grèce*, p. 75 *et seq*
13 *Infra*, p. 261
14 Paus.: VI, 20, 9
15 Liv.: I, 57, 4 *et seq* (trans. G. Baillet)
16 Théopompus: *supra*, p. 48
17 Bücheler: Carm. Lat. Epigr., 52, 8
18 A. Blakeway: *Demaratus*, J.R.S., XXV, 1935, p. 147 *et seq*
19 Liv.: I, 34, 4 (trans. G. Baillet)
20 Paul. Fest.: p. 253 L: *Priscus Tarquinius est dictus, quia prius fuit, quam Superbus Tarquinius*
21 Liv.: I, 41
22 On this transformation of character. J. Heurgon: *Tite-Live et les Tarquins*, L'Inf. Littér., VII, 1955, p. 56 *et seq*
23 Tac.: Ann., II, 34; IV, 21, 2; 22; J. Heurgon: C.R.A.I., 1953, p. 92 *et seq*
24 C.I.L., XIV, 3605–3607
25 Her.: I, 173
26 L. Euing: *Die Sage von Tanaquil*, 1933, p. 16 *et seq*
27 Cic.: Ad Att., II, 1, 8
28 Liv.: I, 46, 4 *et seq*
29 Liv.: I, 48, 5
30 Liv.: I, 46, 6; cf. J. Heurgon: R.E.L., XXXVIII, 1960, p. 38
31 L. Pareti: *La tomba Regolini-Galassi*, 1947. (We summarize here the conclusions of an article in M.E.F.R., 1961)
32 Id.: *ibid*, p. 129
33 G. Q. Giglioli: Arch. Class., II, 1950, p. 85
34 Mon. Ant., XLII, 1955, p. 241 *et seq*
35 Xen.: Econ., IX, 18 (trans. P. Chantraine)
36 Not. Sc., 1915, p. 353 *et seq*; 1937, p. 355 *et seq*
37 F. Altheim: Röm. Gesch., I, p. 106
38 Mon. Ant., XXXVI, 1937, p. 394
39 St Etr., I, 1927, p. 164; cf. XI, 1937, p. 84 *et seq*

40 Mon. Ant., XLII, 1955, p. 450 *et seq*
41 R. Vighi: Not. Sc., 1955, p. 111
42 *Ibid*, p. 46 *et seq*
43 Mon. Ant., *ibid*, p. 565, 595, 802; p. 771
44 Mon. Ant., *ibid*, p. 1057
45 J. Heurgon: M.E.F.R., LXXIII, 1961

CHAPTER FIVE, THE ETRUSCAN COUNTRYSIDE AND PATTERNS OF RURAL LIFE

1 Diod. Sic.: V, 40; cf. *supra*, p. 51
2 Liv.: IX, 36, 11
3 Liv.: XXII, 3, 3
4 Pl. the Y.: Ep., V, 6, 7 *et seq*
5 Dante: Inf., XIII, 9 (tra Cecina e Corneto); XXV, 19; XXIX, 48
6 Plut.: Tib. Gracch., 8, 9; *supra*, p. 76
7 Prop.: El., IV, 10, 27 *et seq*
8 Strab.: V, 2, 3
9 Rut. Nam.: De Red. suo, 285–286
10 Sid. Apoll.: Ep., I, 5
11 L. Domitius Apollinaris: consul suffectus in 97
12 Pl. the Y.: Ep., V, 6, 2
13 M. Pallottino: *Tarquinia*, p. 580
14 Virg.: Aen., X, 184; Rut. Nam.: *De Red.* suo, 282
15 Cat.: Or., II, 20; in *Serv.*: ad Aen., X, 184
16 Liv.: XXVIII, 45, 15 *et seq*
17 Cic.: De Div., II, 50
18 Strab.: V, 1, 7
19 N. Toscanelli: *La Malaria e la fine degli Etruschi*, 1927
20 Pl. Fraccaro: St Etr., II, 1928, p. 197 *et seq*; B. Nogara: *Gli Etruschi e la loro Civiltà*, 1933, p. 116 *et seq*
21 Ed. et Ét. Sergent: *Histoire d'un Marais algérien*, 1947
22 *Cité*, p. 165. – Doctor P. Decouflé who studies the anatomical models which compose many votive offerings tells us that the spleens are always hypertrophied
23 Pl.: N.H., III, 115
24 Liv.: I, 38, 2
25 Liv.: I, 56, 2
26 Cic.: *De Rep.*, II, 11
27 J. Gagé: *Apollon Romain*, 1955, p. 71 *et seq*
28 F. E. Brown: Cosa, I, *History and Topography*, Mem. of the Am. Acad. in Rome, XX, 1951; J. Bradford: *Ancient Landscapes*, 1957, p. 227 *et seq*, pl. 54–55
29 A.E., pl. 57; N.M., fig. 63
30 La Blanchère: *Dict. des Ant. gr.-rom., s.v. cuniculus*, p. 1592
31 Liv.: V, 15, 12; J. Gagé: M.E.F.R., LXVI, 1954, p. 39 *et seq*
32 Varr.: Men., *Quinquatrus*, in *Nonius*
33 Pl.: N.H., XXVI, 16, 30; Sen.: Q.N., III, 15; Plut.: Paule-Émile, 13

34 Ed. and Ét. Sergent: *ibid*, p. 202
35 Cic.: P. Mil., 74
36 Rut. Nam.: De Red. suo, 283 *et seq*
37 Virg.: Aen., VIII, 327
38 Virg.: Georg., I, 128 *et seq*; J. Bayet: *L'Expérience sociale de Virgile*, Deucalion, II, 1947, p. 197 *et seq*
39 Lachmann: Gromatici Veteres, I, p. 350
40 S. Mazzarino: Hist., VI, 1957, p. 101 *et seq*
41 T.L.E., 571
42 T.L.E., 675-677, 689
43 T.L.E., 692
44 T.L.E., 515
45 T.L.E., 632
46 G. Devoto: *Tabulae Iguvinae*, p. 158
47 T.L.E., 570
48 T.L.E., 515; S. Mazzarino: *ibid*, p. 106 and 110, n. 1
49 C.I.L., XI, 3370; J. Heurgon: *Latomus*, XII, 1953, p. 402 *et seq*
50 Cic.: De Div., II, 50
51 Serv. Dan.: ad Aen., I, 2
52 S. Mazzarino: *ibid*, p. 109
53 Papers of the British School at Rome, XXIII, 1955, p. 44 *et seq*; XXV, 1957, p. 67 *et seq*; J.R.S., XLVII, 1957, p. 139 *et seq*
54 Varr.: R.R., I, 9, 5
55 Liv.: II, 34, 5; IV, 52, 5
56 J. le Gall: *Le Tibre, fleuve de Rome dans l'Antiquité*, 1952, p. 56
57 Varr.: R.R., I, 44, 1
58 Pl.: N.H., XVIII, 66
59 Col.: II, 6
60 Ov.: Medic. fac., 65
61 Mart.: XIII, 8
62 Pl.: N.H., XVIII, 87
63 Pl.: N.H., XVIII, 86
64 Pl.: N.H., XVIII, 109
65 Pol.: II, 15, 2; Strab.: V, 1, 12
66 Ath.: XV, 702 b
67 Dion. Hal.: I, 37, 2
68 Mart.: XIII, 118, 2
69 Pl.: N.H., XIV, 68
70 Id.: *ibid*, 67, with notes by J. André in his edition
71 Hor.: Sat., II, 3, 143; Pers.: V, 147; Mart.: I, 103, 9; II, 53, 4; III, 49, 1
72 Pl.: N.H., XIV, 67
73 Id.: *ibid*, 24
74 T.L.E., 678
75 Pl.: N.H., XIV, 36
76 Id.: *ibid*, 38, cf. 35
77 Liv.: V, 33, 2
78 Sil. Ital.: Pun., IV, 223

79 Grat.: Kyneg., 36; Pl.: N.H., XIX, 10; J. Aymard: *Les Chasses romaines*, 1951, p. 213
80 Pl.: N.H., XV, 1
81 Cat.: De Agr., 42 *et seq.*, 64 *et seq.*, 143 *et seq*
82 T.L.E., 762; G. Buonamici: St Etr., XII, 1938, p. 317
83 Varr.: R.R., I, 2, 6
84 Virg.: Georg., IV, 125 *et seq*
85 Pl.: N.H., XV, 102
86 Pl.: N.H., XXIII, 105
87 St Gsell: *Hist. anc. de l'Afr. du Nord*, IV, p. 18 *et seq*
88 J. André: *Lex, des termes de botanique en latin*, 1956, p. 93
89 Id.: *ibid*, p. 81
90 References in H. Nissen: *Ital. Landeskunde*, I, p. 457
91 Ov.: Am., III, 13, 1
92 Cat.: *De Agr.*, 156 *et seq*
93 H. Nissen: *ibid*
94 R. Pampanni: St Etr., IV, 1930, p. 293 *et seq*; A. Neppi Modona: in *A Ciba Symposium* . . ., p. 68
95 St Gsell: *ibid*, p. 32
96 P.E., p. 57 and 75
97 P. Grimal: *L'Art des jardins*, 1954, p. 20
98 Macr.: Sat., III, 20, 3
99 G. Vitali: St Etr., II, 1928, p. 409 *et seq*; IV, 1930, p. 427 *et seq*; VII, 1933, p. 321
100 Macr.: Sat., V, 19, 13
101 Pl.: N.H., XVIII, 173
102 E. Saglio: *Dict. des Ant.* gr.-rom., s.v. aratrum; F. Benoit: *L'Outillage rural et artisanal*, 1947, p. 30 *et seq*
103 A.E., pl. 410, 3
104 A.E., pl. 82; A. Grenier: *Bologne villanovienne et étrusque*, 1912, p. 371 *et seq*
105 A.E., pl. 253
106 Varr.: R.R., I, 18, 6
107 Id.: *ibid*, I, 2, 25 *et seq*
108 Id.: *ibid*, I, 2, 22
109 Id.: *ibid*, I, 16, 5
110 Id.: *ibid*, I, 18, 2 *et seq*
111 Id.: *ibid*, I, 19, 1
112 G. E. F. Chilver: *Cisalpine Gaul*, 1941, p. 146 *et seq*
113 Mart.: VI, 73
114 Col.: VI, 1, 1; Ov.: Am., III, 13, 13
115 Pl.: N.H., XI, 241; Mart.: XIII, 30
116 Pol.: XII, 4; Varr.: R.R., II, 4, 20
117 Rut. Nam.: *De Red. suo*, 615 *et seq* (trans. J. Vessereau)
118 Virg.: Aen., VII, 651; J. Aymard: *Les Chasses romaines*, p. 26 *et seq*
119 Stat.: Silv., IV, 6, 10
120 A.E., pl. 82; M. Pallottino: *Tarquinia*, p. 57
121 Varr.: R.R., III, 12, 1

122 *Infra*, p. 245
123 J. Aymard: *ibid*, p. 10
124 B. Bonacelli: St Etr., VI, 1932, p. 341 *et seq*; A. Neppi Modona: A Ciba Foundation Symposium . . ., p. 73
125 A.E., pl. 204
126 St Gsell: *Hist. anc. de l'Afr. du Nord*, I, p. 109
127 Ath.: XII, 18 f.
128 Pl.: Pœn., 1074
129 T.L.E., 811; Strab.: XII, 626, 4, 6; Pl.: N.H., XIII, 82; Bonacelli: *ibid*
130 Pl.: N.H., X, 37
131 T.L.E., 807, 810, 821
132 V. Baldasseroni: St Etr., III, 1929, p. 383
133 P.E., p. 49 *et seq*; R. Bloch: *L'Art étrusque*, pl. 32–33
134 Strab.: V, 2, 6; Ath.: VI, 224 c; Col.: VIII, 16
135 H. Nissen: *Ital. Landesk.*, I, p. 432; II, p. 301
136 *Supra*, p. 127
137 Virg.: Aen., VIII, 599; IX, 521; Theophr.: Hist. pl., V, 8; Strab.: V, 2, 5
138 Pl.: N.H., XXXVI, 168; cf. 135; M. Pallottino: *Tarquinia*, p. 437
139 G. Vallet: *Rhégion et Zancle*, p. 57, n. 1
140 Virg.: Aen., X, 174; A. Minto: St Etr., XXIII, 1954, p. 291 *et seq*; L. Cambi: *dans Tyrrhenica*, 1957, p. 97 *et seq*; A. Neppi Modona: A Ciba Foundation Symposium . . ., p. 65
141 Strab.: V, 2, 6
142 R. Dion: *Latomus*, XI, 1952, p. 306 *et seq*; J. Carcopino: *Promenades historiques aux pays de la Dame de Vix*, 1957, p. 24 *et seq*; see also G.-Ch. Picard: *La Vie quotidienne à Carthage*, 1958, p. 169 *et seq*; and F. Villard: *La Céramique grecque de Marseille*, 1960, p. 137 *et seq*
143 R. Joffroy: *Mon. Piot.*, XLVIII, 1, 1954
144 Two Villanovian bronzes from Etruria have shown the same proportion on analysis: 8, 15 and 11, 6 p. 100
145 G. Germain: *Essai sur les origines de certains thèmes odysséens*, 1954, p. 172; Macr.: Sat., V, 19, 11 *et seq*.; Minto: *ibid*, p. 313 *et seq*
146 A. Minto: *ibid*, p. 299; L. Cambi: *ibid*, p. 107
147 A. Minto: *ibid*, p. 304
148 Ps. Arist.: Mir. Ausc., 93
149 Strab.: V, 2, 6
150 Diod. Sic.: V, 13, 1–2
151 Its prosperity and the development of its economic activity are vouched for by the creation of a gold and silver coinage which was the most plentiful in the whole of Etruria
152 *Supra*, p. 127
153 Diod. Sic.: *ibid*
154 Lucil.: 122 M; Ch. Dubois: *Pouzzoles antique*, 1907, p. 126
155 Cat.: *De agr.*, 135: one buys iron tools at Cales and Minturno

156 The allusion to arms (oplon) is a correction of the text which refers, nonsensically, to birds (oiseaux)
157 Pl.: N.H., XXXIV, 146
158 Rut. Nam.: *De Red. suo*, 411 *et seq*
159 Th. Ashby: St Etr., III, 1929, p. 177
160 R. Bianchi-Bandinelli: *Sovana*, 1929, p. 27
161 Liv.: X, 47, 4
162 P. Romanelli: Not. Sc., 1948, p. 223
163 H. Koch, E. von Mercklin, C. Weickert: *Röm. Mitt.*, XXX, 1915, p. 190 *et seq*
164 M. W. Frederiksen, J. B. Ward Perkins: Papers of the British School at Rome, XXV, 1957, pp. 117 and 141
165 P. Romanelli: Not. Sc., 1948
166 C.I.L., XI, 5265
167 A. Minto: *Populonia*, 1943, p. 131; L. Pareti: *La tomba Regolini-Galassi*, p. 252
168 A.E., pl. 87–90
169 *Infra*, p. 258
170 F. de Ruyt: *Charun*, 1934, p. 48 *et seq*
171 Id.: *ibid*, n° 75, p. 70, fig. 33
172 Id.: *ibid*, n° 74, fig. 32; A.E., pl. 402, 1; *Dict. des Ant.* gr.-rom., s.v. *carpentum et camara*
173 Liv.: I, 34, 7 *et seq*
174 Ov.: Fast., I, 619
175 Liv.: I, 48, 5
176 Prop.: El., IV, 8, 23
177 Liv.: V, 25, 9
178 Liv.: XXXIV, 3, 9
179 Tac.: Ann., XII, 42
180 Suet.: Cal., 15
181 R. Cagnat, V. Chapot: *Man. d'Archéol. rom.*, II, p. 292, fig. 516
182 A. Ernout, A. Meillet: s.v. carrus; J. Carcopino: *Les Etapes de l'Impérialisme romain*, 1961, p. 239 *et seq*; P. M. Duval: *La Vie quotidienne en Gaule*, 1952, p. 245
183 Liv.: XXXI, 21, 17; Flor.: I, 18, 27
184 J. Carcopino: *ibid*

CHAPTER SIX, THE TOWNS AND THE SETTING OF URBAN ACTIVITIES

1 P. Ducati: *La Città etrusca*, Historia, IX, 1931, p. 3 *et seq*
2 E. Kornemann: *Polis und Urbs*, Klio, V, 1905, p. 72 *et seq*
3 Fest.: p. 258 L
4 P. Lavedan: *Hist. de l'Architecture urbaine*, 1926, p. 99
5 Serv.: ad Aen., I, 422
6 *Corp. agrim. Rom.* (Thulin), I, p. 145
7 I. Falchi: Not. Sc., 1895, p. 274, fig. 1; P. Ducati: *Etruria antica*, II, 94; *Stor. dell' Arte etrusca*, fig. 420

8 R. Bianchi-Bandinelli: *Sovana*, p. 15
9 F. Castagnoli: *Ippodamo di Mileto e l'urbanistica a pianta ortogonale*, 1956
10 G. Devoto: St Etr., II, 1928, p. 331
11 On the date of the founding of Capua, M. Pallottino: *La parola del passato*, XLVII, 1956, p. 85
12 J. Heurgon: *Capoue préromaine*, 1942, p. 8 *et seq*
13 Cic.: *De Leg. agr.*, II, 96
14 A. Grenier: *Bologne villanovienne et étrusque*, with fig. p. 116, pl. III; P. Ducati: *Etruria antica*, II, p. 93. On the recent excavations, *Fasti Archeologici*, VI (1951), 2530; VIII (1953), 2198; IX (1954), 2904. It is possible that the remains date only from a reconstruction of the town in the third century
15 N. Alfieri: *Spina e le nuove scoperte. Problemi archeologici e urbanistici* (*Atti del I. Convegno di Studi Etruschi*, 1959), p. 25 *et seq*
16 *Fasti Archeologici*, X (1955), 2479. A report on current excavations was given in May 1955 at the III Congresso degli Studi Etruschi, by Mlle Fogolari
17 G. Vallet: *Athènes et l'Adriatique*; M.E.F.R., LXII, 1950, p. 33 *et seq*
18 R. Chevallier: R.E.A., LIX, 1957, p. 446
19 P. Romanelli: Not. Sc., 1948, p. 193 *et seq*
20 R. Bloch: M.E.F.R., LIX, 1947, p. 9 *et seq*; LXII, 1950, p. 53 *et seq*
21 R. Bartoccini: in *Tyrrhenica*, p. 52 *et seq*; St Rom., VI, 2, 1958, p. 126 *et seq*; C. M. Lerici, E. Carabelli, E. Segre: *Prospezioni geofisiche nella zona archeologica di Vulci*, I, 1958
22 G. Lugli: *L'Urbanistica delle Città italiche, le mura di fortificazione*, 1946–1947, p. 43 *et seq*; *La Tecnica edilizia romana*, 1957, p. 83 *et seq*
23 A. Boscotrecase, villa rustica de Ti. Claudius Eutychus, with 9 cellae on the ground floor, and 9 others on top (Not. Sc., 1922, p. 459); à Gragnano, villa rustica with 19 cubicula and a large ergastule (Not. Sc., 1923, p. 275 *et seq*)
24 J. Carcopino: *La Vie quotidienne à Rome*, p. 39 *et seq*. For what follows, LIV: XXI, 62, 3; Diod.: XXXI, 18, 2; Cic.: De Off., III, 66; De L. a., II, 95; P. Cael., 18
25 R. Bianchi-Bandinelli: *Sovana*, p. 104 *et seq.*; C. Weickert: Röm. Mitt., XXX, 1915, p. 291, fig. 84; A.E., pl. 425, 1 and 2
26 K. J. Beloch: *Bevölkerungsgesch. Italiens*, 1937, I, p. 1 *et seq*; II, p. 57; p. 132
27 B. Nogara: *Gli Etruschi e la loro Civiltà*, p. 46; R. Mengarelli (St Etr., I, 1927, p. 145) did not hesitate at computing the population of Caere, at its greatest, at eighty thousand
28 A Ciba Foundation Symposium, p. 80 *et seq*
29 J. Bradford: *Ancient Landscapes*, p. 116: 'more than 1,000 acres'
30 G. Ricci: *Mon. Ant.*, XLII, 1955
31 Pl. XI

32 Pl. X
33 *Supra*, p. 45
34 *Supra*, p. 114
35 R. Vighi, G. Ricci, M. Moretti: *Mon. Ant.*, XLII, 1955
36 J. Bradford: *ibid*, p. 116 *et seq*, pl. 30–32, fig. 8 and 9
37 G. Ricci: *ibid*, p. 233 *et seq*
38 Id.: *ibid*, p. 346 *et seq*
39 R. Bloch: Bull. Soc. Ant. de Fr., 1957, p. 57 *et seq*; S. M. Puglisi: *Mon. Ant.*, XLI, 1951, p. 1 *et seq*
40 G. Ricci: *ibid*, p. 313 *et seq*
41 Id.: *ibid*, p. 329, n. 1
42 Id.: *ibid*, p. 233
43 Id.: *ibid*, p. 803, fig. 181
44 Id.: *ibid*, p. 241 *et seq*
45 M. Moretti: *ibid*, p. 1065 *et seq*
46 G. Ricci: *ibid*, p. 450 *et seq*
47 R. Vighi: Not. Sc., 1955, p. 106, fig. 72–73
48 G. Lugli: *Roma antica, Il Centro monumentale*, 1946, p. 459, fig. 136
49 R. Cagnat, V. Chapot: *Man. des Ant. rom.*, I, p. 283, fig. 147
50 A. von Gerkan, F. Messerschmidt: *Das Grab der Volumnier bei Perugia*, Röm. Mitt., LVII, 1942, p. 122 *et seq*
51 F. Messerschmidt: *Nekropolen von Vulci*, Jahrb. d. Inst., Erg. Heft, XII, 1930, p. 62
52 Varr.: de L. L., V, 161; P. Ducati: *Etruria antica*, II, p. 94 *et seq*
53 Varr.: *ibid*: *ab Atriatibus Tuscis*; Paul. Fest.: 12 L
54 *Supra*, p. 170
55 T.L.E., I
56 Paul. Fest.: 12 L
57 G. Patroni: *Rend. Acc. Linc.*, 1936, p. 808 *et seq*
58 E. Saglio: *Dict. des Ant. gr.-rom.*, s.v. atrium
59 P. Grimal: *Les Jardins romains*, 1943, p. 216
60 E. Saglio: *Dict. des Ant. gr.-rom.*, s.v. cavaedium, p. 982
61 Vitr.: VI, 3
62 E. Saglio: *ibid*, fig. 1274
63 E. Saglio: *ibid*, fig. 1275
64 Pl. the Y.: Ep., II, 17, 4
65 Id.: V, 6, 15
66 *Supra*, p. 50
67 Vitr.: IV, 7; R. Cagnat, V. Chapot: *Man. d'Archéol. rom.*, I, p. 33 *et seq*
68 M. Pallottino: *La Necropoli di Cerveteri*, p. 13
69 G. Ricci: *ibid*, p. 450 *et seq*, fig. 102
70 G. Q. Giglioli: Not. Sc., 1916, p. 41 *et seq. On the Etruscan column*, lastly, P. J. Riis., *An introduction to Etruscan art*, 1953, p. 51 *et seq* and pl. 22
71 G. Rosi: *Sepulchral Architecture as illustrated by the Rock Façades of Central Etruria*, J.R.S., XV, 1925, p. 1 *et seq*

72 Id.: *ibid*, fig. 49–51, 53, 55–56
73 G. Ricci: *ibid*, p. 966 *et seq* and pl. XV; J. Bradford: *Ancient Landscapes*, p. 122
74 G. Ricci: *ibid*, p. 829 *et seq* and pl. XI
75 Juv.: Sat., III, 191
76 G. M. Richter: *Ancient Furniture*, 1926
77 Cf. In the Tomb of the Shields at Tarquinii (P.E., p. 105 and 107), and the Urn of Chiusi reproduced in A.E., pl. 136, 1
78 G. M. Richter: *Were there Greek Armaria?* Homm. Deonna, p. 418 *et seq*
79 Cf. the Tomb of Orco at Tarquinii (M. Pallottino: *ibid*, p. 114)
80 Ath.: I, 28 b
81 A.E., pl. 199, 1
82 P.-M. Duval: *La Vie quotidienne en Gaule*, p. 79 and 88
83 A.E., pl. 60, 62, 63
84 A. Grenier: Bologne, p. 371 and 397
85 A.E., pl. 17, 1; L. Pareti: *La Tomba Regolini-Galassi*, pl. 23
86 A.E., pl. 316, 1
87 G. Ricci: *ibid*, p. 893 *et seq*, pl. XIII–XIV
88 G. Ricci: *ibid*, p. 722
89 W. Schultze: *Zur Gesch. d. lat. Eigennamen*, p. 274 *et seq.*
90 R. Mengarelli: Not. Sc., 1937, p. 402
91 The inscriptions will be found in G. Ricci: *ibid*, p. 911
92 T.L.E., 51
93 Cf. E. Fiesel: *Das grammatische Geschlecht im Etruskischen*, 1922. We have modified his genealogy at one point, taking account of the new reading, by G. Ricci, of the patronymic of Ramta Matunia (XIII)
94 P. Mingazzini: Archeol. Class., VI, 1954, p. 292 *et seq*
95 A. Stenico: St Etr., XXIII, 1954, p. 201 *et seq*
96 Varr.: de L. L., X, 22; Arch. Anz., 1941, p. 618 *et seq*
97 A. Stenico: *ibid*, p. 197 *et seq*
98 A.E., pl. 104, 6; D. Levi: *Il Museo Civico di Chiusi*, fig. 64 and p. 118
99 Theocr.: XV, 21 *et seq*
100 P.E., p. 105 and 107
101 A.E., pl. 369; on the date, B. Schweizer: *Die Bildniskunst d. röm. Republik*, 1948, p. 8; P. J. Riis: *ibid*, p. 109 *et seq*
102 Cat.: De Agr., 59
103 P.E., p. 87; R. Bloch: *L'Art étrusque*, pl. 53
104 G. Glotz: *La Civilization égéenne*, p. 88
105 P.E., p. 68, 78, 87; R. Bloch: *ibid*, pl. 45–54
106 Stat.: Silv., II, 1, 130
107 P.E., p. 45; R. Bloch: *ibid*, pl. 22
108 A.E., pl. 136, 2: 142, 4; 144, 1 and 3, etc.; N.M., fig. 83
109 Ath.: XII, 519 b
110 Ath.: XII, 541 a; J. S. Callaway: *Sybaris*, 1950, p. 76
111 O. Mueller, W. Deecke: *Die Etrusker*, I, p. 247, with texts

112 Pol.: VIII, 2
113 Dion. Hal.: III, 61, 1
114 A. Ernout: *Philologica*, I, p. 27
115 Poll.: *Lex.*, p. 584, 17
116 Dion. Hal.: II, 60, 2; III, 61, 1
117 A.E., pl. 108, 1; A. Alföldi: *Frühröm. Reiteradel u. seine Ehrenabzeichen*, 1952, p. 36 and pl. 1
118 A.E., pl. 109, 1; P.E., p. 37; R. Bloch: *ibid*, pl. 14–18
119 A.E., pl. 115, 2; N.M., fig. 67
120 A.E., p. 265; P.E., p. 121; R. Bloch: *ibid*, pl. 81–82
121 R. Lambrechts: *Essai sur les Magistratures des républiques étrusques*; cf. especially pl. II, VII, XXII
122 A. Alföldi: *Gewaltherrscher und Theaterkönig*, Stud. A. M. Friend, p. 15 *et seq*
123 Cf. R. Cagnat, V. Chapot: *Man. d'Archéol. rom.*, II, p. 367
124 P.E., pp. 55 and 57; R. Bloch: *ibid*, pl. 14–16, pl. 29, pl. 32
125 Cic: De Nat. Deor., I, 82
126 A.E., pl. 108; *Dict. des Ant. gr.-rom.*, s.v. calceus, fig. 1021; A. Alföldi: *Frühröm. Reiteradel*, p. 60, pl. I
127 A.E., pl. 116; *Dict. des Ant. gr.-rom.*, *ibid*, fig. 1022
128 O. Mueller, W. Deecke: *ibid*, I, p. 254 *et seq*, with texts
129 N.M., fig. 44; G. Ricci: *Mon. Ant.*, XLII, 1955, p. 592
130 P.E., p. 107; R. Bloch: *ibid*, pl. 78
131 A. Alföldi: *ibid*, p. 54 *et seq*
132 *Dict. des Ant. gr.-rom.*, *ibid*, fig. 1017; N.M., fig. 42
133 Virg.: Aen., VIII, 457
134 A.E., pl. 119
135 A.E., pl. 115, 2
136 A.E., pl. 122, 2 and 3
137 A.E., pl. 124, 3
138 Varr.: De L. L., VII, 44; Fest., 484 L
139 E. Coche de la Ferté: *Les Bijoux antiques*, 1956, pl. 34, 1 and 2, and p. 120
140 M. Pallottino: *ibid*, p. 101; R. Bloch: *ibid*, pl. 72
141 Neppi Modona: fig. 99
142 Id.: fig. 100
143 Id.: fig. 72
144 E. Coche de la Ferté: *ibid*, p. 72 *et seq*
145 A.E., pl. 23–27; R. Bloch: *ibid*, pp. 8–9; *Cat. de l'Expos. de* 1955, fig. 21, n° 104
146 A.E., pl. 19; Cat., fig. 20, n° 94
147 Cat., fig. 17, n° 85
148 E. Coche de la Ferté: *ibid*, p. 16
149 Id.: *ibid*, p. 82
150 Id.: *ibid*, pl. 37; Cat., fig. 22, n° 112; R. Bloch: *ibid*, pp. 28–29
151 Id.: *ibid*, p. 72
152 A.E., pl. 66; Cat., n° 102
153 On the origins of Etruscan stone sculpture, particularly at

Vetulonia. A. Hus: M.E.F.R., LXVII, 1955, p. 71 *et seq*; LXVIII, 1956, p. 37 *et seq*
154 G. Vallet: *Rhégion et Zancle*, p. 57, n. 1

CHAPTER SEVEN, SOME ETRUSCAN DIVERSIONS: BANQUETS AND GAMES

1 Shown on mirrors, and mentioned in the ritual of Zagreb
2 Tac.: Germ., 11; Cic. ap Serv.: ad Aen., I, 738; VI, 535
3 Varr. ap Gell: N.A., III, 2, 6; Pl.: N.H., II, 188
4 T.L.E., 181
5 Macr.: Sat., I, 15, 14
6 Macr.: Sat., I, 15, 13
7 T.L.E., 801, 805, 818, 824, 836, 854, 856, 858
8 M. Pallottino: St Etr., XI, 1937, p. 213
9 E. Fiesel: St Etr., X, 1936, p. 324
10 E. Benveniste: B.S.L., XXXII, 1931, p. 68 *et seq*
11 Liv.: VII, 3, 7
12 Censor: 17, 6; C. O. Thulin: *Die etr. Disciplin*, III, p. 63 *et seq*
13 Diod.: V, 40; *supra*, p. 50
14 J. Carcopino: *La Vie quotidienne à Rome*, p. 304 *et seq*, from whom we have borrowed the details following
15 Suet.: Vit. 13, 1
16 Sen.: ad Luc., 103, 6; Pl. the Y.: Ep., III, 5, 10 *et seq*
17 Cic.: Phil., II, 104
18 Plat. Le Comique ap. Ath.: I, 47 d
19 G. Conestabile: *Pitture murali*, 1865; J. Martha: *L'Art étrusque*, fig. 266, 279, 292; N.M., fig. 74; P.E., p. 97 *et seq*; R. Bloch: *L'art étrusque*, pl. 74-76. Inscriptions in T.L.E., 220 *et seq*. But see now by the same *Eutruscologia*, 4th ed. 1957, p. 362, 5th ed. 1963, p. 397
20 C.I.L., I, 364; A. Ernout: *Textes lat. arch.*, p. 36
21 App. Verg.: Mor., 92 *et seq*
22 Varr.: ap. Diom., G.L.K., I, P. 486
23 Apic: VIII, 8, 1; VI, 9, 1. Note 'the aromatic wine of Chiusi' (conditum Camerinum, I, 2) and the 'Kid à la Tarpeiane' (haedus Tarpeianus, VIII, 2, 9)
24 Obviously an anachronistic translation which gives rise to the study of P. Grimal on *La véritable nature du 'garum'*, R.E.A., Liv, 1952, p. 27 *et seq*
25 Varr.: de L. L., VII, 35; Fest.: 403 L
26 M. Pallottino: *Stud. Funaioli*, p. 304
27 O. Danielsson: Gl., XVI, p. 86; T.L.E., 715
28 Walters-Smith: Cat. Brit. Mus., IV, p. 8, fig. 17 (F 470-472)
29 R. Demangel: *La Frise ionique*, p. 437 *et seq*; A. Amdren: *Architectural Terracottas from Etrusco-Italic temples*, p. LXXXV *et seq*, fig. 11
30 F. Villard: *Les Vases grecs*, p. 71, 77, pl. I, 1: XXIX, 3, etc

31 P.E., p. 107; R. Bloch: *L'Art étrusque*, pl. 78
32 P. Ducati: *Stor. dell' Arte etrusca*, fig. 232; Neppi Modona: fig. 87
33 P.E., p. 67; R. Bloch: *ibid*, pl. 44 and 48
34 *Supra*, p. 50
35 Cic.: Verr., II, 1, 86
36 Cic.: Verr., II, 4, 58
37 P.E., p. 67; R. Bloch: *L'Art étrusque*, pl. 44 and 48
38 P.E., p. 107; R. Bloch: *ibid*, pl. 78
39 Ath.: I, 28 b; cf. *supra*, p. 200
40 N.M., fig. 87, p. 117
41 J. D. Beazley: *Etruscan Vase Painting*, p. 284 *et seq*
42 Pl.: Stich., 694 *et seq*
43 Liv.: XXVIII, 38, 5
44 Liv.: XXXVII, 59, 5
45 Gell.: N.A., II, 24
46 R. Bianchi-Bandinelli: *Clusium, Mon. Ant.*, XXX, 1925, p. 306
   et seq; N.M., fig. 73, p. 114
47 Her.: I, 167
48 J. Heurgon: *L'Etat étrusque*, Hist., VI, 1957, p. 88, with the texts
49 *Supra*, p. 75
50 Th. Reinach: *La Musique grecque*, 1926; P. Boyance: *Le Culte des
   Muses chez les philosophes grecs*, 1937; H. I. Marrou: *Hist. de
   de l'Éducation dans l'Antiquité*, 1948
51 Theogn.: I, 791; H. I. Marrou: *ibid*, p. 75
52 Th. Reinach: *ibid*, p. 132
53 Arist.: F.H.G., II, p. 178
54 Plut.: De cohib. ira, 460 c
55 Ath.: XII, 518 b
56 Ael.: Nat. an., XII, 46
57 Arist.: Hist. an., IX, 5, 611 b; J. Aymard: *Les Chasses romaines*,
   p. 336 *et seq*
58 E. Mérite: *Les Pièges*, cité par J. Aymard: *ibid*
59 H. I. Marrou: *ibid*, p. 189
60 Virg.: Georg. II, 193; Pl.: N.H., XVI, 172
61 Dion. Hal.: VII, 72, 5
62 A.E., pl. 407, 4
63 Ath.: XIII, 607
64 Liv.: IX, 30, 5
65 Mueller-Deecke: *Die Etrusker*, II, p. 206, with texts; Esch.:
   Eum., 567
66 Virg.: Æn., VIII, 526
67 Liv.: I, 20, 5
68 R. Bloch: M.E.F.R., 1958, LXX, p. 7 *et seq*
69 Fest.: 334 L
70 Virg.: Aen., V, 545 *et seq*
71 G. Q. Giglioli: St Etr., III, 1929, 111 *et seq*; A.E., pl. 80
72 F. Bömer: *Rom. und Troia*, 1951, p. 18 *et seq*
73 J. Heurgon: M.E.F.R., 1929, XLVI, p. 3 *et seq*

74 Ch. Picard: *Genava*, 1935, XIII, p. 63 *et seq*
75 Dion. Hal.: VII, 72, 10 *et seq*; A. Piganiol: *Rech.*, *sur les jeux romains*, 1923, p. 15 *et seq*
76 P.E., p. 43
77 Id.: *ibid*, p. 45; R. Bloch: *L'Art étrusque*, pl. 21
78 J. D. Beazley: *Etruscan Vase Painting*, p. 114
79 Liv.: VII, 2, 6
80 Ov.: A.A., I, 111
81 Pl.: Curc., 150
82 Liv.: I, 35, 9
83 Pl.: N.H., X, 71
84 R. Bartoccini, C. M. Lerici, M. Moretti: *La tomba delle Olimpiadi*, 1959
85 Plut.: Publ., 13, 4; Fest.: 340 L; J. Hubaux: *Bull. de l'Acad. royale de Belgique*, XXXVI, 1950, p. 341 *et seq*; J. Gage: *Bull. de la Fac. des Lettres de Strasbourg*, XXXI, 1953, p. 163 *et seq*
86 P.E., p. 39; R. Bloch: *ibid*, pl. 19; cf. P. Demargne: C.R.A.I., 1952, p. 167; *Fouilles de Xanthos*, I, 1958: two fat wrestlers holding each other by the neck
87 N.M., fig. 67
88 A.E., pl. 115, 2; M. Pallottino: *Etruscologia*, 3e éd., pl. 57
89 *Supra*, p. 255
90 A.E., pl. 149; E. Gabrici: St Etr., II, 1928, p. 73 *et seq*
91 A.E., pl. 204; P.E., p. 65 *et seq*
92 A. Grenier: *Bologne*, p. 401
93 W. Borgeaud: *Les Illyriens en Grèce et en Italie*, 1943, p. 144; R. Bloch: *Bull. Soc. Ant. de Fr.*, 1959, p. 97
94 Hom.: Il., XXIII, 175
95 J. D. Beazley: *Etruscan Vase Painting*, p. 90
96 Her.: I, 167
97 Liv.: VII, 15, 10
98 Suet.: Aug., 15, 2
99 Ath.: IV, 153 f; Liv.: Per., XVI
100 Isid. de Sev.: Or., X, 159; Ernout-Meillet: Dict. étym., s.v. lanista
101 Tert.: Ap., 15, 5
102 F. Weege: Osk. Grabmalerei, Jahrb. d. Inst., XXIV, 1909, p. 99 *et seq.*; P. Sestieri: *Tombe dipinte di Paestum*, Riv. dell' Ist. di Archeol. e Stor. dell' Arte, V–VI, 1956–1957, p. 65 *et seq*
103 J. Heurgon: *Capoue préromaine*, p. 431
104 F. de Ruyt: Charun, p. 30, points out, hypothetically, a representation of this kind on an urn from the vicinity of Perugia
105 A.E., pl. 109, 2
106 R. Bartoccini, C. M. Lerici, M. Moretti: *La tomba delle Olimpiadi*, fig. 14
107 Tert.: Spect., 12, 4
108 P.E., p. 41; R. Bloch: *L'Art étrusque*, pl. 17
109 P. Romanelli: *Tarquinia*, fig. 33
110 F. Altheim: *Maske und Totenkult, dans Terra Mater*, 1931, p. 48

et seq; J. Heurgon: *Capoue préromaine*, p. 434 *et seq*; H. Rheinfelder: *Das Wort 'Persona'*, Zeitschr. f. roman. Philol., Beiheft 77, 1928

111 Fest. Paul.: 115 L; cf. 52 and 281
112 Ap.: Apol., 13, 7
113 P. Frassinetti: Fab. Atell. Fragm., p. 22
114 Fest.: 238 L
115 On the mines of the Atellanus, most recently, P. Frassinetti: *Fabula Atellana*, 1953, p. 65 *et seq*
116 On the ludi Osci, Cic.: Fam., VII, 1, 3

CHAPTER EIGHT, ETRUSCAN LITERATURE

1 G. Buonamici: *Epigrafia etrusca*, 1934, p. 111 *et seq*; J. G. Fevrier: *Hist. de l'Écriture*, 2ᵉ éd. 1959, p. 440 *et seq*; M. Lejeune: *Observations sur l'alphabet étrusque*, *Tyrrhenica*, 1957, p. 158 *et seq*.
2 A. Minto: *Marsiliana d'Albegna*, 1921, p. 122 and 236, pl. XX; A. Grenier: M.E.F.R., 1924, XLI, p. 1 *et seq*; A.E., pl. 30, 2; M. Pallotinno: *Etruscologia*, 3ᵉ éd., pl. 64
3 L. Pareti: *La tomba Regolini-Galassi*, p. 132, pl. 46; T.L.E., 55
4 F. Weege: *Vasculorum Campanorum Inscriptiones Italicae*, 1–3
5 M. Lejeune: R. Ph., 1952, XXVI, p. 199 *et seq*; R.E.A., 1953, LV, p. 58 *et seq*
6 Id.: R. Ph., 1952, XXVI, p. 204
7 H. I. Marrou: *Hist. de l'Éducation dans l'Antiquité*, p. 211
8 M. Lejeune: *Tyrrhenica*, p. 161, n. 6
9 T.L.E., 423
10 T.L.E., 472; B.N., p. 385, fig. 229
11 T.L.E., 2, 62; 570
12 T.L.E., 69
13 T.L.E., 601
14 T.L.E., 131
15 C.I.E., 5288, p. 227; T.L.E., 91; A.E., pl. 388, 2; F. de Ruyt: *Charun*, p. 131
16 Gerhard-Körte: *Etr. Spieg.*, V, 127; cf. *supra*, p. 64 and n. 25
17 F. de Ruyt: *Charun*, p. 158 *et seq*
18 Strab.: V, 2, 9; N. Lewis: *L'Industrie du papyrus dans l'Égypte gréco-romaine*, 1934, p. 14
19 M. Pallottino: St Etr., VI, 1932, p. 559 (MS. p. 254, Author's addition)
20 Liv.: IV, 7, 12; 13, 7; 20, 8
21 The fragments of the Etruscan linen book preserved in the Museum of Zagreb are the subject of a monograph, apart from C.I.E., *Libri Lintei Etrusci fragmenta Zagrebiensia*, 1919–1921, by G. Herbig and O. Danielsson. For the interpretation we cite particularly M. Pallottino: *Il contenuto del testo della Mummia di Zagabria*, St Etr., XI, 1937, p. 203 *et seq*; K. Olzscha: *Interpretation der Agramer Mumienbinde*, Klio, Beih. XL, 1939

22 *Supra*, p. 88
23 K. Olzscha: *Die Kalenderdaten der Agramen Mumienbinden*, *Aegyptus*, 1959, p. 340 *et seq*
24 Th. Birt: *Die Buchrolle in der Kunst*, 1907, p. 215 *et seq*
25 Lucr.: VI, 381–382
26 Cic.: *De Div.*, I, 20, v. 47; J. Carcopino: *La Louve du Capitole*, 1925, p. 34 *et seq*
27 C. O. Thulin: *Die Etr. Disciplin*, 1909, III
28 Fest.: 358 L
29 Reference in C. O. Thulin: *ibid*, III, p. 86 *et seq*
30 Cic.: *De Haruspicum responso*
31 A. Piganiol: *Le Calendrier brontoscopique de Nigidius Figulus*, Stud. A. C. Johnson: 1951, p. 79 *et seq*
32 A. Grenier: *Les Religions étrusque et romaine*, 1948
33 Collection of texts in M.D., II, p. 23 *et seq*; A. Grenier: *ibid*, p. 27
34 Liv.: I, 7, 4 *et seq*; J. Bayet: *Les Origines de l'Hercule romain*, 1926, p. 203 *et seq*
35 *Supra*, p. 274
36 Hom.: Od., IV, 351 *et seq*; Virg.: Georg., IV, 387 *et seq*
37 Lachmann: *Gromatici Veteres*, I, p. 350; St Weinstock: *Vegoia*, in Real-Enc., VIII, A 1, p. 577 *et seq*; J. Heurgon: The date of Vegoia's prophecy, J.R.S., 1959, p. 41 *et seq*; cf. *supra*, p. 133
38 S. Mazzarino: Hist. VI, 1957, p. 109
39 J. Marouzeau: *L'Ordre des mots en latin*, 1953, p. 7 *et seq*
40 Cic.: De Div., I, 92; cf. Val. Max.: I, 1, 1
41 Cic.: De Leg., II, 21
42 Tac.: Ann., XI, 15
43 Cic.: De Div., II, 51
44 Cat.: De Agr., 5, 4; Cic.: *ibid*, I, 132
45 C.I.L., IX, 5824
46 Cass. Dio.: LVI, 25
47 C. O. Thulin: *ibid*, III, p. 136 *et seq*
48 Zosim.: V, 41 *et seq*
49 C. O. Thulin: *ibid*, III, p. 142
50 On *Herennius Siculus*, Val. Max.: IX, 12, 6; Vell. Pat.: II, 7, 2; F. Münzer: in Real-Enc. (46); E. Babelon: Descr. hist. des monn. de la Rép. rom., I, p. 567. *Sur Postumius*, Cic.: De Div., I, 172; Val. Max.: I, 6, 4. *Sur Spurinna*, Cic.: Fam., IX, 24; De Div., I, 119; Suet.: Caes., 81; Val. Max.: VIII, 11, 2
51 J. Heurgon: *Tarquitius Priscus, Latomus*, 1953, p. 402 *et seq*
52 App. Verg.: Cat., V, 3
53 C.I.L., XI, 3370, 7566
54 F. Münzer: in Real-Enc., III
55 Not. Sc., IX, 1955, p. 114 *et seq*
56 Cic.: Pro Caecina; Fam., VI, 5–8
57 Cic.: Fam., VI, 6, 3
58 T.L.E., 131; J. Heurgon: *Influences grecques sur le religion étrusque*, R.E.L., XXXV, 1957, p. 106 *et seq*

59 *Supra*, p. 275, n. 19
60 J. Carcopino: *La Basilique pythagoricienne de la Porte Majeure*, 1927, p. 183
61 Hom.: Od., XV, 225; Suidas: III, 419, p. 349 A
62 Drac.: Romul., VIII, 480
63 *Supra*, p. 50
64 P. Ducati: *Etruria antica*, I, p. 164
65 B.N., p. 405 *et seq.*
66 Liv.: IX, 36, 3; cf. *supra*, p. 76
67 H. I. Marrou: *Hist. de l'Éducation dans l'Antiquité*, p. 329 *et seq*
68 Dion. Hal.: I, 21, 2
69 Serv. Dan.: ad Aen., VIII, 285
70 *Supra*, p. 249
71 Hor.: Ep., II, 1, 139 *et seq*; Fest. Paul.: 75 L; G. Wissowa: Real-Enc., VI, p. 2223 *et seq*
72 *Supra*, p. 264 *et seq*
73 *Infra*, p. 303
74 Liv.: VII, 2
75 J. H. Waszink: Varro, Livy and Tertullian, Vig. Christ. II, 1948, p. 224 *et seq*
76 The lyre player of the Tomb of the Lionesses has the mouth shut. That on the tomb of the Citrarede if one can believe the drawin which is all that remains of it, has the lips parted, and it is possible his music had words (J. Martha, *L'Art Étrusque*, fig. 289, p. 438)
77 P. Wuilleumier: Tarente, 1939, p. 612 *et seq*
78 A. Piganiol: *Recherches sur les jeux romains*, 1923, p. 32 *et seq*
79 Brunn-Körte: *Rilievi delle Urne etrusche*, I, pl. 73, 2-3; pl. 80, 11; II, pl. 20–26; A.E., pl. 355, 1; 356, 1–3
80 Brunn-Körte: *ibid*, I, 1, 4; 4, 11; II, 13; 18; A.E., pl. 400, 3; 404, 1; 405, 1
81 Brunn-Körte: II, 2; Pacuv.: Medus, 397 R; Lucil.: 587 M
82 Brunn-Körte: II, pl. 89–92
83 E. Fiesel: *Namen des griech. Mythos im Etruskischen*, 1928
84 Pl.: Men., 144
85 Varr.: L.L., V, 55
86 A. Ernout: Etymologica, I, p. 117; G. Dumezil: *L'Héritage indo-européen à Rome*, p. 191
87 Censor.: 17, 6; C. O. Thulin: Die etr. Disziplin, III, p. 63 *et seq*
88 C.I.L., XIII, 1668; P. Fabia: *La Table Claudienne de Lyon*, 1929
89 Schol. Veron.: ad Aen., X, 200; A. H. G. Zimmermann: De A. *Caecina scriptore*, 1852
90 F. Altheim: Röm. Gesch., I, p. 191 *et seq*
91 A.E., pl. 189–196; *les nouveaux fragments dans* M. Pallottino: *La Scuola di Vulca*, 1945; Archeol. Class., II, 1950, p. 122 *et seq*; *Etruscologia*, pl. 10
92 P.E., p. 31; R. Bloch: *L'Art étrusque*, pl. 11; *supra*, p. 263
93 For example, the myth evoked by Porsenna, Brunnkörte: III, pl. 8, 1; A.E., pl. 401, 1; cf. Pl.: II, 140

94 *Supra*, p. 65 *et seq*; P.E., p. 115 *et seq*; R. Bloch: *ibid*, pl. 80–82
95 Virg.: Aen., VI, 88–89
96 Liv.: V, 33, 3; Dion. Hal.: XIII, 14 *et seq*
97 Gell.: N.A., XVII, 14, 4
98 Pol.: II, 17, 3
99 T.L.E., 471
100 W. Schulze: *Zur Gesch. d. lat. Eigennamen*, p. 287
101 J. Perret: *Les Origines de la légende troyenne de Rome*, 1942, p. 458 *et seq*
102 Plut.: Rom., 2 (trans. R. Flaceliere)
103 Dion. Hal.: IV, 2, 1; F. Altheim: *Griech. Götter im alten Rom*, 1930, p. 51 *et seq*
104 L. Ross Taylor: *Local Cults in Etruria*, 1923, p. 120
105 M. Pallottino: Archeol. Class., IX, 1957, p. 206 *et seq*; X, 1958, p. 315 *et seq*
106 P. Romanelli: Not. Sc., 1948, p. 260 *et seq*
107 A. Degrassi: Inscr. Italiae, XIII, III, 1937
108 J. Heurgon: M.E.F.R., LXIII, 1951, p. 119 *et seq*; M. Pallottino: Etr., XXI, 1950–1951, p. 147 *et seq*
109 P. Romanelli: *ibid*, n° 44; The M is certain which excludes the reconstruction of M. Pallottino: *ibid*, p. 170: *bello Hannibalico*. Perhaps it should be Hamertes instead of Camertes
110 P. Romanelli: *ibid*, n° 48; Ann. ép., 1951, n° 146. On Aquila reservations by E. Vetter: Gl., XXXIV, 1954, p. 59
111 U. Kahrstedt: Symb. Osl., XXX, 1953, p. 68
112 J. Heurgon: *ibid*, p. 131; M. Pallottino: *ibid*, p. 162
113 F. Della Corte: St Etr., XXIV, 1955, p. 75
114 J. Heurgon: *ibid*, 133, after a suggestion by J. Bayet
115 P. Romanelli: *ibid*, n° 77, completed by number 18 which corresponds there
116 M. Pallotting: *Tarquinia*, p. 584; inscr. étrusques de Norchia, T.L.E., 164 *et seq*; *supra*, p. 195
117 Pl.: N.H., XXXV, 6
118 Juv.: Sat., VIII, 1 *et seq*
119 Pers.: Sat., III, 28
120 Hor.: Carm., III, 29, 1; Prop.: El., III, 9, 1
121 Hor.: Sat., 1, 6, 1 *et seq*
122 Pl.: N.H., XXXV, 26
123 Tac.: Ann., VI, 11, 3
124 Vell. Paterc.: II, 88, 3
125 P. Boyance: Bull. Ass. G. Budé, 1959, p. 332 *et seq*
126 Cic.: P. Clu., 153
127 Prop.: El., III, 9, 29
128 Hor.: Sat., 1, 5, 29
129 Cass. Dio.: LII, 1–41
130 Sen.: De Clem., 1, 9
131 P. Grimal: *Le Siècle d'Auguste*, p. 58 *et seq*
132 The title of a memorable work by Sir Ronald Syme: *The Roman*

Revolution, 1939, which studies the arrival of a new ruling class during the reign of Augustus

133 Stendhal: *La Chartreuse de Parme*, chap. VI.
134 Sen.: ad Luc., 114, 4
135 Fr. Goethert: *Zur Kunst der röm. Republik*, 1931
136 Sen.: ad Luc., 92, 35
137 Juv.: Sat., 1, 66; XII, 38 *et seq*; Pl.: N.H., VIII, 174
138 Suet.: Vit. Hor., p. 45 R
139 Sen.: ad Luc., 114, 6
140 Pl.: N.H., VII, 172
141 Sen.: De Prov., 1, 3, 10
142 Macr.: Sat., II, 4, 12
143 They have been collected and studied by F. Harder, Progr. Berl. 1889, and P. Lunderstedt, Comment. Philol. Ienenses, IX, 1, 1911
144 Sen.: ad Luc., 92, 35
145 Sen.: ad Luc., 101, 11
146 Suet.: Aug., 86, 3; Sen.: ad Luc., 114, 4
147 H. Bardon: *La littérature latine inconnue*, II, p. 13 *et seq*
148 Sen.: ad Luc., 19, 9. The fragments which follow in 114, 5 *et seq*
149 F. Cumont: *Lux perpetua*, p. 82 *et seq*, 396 *et seq*
150 M. Renard: *Pline l' Ancien et le motif de l' 'assarotos oikos'*, Homm. Niedermann, p. 307 *et seq*
151 Virg.: Aen., VI, 599

CONCLUSION

1 Liv.: 1, 40, 2: Tarquin is not Italicae Stirpis because son of the Corinthian Demaratus
2 Fest.: p. 222 L
3 Her.: IV, 76 *et seq*
4 A. Hus: *Les Etrusques*, 1959, p. 155

INDEX

Nuceria, 12
numbers, names of, 17, 18, 29, 168
Nun-painter, 28

obesity, 24, 25–7
Ogre, Tomb of the, 180
Oinarea (or *Oina*), 59, 60
olives, 112
Ombrici, 4
Ombrone river, 98
'omen books', 121
omens, interpretation of, 5, 36, 38–9, 224–7
'Orator' statue, 172, 176, 177, 179
Orcia river, 98
Orcle, 258
Orient: influence of, 11, 20–1; possible origin in, 2, 3–7, 8, 20–1, 77
origins, 2, 3–9; medico-biological view, 20–2; Oriental, 2, 3–7, 8, 20–1, 77
Orvieto, 54, 59, 77, 137, 146, 169, 186, 188, 192
Oscan games, 215
Ostia, 145, 161
Ovid, 110, 113, 132, 203

Paestum, 243
Paglia, valley
painting, 27–8, 119, 121–2, 148. *See also* frescoes
Pais, Ettore, 15
Palestrina, 10
pallium (cloak), 263, 264
Pallottino, M., 93, 122, 202
papyrus, 220, 222
parental terms, 75
Pareti, Luigi, 90
Parma, 12
Paros, 126
Partunu tomb, 25, 123
pasta, 111
pater familias, 63, 65, 74, 93, 94, 267
Patroclus, 210
Paulus, Aemilius, 67
peasants, 56–9, 61–5
pecorino (cheese), 117
Pelasgians, 24
penestes (free men), 57–8, 61
peristyles, 157–9
Perugia, 10, 15, 18, 23, 43, 57, 68, 69, 71, 73, 75, 101, 108, 109, 110, 122, 137, 146, 154, 198, 210, 218, 230

Petronii family, 75
Phaedra, 96
Phersu, game of, 212–15, 241
Phocaea, 32
Phocaeans, 13
physical characteristics, 20–31, 264
Piacenza, 5
Picard, Charles, 22
piety, 38–9
pig-breeding, 117–18
Piganiol, André, 244
pilentum (ceremonial vehicle), 133
Piombino, 123
piracy, 12, 42
Pisa, 110–11, 118, 122–3, 129, 146
Pithecusa (Ischia), 120, 123
Plato, 198, 224
Plautius Pulcher, M., 84
Plautius Silvanus, M., 83–4
Plautus, 76, 120, 192, 204, 215, 231
plays, 214–15, 241, 244–6
Pliny the Elder, 64–5, 104, 121, 123, 128, 186, 198, 233, 234, 260, 264
Pliny the Younger, 98–9, 100, 117, 157
ploughs, 114–15
Plutarch, 56, 196, 206, 254–5
Po river, 104, 140, 141
poetry, 240–1
Poggio a Gaiella, 156
Pollenius Auspex, 236
Polles, 236
Polybius, 72, 118, 175, 252
pomegranate, 114
pomerium, 108, 136
Pompeii, 12, 154, 156, 219, 243, 256
Pomponius, 231
population, 145–8
Populonia, 11, 58, 59, 101, 122, 123, 125, 126–7, 128, 131, 146
Porsenna, king of Clusium, 41, 48, 141, 253
Porto Clementino, 100
Portonaccio, temple of, 42
Posidonius of Apamea, 35–7, 55, 127, 128, 143, 144, 145, 156, 172, 185, 191, 192, 193, 237
Postumius (*haruspex*), 232–3
pottery, 91–2, 149, 150, 151, 181, 192, 207
Pozzuoli, 127–8, 129
Praeneste (Palestrina), 10, 11, 14, 123, 130, 163; Bernardini tomb, 10–11, 90